December 1–2, 2015
London, United Kingdom

**Association for
Computing Machinery**

Advancing Computing as a Science & Profession

ACM DEV-6 (2015)

Proceedings of the 2015 Annual Symposium on
Computing for Development

Association for Computing Machinery

Advancing Computing as a Science & Profession

The Association for Computing Machinery
2 Penn Plaza, Suite 701
New York, New York 10121-0701

Notice to Past Authors of ACM-Published Articles

ISBN: 978-1-4503-3490-7 (Digital)

ISBN: 978-1-4503-4110-3 (Print)

Additional copies may be ordered prepaid from:

ACM Order Department
PO Box 30777
New York, NY 10087-0777, USA

Phone: 1-800-342-6626 (USA and Canada)
+1-212-626-0500 (Global)
Fax: +1-212-944-1318
E-mail: acmhelp@acm.org
Hours of Operation: 8:30 am – 4:30 pm ET

Printed in the USA

From the Chairs

We are extremely pleased to welcome you to the Sixth ACM Symposium on Computing for Development (DEV) in London. ACM DEV has become the premier conference for computer science research into computing technologies for emerging regions, and this year's program reflects the variety of research challenges encountered in this rich research area.

DEV 2015 received 63 submissions, of which 50 were full papers and 13 were short papers. As in the past, we solicited full papers that deeply investigated ICTD-focused topics. We accepted 13 full papers. As a new addition to the program this year, we solicited short papers to provide a venue for the dissemination of the experiences of practitioners and follow-on work of previously published efforts. We accepted six short papers for presentation at the conference.

Also new this year was the introduction of submission "tracks" (systems, HCI, and data science) to explicitly recognize the interdisciplinary nature of DEV and the unique perspectives and methodologies brought by the different disciplines. Authors were asked to select the track(s) that best characterized their contribution in order to match their submission with the expertise of the reviewers. As in previous years, the review process was double blind. All papers were reviewed by at least three program committee (PC) members. In a few cases, we solicited extra reviews from outside experts and additional reviewers from within the PC. The final decisions were based on reviews, online discussions, and a three hour long program committee conference call. We would like to thank our talented and hard working PC for their rigorous reviewing and generous donation of their time.

This year we also introduced a best paper award and selected a small committee from our PC for this decision.

As a community our experiences have helped our techniques and approaches mature over the past six years. This year's program both broadens and coalesces the themes from past DEV conferences and includes new approaches to development challenges. The program consists of work ranging from connectivity challenges to network performance, from systems building to applications and interfaces, and from crowds to specific communities. This year's program reflects the strong quality and innovative creativity of the DEV research community. Other highlights this year include keynotes from Ken Banks, creator of FrontlineSMS and Ed Cutrell, a Senior Researcher in the Technology for Emerging Markets group at Microsoft Research India. In addition, we look forward to a lively panel led by Joshua Blumenstock of the University of Washington.

We look forward to seeing you at ACM DEV-6!

Arjuna Sathiaseelan
University of Cambridge, UK

Elizabeth Belding
University of California, Santa Barbara

Marco Zennaro
ICTP

Jay Chen
New York University, Abu Dhabi

From the Technical Program Chairs

We are extremely pleased to welcome you to the Sixth ACM Symposium on Computing for Development (DEV) in London. ACM DEV has become the premier conference for computer science research into computing technologies for emerging regions, and this year's program reflects the variety of research challenges encountered in this rich research area.

DEV 2015 received 63 submissions, of which 50 were full papers and 13 were short papers. As in the past, we solicited full papers that deeply investigated ICTD-focused topics. We accepted 13 full papers. As a new addition to the program this year, we solicited short papers to provide a venue for the dissemination of the experiences of practitioners and follow-on work of previously published efforts. We accepted six short papers for presentation at the conference.

Also new this year was the introduction of submission "tracks" (systems, HCI, and data science) to explicitly recognize the interdisciplinary nature of DEV and the unique perspectives and methodologies brought by the different disciplines. Authors were asked to select the track(s) that best characterized their contribution in order to match their submission with the expertise of the reviewers. As in previous years, the review process was double blind. All papers were reviewed by at least three program committee (PC) members. In a few cases, we solicited extra reviews from outside experts and additional reviewers from within the PC. The final decisions were based on reviews, online discussions, and a three hour long program committee conference call. We would like to thank our talented and hard working PC for their rigorous reviewing and generous donation of their time.

This year we also introduced a best paper award and selected a small committee from our PC for this decision.

As a community our experiences have helped our techniques and approaches mature over the past six years. This year's program both broadens and coalesces the themes from past DEV conferences and includes new approaches to development challenges. The program consists of work ranging from connectivity challenges to network performance, from systems building to applications and interfaces, and from crowds to specific communities. This year's program reflects the strong quality and innovative creativity of the DEV research community. Other highlights this year include keynotes from Ken Banks, creator of FrontlineSMS and Ed Cutrell, a Senior Researcher in the Technology for Emerging Markets group at Microsoft Research India. In addition, we look forward to a lively panel led by Joshua Blumenstock of the University of Washington.

Finally, we would like to thank the steering committee for their advice and guidance, and our general chairs, Arjuna Sathiaseelan and Marco Zennaro, for their help with logistics and their conference planning efforts.

Elizabeth Belding
University of California, Santa Barbara
ebelding@ucsb.edu

Jay Chen
New York University, Abu Dhabi
jchen@cs.nyu.edu

Table of Contents

Session: Network Performance

ACM DEV 2015 Conference Organization

General Chairs

Arjuna Sathiaseelan	University of Cambridge
Marco Zennaro	International Centre for Theoretical Physics

Technical Program Committee Chairs

Elizabeth Belding	University of California, Santa Barbara
Jay Chen	NYU Abu Dhabi

Technical Program Committee

Aaditeshwar Seth	IIT Delhi, India
Agha Ali Raza	Information Technology University
Andrew Dearden	Sheffield Hallam University
Azza Abouzied	NYU Abu Dhabi
Barath Raghavan	ICSI
Bhaskaran Raman	IIT-Bombay
Bill Thies	Microsoft Research India
Bill Tucker	University of Western Cape
Brian DeRenzi	University of Cape Town
David Johnson	CSIR
Ed Cutrell	Microsoft Research India
Ellen Zegura	Georgia Tech
Fred Xue	Google
Jon Crowcroft	University of Cambridge
Josh Blumenstock	University of Washington
Kentaro Toyama	University of Michigan
Mahesh Marina	University of Edinburgh
Mariya Zheleva	University at Albany, SUNY
Michael Best	UNU Institute on Computing and Society
Neha Kumar	University of Southern California
Nicola Dell	University of Washington
Nithya Sambasivan	Google
Richard Anderson	University of Washington
Roni Rosenfeld	Carnegie Mellon University
Rumi Chunara	New York University
Shankar Kalyanaraman	Facebook
Sibren Isaacman	Loyola University
Susana Munoz Hernandez	U. Politecnica de Madrid
Tapan Parikh	University of California, Berkeley
Vanessa Frias-Martinez	University of Maryland

Poster Technical Program Chair

Veljko Pejovic   University of Ljubljana

Webmaster

Liang Wang   University of Cambridge

Sponsor:

Supporters:

INTERDIGITAL

Microsoft
Research

Institutional donor/supporters logos:

 Queen Mary
University of London

Hackers, Fixers and Lone Rangers: The Future of Technology for Development?

Ken Banks
kiwanja.net
ken.banks@kiwanja.net

ABSTRACT

Classes in social innovation, technology-for-development and design thinking have become increasingly popular in recent years. On the one hand, this might be seen as a good thing. After all, the world needs as many smart, engaged citizens as it can get, particularly when you consider the multitude of challenges we face as a planet. But does a career in social change really begin in the classroom, or out in the real world? How much social change is planned, and how much accidental? And which approach tends to lead to the most meaningful, lasting or impactful solutions? In his talk, Ken Banks will talk about the rise of innovation 'outside the system', and how this is beginning to challenge conventional thinking around social innovation and the source of technology-for-development projects and interventions.

Categories and Subject Descriptors

H.5.m. Information interfaces and presentation (e.g., HCI): Miscellaneous.

Keywords

ICTD; Global Development; Accessibility

BIO

kiwanja.net helps social innovators, entrepreneurs, engaged citizens and non-profit organisations make better use of information and communication technologies in their work. Founded by Ken Banks in 2003, kiwanja.net specialises in the application of mobile technology, with a particular emphasis on its role as a driver of innovation, entrepreneurship and social change around the world. He has worked at the intersection of technology, anthropology, conservation and development for the past twenty years and, during that time, has lived and worked across the African continent. In 2005 he created FrontlineSMS, one of the most widely used messaging platforms in the non-profit sector today. He is a PopTech Fellow, a Tech Awards Laureate, an Ashoka Fellow and a National Geographic Emerging Explorer, and has been internationally recognised for his technology-based work. In 2013 he was nominated for the TED Prize, and in 2015 he was invited to RMIT University in Melbourne, Australia, as a Visiting Fellow. Ken is also a published author, with his first edited book, "The Rise of the Reluctant Innovator", released in late 2013. His latest project, Means of Exchange, looks at how everyday technologies can be used to democratise opportunities for economic self-sufficiency, rebuild local community and promote a return to local resource use.

ACM DEV 2015, December 1–2, 2015, London, United Kingdom.
ACM 978-1-4503-3490-7/15/12.
DOI: http://dx.doi.org/10.1145/2830629.2830651

The Challenges of Scaling WISPs

Shaddi Hasan
UC Berkeley
shaddi@cs.berkeley.edu

Yahel Ben-David
De Novo/UC Berkeley
yahel@eecs.berkeley.edu

Max Bittman
Sudo Mesh
maxb@sudoroom.org

Barath Raghavan
ICSI
barath@icsi.berkeley.edu

ABSTRACT

Wireless ISPs (WISPs) are one of the primary means of delivering broadband Internet access to rural and underserved areas of the world. However, WISP operators often struggle to maintain let alone grow their operations. We set out both to understand what challenges WISP operators face and to develop new approaches to help them in managing their networks. First, we present a study we conducted of operating WISPs to understand what barriers they face. Second, we describe our experiences building and using a software system for WISP management, and a new WISP we have built from the ground up using that system. We found that WISPs appear to reach natural scaling limits, and that despite excitement in the networking community about the promise of Software Defined Networking (SDN) in new environments, more mundane functionality like subscriber management provides much of the actual benefit to WISPs.

Categories and Subject Descriptors

C.2.3 [**Computer Communication Networks**]: Network management

General Terms

Design, Economics, Management

Keywords

Wireless, Rural, Network Operations

1. INTRODUCTION

Over the last few years, connecting the vast globally disconnected population of potential users—the next billion—to the Internet has attracted significant attention both in the research community (e.g. via GAIA) and among large industrial players such as Google and Facebook. Rural users are most difficult to connect due to lower subscriber density making profitable operation challenging. The task of connecting these *last* billions of rural users has been taken up by small Wireless ISPs (WISPs), taking advantage of low-cost wireless equipment to build networks in areas often lacking any other Internet infrastructure. These WISPs are small network operators, leveraging low-cost fixed wireless infrastructure to build their networks.

While Internet access, speeds, and the diversity of applications available via that access has, in densely populated areas around the world, rapidly increased in the past decade, rural access has not improved at the same rate. Speeds delivered by many rural WISPs have not scaled with the increasing bandwidth needs of modern applications; some WISPs we became familiar with in the course of this work have neither substantially increased the bandwidth they deliver to subscribers nor decreased prices in a decade.

In this paper, we set out to understand why this situation exists, drawing on our own experiences and those of others, and to use that understanding to develop new systems to help WISPs operate more effectively. We contribute three insights into the problems faced in developing rural Internet access. First, we describe the context of rural Internet access through two studies of WISPs that we conducted. Second, we detail how assumptions about scaling networks and growing Internet access must be rethought to address the problems that WISPs face. Third, we describe a new software system, Celerate, that we are building to meet the needs of new WISP operators; we have actively been using this system for over a year to manage a new WISP we have built in a rural area of North America.

To calibrate our thinking on rural Internet access in general and WISPs in particular, we conducted two studies on WISPs, collectively representing responses from 83 WISPs operating across North America. We found that North American WISPs ability to succeed was driven largely by financial, regulatory, and business factors, rather than shortcomings in network-level tools.

The results of these studies guide our work. First, our findings suggest that there may be natural limits to the size of rural WISPs, and thus the approach to scaling Internet access for the last billion users will require scaling not merely the size of networks but the number of distinct WISP operators. To do so, we concluded that a new architecture for WISP operation is needed to help these new operators build and manage their networks, thereby lowering the barrier for starting and sustaining a WISP. Second, at the outset of our work, we hypothesized that SDN, in some form, could help WISPs and thus help address the problems of rural Internet access. In concept SDN has much to offer to simplify network management and implement complex network policies, but in practice we found more mundane functionality, such as integrating billing with subscriber data, yields more immediate benefits for WISPs. Thus, our development effort focuses on mundane but ultimately more useful management functionality at the expense of sophisticated but unnecessary SDN functionality.

ACM DEV 2015, December 1–2, 2015, London, United Kingdom.
© 2015 ACM. ISBN 978-1-4503-3490-7/15/11 ...$15.00.
DOI: http://dx.doi.org/10.1145/2830629.2830637.

To validate our findings and to have a testbed for our work on our new architecture, we built and continue to grow an operational WISP to provide broadband Internet to a rural community and indigenous tribe in North America. We describe our experiences in building the network and how we have leveraged it in testing new approaches to be replicated at WISPs elsewhere. To manage our WISP network, we are building Celerate, an architecture for WISP network management. Our aim is to provide a structure for all aspects of starting, operating, and growing a WISP in rural areas. Some of the components of Celerate build upon conventional SDN designs, while some relate to aspects that are either unique to WISPs or are simply ignored in traditional SDN deployments. Architecturally Celerate differs from many SDN systems in that it makes explicit two additional planes—the management subsystem and the operations subsystem—that are typically viewed as outside the scope of the network's design. These planes are essential to managing many networks, especially WISPs, and by making them explicit we clearly define the ways in which the human operators interact with the system. Our aim is to create a system that meets the needs of small WISPs anywhere in the world, and as such we have incorporated the feedback of numerous WISPs into our designs. Our system is open source and is in the early stages of use beyond our primary deployment in a partner WISP who plans to independently leverage it [7].

2. THE CHALLENGES OF WISPS

In mid-2012 we conducted a systematic survey of WISPs throughout the United States, and in 2014 conducted a more focused but informal survey of WISPs in a specific region in North America. WISPs provide service to millions of subscribers throughout the US. Those who are unfamiliar with the WISP industry are often surprised by its size: over two million subscribers are served by WISPs in the US alone, and in rural areas, WISPs can be the only source of broadband Internet access besides satellite [3]. WISPs have an even larger impact outside the US. Ubiquiti, a leading hardware vendor for WISPs, reports that "the substantial majority of [their] sales occur" outside the US, and sees emerging markets as a major opportunity for their growth [28]. These facts are unsurprising when one considers the fundamental reduction in capital expenditure required to build a wireless ISP network compared to a traditional wired one. Falling costs and rising performance of commodity wireless equipment, driven by the popularity of WiFi, have allowed the industry to grow as availability of unlicensed spectrum has increased globally. Early research from the academic community demonstrated that the same chipsets used in laptops and phones could be used to build long-distance WiFi links [17]; since then, similar technologies have been commercialized and are widely available. Radio equipment for a 50km link providing more than 50Mbps of throughput can be had for under $200, with each radio consuming under 5W.

Despite the importance of WISPs for providing economical broadband service to rural areas, there has been little study by the academic community of the WISP industry. We set out to rectify that situation by answering the following questions: a) what are the demographics of rural WISPs, b) what are the key operational challenges WISPs face, and c) what policy support do WISPs require to effectively provide service?

2.1 Methodology

To investigate the operation and characteristics of WISPs in our initial 2012 study, we developed a web-based survey. The survey consisted of 20 questions covering the size of the WISP and its network, budgeting, network failures, and network management.

Size	1–99	100–499	500–999	1000–4999	> 5000
Number	4	17	14	32	5
Percentile	5.5%	29.2%	48.6%	93.1%	100%

Table 1: WISP size (subscriber base) demographics.

After completing the survey, participants were invited to participate in a follow-up semi-structured phone interview. We had a total of 75 responses to our survey; 13 of those participated in a follow-up interview. Twelve of those interviewed were active WISP operators, and of those ten operated networks in rural areas.

We recruited participants via convenience sampling by distributing announcements on three WISP-focused email lists: the Wireless Internet Service Providers Association's (WISPA) public and members-only lists and the Animal Farm Microwave Users Group (AFMUG) list.[1] The WISPA and AFMUG mailing lists have significant overlap, though the latter focuses primarily on users of a particular manufacturer's equipment (Cambium).

The participation rate is difficult to calculate since the membership lists of each list are private. Based on public archive records, 434 unique users posted to the WISPA mailing list in the two years preceding our study; of course, this only captures active list participants on a single mailing list (though likely the largest of the three we contacted). The AFMUG mailing list claims that "list membership exceeds 450 members." Nevertheless, our respondent pool represents a wide cross-section of the WISP industry. The vast majority of our survey respondents were involved in the day-to-day operation of a WISP. Other respondents had operated WISPs in the past, but now served primarily in a management role, often as a result of growing their company through acquisition.

Our second study, conducted in 2014, was a more informal survey of WISPs in the neighboring regions to our target deployment. We talked to 8 WISPs in the region; for all of these, we directly contacted each and spoke with them about their current operations and their potential interest in using Celerate during development. We did not interview any of these WISPs in our 2012 study, though we have no way of knowing if they participated in the web-based survey component.

2.2 Demographics

The WISPs we surveyed were small, by almost any metric one considers. While only 5% of those surveyed had fewer than 100 customers, half had less than 1000, and almost all of those surveyed had fewer than 5000 customers (Table 1). In terms of traffic load, 40% of WISPs surveyed saw a peak traffic demand of under 100Mbps, and 80% had a peak demand of under 500Mbps.

One of the most consistent and striking characteristics of many of our survey respondents was that they often played multiple roles within their WISP's operations. Most survey respondents reported that they filled a combination of business management, technical management, and marketing roles. This is unsurprising, given almost half of respondents had fewer than 5 employees; 90% had less than 25 employees. For the smallest WISPs we talked to, only one or two people were responsible for the entire operation, though hiring part-time or contract workers for specialized tasks such as tower climbing was common.

2.3 Findings

The goal of this study was to develop an understanding of the technical challenges that impacted WISPs, with the hopes of motivating further research on systems to help WISPs operate more efficiently. After collecting data and conducting interviews, we came

---

[1] WISPA is the industry association for WISPs in the United States.

to realize that some of the assumptions we made were misguided. We initially expected WISPs in the US to face struggles similar to those described in the literature about wireless networks in the developing world [25]: flaky hardware, challenging fault diagnosis, and poor local IT expertise. This turned out not to be the case. In contrast to the "hacked together" wireless systems of the mid-2000s, technology, especially commodity wireless hardware, used by WISPs for building their networks has matured sufficiently that operators focus more of their effort on business development than technical issues. One WISP we spoke with in Colorado provided service over a 45,000 sq. mi. area with only 10 employees.

A common concern among WISPs in our study was spectrum scarcity. Of 43 respondents to the free-response question in our web survey "What is the biggest challenge your organization faces?", 22 (51%) expressed concerns relating to spectrum. The next most common group of concerns was around business development (23%), followed by affordability of upstream bandwidth and backhaul (16%). This was an unexpected result: we had anticipated issues around configuration and manageability of WISP networks to be a major concern, but this was not the case.

Spectrum. We asked about spectrum usage in our interviews. All of the rural WISP operators we interviewed operated in unlicensed spectrum, but many used some licensed spectrum as well. In particular, 7 of the 10 rural WISPs used the 3650MHz "lightly licensed" band, which has been very popular for WISP operators due to the relative quiet of the band compared to unlicensed ones. Multiple interview subjects expressed a desire to have spectrum set aside for WISPs due to overcrowding in the unlicensed bands. According to one operator, "basically, we need to use lots of bands because things are so crowded. [The 3.65GHz band] will never have home routers in it. So we can use, especially for backhaul, a relatively obscure chunk of spectrum." Higher frequency licensed spectrum (specifically, the 11GHz band) was used in some capacity by three of the respondents, primarily for high-capacity backhaul links.

On the surface, it surprising that spectrum scarcity would be an issue in areas that are largely underserved, but several factors make this an issue for WISPs. The WISPs we spoke with all had a limited number of tower sites for access points to connect customers to their networks. To reduce capital cost of expansion, these WISPs would take advantage of geographic features, re-use existing towers, or re-purpose other tall structures (e.g., grain silos) to avoid building new towers from scratch. Adding more subscribers thus meant co-locating more access points on each tower, leading to interference at the tower site. The second driver was foliage—WISPs serving forested areas reported heavy usage of 900MHz spectrum due to improved foliage penetration. The 900MHz band is the lowest-frequency band commonly available to WISPs, and is only 28MHz wide (compared to over 150MHz for the more commonly-used 5GHz band) yet is shared with a variety of non-WISP users, such as cordless phone systems and smart meters.

Business development and Financing. An unexpected theme that emerged was the difficulty of obtaining financing to expand network growth and meeting demand for service. Particularly for rural WISPs, the cost of adding a customer to the network is high, with an installation requiring a site survey, a trained technician, customer premises equipment, and physical installation of the hardware. Specifically, in our 2014 survey, we found that WISP growth was often constrained by financing once the natural (often geographic, though sometimes market, cultural, or political) boundaries of the WISP's growth had been reached, as the cost to grow beyond the boundary was a step function. Indeed, we found that this natural boundary to WISP growth seemed to have the same origin for many WISPs even if it manifested differently. For some

WISPs, it appeared as though the WISP operators no longer had an interest in growing their network and reaching new users, but when pressed, this was because the cost (in time, effort, and money) was too great to take a step beyond the current size. For other WISPs this boundary manifested as a more straightforward financial limit to expansion—while the area in which they operated may have been profitable enough to sustain their current size, it was not able to produce enough profit to finance expansion into new markets.

A humorous but sobering comment from one WISP was that they switched to using minivans instead of trucks for service calls due to better fuel economy, yet still spend $2 per user per month on fuel. In an industry with an estimated ARPU of $30 [3], this represents almost 7% of gross revenue. One of our interview subjects stated that their ability to buy used equipment from a bankrupt competitor at a fraction of retail price was instrumental in allowing them to grow their revenue to sustainability.

Another unexpected theme in this area was the relationships among neighboring WISPs. Several of the WISPs we spoke with had cooperative, often informal, relationships with neighboring WISPs. These relationships included infrastructure and backhaul sharing, referring customers near the edge of one's service area to competitors, agreements to not expand into each other's service areas, and in one case even a co-op of several WISPs that made bulk equipment purchases and shared a customer support call center. Another common practice was WISPs buying out neighboring WISPs; three WISPs we spoke with reported having done this.

2.4 Discussion

Most WISPs we spoke with did not need network management tools to grow larger; their challenges were based on financial or regulatory issues. We argue that this is because they have typically already matured to natural size limits (or have failed). At those limits, even if the network is profitable it is likely unable to expand, constrained by inefficient network management and business processes, and unable to finance improving network performance. The high rate of startup failure and the low performance offered by many WISPs suggests that tools for facilitating the creation of new high-performance WISPs would be valuable. One of our 2012 interview subjects who both runs a WISP and consults for new WISPs went so far as to say, "I tell a lot of people that [running a WISP] becomes a lifestyle until you have people, because you have to babysit the network 24/7." Their advice to new WISPs starting out was to focus on automating and integrating as much of their backend processes (billing, subscriber authentication, etc) as possible to improve the odds the WISP would be able to sustain itself and grow. This insight was reflected throughout our interviews, would be reflected in our own experiences starting a WISP, and succinctly motivates the design of Celerate.

3. ASSUMPTIONS

With these results in mind, we now turn to the design of Celerate. We frame the discussion with a collection of assumptions that we brought to the problem. These assumptions are instructive: our exploration of them over the past decade has led us to hone the list of challenges to be addressed.

Target Rural Access. In urban areas density and existing infrastructure—e.g., right of ways for electricity, telephony, or sewage—make building infrastructure for Internet service delivery easier. Even where existing infrastructure deployment is chaotic and underprovisioned, the options available to serve users—wired or wireless—are better than those for rural areas. We thus focused our work on the task of connecting rural users, and began our work with the question: *how can we help rural ISPs scale?*

Design Choice	Reasoning	Comments
Unmodified Commodity Hardware	Wireless hardware is now cheap and high speed, but (sometimes intentionally) difficult to modify, and firmware such as Open-Wrt seldom keeps pace.	With unmodified commodity gear, we can order and ship hardware directly to field sites for immediate deployment, simplifying our pipeline.
Community Relays	Many subscribers are quite close to our relay sites, but lack line of sight. Often one hop to a neighboring house allows us to reach them.	The radio gear necessary at these relays is not generally cost prohibitive, but deciding whether to provide power backups at these sites is difficult as power gear can be very expensive.
Unlicensed and Lightly-Licensed Bands	Hardware for unlicensed and lightly-licensed bands is affordable, and requires minimal hassle. Most WISPs use unlicensed hardware except in rare circumstances.	Using licensed spectrum is in keeping with our goals of matching the demands of WISPs. We do leverage several bands outside of conventional unlicensed spectrum, including those for which we have obtained experimental licenses.
Paid Service	A free network cannot sustain itself after our funding ends, and would not be reflective of a real WISP.	We had some free hotspots at central locations. After our research completes, the network will be handed off to a local nonprofit organization for long-term operation.
No Towers	Building towers is costly and risky, leveraging topography and existing structures is more efficient.	We have recently opted to build a compact tower, but it is one among dozens of sites at which we have avoided to build our own towers.

Table 2: Design choices we made for the rollout of our WISP deployment.

Greenfield is Valuable. As part of answering our question we decided to, and now have built, an ISP from scratch in a rural area in North America, in an area that had no fast or reliable Internet service options; those who had any service at all subscribed to satellite Internet providers. We might not have needed to build yet another ISP to learn lessons from it, but as we began our analysis of how rural ISPs were operated, we concluded that without a real network built from scratch we would inevitably fail to address subtle or seemingly-uninteresting pain points that prevent rural ISPs from starting up, growing, and operating.

Rural ISPs are WISPs. We assumed that rural ISPs are primarily wireless ISPs (WISPs). Specifically we are interested in WISPs of the sort that are built using low-cost point-to-multipoint wireless links, though some also employ wireless meshes and other approaches. We have found that this is true—nearly all rural ISPs are WISPs, though a small fraction still provide dialup service.[2]

Rural Access is Poor. Despite statistics and anecdotal reports to the contrary, our initial exploration of rural connectivity showed that, at least in North America, there is confusion about the state of rural broadband access. In meetings with many existing governmental and nonprofit stakeholders, we found that while the stakeholders' views aligned with ours—that rural access is poor—their *data and maps* said that's not the case. What we found was that since much of their data is submitted by large carriers that have an interest in overstating their coverage, the (inaccurate) maps that are used as ground truth prevent new entrants into rural markets.

SDN Eases Network Management. Our experience with both research and large-scale operational SDN networks indicated to us that SDN can significantly ease the challenges of network management. The promise of SDN is that it makes implementing network-wide policies simpler and eases management complexity in a network with many devices. This has been borne out in the datacenter context, especially in multitenant environments. However, to our knowledge there is little work on SDN or SDN-like architectures for WISPs, and thus it was part of our aim to test this assumption; we discuss this further in later sections.

Rural WISPs Want to Scale. Since our aim is to increase broadband Internet availability in regions that have perennially been without it, a natural aim is to help rural WISPs themselves scale. However, before our greenfield deployment, we were unsure of the pain points of today's WISPs—what is stopping rural WISPs from

scaling? As a part of our effort to understand that, we spoke with numerous WISPs and we brought this assumption with us to those conversations: we assumed that rural WISPs want to scale and to serve a wider area; we expand upon this in the next section.

What we found was striking: WISPs reach their natural boundaries to their growth and stop growing (and often stop attempting to grow) at very small network sizes. Many WISPs are one or two person operations started by individuals without deep networking knowledge; once they became stable and had a user base, the operators ceased expansion. These WISPs typically reached the users within a well-defined geographic area, had set up gear such that it only needed occasional maintenance, and continued providing that service with minimal work thereafter. To expand for these WISPs meant trying to reach far away users, perhaps secure more rights of way, purchase more bandwidth, etc. It was in seeing these successful WISPs that were not growing (which were typically in the topographically easy to serve rural regions), and the WISPs that had failed, that we reframed our aims, as we describe with our next assumption. In large part, the reasons that WISP operators seemed hesitant to scale were not technological: each WISP is naturally limited, by people, finances, and geography.

Scale WISP Numbers, Not Size. After our conversations with WISPs we still believed that new systems and approaches would be valuable for WISPs and expanding rural broadband Internet availability, as many of the existing WISPs relied upon archaic systems to manage their operations when they used such systems at all—it was far from uncommon for a WISP operator to have little or no written or stored documentation of the WISP's topology, devices, configurations, address allocation, or policy. However since these WISPs were often not interested or able to scale their own operations because of non-technological limitations, we concluded that a reframing of the aims was necessary: our new aim is to determine how to scale WISPs in number, not in size. Thus we believe that *the fundamental challenge is to determine how to enable more people to start and operate successful rural WISPs.*

4. DEPLOYMENT

Our deployment provides broadband Internet access to a farming community and indigenous tribe in rural Northern California. In Table 2 we describe design choices we made for the deployment of our WISP network. A private grant covered the cost of physical infrastructure, putting us at a significant advantage over most small WISPs. We are not the first to serve this region, which has a population of only a few thousand individuals scattered in small towns

---

[2]We found dialup speeds are *decreasing* due to aging copper infrastructure; some areas we surveyed in 2014 get just 9600 baud.

Figure 1: A hillside relay site with a small mast we built to host multiple long-distance backhaul radios. At this site we host over a dozen backhaul radios and sectors (not pictured).

over a mountainous coastal region that is 75km North to South and 10km East to West. Indeed, over the past decade, we are aware of at least three other WISPs that have attempted to provide service to the region, and each failed.[3] What makes the lack of service in this region more remarkable is that there is buried long-haul fiber running through the region owned by two Tier-1 carriers, one of whom we negotiated with to purchase bandwidth.

4.1 Hardware

We use commodity hardware from vendors such as Ubiquiti [29] and Mikrotik [13] as most WISPs do. Commodity wireless gear has advanced considerably in the last few years. Several of our core links use Ubiquiti AirFiber systems [2] which cost about $1000 each and can, under ideal circumstances, provide full-duplex 1Gbps links over 10km. Even newer hardware from Ubiquiti and Mikrotik uses 802.11ac with point-to-point and point-to-multipoint radios and can provide hundreds of Mbps per link at much lower cost [14, 22]. Most of the radios in our deployment operate in the 5GHz ISM band, although we do use some devices that are in the 2.4GHz, 3.6GHz, and 24GHz bands in order to cope with a sometimes crowded spectrum. When unthrottled, many subscribers can get 30-60 Mbps symmetric throughput to the Internet with less than 5ms latency within our network, though we throttle them based upon their subscription plan. We also use fanless multi-port embedded Linux boxes at major infrastructure points.

Figure 1 shows directional backhaul radios on a short mast we built. The equipment pictured connects main sites with relatively high-bandwidth links (several hundred Mbps in good conditions). These sites host sector antennas aimed at subscribers who in turn have CPEs (customer-premises equipment) aimed back; some subscribers host short-hop wireless relays to other subscribers.

4.2 Software

Initially we began with the expectation that an SDN-based software stack, coupled with appropriate hardware in the field, might provide significant gains in the management of our network [15, 16, 18, 20]. However, we found the greatest benefit from our software for subscriber and network management. In parallel we have been developing relatively advanced SDN-based tools, but have not seen the value in deploying these in production and so have relegated them to a development testbed. We describe our work on this in Section 5. Our system integrates with Icinga, Cacti, and other classic monitoring tools, but is not tied to them.

---

[3] Anecdotally we learned that they failed due to a combination of technical, geographic, political, financial, and family issues.

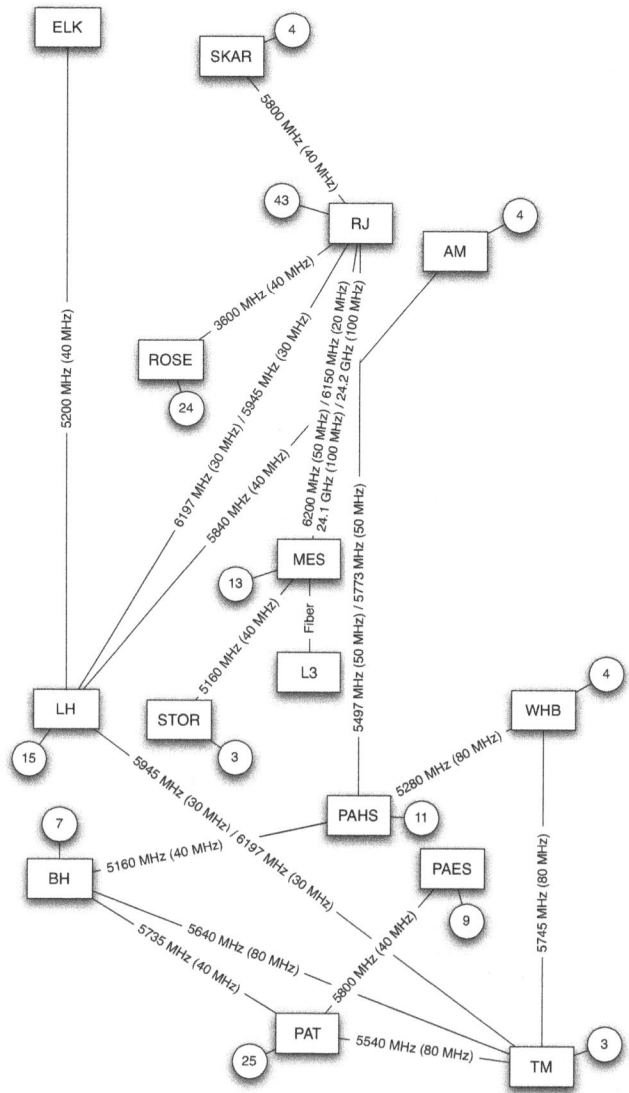

Figure 2: Our WISP network topology as of Q1 2015. Boxes are major sites, labeled by code names. Circles indicate the number of subscribers connected to those sites at that time. Lines depict backhaul links, with frequency and channel width; for full duplex links, we give TX/RX frequencies from South to North.

4.3 Network

Figure 2 shows our major sites and the point-to-point wireless backhaul links that interconnect them; while not to scale, the figure is topographically accurate. Due to numerous hills and forested areas, it is common, as the diagram shows, that nearby sites cannot communicate and must use far away relays. Not shown are the many sector antennas (base stations) that provide point-to-multipoint coverage for connections to subscribers. These sectors are the major source of spectrum contention and interference, which we discuss next. Core sites are bridged and use STP; subscriber nodes only have one path to the gateway.

4.4 Spectrum

Our deployment is in a very rural area, yet there is still significant spectrum contention. There is one other WISP in the region (there was yet another, but it shut down its operations recently), mostly serving different areas, and providing significantly lower

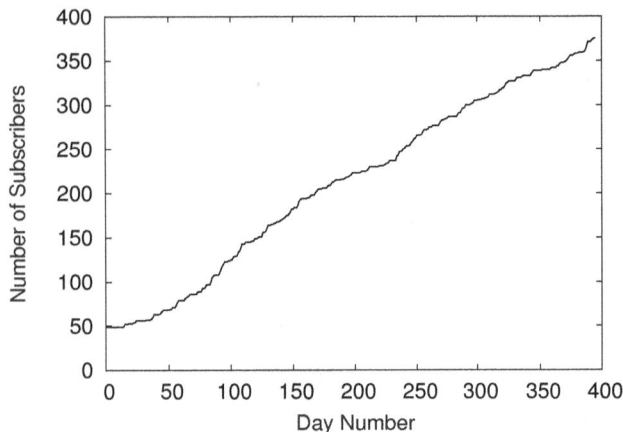

Figure 3: Paying subscribers in our network over time, from 2014-09-01 to 2015-10-01; we began with 49 beta subscribers.

bandwidths. However, we must share certain major sites, such as LH in Figure 2, quickly filling the limited unlicensed ISM bands. At one of our core sites, we have 5 backhaul links and 4 sector antennas that users connect to directly. As a result, we use a radio at 3.6GHz, 7 radios on 5GHz channels, and one radio on a 24GHz channel. The choice of frequencies for our radios at this and other core sites was done manually via careful planning and understanding of the topography, Fresnel zones, weather fade, potential reflections, trees, and spectrum congestion. We had hoped that automated tools, both third-party and our own fledgling efforts, might prove useful, but we found none able to handle the wide range of factors involved in making allocation decisions.

Spectrum regulations constrain our operation, but the situation is improving. For example, in April 2014, the U.S. FCC made several rule changes with regards to (U-NII) devices in the 5 GHz band. This included lifting restrictions on the lower U-NII-1 channels (5.15-5.25 GHz) which had previously been limited to low-power indoor use [10]. It also reiterated the necessity for radios operating on certain U-NII 5GHz channels to use Dynamic Frequency Selection (DFS), a standard for sharing spectrum between radar systems and WiFi devices (the primary and secondary users of this band, respectively). This standard requires secondary devices to listen before transmitting and to move to a different channel if the sense potentially interfering signals. A poor implementation of this can cause a radio to detect "interference" from its own reflected transmissions or choose poor channels to switch to when it must move; this was the cause of an intermittent outage we faced [1].

4.5 Growth

One of the key findings of Section 2 is that WISPs reach natural barriers during network growth: eventually WISPs tend to reach a maximum feasible size and stop growing without external financing. We already see hints of these limits in our own WISP deployment even though we are still in the early stages of network expansion. Figure 3 shows the number of paying subscribers connected to our network over time. The subscriber base of our network frequently reaches plateaus due to natural barriers—a hill beyond which our relays cannot see, for example. Due to our fortunate financial backing, we are often able to circumvent these natural barriers by building new, sometimes expensive relay sites, only to arrive at another barrier after a two-week spurt of growth. Recently we have found that the geographic reach of our network has made it difficult for our technicians to efficiently work at far-flung customer

locations, relay sites, and storage sheds as many hours a day must be spent driving between them despite our best efforts at scheduling. Given our knowledge of the region, we expect our WISP to reach a final plateau at around 700 subscribers in about two years.

5. THE Celerate ARCHITECTURE

Next we describe the design and implementation of Celerate, an architecture for easing the startup and management of WISPs. We use Celerate to manage all aspects of our deployment. Celerate is a work in progress, and will likely require a few years of field deployment and additional refinement before it reaches maturity.

5.1 Challenges

Since Celerate is directly informed by the challenges we have encountered during our deployment and the findings of our WISP studies, we briefly describe the specific challenges that WISPs face that Celerate is designed to respond to. We emphasize that all the challenges listed in this section have both been borne out by our experience and were noted by our study participants. In this we keep squarely in focus our finding that the key way to increase rural broadband connectivity is to help create more WISPs rather than to scale any individual WISP; these new WISP operators are unlikely to have the knowledge or training of existing WISP operators.

Skill Sets. Building a new WISP requires diverse skill sets. Many rural WISPs are operated by a single person, perhaps with part-time contract help for infrastructure work. At small scale, rural WISPs simply can't support a large team of specialists. Thus a single individual is tasked with challenges as diverse as tower and tree climbing, network architecture, carpentry, IP security, negotiating land use, spectrum management, customer support, billing, and reviewing legal agreements. Indeed, it is exactly because of this diversity of required skills—not commonly found in any one individual—that we hypothesized that new tools were needed for such rural WISP networks, to simplify the management of the network and give the WISP operator room to focus on physical infrastructure upgrades, maintenance, and customer support.

Commodity Gear. Almost all WISPs rely upon low-cost commodity wireless hardware and existing software; building custom hardware and implementing custom software is too time consuming, expensive, and requires skills beyond the average WISP operator. In turn commodity wireless hardware vendors operate with thin margins, and as such provide meager software support or flexibility for their hardware. As a result, network management systems, such as SDN systems, cannot leverage support in individual devices, but instead must manage a heterogeneous network of SDN-oblivious commodity devices each with their own quirks.

Operational Issues. The nature of and approaches to resolving operational issues differentiate WISPs from conventional operators. It is not that conventional ISPs or large network operators do not have many of the same operational challenges, but the issues they face are of a different scale: WISPs have a far lower ratio of human expertise and resources relative to the challenges faced in network operation and a far higher ratio of physical and operational challenges relative to the size of the network. This is largely due to dispersed, less-reliable infrastructure and more difficult deployment environments.

Geography and Land Use. In terms of performance, fixed wireless is almost always an inferior option to wired service, and thus is typically used when wired infrastructure is unavailable or is too expensive to deploy. Often, the causes for a lack of wired infrastructure is a lack of population density, rough terrain, or, more often, both. Thus WISPs begin with multiple disadvantages: they must

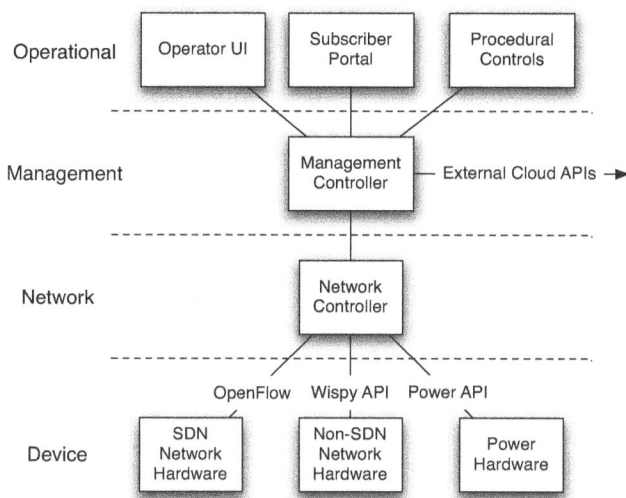

Figure 4: An overview of the subsystems in Celerate.

deliver service to a sparse region (thus making it hard to recoup fixed costs), using wireless instead of wired infrastructure, and do so over challenging terrain. Just because land is not developed in rural areas doesn't mean the landowner will make it available to a (cash-poor) WISP. Lack of existing tower infrastructure with good coverage of the region, especially line-of-sight coverage, means the WISP must build it or find an alternative. Indeed, the best prospects for placement of directional wireless gear is on existing structures such as water tanks, masts, sheds, barns, and the like.

Public Policy. Policy constraints tend to come in two forms: restrictions on spectrum, and restrictions on physical deployments. Spectrum restrictions are not new: WISPs are generally limited to operating on unlicensed spectrum only due to lack of licensing fees, but that spectrum is shared with a variety of other non-WISP devices, complicating spectrum planning. Physical restrictions typically take the form of regulations on tower construction and placement; for example, we found that placement of towers over a certain height under certain zoning required complex permitting and public approval, a process that can take a very long time and can easily end a WISP deployment before it begins.

Summary. The primary challenge posed by geography, land use, public policy, and similar non-technical issues is not the time it takes to resolve them—in due course, WISPs are able to resolve each issue in some way. Instead, the primary challenge is that these issues place non-technical constraints on the design of a WISP network and of the resources that can be deployed to parts of the network; they constrain how WISPs can manage networks on the ground and affect even what hardware they can deploy. It is within these constraints that we aim to address the above challenges to meet the needs of rural WISPs.

5.2 Subsystems

Many of the operational challenges in running a WISP are left out of traditional systems that aim to provide network management support. To make this clearer, next we differentiate between four subsystems of network management that make up Celerate: the device subsystem, the network subsystem, the management subsystem, and the operations subsystem, which we depict in Figure 4. Each of these subsystems corresponds to a plane that communicates with subsystems above and below. As we move up the hierarchy of subsystems from the device subsystem to the operations

subsystem, we deal with a broader technical scope, greater complexity of mechanisms and policy, and slower timescales. Below we provide a sketch of our design for each subsystem and describe initial steps we have taken to realizing these subsystems. We do not claim that the overall structure or the individual pieces of Celerate are novel; indeed, much of it builds upon the canon of networking research over the past two decades. The key difference between Celerate and other network management systems is that it aims to be holistic, since we built it to address the real challenges we faced in building and running a WISP, and we use and improve our Celerate implementation on a daily basis. As mentioned earlier, we have found that the management and and operations subsystems to be most valuable in day-to-day operations.

5.2.1 Device Subsystem

The device subsystem corresponds to the traditional data plane in a networking context. In our context, however, the data plane is just a subset of functionality exposed. For example, in our deployment, the device subsystem includes SDN-enabled networking hardware, commodity non-SDN networking hardware, Power-over-Ethernet (PoE) switches with proprietary interfaces, power monitors, and battery systems. All of these devices provide interfaces for both control and monitoring, but they vary significantly in the interfaces they present. We are in the process of refining and developing APIs to manage these devices; the details of these APIs are relatively mundane, but are exactly what is needed to uniformly control devices that expose different types of functionality. At the moment we expose three APIs to the network controller above: OpenFlow; the Celerate API, which exposes common non-OpenFlow networking functionality such as advanced traffic shaping, SNMP, and wireless control; and the Power API, which exposes the ability to control and monitor power.

Many commodity networking devices actually run forked versions of OpenWrt [9] and thus could run standard Linux networking tools. However, the manufacturers add their own configuration mechanisms, generally in an effort to provide an easy to use GUI. Attempting to connect the network controller directly to these devices would leave a messy, tangled architecture.

5.2.2 Network Subsystem

The network subsytem includes the traditional SDN control plane, as well as extensions to integrate with our higher level management subsystem as well as the diversity of devices exposed by our underlying device subsystem (i.e., devices not traditionally managed by an SDN controller, such as battery backups). Our network subsystem consists of a traditional SDN controller (currently built upon POX [20]) suitably modified to address three of the key challenges we have in managing our dataplane. First, since the device subsystem is highly diverse, the SDN controller has to have support for APIs beyond OpenFlow. Second, the controller receives its ground truth not solely from the network, but as a synthesis of live status of the network from these diverse devices and management state from the subsystem above. Third, the controller requires the ability to speak with the device subsystem, but unlike many SDN deployments (such as in datacenters), we have no easy means of out-of-band communication between the controller and the devices it controls. Thus we have been developing an approach for broadcast-based in-band control for SDN, to ensure the network controller can always communicate with devices in the field.[4]

These two subsystems are the two that SDN typically is concerned with. Beyond them, in industry and academia, a large ar-

---

[4]We believe that this in-band control approach may have broader applicability, but is out of scope for this paper.

ray of diverse and incompatible approaches have been applied to higher subsystem management, usually tailored to specific applications and settings. To our knowledge, none of these higher-layer subsystem approaches are applicable to the unique needs of WISPs, and so we have designed our own, as we discuss next.

5.2.3 Management Subsystem

The management subsystem corresponds to the systems that track a range of information necessary for WISP management: network topology, physical deployments, network site documentation, and subscriber data including information about their physical installations, billing, and configurations. The management subsystem contains the ground truth about the network topology and about users of the network, and conveys this information downward to the network subsystem and upwards to the operations subsystem. We augment this ground truth with periodic automated discovery of new devices that are installed by technicians. We also integrate inventory tracking and management into Celerate.

Our management subsystem implementation is non-traditional for networking software, but an approach that is both flexible and easy to integrate with other systems: we use the Meteor Node.js (Javascript) framework, and our current implementation consists of over 5000 lines of Javascript, 2000 lines of front-end templating code, and hooks into numerous third-party modules and services that provide functionality, such as financial transaction processing, that must remain external to our system.

By separating the management and networking subsystems, we allow for the management subsystem to become disconnected or intermittently connected and not affect the operation of the network. In doing so, we can host and operate the management subsystem elsewhere (using cloud hosting), removing the burden from the WISP operator while not hurting the delivery of Internet service; setting up and running a cloud instance is, to our surprise, hard for some WISP operators we have spoken with, and so this separation allows us to offer it as a hosted service for other WISPs to use. In addition, the management controller can make calls to external cloud-based APIs, something that would be dangerous to do from the network controller.[5]

5.2.4 Operations Subsystem

Finally, the operations subsystem corresponds to the operators and the operational tools used to manage the entire WISP. The operations subsystem is largely human, but also consists of tools for managing and tracking operational and billing issues in the network, monitoring the status of the network, notifying operators about failures, and procedural controls to ensure that operator actions are constrained. This subsystem is a crucial aspect of SDN as applied to WISPs. Indeed, keeping track of subscriber relationship information is the core functionality a WISP needs, and thus is a core of Celerate. In addition, the operations subsystem enables an integrated view of all information needed by a WISP operator, from new-user signups to billing to link status and capacity to power status, and can present a network manager with an entirely new perspective on their network.[6] In addition, we provide a portal

---

[5]One of these external APIs is Stripe, a PCI-compliant credit card processing system which enables us to process credit-card payments without handling credit card data directly [24].

[6]This can be crucial in responding to weather. Our deployment region suffers from heavy storms, which can render our otherwise strong 24GHz backhaul link entirely unusable. We plan to leverage Celerate to enable an operator to anticipate this in advance based upon forecasts and adjust network flows accordingly.

to subscribers similar to that of most large ISPs, so subscribers can see their plan information and pay their bill.

The Operator UI presents a user-friendly interface for technicians in the field to easily search and update this information. Indeed the user-friendliness of the interface, while far from the traditional challenges that are faced by SDN systems, is actually one of the most important, in our experience, to the overall usefulness of the system. Some of the most urgent software fixes we have made are when the operator interface has a bug that prevents field technicians from using it easily on their devices in the field.

While a WISP may have a very professional installation crew, depending upon them to configure hardware in the field—wireless spectrum, routing, services including logging and monitoring, etc.—can be putting too much weight on their shoulders. One of our long-term goals it to enable the operator—with the help of the network management system—to preconfigure devices which can be "plug-and-play". Especially as a WISP starts and begins to grow, not requiring a networking expert to administrate the network can make the difference between success vs failure, or high vs low performance. We hope to deploy our prototype implementation of such support in our network in the coming months.

5.3 Status

We have been developing each of these subsystems independently, have built systems for each, and are integrating them, a process that we expect will require an additional feedback from deployment experience and iteration. Contrary to what we expected at the outset, we have found that we have reaped the most benefit from our work on the management and operations subsystems, and as such much of our development effort has gone into these tools. As a result, we currently use only the management and operations subsystems in our field deployment. Our field technicians have come to rely upon these tools and use them daily when planning, expanding, and debugging the network.

Our challenge has been to define what each subsystem provides to and needs from other subsystems. For example, now that we have delineated for what information the management subsystem holds the authoritative copy (e.g., network topology, power monitoring configurations) vs. the network subsystem (e.g., currently-active links based upon routing decisions, power-cutoff thresholds), there is the potential to fully integrate them.

6. RELATED WORK

For at least a decade researchers have advocated developing networking to meet the needs of poor and rural regions around the world [6]. The potential for WISPs to provide rural Internet access has been recognized for at least that long [4]. Prior work shows low-cost wireless hardware can deliver Internet access affordably and how to modify the MAC and PHY to improve performance [5, 8, 17, 23]. Similar techniques have been adopted by vendors of WISP hardware, making them available to the average WISP operator.

Surana et al. provided an early look at the operational challenges faced in rural wireless networks [25]. More recently, Rey-Moreno et al. describe lessons from the deployment of a community wireless mesh network [21]; this work however focuses on the particular challenges of operating a mesh network and in building a bottom-up community network. Similarly, Gabale et al. describe experiences from managing and a system for monitoring another rural mesh network [11]. While some of our findings and experiences overlap with those of prior work, we focus on the particular challenges around the *business* of operating rural WISPs.

Many WISP-specific management tools exist. HeyWhatsThat [12] is a mapping and link planning tool. Powercode [19],

Swiftfox [27], and Azotel [26] are commercial WISP management systems that provide subscriber, device, and network management tools; TowerDB is a similar open-source project. While exact feature sets vary, all of these and Celerate solve similar problems for WISP operators. Celerate differs from these by supporting deeper integration with network devices and is designed to be a modular, open-source, and SDN-capable platform for WISP management.

7. CONCLUSION AND FUTURE WORK

While our deployment and exploration of the benefits of improved management to WISPs is still young, we believe that our deployment has already showed, to us at least, that these approaches can help new WISPs start up and operate more smoothly. A local partner WISP has repeatedly asked for us to set up our systems for him as he sees that it will have immediate benefits for his operation, and we are in the process of doing so.

We expect that tying the wireless physical layer to SDN is likely to yield benefits for rural WISPs—especially when coordinated across multiple WISP operators—and will further simplify and automate these networks. Our long-term vision is of a WISP network that manages itself—a network that actively diagnoses failures and informs the local operator what to fix. While this vision is not a new one in networking, the context makes it particularly applicable, since WISPs are usually run by very small teams with limited skill diversity. Using SDN to globally coordinate the physical layer and network layer—taking into account RF connectivity, control of electronically steerable antennas, link bitrates, real-time workloads, and multiple backhaul paths through the network—would be beneficial for WISP networks (and would also be an attractive avenue of study, one which we plan to pursue).

We do not claim that our findings are the last word on WISPs, or are even necessarily broadly generalizable. Our surveys covered only a limited number of WISPs in North America, and our system design and experiences are inherently grounded in the particulars of our own network's history and evolution: if nothing else, our work shows that WISPs operate under a diversity of constraints, complexities, and circumstances. That said, our work does provide insight into the state of rural network development today, and importantly we have shown that the low-hanging fruit for WISP deployments comes from easing rather straightforward management burdens. WISPs are small operations constrained by their physical and economic environment, with stages of growth marked by jumps in capital expenditure. While the industry as a whole would benefit from regulatory changes like more allocation of spectrum for unlicensed use (which, happily, is a priority for the FCC), every small WISP that starts must to some extent re-invent and re-discover the best practices and systems necessary to run a sustainable network. To this end, we have developed Celerate as a modular and extensible system for WISP management that addresses the full stack of business concerns of the WISP. In doing so, we believe Celerate can serve to lower the difficulty of starting a WISP, increasing their number and improving access to Internet in rural areas.

8. ACKNOWLEDGEMENTS

We thank Eric Brewer, Jane Cavlina, Fred Coffman, Jason Coleman, Michael Hanson, Julie Lee, Jasper McMurtry, Zean Moore, Troy Nichols, Alex Papazoglou, Jenny Ryan, Krispin Scanlon-Hill, Scott Shenker, and Ron Steinherz for their assistance with this work, along with the Mendocino county community for their support of our efforts. This work was supported by a grant from Google.org and an NSF Graduate Research Fellowship.

9. REFERENCES

[1] IEEE 802.11h Standard. IEEE, 2003.
[2] Airfiber Spec Sheet. http://dl.ubnt.com/datasheets/airfiber/airFiber_DS.pdf.
[3] R. C. Atkinson and I. E. Schultz. Broadband in America: where it is and where it is going, 2009.
[4] F. Bar and H. Galperin. Geeks, Cowboys, and Bureaucrats: Deploying Broadband, the Wireless Way. *African Journal of Information and Communication*, (6):48–63, 2005.
[5] Y. Ben-David, M. Vallentin, S. Fowler, and E. Brewer. Jaldimac: taking the distance further. In *Proceedings of the ACM NSDR Workshop*, 2010.
[6] E. Brewer, M. Demmer, B. Du, M. Ho, M. Kam, S. Nedevschi, J. Pal, R. Patra, S. Surana, and K. Fall. The case for technology in developing regions. *IEEE Computer*, 38(6), 2005.
[7] Celerate. https://github.com/Celerate/celerate-controller.
[8] K. Chebrolu, B. Raman, and S. Sen. Long-Distance 802.11b Links: Performance Measurements and Experience. In *Proceedings of ACM MOBICOM*, 2006.
[9] F. Fainelli. The OpenWrt embedded development framework. In *Proceedings of the Free and Open Source Software Developers European Meeting*, 2008.
[10] FCC 14-30. http://www.fcc.gov/document/5-ghz-u-nii-ro.
[11] V. Gabale, R. Mehta, J. Patani, K. Ramakrishnan, and B. Raman. Deployments Made Easy: Essentials of Managing a (Rural) Wireless Mesh Network. In *Proceedings of the 3rd ACM Symposium on Computing for Development*, page 10. ACM, 2013.
[12] Heywhatsthat. http://heywhatsthat.com/.
[13] MikroTik. http://www.mikrotik.com/.
[14] Mikrotik Netmetal 5. http://i.mt.lv/routerboard/files/NetMetal_4-150106151128.pdf.
[15] OpenDaylight. http://www.opendaylight.org/.
[16] OpenStack. http://www.openstack.org/.
[17] R. K. Patra, S. Nedevschi, S. Surana, A. Sheth, L. Subramanian, and E. A. Brewer. WiLDNet: Design and Implementation of High Performance WiFi Based Long Distance Networks. In *Proceedings of USENIX/ACM NSDI*, 2007.
[18] B. Pfaff, J. Pettit, T. Koponen, M. Casado, and S. Shenker. Extending Networking into the Virtualization Layer. In *Proceedings of ACM SIGCOMM HotNets*, 2009.
[19] Powercode. http://powercode.com/.
[20] POX, Python-based OpenFlow Controller. http://www.noxrepo.org/pox/about-pox/.
[21] C. Rey-Moreno, Z. Roro, W. D. Tucker, M. J. Siya, N. J. Bidwell, and J. Simo-Reigadas. Experiences, Challenges and Lessons from Rolling out a Rural WiFi Mesh Network. In *Proceedings of the 3rd ACM Symposium on Computing for Development*, page 11. ACM, 2013.
[22] Rocket AC Spec Sheet. http://www.ubnt.com/downloads/datasheets/RocketAC/Rocket5ac_DS.pdf.
[23] L. Salameh, A. Zhushi, M. Handley, K. Jamieson, and B. Karp. HACK: hierarchical ACKs for efficient wireless medium utilization. In *Proceedings of USENIX ATC*, 2014.
[24] Stripe. https://stripe.com/.
[25] S. Surana, R. K. Patra, S. Nedevschi, M. Ramos, L. Subramanian, Y. Ben-David, and E. A. Brewer. Beyond Pilots: Keeping Rural Wireless Networks Alive. In *Proceedings of USENIX/ACM NSDI*, 2008.
[26] Azotel Technologies. http://www.azotel.com/.
[27] Swiftfox. http://www.swiftfox.net/.
[28] Ubiquiti Networks. Ubiquiti Networks Q1 Fiscal Year 2015 Earnings, November 2014.
[29] Ubiquiti Networks. http://www.ubnt.com/.

USSD: The Third Universal App

Trevor Perrier
Computer Science &
Engineering
University of Washington
tperrier@cs.washington.edu

Brian DeRenzi
Department of Computer
Science
University of Cape Town
bderenzi@cs.uct.ac.za

Richard Anderson
Computer Science &
Engineering
University of Washington
anderson@cs.washington.edu

ABSTRACT

In this paper we argue for the use of Unstructured Supplementary Service Data (USSD) as a platform for universal cell phone applications. We examine over a decade of ICT4D research, analyzing how USSD can extend and complement current uses of IVR and SMS for data collection, messaging, information access, social networking and complex user initiated transactions. Based on these findings we identify situations when a mobile based project should consider using USSD with increasingly common third party gateways over other mediums. This analysis also motivates the design and implementation of an open source library for rapid development of USSD applications. Finally, we explore three USSD use cases, demonstrating how USSD opens up a design space not available with IVR or SMS.

Keywords

USSD; SMS; ICT4D; M4D; mHealth; mAgriculture; mBanking

1. INTRODUCTION

Mobile phone applications have tremendous impact in global development across the domains of health, agriculture, education, and finance. The field, referred to as Mobiles for Development (M4D), builds upon the ubiquity of mobile phones and standard digital telephony. Two fundamentally different approaches are used for deploying services on mobile phones. One approach is to build services using generic features provided by the mobile operator, such as voice or text, ensuring the service is available on every single mobile phone handset. The other approach is to take advantage of capabilities of specific types of handsets, including installing and executing applications on individuals' mobile phones. Both of these approaches are important, but in this paper we focus solely on the first approach, targeting applications which are intended to have broad reach and high coverage across a population. One strength of this generic approach is that it can be used to reach people owning basic mobile phones. Even though smartphones have a growing market share, a very large number of people will continue to use basic or feature phones over the next decade. Being able to reach owners of basic phones is particularly important for development initiatives reaching the poorest people.

Mobile applications designed to work with carrier provided services, and not utilize features of specific handsets have generally focused on voice through Interactive Voice Response (IVR) and text through Short Message Service (SMS). IVR and SMS are *Universal Apps* in that they make services uniformly available on every mobile handset. There is a third option for a Universal App, which is less frequently used in M4D: Unstructured Supplementary Service Data (USSD). USSD is a protocol defined inside the Global System for Mobile Communications (GSM) standard.[1] USSD is a session based protocol, like IVR, that supports the exchange of text data, like SMS, thus filling a gap in the M4D design space. The most common uses of USSD are for customers interacting with a carrier's services, such as querying airtime or subscribing to information services. This is done by sending a *star code* (such as *144# to check an airtime balance with Safaricom in Kenya) and accessing interactive menu systems. USSD has a number of advantages over SMS, such as providing greater privacy, which makes it a candidate for some important M4D applications. However, until recently, it has been very difficult to deploy USSD applications due to requirements of working directly with carriers. As third party companies have begun making USSD services available, there are growing opportunities for M4D to utilize a new Universal App.

In this paper we explore the application design space for USSD by identifying fundamental considerations and trade offs between IVR, SMS, and USSD. By analyzing existing universal applications we propose methods for USSD to enhance and improve M4D services such as data collection, health messaging, and accessing data. Based on these findings we describe the design and implementation of a library for rapidly building USSD applications. Finally, we develop three detailed use cases to show how USSD applications in different domains provide services that neither SMS or IVR alone can accomplish.

2. BACKGROUND

Prior use of USSD in the ICT4D literature has been limited. A search of the ACM Digital library returns only 52

ACM DEV 2015, December 1–2, 2015, London, United Kingdom.
© 2015 ACM. ISBN 978-1-4503-3490-7/15/12 ...$15.00.
DOI: http://dx.doi.org/10.1145/2830629.2830645 .

---

[1]USSD is not supported on CDMA networks, however GSM covers 90% of the world and is particularly ubiquitous in those regions with the lowest smartphone penetration.

publications using the term "USSD". In two of these publications USSD is either an unrelated acronym or a typo, and 12 of the papers are systems or security papers not related to ICT4D. Of the remaining 38 papers, 32 reference USSD in an incidental manner, leaving only 6 papers with any discussion of USSD in an ICT4D context [19, 18, 37, 17, 38, 23]. Several works have explored the potential of USSD based menus noting that they are feasible in countries using a Latin based scripts [19] but not those that must access the full range of Unicode characters [18]. Based on observations in Kenya, Whyche and Murphy [37] strongly advocate for USSD as a mechanism for reaching the users at the bottom of the pyramid. However, they also note that USSD is not as widely used as SMS or IVR.

Despite a lack of USSD examples in academic deployments, USSD and similar tools such as SIMapps[2] are integral to large scale M4D successes. Perhaps the most well known example is mPesa in Kenya. The wide spread adoption of it and other mobile money programs demonstrates the potential of simple menu based services to reach owners of low-end mobile phones. One reason USSD has not been a primary focus of ICT4D researchers is establishing USSD service has traditionally been more difficult than using SMS or IVR. With SMS and voice, a modem or mobile phone can be the gateway between application logic and the telephone network; however, with USSD a direct connection with a mobile operator (MO) must be established. Most MOs do not support API's with general access, requiring connections through telephony protocols such as Short Message Peer-to-Peer (SMPP) or Signaling System No. 7 (SS7), which have high start up costs and bureaucratic overhead.

However, recently third parties have begun opening up USSD gateways. The APIs have HTTP end points for establishing new USSD sessions and interacting with ongoing ones. Each time a new request comes, the gateway will forward it to all callback URL with the message, phone number, and session ID. The web service is responsible for responding with a correctly formatted message to display. This makes creating USSD applications no more complicated then IVR or SMS. Besides HTTP gateways many software as a service (SaaS) cloud hosted solutions have appeared. These services already connect to existing gateways and have interfaces for creating and managing contacts, messaging campaigns, and data collection flows. However, none of these companies currently support higher level USSD features such as menu creation, managing state, and storing personal information. Table 1 lists some of these gateways, split into gateway only providers and SaaS solutions. This is not a comprehensive list and many similar gateways can be found with global coverage or local focus.

There is a large body of work showing that universal applications built on top of SMS and voice have a significant part in the ICT4D design space. These projects have shown how universally accessible mobile applications can be used as a catalyst for change and demonstrate the role USSD plays in this design space. One of the first ICT4D projects showing the potential of SMS to simplify interactions and reach end users was Warana Unwired [36] which converted a kiosk based information system into an SMS query system.

Since then many more projects have explored the SMS M4D design space which we will analyze in Section 3.

Within the field of mHealth there is mounting evidence for the importance of SMS and IVR at engaging patients to improve health outcomes. WelTel [16], one of the first SMS based mHealth studies, showed that sending simple, single word SMS messages significantly decreased HIV viral load among ART patients. Following on this work other projects have shown that IVR can offer a richer user experience for patient engagment [14, 22].

Besides messaging, another major use for IVR and SMS solutions has been data collection in the field. Patnaick et al. [25] did an early study in India comparing forms, SMS, and voice and showed that while voice was the most costly it was also more accurate than SMS prototypes. However, Danis et al. [7] showed that SMS based surveys were successfully answered in Uganda. One reason for these seemingly contradictory results just one year apart is the different demographic and cultural context between Uganda and Gujarat, India.

3. UNIVERSAL GSM APPLICATIONS

SMS, IVR, and USSD can be considered universal applications since each protocol is outlined in the GMS specification and works on every single handset. Universal mobile applications are well suited for M4D deployments that aim to reach end users. There is no need to customize applications for individual handsets as J2ME deployments require or provide standardized hardware to all participants, both of which hamper the ability of a project to scale and reach all target users [28]. The use of these communication channels represents a fundamental trade-off between universal access and the richness of user interactions due to the limited user interfaces of universal applications. In the next two sections we explore the design space of universal M4D applications showing how USSD complements existing services. We also layout guidelines that assist organizations starting M4D projects to decide on which technologies suite their design goals and project requirements.

3.1 Design Space and User Interactions

We first analyzes applications built on top of SMS and IVR to understand the types of user interactions and platforms in use. Fogg and Allen [9] identified five categories of SMS applications for health. Even though this work did not focus on a developing world context, the universality of SMS means it can be applied across applications in the M4D domain and onto other universal modes of mobile communication.

Projecting Fogg's persuasive SMS computing model onto the existing literature we examine well known projects and identified five specific application domains for M4D services. In each of these domains there is a substantial body of work demonstrating the effectiveness of both SMS and IVR. USSD has not been as widely adopted, but the few examples of USSD applications show that it is well suited for complicated user interactions.

3.1.1 Data Collection

Data collection is an important domain for ICT4D acting as an enabling tool to improve service delivery and evaluation. For projects that can provide smart- or feature-phones, there are powerful data collection applications such as ODK

---

[2]Built on the SIM Application Toolkit SIMApps interface directly with the SIM card enabling menu driven interactions. See Medic Mobile for an interesting use case: https://medicmobile.org/tools

Table 1: Third party REST gateway providers and SaaS companies.

HTTP Only Gateways	SMS	IVR	USSD	Coverage
Twilio[†], Nexmo[^]	✓	✓		World Wide
txtNation[±]	✓	✓	✓	World Wide
Infobip	✓	✓	✓	9 different countries
Africa's Talking[‡]	✓	✓	✓	Kenya
Ideamart[#], SMSGH[%], Panacea Moible[$]	✓		✓	Sri Lanka | Ghana | South Africa

[†]http://twilio.com/ [^]http://nexmo.com/ [±]http://txtnation.com [*]http://infobip.com
[‡]http://africastalking.com [#]http://ideamart.lk [%]http://developers.smsgh.com [$]http://panaceamobile.com

SaaS Enabled Gateways	SMS	IVR	USSD	Coverage
VumiGo[§]	✓		✓	11 countries across Africa
Voto Mobile[¶]	✓	✓		Ghana, Tanzania, South Africa
TextIt[♣]	✓	✓		Android, Twilio
Telerivet[◇] Frountline Cloud[♠]	✓			Android, Twilio, Nexemo

[§]http://vumi.org [¶]http://votomobile.org [♣]http://textit.in/ [◇]https://telerivet.com [♠]http://frontlinesms.com

Collect [13] and CommCareHQ. However, when data collection is required across large populations or must be accessible on personal mobile phones, default GSM solutions are the most feasible option. In this case the universality of SMS, IVR, and USSD trumps the improved UI and features of device specific applications.

While, SMS has been a common choice for data collection, the unstructured and asynchronous nature requires special syntax for submitting data. In the SMS for Life project, weekly SMS reports were collected containing stock levels for antimalarial medications and rapid diagnostic tests in rural Tanzania [4]. Each tracked resource was assigned a single letter code. By combining these codes, all necessary fields were reported in a single SMS. This allowed structured data to be automatically parsed from incoming SMSs. Data showed a high average response rate (95%) and low average error rate (7.5%) indicating that, at least in rural Tanzania, simple SMS reporting is feasible at large scale.

Beyond simple data collection, various methods have been developed to capture large amounts of structured data via SMS. Using a RapidSMS based system, Assiimwe deployed reporting system that captured weekly disease counts and stock levels [3]. With almost 40 data fields, a single SMS per field was cumbersome and expensive, while putting all fields into a single SMS was complicated. Instead, four different SMS messages were created with the assistance of a paper job aid. This eliminated much of the syntax while maintaining an average error rate of 8.8%. Other examples of job aids assisting message creation include the Reporting Wheel from Instedd [3] to help translate data into nine digit numbers for easy submission and parsing.

SMS data collection can also be accomplished with a multi-SMS survey form. This type of data collection is exemplified by early work from Text for Change sending HIV related quizzes via SMS in Uganda [7]. Each question is a single SMS and participants are asked to respond with a question specific key word prefixed to their answer. These multi-SMS surveys have been standardized as part the SaaS IVR and SMS services from Table 1 as well as services dedicated to data collection such as CommCareHQ.

Voice data collection is a good option for low literacy users [18]. Previous results have shown that voice data collection can be more accurate than both SMS and digi-

tal forms [25]. Using an IVR system numeric and multiple choice questions can be recorded using Dual Tone-Multi Frequency (DTMF) touch tones and open ended verbal responses can be recorded for later analysis. Multiple projects have used IVR for data collection [11, 15] and just like with SMS, third-party SaaS services have emerged to provide voice data collection.

By using USSD for data collection, the user experience and work flow can be improved in three ways. First, including all transactions in a single session simplifies the user experience around multi-SMS forms. Second, the menu system acts as a built in job aid eliminating the need for complex syntax to fit as much information as possible into a single SMS. Third, using USSD for data collection allows for immediate data validation during the session flow. These advantages of USSD are most helpful for organizations who can not train all end users or when data collection may happen infrequently and enumerators never have time to become comfortable with complex SMS syntax.

3.1.2 Messaging for Awareness

Messaging for awareness and engagement was a cornerstone of Fogg's persuasive technology SMS framework and has become an integral aspect of ICT4D work. The theory behind messaging campaigns is grounded in behavior change communication and relies on two main assumptions: (1) open communication channels improve uptake of available services and (2) frequent small reminders help with the adoption and maintenance of new practices.

The Kenya WelTel project was among the first controlled studies measuring the effectiveness of messaging for awareness [16]. For 12 months patients initiating antiretroviral therapy (ART) received a weekly SMS with the single word *Mambo* (How are you). They were asked to reply with either *Sawa* (Fine) or *Shida* (Not Fine). Even with such simple messaging content, the WelTel study found a significant decrease in HIV viral load between those receiving and not receiving SMSs.

The low cost, quick content creation, and ease of sending SMSs has meant many other projects use it for awareness and engagement. Across the medical domain, projects focused on both health workers [39, 3, 8] and patients [27, 30, 26] have demonstrated high levels of engagement and changes in behavior. In places with low literacy similar

---

[3]http://instedd.org/technologies/reporting-wheel/

projects have targeted maternal health outcomes using voice such as making automated voice calls from a doctor to pregnant women about iron supplements [22].

A review paper on mHealth found that one reason to prefer IVR over SMS is to ensure privacy for vulnerable populations [12]. For example, a project working with men who have sex with men decided to use voice calls instead of SMS primarily to ensure messages were not saved on shared phones. Recent work with HIV positive youth in Kampala, Uganda has shown that privacy is paramount when sending SMSs [29]. In this respect USSD has the same level of privacy of voice based systems. By requiring a PIN before accessing medically sensitive information, a USSD system can more directly address individuals needs while at the same time protecting doctor patient confidentiality - especially if the phone is shared among individuals.

3.1.3 Accessing Information

Ubiquitous, on demand access to information is one of the most revolutionary features of mobile computing. Enabling end users at the bottom of the pyramid to find information when they need it has been a major challenge in ICT4D. An early project using mobile phones for information access was Warana Unwired [36] which replaced a PC-based kiosk system for information retrieval with an SMS interface at a sugarcane cooperative in India. This system used a smartphone connected to computer to allow correctly formatted SMS queries to access information previously only accessible via a computer. Another ICTD project enabled SMS querying of taxi arrivals in Kyrgyzstan [2]. One finding from that work was that USSD would be more cost effective and user friendly.

The fact that SMS is always available has been a major driver for query based systems. Google and Yahoo both had SMS interfaces [31] prior to more data intensive and graphical interfaces enabled by smartphones. The limiting nature of the SMS responses has lead to work optimizing for this low bandwidth channel [33]. Chen et al. created an SMS based web search system specifically designed for SMS results on low end phones [5]. Voice channels have not been used for data querying largely due to the fact that automatic speech recognition does not work well for the vast majority of languages in the world. The primary use case for voice channels has been to create call in hot-lines accessing information through a live operator [6] [25].

Creating applications for information access over USSD adds a layer of interactivity to SMS based systems. For example in a series of prompts the Vumi Wikipedia Zero application[4] allows the user to narrow down a search before returning the first 180 words of the page and section requested. With the user interface of USSD a sugarcane cooperative could provide a menu driven application for accessing individual information as well as a query interface for in formation about best practices or new procedures. Like SMS, USSD works best with short text based responses and requires the development of backend processes specifically designed for this limited channel.

3.1.4 Social Networks and Group Messaging

Since the first Usenet newsgroups, ICT has been connecting individuals, friends, family, and the larger community. It is no surprise that ICT4D research has looked at connecting

beyond the default capabilities of SMS and voice. Odero created Tangazo, as a group messaging platform. Subscribed users could send either voice or SMS messages to custom made groups, and a special SMS syntax was used to manage group membership [21]. Safaricom in Kenya has a small SMS based group SMS messaging service called Semeni[5] that allows users to create groups of up to 10 members managed through a USSD interface.

USSD as a user interface is well suited for small group social networking. Using our library it would be possible to easily create digital groups connecting and strengthening existing community ties. Grassroots community groups are a common mechanism for development. For example, community health workers lead mothers groups and peer HIV support groups and peer structures are fundamental to microfinancing. A USSD menu system could be used to help facilitate group interactions outside of meetings as well as connect different groups.

While Tangazo connected small groups together IVR systems such as CGnet Swara [20] and Avaaj Otalo [24] create voice networks linking large groups of people. At scale curating user submitted content for access over menu systems becomes an issue [34]. In a large USSD based social network similar concerns would arise since search and discoverability are limited to 180 characters. For this reason, we see the benefit of USSD in the social networking domain primarily to help create small focused community based groups.

3.1.5 Complex User Transactions and Interactions

A paradigm shift occurs once useful functions can efficiently and economically be preformed on a mobile device. The mobile is transformed from a one-to-one communication tool into a device for accomplishing tasks and interacting with larger systems. However, it is when complex tasks need to be preformed that the fundamental limitations of universal GSM applications make systems overly complicated. For example, findings from an SMS based agriculture trading system in Uganda showed that almost all the messages received could not be automatically parsed [32]. Again,the study authors suggested that USSD would be a viable alternative to the complex SMS structure.

Because of their session based nature, both IVR and USSD are more suitable for preforming complex user interactions. Many MOs have IVR systems that allow users to top up via DTMF key presses and perform basic administrative features for prepaid lines. One of the most complex IVR universal applications deployed is TAMA which provides treatment support for HIV+ individuals and was tested in India for 12 months [14]. Protected by a PIN patients receive calls from TAMA with reminders to take medication. The system also has the ability to record adherence. Patients can call the system to inquire about symptoms or listen to 30 second health tip messages.

Another example of complex transaction tasks via GSM applications is a pilot project to book train tickets sponsored by the Indian Ministry of Railways [1]. This services is offered on all three universal application GSM channels. The SMS message syntax is quite complex, requiring one SMS with train and station codes plus a correctly formatted date and a second SMS to confirm and authorize mobile billing that has five unique fields. This is in contrast to the USSD interface consisting of a series of menus to select a station,

---

[4]https://github.com/praekelt/vumi-wikipedia

[5]http://www.semeni.co.ke/

date, and ticket type. Authorization of mobile billing with PIN code occurs within the same session and confirmation details that act as an eTicket are sent back via SMS.

3.2 Advantages and Limitations of GSM User Interfaces

In this section, we analyze the three universal GSM applications from the view point of organizations wanting to deploy M4D solutions and the users they target. When launching a mobile based project the choice of underling technology is dependent on many factors including, but not limited to, target demographics, administrative overhead, usability, setup costs, maintainability, and scalability. There is no universal method or technology set for a mobile based project and each deployment must be evaluated individually, based on the target country, demographics and partners.

3.2.1 Setup and Infrastructure

When starting an M4D project the first question an organization must ask is what technology is available. Connecting with the telecommunication system can be difficult with two main pathways. At the do-it-yourself (DIY) level, a commodity phone can be used as a modem. With tools such as IVR Junction [35] and FrontlineSMS, a working system can be setup relatively quickly and with low overhead. However, these solutions do not scale well. A more robust solution is needed if simultaneous voice calls must be handled or a high rate of SMS need to be sent (over 1000 SMS/hour). A second limitation of DIY solutions is the inability to have toll free numbers and short codes. So, while setup up costs might be low, it is expensive for end users. Projects often look for ways to send airtime reimbursements [10]. There is also a reliability concern for DIY solutions, since the phone-modem is a single point of failure, risking running out of power or airtime, or loss through damage or theft. DIY solutions are not available for USSD, which is a major reason why USSD applications have been limited to large organizations.

At the next level of complexity, there exists an ecosystem of third party gateways who have partnered with mobile operators (MOs) to make available HTTP gateways for voice, SMS, and USSD. Table 1 lists eight of these gateways in two different categories - large multinational and smaller country specific gateways. The multinational gateways can reach many countries because they send messages from international numbers into countries where they do not have a partnership with an existing MO. This makes prices much higher for places like Kenya and Ghana using Nexmio over local gateways that have direct deals with country MOs. In the last few years the the number of these gateways that offer USSD APIs has been rapidly expanding and this is a significant motivation for this work. We expect more USSD gateways to open up in the future. For example InfoBip claims that USSD services will soon be available in Brazil, Peru, India, Thailand, and Ukraine.

3.2.2 Communication Channel Usability

Each GSM transport layer creates a different user experience and choosing the appropriate one depends on the target audience and service complexity. Figure 1 groups each channels based on the mode of communication and the method of interaction. On these axes SMS and USSD are the text based analogs of automated voice calls and IVR. From this

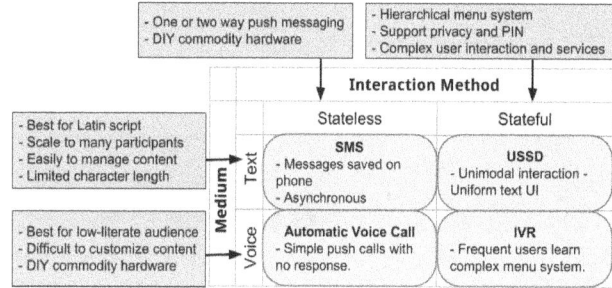

Figure 1: Comparison of GSM applications design space split by communication medium and interaction method.

perspective USSD can be viewed as a bridge between the session based features of IVR and the text based mode of SMS.

There are four primary considerations for choosing between text and voice channels. The first, and primary reason, is that for most projects creating and collecting text based content will have lower administrative cost. For example three hundred preconfigured text messages can be modified with the name of sender and recipient when sending an SMS [26], prerecording these as voice messages means content is not as flexible or customizable. This is a major reason to favor text over voice solutions. However, the second consideration is the literacy proficiency of the end users - which may require that voice be used. A data collection program used by trained CHWs can use SMS [3], while, a program targeting pregnant women from a Mumbai slum should use voice [22]. Another reason to potentially prefer voice over text is that non-Latin script support on low end phones is often poor [17]. Lastly, it is important to consider the bandwidth and cost requirements of each channel. While SMS and USSD have extreme character restrictions (160 and 180 chars respectively) they can easily scale to many thousands of messages an hour. Voice, on the other hand, scales well with larger content but establishing multiple simultaneous voice lines raises costs. Such concerns are very dependent on each country, for example voice is cheaper relative to SMS in India while it is the reverse in Kenya.

3.2.3 Stateful and Stateless Messaging

The requirements of an individual project will also require a decision between the session based interaction which maintains state, and stateless automated calls or SMS messages. Stateful applications allow for a broader design space but come with increased setup and maintenance cost. If an intervention simply needs asynchronous messaging there is no need to move beyond SMS or automatic voice calls. The SaaS SMS solutions from Table 1 have a backends that simulates stateful connections over SMS in the same way web servers convert HTTP from a stateless to stateful protocol.

However, for certain applications the true session based interaction of USSD and IVR cannot be mimicked. First, session based interactions are not saved on the mobile phone. This is extremely important for guaranteeing privacy from friends and family, particularly when a shared phone is involved and sensitive health topics such as TB, HIV, or family planning are discussed. An additional layer of privacy is gained by entering a PIN before taking any actions. Although not secure against man-in-the-middle or operator snooping, this is secure against friends and family from learning about a sensitive medical condition. Other reasons to prefer a session based medium are that hierarchical menus are much easier to implement, real time validation is smoother, and interactions happen in real time.

4. USSD LIBRARY DESIGN

We next describe our library designed to create USSD based applications that work with existing third party USSD gateways. The library is created with the Django web-framework facilitating integrating with Python based message routing platforms such as Vumi and RapidPro. The intention behind this open source reference library is two fold: first to help define the building blocks of generic USSD applications; and second, to provide M4D deployments targeting end users a third option besides SMS and IVR. Currently, the intended user of this library is an organization that has accesses to programming experience, but we are working on methods to create USSD menu systems and questions using Excel worksheets or a graphical flow visualizer. Eventually we hope that third party SaaS messaging providers will incorporate these USSD features into the services they provide.

The library is a set of Python class that can be extended to quickly implement the flow and organization of a USSD menu system. By extending the basic *USSDTransport* class applications with the particular variables required by a third-party USSD HTTP APIs our framework assists with establishing text based sessions. Currently our prototype implementation interacts with the Ideamart USSD simulator[6] (Figure 2) and the Panacea Mobile USSD gateway[7] via their HTTP API.

Unlike stateless SMS applications a USSD application must maintain the users state throughout each session. Both Panacea Mobile and the Ideamart USSD simulator interact over the stateless HTTP protocol, so an important feature provided by the library is the seamless management of session state. This is done by using the session ID provided by each USSD gateway API as a UUID for a Django HTTP session. In this way each initiated USSD session maintains its own current position and state on the server side and can determine the next USSD screen to send based on the current state and user input.

A USSD applications is defined by a linked graph of nodes called *USSDScreens*. The most basic node is a TextNode that simply renders a template string to be sent to the user's phone. Each screen is rendered using context variables associated with the current session and user. For example if each contact has a next visit date, preferred language, and age variable linked with them these variables become available in template strings. Two additional nodes extend from TextNode. The MenuNode links other nodes together attaching numbered options that map to other USSDScreen instances. MenuNodes provide consistent navigation throughout the library; the numbers one through eight jump to a next node while '0' goes to the last screen, '9' goes to the

[6]www.ideamart.lk/idea-pro/ussd
[7]www.panaceamobile.com/gateways/ussd-gateway/

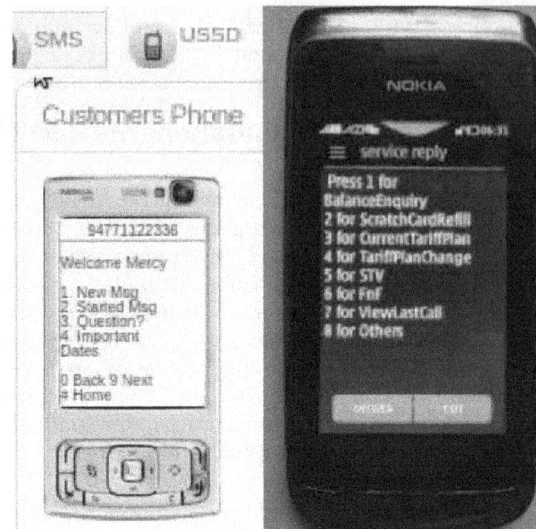

Figure 2: Left: Example Maternal Health USSD application running on IdeaMart USSD Simulator; Right: USSD home screen for Indian mobile operator BSNL.

next screen of a long list, and '#' will go back to the home screen. The characters for all of these actions are easily configurable and can also be disabled on individual screens. We also implement the QuestionNode, which validates response and establishes branching logic for the next node based on the response making it possible to create simple forms with a few Python classes. For more specific applications the TextNode class can be extended.

The library also has optional screens that can be added before the home screen is shown. This can be used to present the user with the option of initiating the USSD session where they left of last time or requiring that a correct PIN number be entered before the home screen is shown. Because the USSD library is built on top of the Django framework it also makes it easy to have a web accessible admin interface. Administrative tasks include replying to messages left by users in the USSD system, monitoring usage statistics, and exporting collected data. The library also makes it easy to open a web accessible front end that mimics the workflow of the USSD system. Thus users who have a data enabled phone can access the application over USSD or a web browser. We are also working on an Android application to access the same information over a built in API. Using this library we have built a prototype Maternal Health application for testing the work flow and integration of the libraries building blocks. (Figure 2)

5. USSD USE CASES AND PERSONAS

In this section we explore how the building blocks of our USSD library can create applications that improve the usability and quality of universal GSM applications. These use cases illustrate several advantages of USSD over SMS, practicality when it comes to real time interactions and privacy. Although some parts of these services have been implemented with SMS or IVR, the full USSD implementation is not replicable on any other default GSM medium. They also highlight how the general flow of USSD applications is easily extended beyond the traditional financial services application. However, they also expose limitations of basic GSM applications and why for some cases it might make sense to target phone specific applications utilizing a data channel.

We introduce each use case through a target user's persona and demonstrate how she or he would utilize different USSD applications to accomplish tasks and access services.

5.1 Maternal Health

Mercy is a 20 year old Ugandan living in the informal settlement of Namuwongo, southeast of Kampala. She is among the ninety percent of Namuwongo residents living on less then one dollar a day. Twenty-two weeks into her first pregnancy she has just attended her first antenatal care visit. There was a two and a half hours wait before she had twenty minutes with a nurse who took vital signs, listened to the babies heart, and drew some blood. Mercy was ushered into a room with twelve other first time mothers where they were told what to expect during pregnancy, where to give birth, and given booklets to record clinic visits and their baby's milestones. She thought she was done after this session, but the nurses sent her to another room - this time with just four other expectant mothers. In this room Mercy found out she was HIV positive.

There was a torrent of information and although the nurses tried to be understanding Mercy found it difficult to focus on this new reality. The nurse asked her for a four digit personal identification number so she chose the last two digits of her and her sisters birth years. They told her that if she called a special number - it looked like a code to top up a phone - she could enter her name and the secret number to access information and ask a nurse questions. Before leaving each of them practiced logging into the system.

Later when Mercy tried the system she liked how the first screen did not mention HIV or being pregnant, rather it displayed a generic health tip with a box to type her name. After hitting send a new health tip displayed with another box, Mercy didn't know what to do with this box so she just hit send again. This time the system told her she had used her two health tips and to call again. That reminded her what the second box was for, her PIN number. After correctly signing in she was presented with four options. Press 1 for New Messages, Press 2 for Starred Messages, Press 3 For Questions, Press 4 for Important information. Going to the new messages Mercy saw the welcome messages, the nurses had told her that this message would change every week. Mercy followed instructions to star the welcome message since it was the only message she had. The screen told her to press # to go to the beginning and from there she checked the important dates menu which told her how many days until her next visit and when her due date was.

This use case demonstrates how USSD can augment existing SMS based systems that support marginalized individuals living with HIV. By requiring a user name and password to access the USSD system mothers who share a phone with family members can call from any available phone. The application looks like a generic health tip service without proper credentials. We acknowledge that this system still has some security vulnerabilities since USSD communication is not encrypted - but is is an improvement on SMS only solutions.

5.2 Agriculture

Solomon is a Ghanaian farmer living in Gushie, 50km north of Tamale - the capital of the Northern Region. He and his brothers grow cassava, yams, kola nuts, and bananas for a regional farmers cooperative based in Tamale. The cooperative runs a marketplace to help match produce buyers and sellers. Every time Solomon goes to Tamale, he checks the records for how much his farm has sent to the cooperative, when the number doesn't match his expectations it can take awhile to sort out. The cooperative is also a great place to exchange information with farmers from villages Solomon doesn't visit often. There is a bulletin boards with fliers from the Ministry of Agriculture and NGO's advertising new, and sometimes old, techniques or tools. Solomon doesn't always trust this information and likes to ask what theories his friends have about it before he goes home.

This time when Solomon visited the cooperative they advertised a special star code to call and access information that would be useful to him. He had received SMSs from the cooperative before containing information about when crops would be collected or that the road into Tamale was bad. He also knew there was a way to post crops to the cooperative exchange via SMS. However, he personally didn't know any farmers who had used it and he heard rumors that it didn't always work if you typed information incorrectly.

The next week Solomon received another SMS reminding him about the star code and he decided to call it. The home screen was a menu with the following choices: 1. Weather, 2. Personal Account 3. Exchange Market 4. Community 5. Tips. After sending back 5 the next screen had the title of 6 new tips. The last line told him that 0 would go back and 9 would go to the forward in the list. The first tip was about about using herbicide for weed management - something the cooperative was always pushing and Solomon never had the savings to get. Though he wished to someday to use herbicide. There was an option to give feedback on the tip, so he reported that it wasn't very helpful since it was information he already knew. Solomon pressed 0 to go back and then went to the community forum. This was a message board with six different categories for posts. Solomon went into the section for cassava and found a list of posts by other farmers. He found out that he could make his own post by entering '+' and the '@' symbol would reply to someone. The last thing Solomon did was check the market place where he found a series of menus to help post crops to the exchange and see what the current prices were.

5.3 Data Collection

Josephine is a manager working with the National Immunization Program (NIP) in Kigoma, a district capital in Tanzania on Lake Tanganyika. She needs to receive information on a regular basis from health facilities, including weekly reports on vaccine stocks, as well as immediate notifications of stock outs and refrigerator failures. She is excited about the introduction of a USSD based system for data collection from rural facilities, as she has found using USSD to send money to relatives on mPesa both useful and reliable.

As part of the introduction of the new system, Josephine is leading training sessions throughout the district. Health workers from the rural areas have been attending these sessions where the NIP confirms that the current database is current. They use a web based management system to add contact phone numbers for each facility. When a number assigned with a health facility dials the USSD short code they get a simple menu system: 1. Submit Weekly Report, 2. Stock Out, 3. Fridge Status, and 4. Report Histories. The weekly report is a series of questions collecting the stock of six key vaccines as well as case reports for ten diseases. Josephine likes the fact that if the system detects format errors it replies with hints asking for the data to be resubmitted.

When Josephine calls the USSD number, she gets a different menu system from the health facility version. This admin USSD interface allows her to enter and view data for any facility while on the road. She can also associate new phone numbers with a health facility and manage information on the refrigerators. This is useful when she visits health facilities, because sometimes the data recorded can be inaccurate and, even on her smartphone, she has found it impossible to access the web interface on poor data connections at rural facilities.

6. DISCUSSION AND FUTURE WORK

While we have identified several use cases for USSD that extend the capabilities of GSM universal applications, we acknowledge that USSD is only a piece of the broader ICT4D toolkit. Organizations must survey available options in the context of the requirements of their individual project. If primary audience for a service is non-literate, IVR may be the best solution. If a project needs only simple messaging and privacy is not a concern or if frequent data collection will be done, SMS is a feasible option. And when there are few primary users a custom device specific application may work. However, there are three situations where USSD enables services that otherwise could not be offered as universal GSM applications. (1) when sensitive text based information must be shared, (2) when data collection is infrequent and complex, (3) when complex user interactions must take place.

The feasibly of USSD for large scale applications such as mobile money and interacting with mobile carriers is well documented. The framework presented in this paper shows how USSD can also be used for smaller scale operations similar to IVR and SMS. This opens up a large new design spaces to explore. There is a need to do user studies to understand the limitation of PIN and username based systems, which although the easiest from a technical stand point may not be the most user friendly. Systems should be designed that push the boundaries of what text based USSD systems can do such as creating a digital marketplace or math tutor. The user experience for these systems should be better studied to understand how to scale communities and improve services.

The principal motivation for this work originated in discussions with the Kenyan Ministry of Health (MOH) around SMS applications for maternal health and HIV awareness. Concern was expressed about the safety and ethics of distributing medical information over SMS. USSD seemed to be a solution that offed more privacy, even on the least expensive phones, as well as improved user experience and expanded design space. We were pleasantly surprised to find already existing third party operators offer USSD services. We now are currently in the process of testing the feasibly and design of our maternal health USSD application and working with the MOH to establish guidelines around its use.

7. CONCLUSION

The recent emergence of third party USSD gateways has opened up the design space for M4D applications that can reach users on the most basic phones. Traditionally USSD has only been used for banking and cellular operations, but by examining the existing ICT4D literature we can identify how USSD will complement and extend current uses of SMS and IVR for data collection, messaging, information query, social networking and making complex transactions. We built a prototype USSD application using an new library that provides the basic building blocks for general USSD applications. We have identified when M4D projects should consider using USSD as a solution and our USSD library will well in creating innovative services aimed at marginalized users throughout the world.

8. ACKNOWLEDGMENTS

The authors would like to acknowledge NSF grant IIS-1111433 which funded part of the work. We also thank Aditya Vashistha for photos of USSD systems in India.

9. REFERENCES

[1] Now book railway tickets on your mobile without internet connection. http://www.pib.nic.in/newsite/efeatures.aspx?relid=97308. Accessed: 2015-07-01.

[2] R. E. Anderson, W. Brunette, E. Johnson, C. Lustig, A. Poon, C. Putnam, O. Salihbaeva, B. E. Kolko, and G. Borriello. Experiences with a transportation information system that uses only GPS and SMS. ICTD '10.

[3] C. Asiimwe, D. Gelvin, E. Lee, Y. B. Amor, E. Quinto, C. Katureebe, L. Sundaram, D. Bell, and M. Berg. Use of an Innovative, Affordable, and Open-Source Short Message Service-Based Tool to Monitor Malaria in Remote Areas of Uganda. *The American Journal of Tropical Medicine and Hygiene*, 85(1), July 2011.

[4] J. Barrington, O. Wereko-Brobby, P. Ward, W. Mwafongo, and S. Kungulwe. SMS for Life: a pilot project to improve anti-malarial drug supply management in rural Tanzania using standard technology. *Malaria Journal*, 9, Oct. 2010.

[5] J. Chen, L. Subramanian, and E. Brewer. Sms-based web search for low-end mobile devices. MobiCom '10.

[6] J. Corker. "ligne verte" toll-free hotline: using cell phones to increase access to family planning information in the democratic republic of congo. *Cases in Public Health Communication & Marketing*, 4, 2010.

[7] C. M. Danis, J. B. Ellis, W. A. Kellogg, H. van Beijma, B. Hoefman, S. D. Daniels, and J.-W. Loggers. Mobile phones for health education in the developing world: SMS as a user interface. ACM DEV '10.

[8] B. DeRenzi, L. Findlater, J. Payne, B. Birnbaum, J. Mangilima, T. Parikh, G. Borriello, and N. Lesh. Improving community health worker performance through automated sms. ICTD '12.

[9] B. Fogg and E. Allen. 10 Uses of Texting to Improve Health. Persuasive '09, New York, NY, USA. ACM.

[10] S. Githinji, S. Kigen, D. Memusi, A. Nyandigisi, A. M. Mbithi, A. Wamari, A. N. Muturi, G. Jagoe,

J. Barrington, R. W. Snow, et al. Reducing stock-outs of life saving malaria commodities using mobile phone text-messaging: Sms for life study in kenya. *PLoS One*, 8(1), 2013.

[11] A. S. Grover, K. Calteaux, E. Barnard, and G. van Huyssteen. A voice service for user feedback on school meals. ACM DEV '12.

[12] T. A. Gurman, S. E. Rubin, and A. A. Roess. Effectiveness of mHealth Behavior Change Communication Interventions in Developing Countries: A Systematic Review of the Literature. *Journal of Health Communication*, 17(sup1), May 2012.

[13] C. Hartung, A. Lerer, Y. Anokwa, C. Tseng, W. Brunette, and G. Borriello. Open Data Kit: Tools to Build Information Services for Developing Regions. ICTD '10, New York, NY, USA. ACM.

[14] A. Joshi, M. Rane, D. Roy, N. Emmadi, P. Srinivasan, N. Kumarasamy, S. Pujari, D. Solomon, R. Rodrigues, D. Saple, K. Sen, E. Veldeman, and R. Rutten. Supporting Treatment of People Living with HIV / AIDS in Resource Limited Settings with IVRs. CHI '14, New York, NY, USA.

[15] A. Lerer, M. Ward, and S. Amarasinghe. Evaluation of ivr data collection uis for untrained rural users. ACM DEV '10.

[16] R. Lester, P. Ritvo, E. Mills, A. Kariri, S. Karanja, M. Chung, W. Jack, J. Habyarimana, M. Sadatsafavi, M. Najafzadeh, C. Marra, B. Estambale, et al. Effects of a mobile phone short message service on antiretroviral treatment adherence in Kenya (WelTel Kenya1): a randomised trial. *The Lancet*, 376, 2010.

[17] I. Medhi, S. N. Gautama, and K. Toyama. A comparison of mobile money-transfer uis for non-literate and semi-literate users. CHI '09, 2009.

[18] I. Medhi, S. Patnaik, E. Brunskill, S. N. Gautama, W. Thies, and K. Toyama. Designing Mobile Interfaces for Novice and Low-literacy Users. *ACM Trans. Comput.-Hum. Interact.*, 18(1), May 2011.

[19] J. Merrill, R. Hershow, K. Gannett, and C. Barkley. Pretesting an mHealth Intervention for At-risk Adolescent Girls in Soweto, South Africa: Studying the Additive Effects of SMSs on Improving Sexual Reproductive Health & Rights Outcomes. ICTD '13.

[20] P. Mudliar, J. Donner, and W. Thies. Emergent Practices Around CGNet Swara, Voice Forum for Citizen Journalism in Rural India. ICTD '12, New York, NY, USA.

[21] B. Odero, B. Omwenga, M. Masita-Mwangi, P. Githinji, and J. Ledlie. Tangaza: frugal group messaging through speech and text. ACM DEV '10.

[22] N. Pai, P. Supe, S. Kore, Y. S. Nandanwar, A. Hegde, E. Cutrell, and W. Thies. Using Automated Voice Calls to Improve Adherence to Iron Supplements During Pregnancy: A Pilot Study. ICTD '13, New York, NY, USA.

[23] S. Panjwani and E. Cutrell. Usably secure, low-cost authentication for mobile banking. SOUPS '10, 2010.

[24] N. Patel, D. Chittamuru, A. Jain, P. Dave, and T. S. Parikh. Avaaj Otalo: A Field Study of an Interactive Voice Forum for Small Farmers in Rural India. CHI '10, New York, NY, USA.

[25] S. Patnaik, E. Brunskill, and W. Thies. Evaluating the Accuracy of Data Collection on Mobile Phones: A Study of Forms, Sms, and Voice. ICTD'09.

[26] T. Perrier, N. Dell, B. DeRenzi, R. Anderson, J. Kinuthia, J. Unger, and G. John-Stewart. Engaging Pregnant Women in Kenya with a Hybrid Computer - Human SMS Communication System. CHI '15.

[27] J. R. G. Raifman, H. E. Lanthorn, S. Rokicki, and G. Fink. The Impact of Text Message Reminders on Adherence to Antimalarial Treatment in Northern Ghana: A Randomized Trial. *PLoS ONE*, 9(10), Oct. 2014.

[28] A. Ramanujapuram and A. Akkihal. Improving performance of rural supply chains using mobile phones: Reducing information asymmetry to improve stock availability in low-resource environments. In *Proceedings of the Fifth ACM Symposium on Computing for Development*, pages 11–20. ACM, 2014.

[29] Y. Rana, J. Haberer, H. Huang, A. Kambugu, B. Mukasa, H. Thirumurthy, P. Wabukala, G. J. Wagner, and S. Linnemayr. Short Message Service (SMS)-Based Intervention to Improve Treatment Adherence among HIV-Positive Youth in Uganda: Focus Group Findings. *PLoS ONE*, 10(4), Apr. 2015.

[30] S Lund. Mobile phones as a health communication tool to improve skilled attendance at delivery in Zanzibar: a cluster-randomised controlled trial. *BJOG : an international journal of obstetrics and gynaecology.*, 119(10), 2012.

[31] R. Schusteritsch, S. Rao, and K. Rodden. Mobile Search with Text Messages: Designing the User Experience for Google SMS. CHI EA '05.

[32] R. Ssekibuule, J. A. Quinn, and K. Leyton-Brown. A mobile market for agricultural trade in uganda. ACM DEV-4 '13.

[33] M. Suktarachan, P. Rattanamanee, and A. Kawtrakul. The Development of a Question-answering Services System for the Farmer Through SMS: Query Analysis. KRAQ '09, Stroudsburg, PA, USA, 2009. Association for Computational Linguistics.

[34] A. Vashistha, E. Cutrell, G. Borriello, and W. Thies. Sangeet swara: A community-moderated voice forum in rural india. CHI '15.

[35] A. Vashistha and W. Thies. Ivr junction: Building scalable and distributed voice forums in the developing world. In *6th USENIX/ACM Workshop on Networked Systems for Developing Regions*, 2012.

[36] R. Veeraraghavan, N. Yasodhar, and K. Toyama. Warana Unwired: Replacing PCs with mobile phones in a rural sugarcane cooperative. ICTD '07.

[37] S. P. Wyche and L. L. Murphy. "Dead China-make" Phones off the Grid: Investigating and Designing for Mobile Phone Use in Rural Africa. DIS '12.

[38] S. P. Wyche, S. Y. Schoenebeck, and A. Forte. "facebook is a luxury": An exploratory study of social media use in rural kenya.

[39] D. Zurovac, R. K. Sudoi, W. S. Akhwale, M. Ndiritu, D. H. Hamer, A. K. Rowe, and R. W. Snow. The effect of mobile phone text-message reminders on Kenyan health workers' adherence to malaria treatment guidelines: a cluster randomised trial. *The Lancet*, 378(9793), Sept. 2011.

DUCES: A Framework for Characterizing and Simplifying Mobile Deployments in Low-Resource Settings

Samuel R Sudar
Unversity of Washington
Seattle, USA
sudars@cs.uw.edu

Richard Anderson
Unversity of Washington
Seattle, USA
anderson@cs.uw.edu

ABSTRACT

Mobile devices are increasingly being used in data-focused workflows in low-resource settings. These deployments are frequently orchestrated by organizations with limited technical capacity, making fundamental architectural decisions difficult. We present DUCES, a framework for characterizing mobile deployments along five axes of design. DUCES allows organizations to better understand deployment requirements and simplify decisions regarding deployment architectures. It focuses on the workflow's **D**ata flow, **U**ser interface, **C**onnectivity model, **E**dit mode, and **S**erver requirements. We discuss five case studies of data-focused mobile deployments and evaluate them using the DUCES framework. We conclude by discussing how the DUCES framework can be used as a lens by organizations and researchers to understand and simplify mobile deployments.

Keywords

ICTD; mobile devices; application, app design

Categories and Subject Descriptors

H.4.0 [**Information Systems Applications**]: General; D.2.1 [**Software**]: Software EngineeringRequirements/Specifications[methodologies]

1. INTRODUCTION

Mobile devices are deployed in many low-resource settings for data-focused applications. Creating these applications is nontrivial, consuming considerable time and resources [8]. Successful custom-built deployments can require years of iterative refinements to work out stable technical architectures [11]. Smaller scale deployments often do not involve developers, making reasoning about technology difficult. We present the DUCES framework, which can be used to deepen understanding of a deployment and its requirements as well as to highlight which requirements are most challenging technically. If these can be altered in a way that simplifies the architecture, the deployment will become more sustainable without external expertise.

ACM DEV 2015, December 1–2, 2015, London, United Kingdom.
© 2015 ACM. ISBN 978-1-4503-3490-7/15/12 . . . $15.00.
DOI: http://dx.doi.org/10.1145/2830629.2830653.

We have observed that a number of common paradigms exist in data-focused mobile deployments conducted by groups in low-resource settings. Based on our experience, we characterize these deployments along five axes of design: whether the **D**ata flow is unidirectional or bidirectional; whether the **U**ser interface (UI) is form-based or non-form-based; if **C**onnectivity is required to function; if **E**dits are non-transactional or transactional; and if the supporting **S**erver is merely a data repository or if it encapsulates logic. Using technology always presents challenges. It is easy to argue for simplification, but developing intuitions around how to do so can take years of experience and can be specific to a single technology. The DUCES framework provides a way to approach simplification that is generalizable to a wide range of scenarios and tools.

DUCES is aimed at small and medium-sized organizations seeking to leverage mobile technology in low-resource settings. These organizations generally do not have the resources to devise a custom technical solution. They are not creating new technical frameworks and they do not have a developer on staff. They are seeking to build on top of existing solutions to leverage mobile technology. Such organizations frequently face difficulties when trying to reason about diverse requirements and their implications [4]. In these organizations, deployment architects are generally not developers themselves. This frequently makes the implications of requirements opaque. Many deployment architects lack even basic intuitions about what is easy and what is hard. For example, supporting two languages is a fundamentally different problem than working in the absence of an internet connection. Sending SMS reminders automatically based on HIV status is more challenging than capturing GPS data. Organizations frequently treat all requirements as equal, even though disconnected operation or server-side automation might complicate the deployment by orders of magnitude.

In this paper we explore five case studies of mobile deployments that leverage technology in different ways. We analyze these deployments to gain a comprehensive understanding of the various technical requirements that exist in mobile workflows in low-resource settings. The contributions of this paper are to formalize a framework for understanding and simplifying these mobile-based workflows. This framework, which we refer to as DUCES, elucidates characteristics and intuitions that are latent in many data-focused mobile apps, including those in high-resource environments, but that take on increased importance in low-resource settings. Using DUCES, organizations can identify early in their process what components are likely to require outside technical support and what should be able to be accomplished in-house.

The paper is structured as follows. In Section 2 we outline five case studies of mobile deployments in low-resource settings. We summarize the requirements and goals of each case study. In Section 3 we describe the five axes of design that define the DUCES framework. We revisit each case study, exploring how the requirements of the deployment impacted the deployment architecture. In Section 4 we discuss how the traits of our framework highlight fundamental challenges that exist in mobile deployment architectures, how certain features are in tension with one another, and the ramifications of these considerations on mobile deployments. We revisit each case study to describe how DUCES was used to simplify or could potentially simplify each architecture. We close by discussing the ramifications this work has on organizations deploying mobile apps in low-resource settings.

2. CASE STUDIES

The goals of a mobile deployment define the technical requirements. This is not always a straight forward process. In this section we present five data-focused mobile deployments to serve as case studies. They were chosen to provide a broad sample of requirements. Characterizing them through the lens of the DUCES framework lends insight into what sorts of technical solutions are appropriate given the constraints of the deployment. Three of these case studies have been conducted by the authors, allowing insight into how DUCES was used during development of the deployment.[1] All have been deployed and used in the field. Two case studies are based on published literature.

2.1 Longitudinal HIV Study

The first deployment is support for a study of HIV discordant couples in Kenya [13]. The study itself was designed by global health researchers in order to longitudinally monitor couples where one partner is HIV-positive and the other is not. Participants are screened, at which point data is collected, and at time points in the future additional sets of data are collected. For both screening and follow ups participants are administered a survey on a mobile device. Different data is collected at different time points about male and female participants. A particular form is administered to a participant based on the time they have been enrolled in the study and their gender. This model of an entry form with follow up forms is common in research studies [7].

Each day study coordinators perform basic analysis and create a list of participants that require follow up. This data includes the subject's unique identifier and the form that is required to be completed. Enumerators are hired to take this information into the field, locate the subject, and complete the specified form. They are equipped with mobile devices that render the forms and provide a simple app-like user interface. Upon opening the app, enumerators arrive at a home screen and are trained that they can screen a new participant, perform a follow up interview, or submit collected data to the server. Sample screens are shown in Figure 1.

2.2 Tuberculosis Test Results

In 2009 a digital form-based workflow was deployed in Lima, Peru to digitize tuberculosis (TB) test results [2]. Sputum smears are collected at local health centers and the test results are written in a ledger. Enumerators visit these health centers with personal digital assistants (PDAs) that are equipped with digital forms. The forms have been designed to collect the information that has been written in the ledger, and enumerators transcribe the contents of the ledgers to the digital forms on the PDA. Upon returning to the central office, the data is uploaded from the PDAs to an Oracle databased managed by Partners in Health, a non-governmental or-

---

[1]Two of these three deployments are presented here for the first time.

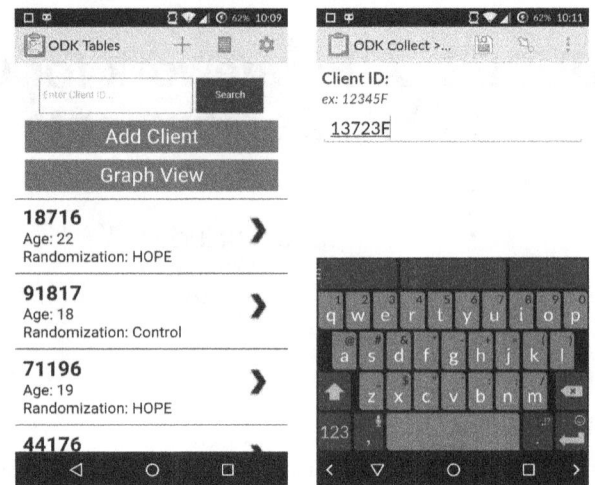

Figure 1: Examples of the mobile app for the HIV study. The participant list supports prepopulation of identifiers (left). If not available, the identifier can be entered manually (right).

ganization (NGO) operating in Lima. Data upload takes place over the internet using the open database connectivity (ODBC) standard. The study designers also extended the database to include automated processing of the data as well as web pages that allow for summaries of the data and provide data quality checks. With this workflow, processing times for samples were greatly improved.

2.3 Supply Chains Using Mobile Phones

Mobile devices have been deployed to improve the performance of rural supply chains in resource-constrained environments [12]. For this deployment an organization (Logistimo) noticed that stock outs were occurring at health centers in large part due to poor information management and communication. They created a Java application for feature phones that allows pharmacists to enter stock-related data, including the sale of items and stock counts. This data is transmitted to a server via a cellular data connection or SMS. The server component processes the data and removes duplicates that have arisen due to network errors. The server is also responsible for sending alerts to supervisors via SMS or voice calls. The server also provides a "bulletin board" web application that shows streaming information about the state of the supply chain. Synthesizing data in this way created actionable items that resulted in a drastic increase of availability of vaccines at local health centers.

2.4 Chimpanzee Monitoring

The Jane Goodall Institute (JGI) has employed a complex chimpanzee monitoring system for a number of years. Under the system, a ranger follows a group of chimpanzees through the forest over the course of a day with a complex paper worksheet. This activity is referred to as a "follow", and is broken into 15 minute time intervals. Data is collected about each interval. Various data is recorded, including when chimps arrive and depart, the estrus state of the female chimps, the foods consumed by the chimps, and the presence of other species. All this information is captured on a dense paper worksheet consisting of a matrix with 15 minute intervals on the y-axis and chimp identifiers on the x-axis. Arrivals and departures indicated by drawing a line in the corresponding 15 minute interval. A copy of the paper form is shown in Figure 2 in order to convey the density of information on the worksheet. These sheets

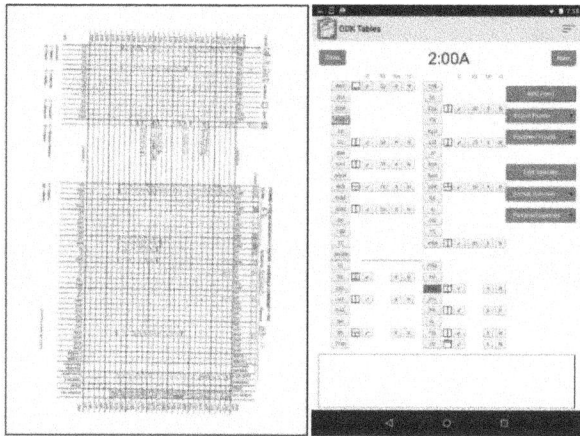

Figure 2: The Chimpanzee Monitoring Worksheet (left) and Application (right) The left image shows the paper worksheet employed by JGI rangers. It permits continuous review of data as it is updated. The right image shows this technique replicated in our application. This permits stylized reviews mimicking the paper-based workflow.

are periodically sent to researchers that transcribe the data into a database.

One of the strengths of this model is that rangers are able to see a summary of the day's data at a glance, making it easy to visually audit data and revisit time points as the day progresses. It also facilitates non-standard data entry. For example, times are not recorded by writing an hour and a minute. Instead the ranger draws a line in the first third of the box representing 9:00 to 9:15 to show that the chimp arrived or departed between 9:00 and 9:05. We designed an application to run on a 10 inch tablet that mimics this workflow. The tablet was smaller than the normal paper form employed by the rangers and displayed data of a single 15 minute interval at a time instead of the whole day's data. Crucially, however, data is displayed as it can be edited, affording rangers similar auditing power to the original paper form. The application also uses icons to achieve the same pictographic data entry to represent time that is provided by paper. The familiar tabular structure is preserved. A comparison of the paper form and the tablet application is shown in Figure 2.

2.5 Aid Distribution

The International Federation of Red Cross and Red Crescent Societies in the Americas (IFRC) often handles aid distribution after natural disasters. They recently piloted a program where debit cards were distributed instead of physical goods. We devised a mobile system to support this workflow. The pilot took place over two days in Kingston, Jamaica, and involved 93 participants at two locations.

Registration and distribution are separated into two distinct phases. In the registration phase, beneficiaries are entered into the system using digital forms on four mobile phones. Basic data like name and address are collected. Each beneficiary is also be assigned a paper card with a bar code that will later entitle them to receive their debit card. After screening and before distribution, each screened patient is assigned a debit card number. Distribution occurs an hour later. During the distribution phase, beneficiaries present their beneficiary card and bar code, which is used by the mobile app to retrieve their information. After confirming that it is correct, they are

presented with the cash card and marked in the database as having received the card.

3. THE DUCES FRAMEWORK

The DUCES framework provides a way to characterize mobile deployments. The framework can be applied to mobile-based workflow, including applications produced by organizations with significant resources. However, it is most useful in low-resource contexts where many simplifying assumptions appropriate in high-resource settings are inadequate. DUCES consists of five axes of design:

1. Data Flow (Unidirectional vs Bidirectional)

2. User Interface (Form-Based vs Non-Form-Based)

3. Connectivity Model (Connected vs Disconnected)

4. Edit Mode (Non-Transactional vs Transactional)

5. Server Model (Bucket-Based vs Processed)

Understanding where a deployment falls along these axes provides meaningful insight into the technical requirements of a deployment. Deployment architects without a strong technical background often lack sound intuitions surrounding mobile deployments. For example, we have seen non-technical collaborators assume that altering the text accompanying a question in a form will be as difficult as adding bidirectional data flow to an existing data entry tool. DUCES is intended to better scaffold reasoning about deployment requirements in order to prevent this sort of misunderstanding. If a deployment requires a bidirectional data flow, a data entry tool that does not support the bidirectional movement of data can be discounted out of hand. Better still, the bidirectional data flow requirement might be obviated by a slight change in deployment protocol. DUCES provides a set of primitives that can guide an understanding of technical requirements.

In the following sections, each axis of design is described in detail. The case studies from Section 2 are used to illustrate how DUCES can be used to describe a variety of mobile deployments.

3.1 Data Flow

Mobile devices are frequently used to collect and manage data, aggregating it on a server. DUCES asks if this flow of data is unidirectional or bidirectional. In other words, does collected data move only from the mobile device to the server, or does it also move from the server to the mobile device? A unidirectional data flow is simpler to implement than a bidirectional data flow, but it is also less versatile. Deployments can use each design to great effect.

3.1.1 Longitudinal HIV Study

The HIV study is a **unidirectional** data flow. Subject data is collected using forms and later submitted to a central server. Data is never sent from the server back to the device. Enumerators are essentially replicating a paper-based data collection workflow, which is a unidirectional data flow.

3.1.2 Tuberculosis Test Results

This too uses a **unidirectional** data flow. Data is transcribed from the ledgers at health centers into the forms on the PDAs carried by enumerators. At their central office they then submit data to the server.

3.1.3 Supply Chains Using Mobile Phones

In this case the data flow is **bidirectional**. Pharmacists use a Java-based application for feature phones that sends sale and stock count information to the central server. The server processes this data and broadcasts resultant information to all users of the system via SMS. Further, the list of materials at each health center is pulled from a central server. The authors of the tool took care to degrade gracefully in the case of poor connectivity, but the flow of data in the deployment is still bidirectional.

3.1.4 Chimpanzee Monitoring

Data collected by rangers is stored locally. It can be reviewed and revised until it is pushed to the central server. No data is ever sent from the server to the device. Further, this deployment is a replacement for paper-based data collection. All of these characteristics indicate that it employs a **unidirectional** data flow.

3.1.5 Aid Distribution

Beneficiary information is entered on mobile devices in a digital form. Screening takes place on four mobile devices. During distribution, beneficiaries must be able to be processed on any device, not just the device that screened them. This indicates that data must be shared between devices, indicating that the data flow is **bidirectional**.

3.2 User Interface

Mobile deployments can be described in terms of two distinct modes defining their users' interactions: form-based and non-form-based. The distinction between these modes is motivated by two factors. First, form-based data entry is extremely common in low-resource deployments [7]. Second, a large number of tools exist that facilitate form-based data collection on mobile devices. Many are designed specifically to be leveraged by lightly technical users. This host of data-entry applications includes Google forms, Cyber-Tracker [1], Red Cap [9], Open Data Kit (ODK) Collect [10], ODK Survey [3], Pendragon Forms, Magpi, CommCare, and many others.

One hallmark of form-based tools is that deployment architects do not normally need sophisticated control over the presentation layer of form-based data entry: presenting a piece of text indicating what data should be entered is usually sufficient. In a form-based UI, a user is making changes to the database by stepping through a series of questions, potentially with branching based on responses. Non-form-based UIs do not have as clearly defined workflow. Almost all mobile applications produced by highly technical organizations and aimed at high-resource settings (e.g. email apps, to-do lists, calendars, and chat clients) do not use a form-based workflow. This stands opposed to the applications used by organizations in low-resource settings, where workers are often employed to collect data using mobile phones.

Any workflow can be viewed through these two modes, but they have increased relevance in low-resource settings. Which of these modes is appropriate and necessary for a given deployment can define immediately the types of interactions users will have with mobile devices. Understanding and describing a deployment can be greatly simplified if deployment architects identify early if they can model their deployment's user interface using a form-based workflow. In general, the more a deployment can be forced to follow a form-based workflow, the easier it will be to manage by local organizations with tools that have a relatively low barrier to entry.

3.2.1 Longitudinal HIV Study

The HIV study employs a predominantly **form-based** user in-terface. Forms were designed for screening participants and for a number of follow up visits. A lightweight non-form-based skin was designed to present a list of existing participants, but the vast majority of enumerators' time is spent completing digital forms.

3.2.2 Tuberculosis Test Results

Here again the user interface is predominantly **form-based**. Pendragon Forms was used to create forms mimicking the data collected on paper ledgers and transcribed on PDAs. A non-form-based component was used to perform data quality checks on the server, but enumerators spent most of their time completing digital forms.

3.2.3 Supply Chains Using Mobile Phones

Pharmacists in the supply chain deployment used a custom-built Java app for feature phones. The bulletin board aggregating results from pharmacists was written as a web page. Thus the user interface was **non-form-based**.

3.2.4 Chimpanzee Monitoring

Although the JGI was replicating paper-based data collection, the tablet-based app did not follow a standard digital form workflow. Unlike in conventional forms, the JGI had strict requirements for the presentation layer: it must be tabular, show previously entered data to allow visual auditing, and data entry must employ stylized icons rather than text. This workflow was **non-form-based**.

3.2.5 Aid Distribution

Both screening and distribution phases took place using digital forms, making this a **form-based** user interface.

3.3 Connectivity Mode

Mobile deployments can follow one of two connectivity models: connected and disconnected. A disconnected model is one where full functionality is capable without connecting to a central server. In this model, workers would be able to go into the field for periods of time and use a mobile tool without degraded quality. For example, data enumerators might leave the city for several weeks at a time collecting data about the state of a country's refrigeration infrastructure at its health centers. When they return they submit their information to their supervisor. The tasks they were expected to perform were not dependent on a reliable connection to the internet or to their superior via a telephone.

Connected operation, on the other hand, requires a connection to achieve the full functionality of an application. Mobile deployments in low-resource environments can adopt either model: organizations might have an enumerator in the field without connection or a researcher working at a large hospital with a strong wifi connection.

3.3.1 Longitudinal HIV Study

Many of the participants in the HIV study are expected to be contacted in the field without internet connectivity. The mobile app was designed to work entirely offline, with forms created using ODK Collect. Collect permits data entry offline, storing data locally until it is uploaded when internet connectivity becomes available. Enumerators thus were able to use the app's full functionality without an internet connection, making this a **disconnected** connectivity model.

3.3.2 Tuberculosis Test Results

Data was entered on PDAs using Pendragon Forms. This did not require connectivity until data was uploaded at a central office.

This is a **disconnected** model, as full functionality did not require a connection.

3.3.3 Supply Chains Using Mobile Phones

The authors of the supply chain intervention took great care to ensure that their mobile devices would accommodate a **disconnected** connectivity model. After an initial download, data is persisted locally. Service degrades gracefully, defaulting to SMS data transfer if an internet connection is not available, and allowing full offline entry if neither SMS or data is available.

3.3.4 Chimpanzee Monitoring

The mobile tool for the JGI was designed from the outset to embrace a **disconnected** connectivity model. Data can be collected entirely offline and only requires an internet connection to send data to a server.

3.3.5 Aid Distribution

The aid distribution deployment requires a **connected** connectivity model. Distribution cannot follow screening without first aggregating all the data centrally, pairing beneficiaries with a debit card, and downloading this new information to all the devices. Further, without a connection workers cannot prevent double distribution—a beneficiary might visit two distribution stations.

3.4 Edit Model

Data edits within a deployment can also be characterized as non-transactional or transactional. Transactional data is data where edits are dependent on one another. The order of edits matter and are conceived of as a unit. Non-transactional data is data where the order does not matter and edits are independent of each other. For example, records of medical visits are non-transactional. Each record refers to a separate visit. Reports may be submitted out of order and remain coherent. Transactional data, meanwhile, places stricter requirements on ordering. An example is financial data, where a sequence of withdrawals and deposits must be ordered to ensure that the balance is sufficient to address subsequent requests.

3.4.1 Longitudinal HIV Study

The HIV study treats data entry as a sequence of reports. The six month follow up is not dependent on the six week follow up. This is a **non-transactional** edit model.

3.4.2 Tuberculosis Test Results

Again each collected data point is isolated and independent of the others, making this a **non-transactional** edit model.

3.4.3 Supply Chains Using Mobile Phones

In this case data collected from pharmacists consists of stock counts and stock disbursements. This data is only useful if ordered. If all stock disbursements were sent two days late, the functionality of the bulletin board system would be severely impacted. Consequently this deployment requires a **transactional** edit model.

3.4.4 Chimpanzee Monitoring

Data is collected about each time point and is independent of the others, making this a **non-transactional** edit model.

3.4.5 Aid Distribution

A cagey beneficiary might try and cheat the system by visiting two distribution systems in order to receive double aid disbursement. This implies that ordering matters and edits are not independent of each other, making this a **transactional** edit model.

3.5 Server Requirements

Broadly speaking, the server requirements for a mobile deployment can be bucket-based or processed. Bucket-based servers are the simplest, acting as receptacles or sources for data. Processed servers are everything else. This distinction is purposefully broad, as the moment a server stops being bucket-based it becomes significantly more complicated. Bucket-based servers are those where all form data is submitted to a single location or pulled from a single location. Processed servers might serialize data for consumption or analyze data and perform notifications. Bucket-based server workflows can be replicated with a wide variety of tools, while processed servers require more customization and configuration.

3.5.1 Longitudinal HIV Study

This is a classic **bucket-based** server configuration. Data from each form is sent to a table on a server. No processing is required. The forms are written using ODK Collect and the bucket-based workflow is facilitated by ODK Aggregate, which serves as a bucket for form data.

3.5.2 Tuberculosis Test Results

This deployment uses Pendragon Forms to send data to an Oracle database. A module was added to the back-end that supported validation of submitted data, highlighting errors in red. This represents a **processed** server requirement.

3.5.3 Supply Chains Using Mobile Phones

The server in this deployment performs a number of tasks. It supports bidirectional data flow of JSON data to the Java feature phone application, it synthesizes data and presents it on a helpful bulletin board, and it sends broadcasts to registered users of critical events. This represents a high degree of customization and configuration and demonstrates what can be accomplished with a **processed** server.

3.5.4 Chimpanzee Monitoring

Data is collected locally and sent to the server. Nothing is required of the server beyond being a receptacle for data, making it **bucket-based**.

3.5.5 Aid Distribution

Screening and distribution data is entered using a digital form and submitted using a **bucket-based** server configuration.

4. DISCUSSION

The power of the DUCES framework is twofold. First, it provides a schema by which to understand the requirements of a mobile deployment. Second, it provides a means by which to simplify a deployment.

4.1 Understanding

DUCES permits deep insight into the requirements of mobile deployments in low-resource settings. With appropriately scoped requirements, solutions can be created by leveraging existing technology. With sufficient technical knowledge and resources, custom-built solutions can be created to meet any set of requirements. Electronic medical record systems have been deployed successfully on custom technology using commercial-quality servers and custom work stations in Haiti for thousands of patients [11]. Touchscreen PCs running custom software have been used in Malawi to improve point of care treatment and provide immediate reporting to doctors in the field [5]. These are testaments to the potentially transformative power of technology, but unfortunately such technical feats are not available to a number of organizations with fewer resources.

A crucial observation is that the axes of design underpinning DUCES do not exist in isolation. A bidirectional data flow might affect server requirements, for instance, perhaps necessitating a processed configuration. The supply chain case study used bidirectional data flow to send lists of items and alerts to mobile phones. Consequently they required a processed server to synthesize data and generate alerts as well as to present a list of items to mobile phones in a specialized format (JSON). Unfortunately, however, there are no hard and fast rules when reasoning about the impacts of architectural decisions. The aid distribution case study, for example, similarly uses a bidirectional data flow but manages to use a bucket-based server. This seeming contradiction is one example of why it can be difficult for organizations to hone their intuitions surrounding technology requirements.

Why the discrepancy? In short, the supply chain case study required logic on the server that would create events and broadcast them to registered devices. It also needed to expose data using a custom format—JSON—that could be consumed by devices. The aid distribution study, meanwhile, was implemented using ODK Survey and Aggregate, which supports an out-of-the-box bucket-based server for producing and consuming data. This is difficult to recognize prima facie without extensive knowledge of the capabilities of the tools being used to implement the study. For deployment architects without a strong technical background, this will be an especially difficult conclusion to draw.

Instead, DUCES claims that the most easily satisfied configuration is **unidirectional**, **form-based**, **connected**, **non-transactional**, and **bucket-based**. If a set of requirements can be modeled using this configuration, it will be more likely to be managed successfully without outside technical resources. Deviations from this model will create additional dimensions and edge cases that will complicate the deployment and potentially require technical assistance.

For example, consider trying to support transactional data using a disconnected workflow. In the aid distribution scenario, the edit model is transactional. This is necessary as it is important that aid is not distributed twice to the same beneficiary. If errors cannot be tolerated, this requires a connected connectivity model. This is a familiar problem in distributed systems, as it is essentially an extension of the CAP theorem [6]. The CAP theorem states that a system cannot be partition tolerant, available, and provide a consistent view of the data simultaneously. In the context of the aid distribution case study, no worker would be able to become disconnected (essentially partitioning the network) while the other users are able to maintain a consistent view of the data (not double distributing) but not have to wait for all users to reconnect. This highlights a fundamental tension between a transactional edit model and disconnected workflows. The supply chain case study was able to use both transactional data and a disconnected workflow by adding processing logic to their server and, in the worst case, simply tolerating late data that was no longer actionable. This was acceptable in their deployment and was a necessary concession to support disconnected operation.

DUCES also provides insight into why mobile deployments in low-resource settings are fundamentally challenging. The simplest configuration can be at odds with the realities of the environment. It is common for many deployments to require disconnected operation, for instance, because they occur in regions without reliable data connectivity. As we have seen, this complicates the handling of transactional data but is simply unavoidable in some settings. To take another example, the chimpanzee monitoring study required a non-form-based workflow to be effective. The JGI had previously tried to encode the workflow using traditional form-based building tools without success. In the end they required a custom solution that could support their non-form-based workflow.

4.2 Simplification

DUCES can also be used to guide the simplification of mobile deployments. It posits that deviations from the simplest configuration of **unidirectional**, **form-based**, **connected**, **non-transactional**, and **bucket-based** will invite technical complications that may be insurmountable without the aid of a developer.

For example, bidirectional data flow is more difficult to support than unidirectional data flow. If a bidirectional data flow requirement can be loosened to a unidirectional data flow, this will have positive ramifications for the sustainability of the deployment. In many cases it is easier to alter the requirements of a deployment than to devise a sophisticated technological solution that will add complexity and hurt sustainability. We now discuss the five case studies in the context of simplification using the DUCES framework.

4.2.1 Longitudinal HIV Study

This study has been running successfully for over 24 months in a hospital in Kenya. The researchers first requested a bidirectional data flow and a processed server model. Five to ten phones were to be shared between enumerators and used to screen participants and perform follow up interviews. The researchers had previously seen enumerators make errors typing subject identifiers, making it difficult to perform post-hoc analysis. They reasoned that bidirectional data flow would allow all participant records to exist on all phones. Whenever a participant was contacted for follow up, enumerators would not have to re-type the identifier, reducing the likelihood of errors.

However, supporting bidirectional data flow would complicate requirements. First, the server would have to support presenting captured data in a machine-consumable way, similar to how the supply chain example provided JSON. Second, it might require authentication and access control to prevent the collected HIV data from being visible to non-study devices. Third, enumerators would have required a stable internet connection at headquarters before leaving for the field. If a connection issue interrupted the bidirectional data flow, the flow might be interrupted.

Instead, the study designers were able to refine their study procedures to work within the confines of a unidirectional data flow. Enumerators were made responsible for the same cohort of patients and assigned specific devices rather than a shared device. This greatly increased the likelihood that a participant would already be present on the device without requiring bidirectional data flow. However, participants might still be seen for follow up interviews on devices that were not used to screen them. This might occur if the screening device was lost or stolen or if they were visited by a new enumerator for logistical reasons. To accommodate this eventuality, the follow up workflow was modified to allow entering an existing patient identifier. This was not completely in-line with the original requests of the researchers, as they requested that the identifier not be entered manually more than once, but with the advent of individually assigned devices the likelihood of a manually entered identifier was less common and was deemed acceptable.

A processed server was desired to calculate when participants were due for follow up visits. This information would be generated each morning and provided to study coordinators. Automating this task would not be complicated for a computer scientist, but the smooth operation of the study would depend on this task functioning without interruption. This might prove difficult without a technical staff capable of supporting the server. Instead, the researchers directed study staff to manually review the data on the bucket-based server and generate a list of follow up participants each day by hand. This might seem less than elegant to a computer scientist, but it is much more sustainable with local talent.

In this way a bidirectional, processed workflow was transformed and simplified to use a unidirectional, bucket-based workflow. These simplifications are a large part of the reason that the study has remained in successful operation with limited involvement from outside technical staff for over two years.

4.2.2 Tuberculosis Test Results

The authors were not involved in this deployment, so DUCES will be used to describe how the deployment might have been further simplified from its current incarnation rather than how it was simplified in practice. The configuration was almost an ideal DUCES configuration, being unidirectional, form-based, disconnected, and non-transactional. The server, however, was processed, performing validation logic and displaying it as a web page. This required adding a module to an Oracle back end managed by an NGO [2].

Although the authors do not state it, this likely required a developer with the technical ability to create a web page and encode validation logic. This processed server requirement may have been able to yield to an unprocessed server if server-side validation was not automated. Instead, data could have been exported to a format like comma-separated values (CSV) that can be consumed by a number of programs. At that point it could be manually validated by a staff member, or validation logic could be encoded in a Microsoft Excel worksheet rather than a web page. This would slow the cycle of validation but would not require web programming skills. Alternatively, validation logic is supported by a number of form-based data entry tools. The researchers could instead have performed validation upon data entry rather than during server auditing. Both of these solutions would yield a near optimal configuration under the DUCES framework.

4.2.3 Supply Chains Using Mobile Phones

This deployment serves as a testament to the rich functionality that can be achieved using custom solutions. A custom Java application for feature phones communicated with a custom processed server capable of performing analysis and broadcasting alerts to users. Here again the authors were not involved with the deployment, so application of the DUCES framework will be aim to demonstrate how an organization with less technical resources might try to replicate the success of this workflow.

First, the non-form-based workflow for feature phones could be replaced by a form-based data entry tool for smart phones. As discussed in Section 3.2, a number of form-based data entry tools have been designed to support use by non-programmers.

The processed server model is crucial to this deployment. The authors of the study argue that consumers of the information submitted by the mobile devices are too busy to synthesize the reports without automation. This domain knowledge suggests that simply converting to a bucket-based server model is inappropriate. The authors also note explicitly that their edit model is transactional and that their mobile application functions offline. It is informative to look at how they circumvent the requirement put forth in Section 4.1 that transactional workflows require connectivity.

The answer is twofold. First, they apply server-side processing to deduplicate and process errors that are created as a result of network errors. Second, although their data is transactional, they are able to tolerate errors. In terms of the CAP theorem, they are able to tolerate a loss in consistency as long as the system remains available during periods of no data connectivity. The ramifications for the deployment are that events might not be shown on their web-based bulletin board in real-time. A stock out might be reported late, but this is likely uncommon and is thus deemed acceptable.

4.2.4 Chimpanzee Monitoring

The chimpanzee monitoring case study attains a near-optimal DUCES configuration. It fails by being non-form-based and disconnected. In reality the only simplification that might be afforded by a connected model would be that a wider variety of tools could be used to implement the framework. This would thus accommodate a wider range of user interface components and back ends, including potentially a web-based application. Practical implications of this change are low due to the fact that the data is non-transactional and thus ordering is not significant.

Arriving at this configuration was straight-forward, as the JGI was seeking to replace an existing paper workflow. It is important to note that the non-form-based workflow necessitated the involvement of the assistance of developers, which is an added technical burden. The JGI has extensive experience creating form-based workflows, but the creation of a non-form-based workflow requires an additional skill set. In this case the DUCES framework did not simplify the deployment, but it did clearly delineate where external resources would be required.

4.2.5 Aid Distribution

The aid distribution case study was bidirectional, form-based, connected, transactional, and bucket-based. In the HIV case study, the bidirectional data requirement was able to be eliminated by having participants ideally interact with only a single device, obviating the need to share data between multiple devices. This was not possible in the aid distribution case study, as the nature of the distribution environment required that beneficiaries not be confined to an individual device. With this requirement, tools immediately had to be chosen that could support bidirectional data flow. This eliminated some possibilities like Pendragon Forms, Magpi, and ODK Collect, which support only unidirectional data flows.

A connected connectivity model was required to accommodate the transactional nature of the data. In this case, if connectivity was lost, workers might see an inconsistent view of the data. In other words, a beneficiary may have received aid from one disconnected distribution station and then received aid from a second station that was not aware aid had already been distributed. To prevent this, the system required a connected model. This would in turn require that whatever tools were used to implement the deployment support an online, connected workflow. However, this requirement was able to be circumvented by the real-world details of the aid distribution.

In this case the aid itself was a debit card that had been uniquely assigned to each beneficiary. Once distributed, it could not be distributed again, preventing double distribution. This relaxes the requirement slightly, although at the cost of masking errors during distribution. Coordinators would know a card was missing, but they would not know if it had already been given to the correct recipient or had simply been lost or misplaced. Further, this approach would not accommodate distribution of goods that were not uniquely paired to beneficiaries.

5. CONCLUSION

Mobile devices are increasingly integrated into the workflows of organizations working in low-resource settings. We have presented the DUCES framework as a means to elucidate the requirements of data-focused mobile deployments. We have described five case studies with varying aims and requirements and discussed how they can be evaluated under the DUCES framework, permitting both a meaningful understanding of requirements and guiding simplifying assumptions. Using this framework, deployment architects can start to identify what requirements will add significant complexity. This in turn facilitates the selection of technologies. If a deployment requires bidirectional data flow and that requirement cannot be loosened, technologies that do not support bidirectional data flow can be discounted immediately.

It is important to note that the DUCES framework is not simply an attempt at formalizing a series of known tradeoffs in system design. For example, encrypting data can result in decreased usability while increasing data security. DUCES instead provides a mental scaffold by which a single set of requirements can be described and satisfied in a number of different ways. A processed server might require a custom-built solution with a custom database and a suite of scripts running every night. It instead might be transformed into a bucket-based server by having an administrator copy relevant rows between data sinks and data sources. This would seem an ugly solution to a computer scientist that prefers to automate all tasks. However, it would elegantly allow a lightly skilled deployment architect to compose simple tools in a powerful way that meets the needs of their deployment while remaining comfortably within their skill set.

Some things will always remain difficult in mobile deployments conducted by organizations and groups with limited resources. Transferring data between back-ends is a prime example. Inputting data collected into another system will always be difficult. No choice of tools will completely allay this difficulty unless a programmer has already taken the time to create a method by which data can be exported in a form consumable by the tool in question. Organizations are better off recognizing that this will require technical expertise than they are limiting their technological solutions to one that will be compatible with their current target repository out of the box.

The DUCES framework provides a useful set of considerations for architects of mobile deployments and data-based workflows. The framework can be applied to all systems, but it is most effective when considered by deployment architects operating in low-resource settings. In these environments DUCES can be used to re-imagine requirements in ways that will make mobile workflows easier to deploy and maintain. The DUCES framework is a valuable tool that organizations in low-resource settings can use to characterize and simplify their data-focused mobile deployments.

6. ACKNOWLEDGMENTS

The authors would like to thank USAID, NSF Grant IIS-1111433, the Jane Goodall Institute, the IFRC of the Americas, and the open source community that made this work possible.

7. REFERENCES

[1] Edwin H Blake. 2002. Extended abstract a field computer for animal trackers. *CHI 02 extended abstracts on Human factors in computing systems CHI 02* (2002), 532. DOI: http://dx.doi.org/10.1145/506461.506466

[2] Joaquín a. Blaya, Ted Cohen, Pablo Rodríguez, Jihoon Kim, and Hamish S F Fraser. 2009. Personal digital assistants to collect tuberculosis bacteriology data in Peru reduce delays, errors, and workload, and are acceptable to users: cluster randomized controlled trial. *International Journal of Infectious Diseases* 13, 3 (2009), 410–418. DOI: http://dx.doi.org/10.1016/j.ijid.2008.09.015

[3] Waylon Brunette, Mitchell Sundt, Nicola Dell, Rohit Chaudhri, Nathan Breit, and Gaetano Borriello. 2013. Open Data Kit 2.0: Expanding and Refining Information Services for Developing Regions. *HotMobile '13* (2013), 6. DOI: http://dx.doi.org/10.1145/2444776.2444790

[4] Kuang Chen, Akshay Kannan, Yoriyasu Yano, Joseph M. Hellerstein, and Tapan S. Parikh. 2012. Shreddr: pipelined paper digitization for low-resource organizations. *ACM DEV '12* (2012), 1. DOI: http://dx.doi.org/10.1145/2160601.2160605

[5] Gerald P. Douglas, Oliver J. Gadabu, Sabine Joukes, Soyapi Mumba, Michael V. McKay, Anne Ben-Smith, Andreas Jahn, Erik J. Schouten, Zach Landis Lewis, Joep J. van Oosterhout, Theresa J. Allain, Rony Zachariah, Selma D. Berger, Anthony D. Harries, and Frank Chimbwandira. 2010. Using Touchscreen electronic medical record systems to support and monitor national scale-up of antiretroviral therapy in Malawi. *PLoS Medicine* 7, 8 (2010). DOI: http://dx.doi.org/10.1371/journal.pmed.1000319

[6] Armando Fox and Eric Brewer. 1999. Harvest, yield, and scalable tolerant systems. *Proceedings of the Seventh Workshop on Hot Topics in Operating Systems* (1999). DOI: http://dx.doi.org/10.1109/HOTOS.1999.798396

[7] Hamish SF Fraser, Christian Allen, Christopher Bailey, Gerry Douglas, Sonya Shin, and Joaquin Blaya. 2007. Information Systems for Patient Follow-Up and Chronic Management of HIV and Tuberculosis: A Life-Saving Technology in Resource-Poor Areas. *Journal of medical Internet research* 9, 4 (2007).

[8] Abhishek Gupta, Jatin Thapar, Amarjeet Singh, Pushpendra Singh, Vivek Srinivasan, and Vibhore Vardhan. 2013. Simplifying and improving mobile based data collection. *ICTD '13 - volume 2* (2013), 45–48. DOI: http://dx.doi.org/10.1145/2517899.2517929

[9] Paul Harris, Robert Taylor, Robert Thielke, Jonathon Payne, Nathaniel Gonzalez, and Jose Conde. 2009. Research electronic data capture (REDCap)-A metadata-driven methodology and workflow process for providing translational research informatics support. *Journal of Biomedical Informatics* 42, 2 (2009), 377–381. DOI: http://dx.doi.org/10.1016/j.jbi.2008.08.010

[10] Carl Hartung, Yaw Anokwa, Waylon Brunette, Adam Lerer, Clint Tseng, and Gaetano Borriello. 2010. Open Data Kit: Tools to Build Information Services for Developing Regions. *Proceedings of the International Conference on Information and Communication Technologies and Development* (2010). DOI: http://dx.doi.org/10.1145/2369220.2369236

[11] William B. Lober, Stephen Wagner, and Christina Quiles. 2010. Development and implementation of a loosely coupled, multi-site, networked and replicated electronic medical record in Haiti. *ACM SIGOPS Operating Systems Review* 43, 4 (2010), 79. DOI: http://dx.doi.org/10.1145/1713254.1713272

[12] Arun Ramanujapuram and Anup Akkihal. 2014. Improving Performance of Rural Supply Chains Using Mobile Phones: Reducing Information Asymmetry to Improve Stock Availability in Low-resource Environments. *ACM DEV* (2014), 11–19.

[13] Samuel Sudar, Saloni Parikh, Mitchell Sundt, and Gaetano Borriello. 2013. ODK Tables : Case Studies in Deployment. (2013), 12–14. DOI: http://dx.doi.org/10.1145/2537052.2537077

Towards a 2-way Communication and Analytics Platform for Emergency Response and Post-emergency Recovery Efforts in Sierra Leone

Meenal Pore*, *IBM Research – Africa*
Nuri Purswani, *IBM Research – Africa*
Reginald E. Bryant, *IBM Research – Africa*
Purity Mugambi, *IBM Research – Africa*
Osamuyimen Stewart, *IBM Research – Africa*
*Contact: meenalpore@ke.ibm.com

At the peak of the West African Ebola outbreak in December 2014, the only prospect for containing the Ebola Virus Disease (EVD) was through behavior change to reduce transmission pathways. However, deeply ingrained beliefs, social systems, and cultural practices, combined with a lack of knowledge of the disease, made containment difficult. IBM Research - Africa, in collaboration with Sierra Leone Open Government Initiative (OGI), set up a call and SMS hotline to engage with citizens and understand issues on the ground using free text responses, which started on 19th Sept 2014 (during the first national lockdown). Localized versions of Centre for Disease Control (CDC) public health messages were broadcast on public radio along with a short question on Ebola, and listeners were encouraged to call or SMS the OGI hotline in reply to the question, or to report the current situation in their locality. Messages were categorized using a basic keyword search approach, based on categories that were determined manually, and the results of the analysis were communicated to the government via OGI. The initial deployment showed the potential of using a 2-way communication platform utilizing natural language responses to provide valuable feedback on behaviors and attitudes during a health emergency.

Our presentation will describe the original platform, the outcomes of the analysis performed to date and the current work being undertaken to extend and scale the platform in Sierra Leone.

ACM Categories & Descriptors: J.3 [Life and Medical Sciences]: Health

Keywords: Ebola; SMS; Public Health; Behavior change

DOI: http://dx.doi.org/10.1145/2830629.2830634

Toward Alternative Decentralized Infrastructures

Bill Tomlinson
Department of Informatics
University of California, Irvine
wmt@uci.edu

Bonnie Nardi
Department of Informatics
University of California, Irvine
nardi@ics.uci.edu

Donald J. Patterson
Department of Computer Science
Westmont College
dpatterson@westmont.edu

Ankita Raturi
Department of Informatics
University of California, Irvine
araturi@uci.edu

Debra Richardson
Department of Informatics
University of California, Irvine
djr@uci.edu

Jean-Daniel Saphores
Henry Samueli School of Engineering
University of California, Irvine
saphores@uci.edu

Dan Stokols
School of Social Ecology
University of California, Irvine
dstokols@uci.edu

ABSTRACT

New forms of infrastructure are needed in a world characterized by the burdens of global climate change, a growing population, increasing socio-technical complexity, and natural and human stressors to our human systems. Enabling communities to transition to a more resilient configuration of infrastructures is crucial for establishing a distributed portfolio of processes and systems by which human needs may be met. This paper proposes a potential way to increase infrastructure resilience by supporting the creation of alternative, decentralized infrastructures (ADIs) composed of small-scale, heterogeneous systems and processes. We see two possible roles for these ADIs: first, they could be integrated with existing infrastructures in the industrialized world, thereby providing some redundancy during times of strain on larger centralized systems; and second, they could help developing communities leapfrog centralized and more capital intensive conventional infrastructure. We present a model for how ADI systems may be built, based on principles from software engineering. Finally, we identify some challenges that go beyond technical implementation details in the instantiation of ADIs, and offer some thoughts on how to address them.

Categories and Subject Descriptors

H.5.m [**Miscellaneous**]; J.7 [**Computers in Other Systems**]

General Terms

Human Factors

Keywords

Infrastructure; Software Engineering; ICT4D; Sustainability

1. INTRODUCTION

This paper seeks to increase the resilience of infrastructures that support life around the world. We use Holling's definition of resilience as "a measure of the persistence of systems and of their ability to absorb change and disturbance" [20]; see also [43]. Resilient systems are not static, and may fluctuate, but still persist in recognizable form [20]. An infrastructure, as defined by the US National Science Foundation, is "a network of man-made systems and processes that function cooperatively and synergistically to produce and distribute a continuous flow of essential goods and services." [12] Persistence is achieved when the infrastructure's basic services continue in spite of change and disturbance. Because forces of disturbance such as climate change, resource depletion, pollution, and growing income disparity [24] point to a future where infrastructures must be adapted to absorb such stresses, our work examines how to transition to a world that gracefully integrates decentralized infrastructures, and potentially couples them with centralized infrastructures.

Throughout this paper, we refer to centralized interdependent critical infrastructures as ICIs. The US Department of Homeland Security lists sixteen main categories of ICIs: chemical; commercial; communications; critical manufacturing; dams; defense industrial base; emergency services; energy; financial services; food and agriculture; government facilities; healthcare and public health; information technology; nuclear reactors, materials, and waste; transportation systems; and waste and wastewater systems [11]. In many developed regions, critical goods and services in these sectors are provided by centralized, government- or corporate-controlled institutions.

In addition to ICIs, though, many small-scale alternative, decentralized infrastructures have been developed around the world to serve human needs and lie outside the purview of ICIs, either due to a lack of ICIs (e.g., in developing contexts) or due to residents' dissatisfaction with ICIs (e.g., their quality, sustainability, etc.). Examples include urban gardens, biofiltration systems, home solar panels, DIY activities, and numerous others (cf., [15, 21, 30, 35]). Although these decentralized infrastructures do not enjoy the economies of scale of conventional/centralized infrastructures (e.g., rooftop gardening vs. agribusiness), they are typically a lot more environmentally benign per unit produced (e.g., rooftop gardening typically uses a lot less pesticides and fertilizers than industrial agriculture and solar panels do not emit GHG). These decentralized infrastructures currently tend to be isolated, inefficient activities that do not address regional, community-based needs. We envision that they could be integrated together, serving as elements in a greater whole. Adapting the NSF definition of infrastructure above, we define an ADI as a "network of small-scale, heterogeneous, human-made systems and processes that dynamically integrate with each other and function cooperatively and synergistically to produce and distribute a continuous flow of essential goods and services" (adapted from [12]). Throughout this paper we refer to the specific systems that could be brought together to constitute an ADI as *elements* of that ADI. For example, an urban garden would be an element of a food ADI.

The core question addressed in this paper is this: What if ADIs could be scaled up through intelligent, computer-based management, adhering to the principles of good software design, to produce a transition to more integrated, regional structures?

The structure of the paper is as follows. First, we describe the role that ADIs could play in a selection of sectors in developed and developing contexts. Second, we describe how an ADI system could be implemented, based on principles from software engineering, and integrated with sensors to provide with up-to-date information about its elements. Finally, we present a number of key challenges facing ADIs, and potential plans for addressing these challenges.

2. ADI SYSTEMS IN USE

Extensive computer systems exist to manage centralized infrastructures for water, energy, transportation, and many other critical infrastructure sectors discussed above. However, small-scale systems, managed locally, are frequently integrated in an ad hoc fashion, if at all. We envision a world in which human needs such as food, water, and energy are met, at levels currently enjoyed in the industrialized world, not primarily by large-scale, corporate- or government-controlled infrastructures, but rather by well coordinated, distributed collections of small-scale systems and services. This section describes the role ADI systems could play across various different sectors.

2.1 Food

In many parts of the world, food is provided by industrial agricultural systems. In others, the primary sources of nutrition are subsistence agriculture and other small-scale activities. In an ADI system, food would be produced, processed (e.g. dried, milled, deboned, and packaged), and distributed via many small-scale farms, processing systems, and transportation activities that together are able to perform at the efficiency of industrial agriculture, but with significantly greater robustness. These production, processing, and distribution systems would be dynamically coordinated by computational systems that allow for individual elements entering or leaving the system. For example, as people move from place to place, a farm may disappear in one location and arise in a new location. If a family bought a truck, they could quickly be included in the routing mechanisms that enable food to be moved from place of production to place of consumption. If climate change compromised the viability of one crop, farms growing different crops and therefore needing different distribution processes and routes could be gradually integrated into the system as a whole.

By coordinating and connecting individual elements, network economies could be realized that would lead to greater production efficiency without the large external costs of current ICIs. Information from the various elements of the ADI system would be uploaded to the computational algorithms via a combination of automatic sensors (e.g., GPS locations of vehicles) and guide human effort (e.g. number of squash harvested on a given day). This could enable optimization of the flows of resources through the food system, provide metrics to measure performance, and allow for other forms of system analysis. ADIs could integrate with tools such as KrishiEkta [2], OneFarm [1], and KrishiMantra [26] to provide farmers across a region with important information regarding opportunities within the local food system.

2.2 Water

The provision of water takes many different forms around the world, from centralized, government-controlled water infrastructures such as those found in many industrialized nations, to systems where people carry containers of water each day from hand pumps, rivers, or streams to their homes (e.g., [44]).

An ADI system could integrate numerous different forms of available water (from rivers, reservoirs, hand pumps, greywater collectors, desalinization plants, fog harvesters, biofiltration systems, etc.), and help coordinate the production of different levels of water quality to satisfy local needs. Water flow and water quality sensors could be systematically integrated into these water sources to optimize the value of their services to humans without compromising the value they provide to other organisms and the long-term viability of our ecosystems more broadly.

As an example of the potential benefits of an ADI system, rather than watering a garden with fresh water or reclaimed water, a greywater collection system from nearby homes could provide water of high enough quality for that purpose. Where such a greywater system does not exist, an ADI system could provide suggestions for potential ways to improve the overall functionality of the system by finding bottlenecks and suggesting opportunities for improvement. Water ADIs could make use of currently unclaimed water resources, such as greywater, and allow several local sources to pool their resources to benefit the community.

2.3 Energy

In the energy domain, as with food and water, there are numerous pathways by which energy is generated and distributed. From centralized fossil fuel-based power companies to solar charging kiosks [23] to energy distribution via discarded laptop batteries [7], various communities have developed a diverse array of ways to meet the need for energy. In an ADI system, these diverse pathways that energy enters and travels within human communities would be integrated, monitored, and routed algorithmically. Given the increasing policy emphasis on reducing our dependence on fossil fuels to cut our emissions of greenhouse gases, local alternative sources of energy such as wind and solar power will become increasingly important and require much better management to smooth weather related variations in order to satisfy demand for energy.

2.4 Information Technology

As with each of the above, access to information technology currently occurs through a range of channels. As well as increasing use of mobile, desktop, and internet technologies in industrialized nations, there are numerous smaller-scale IT activities throughout the world (e.g., [9, 10]). By providing a rigorous way of documenting people's IT needs/wants, the IT resources available, and dynamically connecting them, an ADI system could improve the effectiveness with which a large collection of small-scale, heterogeneous IT systems could be provided to people.

There is also significant interest in creating alternative networking systems: from work on enabling local voice communication through a mesh network [17], to providing universal Internet access to deprived regions through WiFi sharing [39]. These are all potential elements of an ADI system that would equip people with a range of networking and communication services appropriate to their geography.

2.5 Integration Across Infrastructures

An important contribution that an ADI system could make lies not just within a particular sector (e.g., food, water), but also in the process of integrating across different infrastructures. In the first example above, the linkages between food and transportation were evident. Similarly, an ADI system could be helpful in harnessing the complex linkages between IT and energy (e.g., powering devices), between water and food (e.g., watering food plants), between food and energy (e.g., biofuels), between energy and water (e.g., cooling or pumping water), and other more tenuous interactions. Allowing all of these small-scale, heterogeneous, distributed infrastructural elements to work together would hopefully better satisfy human needs than conventional industrial infrastructures, with significantly improved robustness and resilience.

2.6 ADIs in Developed and Developing Contexts

ADIs have potential application in both developed and developing contexts. If an ADI system were deployed to work jointly with conventional infrastructure, the elements that make up the ADI could provide a complement to the centralized infrastructure, thereby enabling more sustainable lifestyles, more effective utilization of resources, and resilience against potential collapse [42]. If the ADI system were deployed in a context where reliable infrastructures are lacking, the dynamic coordination could link together many existing but not-yet-well-connected mechanisms for how people's needs are met, streamlining the process and making apparent those places where new ventures and other forms of development are most needed [35]. In addition, where conventional/centralized, large-scale infrastructures are missing, such as in developing communities, ADIs could provide a mechanism to leapfrog their developed counterparts [8], as illustrated by the development of cellular communications that made obsolete the need to install landlines.

In many developing regions people have begun creating alternative decentralized infrastructures already, driven by need and implemented with materials readily available. Often though, they are interfacing with more centralized infrastructures, but in an *ad hoc* way. For example, electricity grids may be subject to parasitic loads from unsanctioned line splitting, and typically semi-centralized resource distribution (for example fuel) is augmented with individuals buying, selling and transporting small amounts on a gray market. The development of well-structured ADIs could actually facilitate these kinds of relationships, but in a way that would benefit traditional suppliers and the *ad hoc* suppliers as well. Clearly there is a need because there exist many ADIs, very poorly specified, in developing regions already. As we continue to work on these ideas, we want to be alert to the varied global socieconomic contexts in which ADIs might be deployed. Infrastructural components vary across contexts, yet we believe that the notion of interfaces between centralized and decentralized infrastructures has great generality.

3. HOW AN ADI SYSTEM WOULD WORK

We envision the core of the implementation of such a system being based on ideas arising out of software engineering. This section presents a summary of the technical aspects of a potential ADI implementation. The design of such a system would be informed by interviews with key stakeholder groups to ensure that the technical aspects provide the desired effect on quality of life. For example, interviewees could include:

- scholars and activists with deep expertise in particular ADI domains or the interactions between domains, for example, [15] on food, [38] on water, [33] on energy, and [40] on information technology;

- citizen users of alternative technologies and participants in local community activities geared to sustainability; and

- private sector consultants, regulators, government decision-makers, and politicians whose joint efforts are essential for catalyzing the adoption and expansion of alternative sustainable infrastructures.

These interviews would inform the development of computational models of ADI elements and the interfaces between them, and of the process by which sensors could be enabled to measure aspects of the elements automatically.

3.1 Interfaces Among ADI Elements

A key challenge for integrating many small-scale systems lies at the interfaces between those systems. The software engineering community has well-established principles for rigorously specifying interfaces and building systems around those interfaces. Software engineering has developed sophisticated understandings of the roles and properties of interfaces for specifying interdependencies and interactions among the components of complex software systems, to explore and characterize the interfaces between interdependent infrastructures. Software engineers are also looking at adapting existing practice to cater to infrastructural requirements such as sustainability [37] and resilience [36].

Software engineering focuses on "the application of a systematic, disciplined, quantifiable approach to the development, operation, and maintenance of software" [22]. We see significant potential in bringing this approach to infrastructure analysis. In particular, we propose that coupled decentralized/centralized infrastructures could work efficiently and effectively through intelligently managed interfaces.

A key focus of the ideas presented here is to use insights from software engineering, drawing on the analogous complexities of large-scale software systems with interdependent components that are addressed by disciplined techniques to specify well-defined interfaces that describe component interdependencies. Software interface specifications are carefully defined rules constraining the

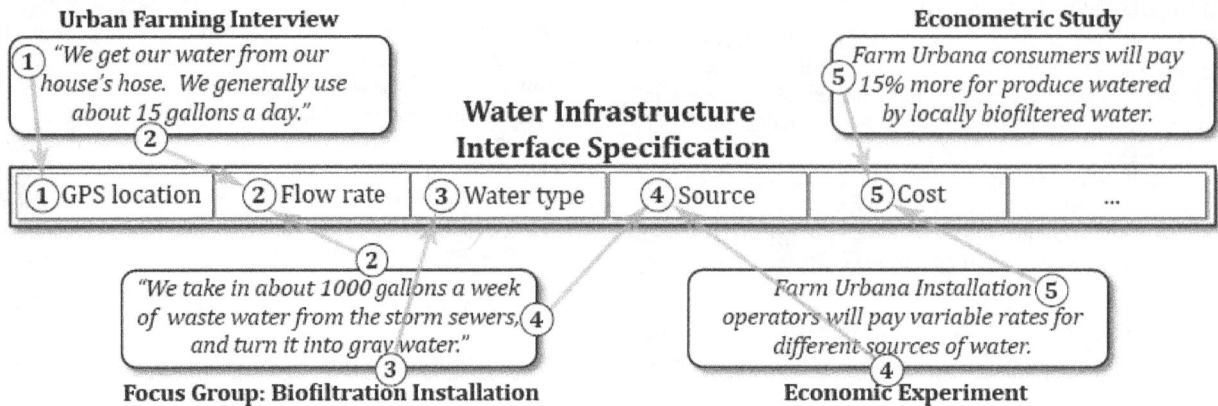

Figure 1: An illustration of how content from stakeholder interviews could inform the infrastructure interface specification model.

interactions of interdependent components, specified using an interface description language (IDL) [27]. Software engineering researchers have evolved IDLs, making it possible to specify not just input/output between components, but a range of additional properties such as dependencies [45], measurements [14], and behavior [28]. A related development in software engineering is Application Programming Interface (API) design [5, 41]. APIs are crafted explicitly to expose only chosen functionality and/or data of a software application (components) while safeguarding other parts of the application. A properly crafted API enables the underlying implementation to change without affecting a client system using the application – in fact, the application can be completely "swapped" with another, so long as the replacing application adheres to the API [29].

We envision that the concept of component interface specification could be fruitfully applied to connecting ICIs and ADIs. The interface specification of an infrastructure would specify the resources provided as well as certain attributes of the resources. We suggest that qualities adapted from software, such as efficiency, reliability, robustness, reusability, visibility, and others should be characterized by the interface specification as well, as such qualities are especially relevant to infrastructures. Interface specifications could enable ADIs to be explored more easily in simulations, and eventually scaled up from local demonstration projects to regional scale innovations that may complement existing, dominant ICIs.

The interface specification model would include several aspects of infrastructure interdependencies, including: (a) resources and other inputs/outputs required and provided along with the attributes of these objects, (b) object and attribute visibility among infrastructures, and (c) other desired/delivered qualities of the infrastructure. The value of such carefully defined interfaces lies both in defining the scope of particular ADIs and the potential to replace one infrastructure (ICI) with an alternative (ADI) satisfying the same API. This ability to "swap" in an alternative infrastructure leads to resiliency in a manner similar to design diversity for software fault tolerance [4] and is similar to dynamic software component "swapping" by RAIC—Redundant Arrays of Independent Components [29].

The goal is to arrive at the minimal interface necessary to capture the characteristics of most interactions that ADIs may have with ICIs or with each other. While such a technical approach may seem unnecessary at first glance (e.g., because an existing ADI already realizes where its inputs are coming from and where its

outputs are going), ensuring consistency across ADIs and ICIs through rigorously defined interface specifications makes it feasible to place the interactions across those systems under computational control.

3.1.1 Inputs/Outputs

An infrastructure interface specification (as with a software interface) should define the input/output objects that are required/provided in its interaction with other infrastructure systems, along with the attributes of those objects. Primary I/O objects are resources, but there may also be parameterization, for instance, to control the magnitude of resources or other inputs controlling infrastructure functionality as there may be other outputs denoting infrastructure state.

The interface must cover not only the commonalities but also the unique aspects of interactions. For example, in interfacing with the water sector (see Figure 1), the attributes "flow rate," "water type," and "location" may be shared across most water sources discussed in stakeholder interviews, but less ubiquitous issues such as a "bacterial content" attribute could surface in rarer instances. Each attribute must also be defined by the appropriate measurement or units (e.g., gallons per day vs. cubic feet per second, or cold | cool | warm | hot | boiling vs. degrees Fahrenheit/Celcius), ways of converting from one unit to another ("cool equals 55-85°F"), and sensible default values.

3.1.2 Object Visibility

A second key aspect of infrastructure interface specification relates to object and attribute visibility. Continuing with water as an example, an organization may be comfortable sharing the flow rate out of a bathroom sink drain, but not the water's bacterial content (which could be used to assess the personal health of people who live/work there). Based on stakeholder interviews, we would seek to establish appropriate categories of visibility—e.g., private, friend organizations only, same sector only, other sectors only, public – as well as specific visibility between infrastructures (ADIs or ICIs). We would also seek to establish sensible default visibility values for each object in an interface.

3.1.3 Infrastructure Qualities

A third aspect of infrastructure interface specification focuses on the qualities of the infrastructure system represented by an interface. One key aspect of a critical infrastructure, for instance, is "up-time", which is related to but not equivalent to the software quality of reliability. As an example, regional energy companies in the US have very high levels of up-time, while a local solar

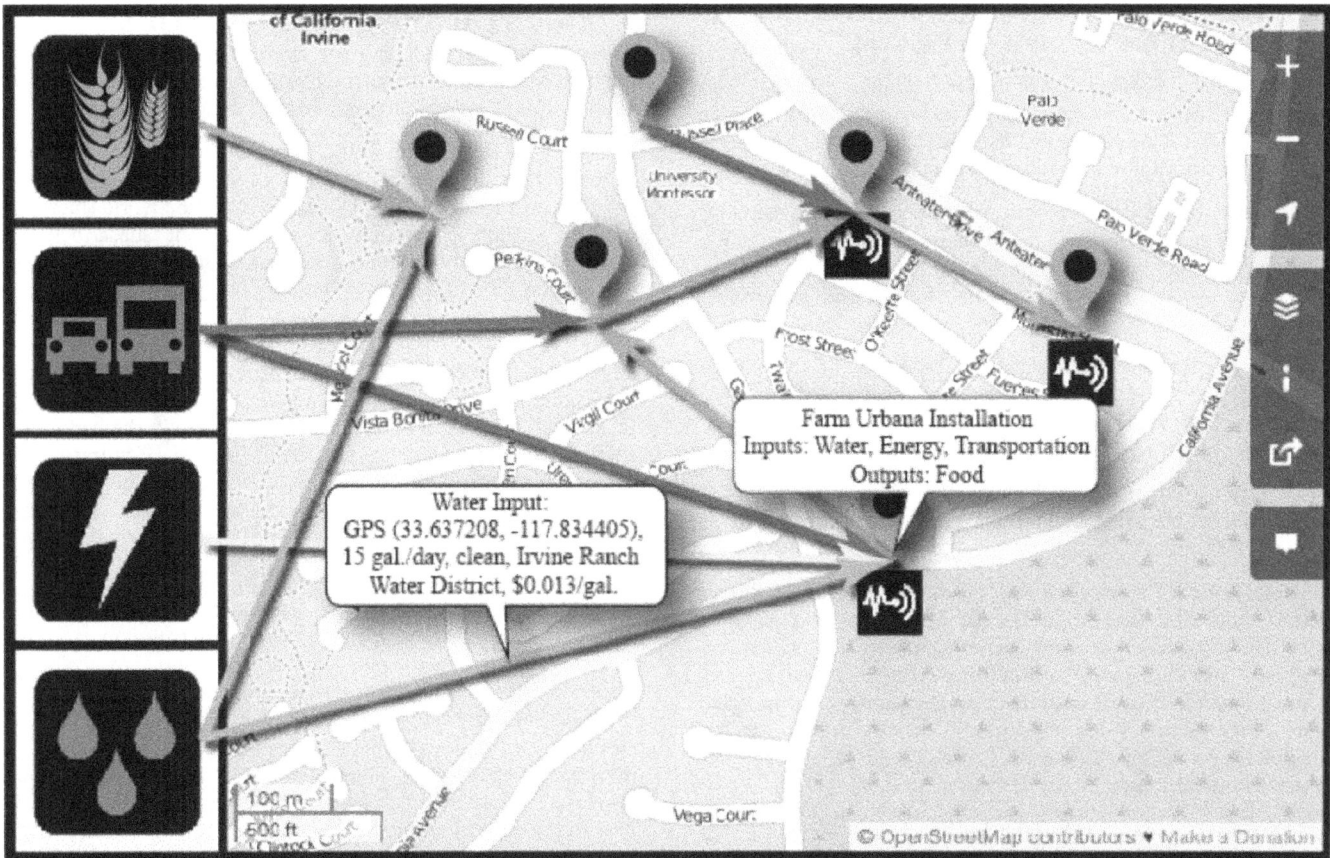

Figure 2: A mockup of a visualization of an ADI system. © <u>OpenStreetMap contributors</u> **and the authors of this paper.**

installation is inherently intermittent based on availability of sunshine. Critical infrastructures are also highly interconnected. Seemingly separate infrastructures such as water and communication can affect the performance of elements in each infrastructure [35], requiring not only the development of resilient networks of elements and infrastructures (e.g., [6]), but also ADIs that are flexible and adaptable. Stakeholder interviews would help determine what software qualities and variants apply to which infrastructures, and allow the interface specification model to be augmented to specify particular qualities.

3.2 ADI Monitor System

Advances in manufacturing efficiencies and the subsequent reduction in prices of sensors have caused their deployment to rapidly increase and their role in infrastructures to grow. From barometers on cell-phones and motion sensors on light switches in offices, to seismographs in civil infrastructure and smart meters in homes, physical sensors are proliferating. In order to facilitate system maintenance and the analysis of data, many of these sensors are connected to applications and to Internet services. Collectively this "Internet of Things" is becoming an increasingly important and pervasive facet of infrastructure interface design (cf., [3]).

At the same time, software, both simple and sophisticated, is being used to create virtual sensors; for example, geographic crowd sentiment analysis derived from Twitter feeds that capture the mood of a city [25, 32], and search engine aggregations that identify disease outbreaks [18]. While the spread of sensors has created increased opportunities for context-aware applications and is tightly coupled with infrastructure [3], it is difficult to manage

the opportunities afforded by the scale of this trend—there are difficulties inherent in discovering, collecting, fusing, and reasoning with data from the heterogeneous set of distributed sensors.

In the face of these trends and challenges, we propose to develop a monitoring network (the "ADI Monitor") that is particularly well suited to the decentralized nature of ADIs (see Figure 2 for a mockup of a visualization of such a system). An initial prototype [6] has been developed of this system, but significant work is still needed in order to allow it to monitor real-world infrastructure interface connections. In our current design the ADI Monitor has computational processes or "nodes" that provide value-added information services on top of networked physical and virtual infrastructure sensors. Conceptually, the "owner" of a sensor pairs one ADI Monitor "node" with one sensor that is already exposed on the internet. Nodes communicate with each other using peer-to-peer networks. Here we describe future work that could extend this monitoring system so that real-world deployments are robust and easy for end-users to operate. The system would enable a range of capabilities, detailed below.

Organization of Existing Sensors: The ADI Monitor would not seek to deploy new sensors, but to integrate existing sensors into our network. In the pairing process of an ADI Monitor node with the underlying sensor, the sensor is exposed to the rest of the ADI Monitor system with a consistent data interface. The node/sensor pairs become searchable through an automated directory and the complexity of gathering data from now-exposed sensors is greatly reduced. Examples of sensors that we are integrating include smart-meters on homes, electric current sensors on solar panels, irrigation system operational status, micro-weather stations, and smart-phone/wearable sensors. We intend to broaden our targets based on feedback from our stakeholder interviews.

Intermittency Tolerance: The ADI Monitor nodes can communicate using a peer-to-peer networking protocol [34] that is itself resilient to intermittency, but also, as a result, supports continued monitoring in the face of partial infrastructure outages.

Scaling: By using a decentralized peer-to-peer network, the ADI Monitor supports extremely large networks of sensors. We anticipate incorporating approximately 10,000 sensor values in our next stage of deployment, many focused on geographic specializations.

Analytics: By incorporating statistical modeling of the sensor values, ADI nodes can be given predictive analytics that enable them to function on par with utility-grade infrastructures.

Operator Reflection: Consistent, reliable access to decentralized sensor systems coupled with high quality user-interfaces would enable ADI owner/operators insight into how to manage their ADIs more effectively.

Research Data: The construction of the ADI Monitor would utilize cloud resources such as Google App Engine and Amazon EC2. By consolidating and exposing sensor systems we potentially introduce new vulnerabilities related to privacy and data exploitation. It is important to have mechanisms that mitigate these concerns by using high-grade encryption and access parameters controlled by sensor owners and designed from stakeholder interviews.

Typical sensor studies focus on a limited sensor portfolio, i.e., researchers build event recognition models by applying machine learning methods to the data collected from one sensor or from a closely coupled set of sensors. Though this demonstrates how powerful a small federation of sensor data can be if interpreted correctly, it ignores the fact that our world is a much more broadly instrumented multisensory environment now. Such an environment should enable new events to be recognized for the first time. We hypothesize that the state of infrastructures is just such a new category of context. Each of the many sensors provides a different perspective and complements information from other sensors to construct a comprehensive picture. As well as enabling many more sensors to be aggregated by a single application, the ADI Monitor also enables a single sensor to be simultaneously utilized by more than one application.

Applications that are built on top of the ADI Monitor would be able to harvest information from a network of sensors, including physical stationary sensors, mobile and worn sensors, and virtual or physical social sensors, and would provide richer insights and potentially support novel use cases.

The final component of the ADI Monitor would be a mobile application that enables users to connect sensors to the ADI Monitor network and to visualize related data that is already incorporated. For example, an urban farmer may stand next to the location where her outdoor spigot connects to her automated sprinkler system, and use her mobile phone to launch an ADI Monitor node to monitor the sprinkler's operation. In the process, it could reveal assets in her immediate vicinity (e.g., water output from a nearby biofiltration system) that may be useful to her farm and already implemented as ADI Monitor nodes.

4. OUTSTANDING CHALLENGES

The possibility of ADI systems coming into existence brings to the fore a number of significant challenges beyond the technical details of implementation discussed above.

First, an ADI system would rely heavily on a computing infrastructure in order to work well. While such computing infrastructures are available in many parts of the world (more than half the world's population are mobile phone subscribers, and there are more mobile connections (including M2M) than there are people [13, 19], not everyone has equal access to the computing infrastructures that would make ADIs feasible. Therefore, it is possible that, from a quality-of-life perspective, ADIs would preferentially benefit those who already have more than enough. Nevertheless, from a sustainability perspective, those who enjoy such abundance may be exactly the people who should migrate to a more sustainable model of infrastructure. Either way, to address this issue at least in part, ADI implementations should be developed with the goal of utilizing the lowest-tech and most available technologies on which they would be viable.

A second problem involves the question of justice, from an algorithmic perspective. If a computational system is routing resources, who gets to decide what the optimal utilization of resources is? Does the algorithm seek the highest average quality of life, the highest minimum quality of life, the greatest sustainability of the system, or some other goal? There have been discussions about how Google's search algorithm may be a powerful influencer of elections [16]; similarly, the algorithm underlying an ADI would by its nature bias the distribution of life sustaining resources. Therefore, it would be critical to have a wide range of key stakeholders involved in decisions about how the algorithms should function, and transparency in the implementation of those algorithms must be ensured.

A third problem lies in the possibility that, by centralizing the decision-making process controlling the distribution of resources (even if the production of those resources is via small-scale decentralized infrastructure elements), ADIs might create a single point of exploitation for those elements. The elements that would be brought together into an ADI presumably already have some mechanism for distributing their products and services to relevant end-points, even if those mechanisms may not be particularly efficient or robust. Nevertheless, efforts exist to allow digital systems to be as robust as the offline equivalents that they replace (e.g., [31]); the ADI routing systems could hopefully be made similarly robust.

Overall, while challenges are substantial, they are comparable (if not identical) to those found in conventional industrial infrastructures. We hope that the transparency that could be enabled by an ADI system would help address them.

5. CONCLUSIONS

In this paper, we have presented the concept of alternative, decentralized infrastructures (ADIs), and their potential role in providing for human needs around the world. We have laid out a plan by which ideas from software engineering could be brought to bear on the process of implementing ADI systems. By doing so, we seek to elevate the role of small-scale, decentralized aspects of infrastructure in the larger landscape of infrastructures. We hope that the conceptualization of ADIs presented here will help inform policy decisions that facilitate smoother transition to more resilient infrastructure, and societal shifts toward more sustainable ways of life.

6. ACKNOWLEDGMENTS

The authors thank Richard Donovan, Neil Young and the ACM DEV reviewers for their suggestions and contributions to this work.

7. REFERENCES

[1] Aditya, V. and Sasikumar, K. 2013. Nutrient management decision support system for livelihood security of farmers. *Proceedings of the 3rd ACM Symposium on Computing for Development (ACM DEV '13)* (New York, New York, USA, 2013).

[2] Agrawal, R. and Sundari, S.K. 2012. KrishiEkta : Integrated Knowledge and Information Distribution System for Indian Agriculture. *Proceedings of the 2nd ACM Symposium on Computing for Development (ACM DEV '12)* (New York, New York, USA, 2012).

[3] Atzori, L., Iera, A. and Morabito, G. 2010. The internet of things: A survey. *Computer networks.* 54, 15 (2010).

[4] Avizienis, A. and Kelly, J. 1984. Fault tolerance by design diversity: Concepts and experiments. *Computer.* 17, 8 (1984).

[5] Bloch, J. 2006. How to design a good API and why it matters. *In Companion to the 21st ACM SIGPLAN symposium on Object-oriented programming systems, languages, and applications (OOPSLA '06)* (New York, New York, USA, 2006).

[6] Brock, J. and Patterson, D.J. 2015. Cacophony: Building a Resilient Internet of Things. In First Workshop on Computing within Limits. *First Workshop on Computing within Limits (LIMITS 2015).* (Irvine, CA, 2015).

[7] Chandan, V., Jain, M. and Khadilkar, H. 2014. UrJar: A Lighting Solution using Discarded Laptop Batteries. *Proceedings of the Fifth ACM Symposium on Computing for Development (ACM DEV-5 '14)* (New York, New York, USA, 2014).

[8] Chen, J. 2015. Computing within Limits and ICTD. *First Workshop on Computing within Limits (LIMITS 2015).* (Irvine, CA, 2015).

[9] Chen, J. and Subramanian, L. 2013. Interactive web caching for slow or intermittent networks. *Proceedings of the 4th Annual Symposium on ...* (New York, New York, USA, 2013).

[10] Corrigan-Gibbs, H. and Chen, J. 2014. FlashPatch: spreading software updates over flash drives in under-connected regions. *Proceedings of the Fifth ACM Symposium on Computing for Development (ACM DEV-5 '14)* (New York, New York, USA, 2014).

[11] Critical Infrastructure Sectors: 2015. *http://www.dhs.gov/critical-infrastructure-sectors.* Accessed: 2015-09-06.

[12] Critical Resilient Interdependent Infrastructure Systems and Processes (CRISP): *http://www.nsf.gov/pubs/2015/nsf15531/nsf15531.htm.*

[13] Current World Population: 2015. *http://www.worldometers.info/world-population/.* Accessed: 2015-09-06.

[14] Damevski, K. 2009. Expressing measurement units in interfaces for scientific component software. *Proceedings of the 2009 Workshop on Component-Based High Performance Computing (CBHPC '09)* (New York, New York, USA, 2009).

[15] Despommier, D. 2010. *The vertical farm: feeding the world in the 21st century.* Thomas Dunne Books, St. Martin's Press.

[16] Epstein, R. 2015. How Google Could Rig the 2015 Election. *Politico Magazine.*

[17] Gabale, V., Raman, B., Chebrolu, K. and Kulkarni, P. 2010. LiT MAC: addressing the challenges of effective voice communication in a low cost, low power wireless mesh network. *Proceedings of the First ACM Symposium on Computing for Development (ACM DEV '10)* (New York, New York, USA, 2010).

[18] Ginsberg, J., Mohebbi, M. and Patel, R. 2009. Detecting influenza epidemics using search engine query data. *Nature.* 457, 7232 (2009).

[19] Global Data: 2015. *https://gsmaintelligence.com/.* Accessed: 2015-09-06.

[20] Holling, C. 1973. Resilience and stability of ecological systems. *Annual review of ecology and systematics.* 4, (1973).

[21] Hopkins, R. 2008. *The transition handbook: from oil dependency to local resilience.* Chelsea Green Publishing.

[22] IEEE 2010. Systems and software engineering -- Vocabulary. ISO/IEC/IEEE 24765:2010(E). 2010.

[23] Iland, D. and Belding, E. 2014. Open Charging Kiosk: A Business in a Box. *InProceedings of the Fifth ACM Symposium on Computing for Development (ACM DEV-5 '14).* (New York, New York, USA, 2014).

[24] IPCC 2014. *Part A: Global and Sectoral Aspects. Contribution of Working Group II to the Fifth Assessment Report of the Intergovernmental Panel on Climate Change.*

[25] Kouloumpis, E., Wilson, T. and Moore, J. 2011. Twitter sentiment analysis: The good the bad and the omg! *Proceedings of the Fifth International AAAI Conference on Weblogs and Social Media (ICWSM 11)* (2011).

[26] Kumar, V. and Dave, V. 2013. Krishimantra: agricultural recommendation system. *Proceedings of the 3rd ACM Symposium on Computing for Development (ACM DEV '13)* (New York, New York, USA, 2013).

[27] Lamb, D. 1987. IDL: Sharing intermediate representations. *ACM Transactions on Programming Languages and Systems.* 9, 3 (1987).

[28] Leavens, G., Baker, A. and Ruby, C. 2006. Preliminary design of JML: A behavioral interface specification language for Java. *ACM SIGSOFT Software Engineering Notes.* 31, 3 (2006).

[29] Liu, C. and Richardson, D. 2002. RAIC: Architecting dependable systems through redundancy and just-in-time testing. *ICSE 2002 Workshop on Architecting Dependable Systems (WADS)* (Orlando, FL, USA, 2002).

[30] Lydon, M. and Garcia, A. 2015. *Tactical urbanism: Short-term action for long-term change.* Island Press.

[31] Maniatis, P. and Roussopoulos, M. 2005. The LOCKSS peer-to-peer digital preservation system. *ACM Transactions on Computer Systems.* 23, 1 (2005).

[32] Mitchell, L., Frank, M. and Harris, K. 2013. The geography of happiness: Connecting twitter sentiment and expression, demographics, and objective characteristics of place. *PLoS ONE.* 8, 5:e64417 (2013).

[33] Modi, V., McDade, S., Lallement, D. and Saghir, J. 2005. *Energy and the Millenium Development Goals.*

[34] p2p4java: *https://github.com/djp3/p2p4java.* Accessed: 2015-09-06.

[35] Patterson, D.J. 2015. Haitian Resiliency: A Case Study in Intermittent Infrastructure. *First Workshop on Computing within Limits (LIMITS 2015).* (Irvine, CA, 2015).

[36] Penzenstadler, B., Raturi, A., Richardson, D., Silberman, S. and Tomlinson, B. 2015. Collapse (& Other Futures) Software Engineering. *First Workshop on Computing within Limits (LIMITS 2015).* (Irvine, CA, 2015).

[37] Penzenstadler, B., Raturi, A., Richardson, D. and Tomlinson, B. 2014. Safety, security, now sustainability: The nonfunctional requirement for the 21st century. *IEEE Software.* 31, 3 (2014).

[38] Radcliffe, J. 2004. *Water recycling in Australia: a review undertaken by the Australian academy of technological sciences and engineering.*

[39] Sathiaseelan, A. and Mortier, R. 2014. A Feasibility Study of an In-the-Wild Experimental Public Access WiFi Network. *Proceedings of the Fifth ACM Symposium on Computing for Development (ACM DEV-5 '14)* (New York, New York, USA, 2014).

[40] Smarr, L. 2010. The Growing Interdependence of the Internet and Climate Change. *IEEE Internet Computing Magazine.* Jan/Feb, (2010).

[41] Stylos, J. and Myers, B. 2007. Mapping the space of API design decisions. *Proceedings of the IEEE Symposium on Visual Languages and Human-Centric Computing (VLHCC '07).* (Washington DC, USA, 2007).

[42] Tomlinson, B., Silberman, M., Patterson, D., Pan, Y. and Blevis, E. 2012. Collapse informatics: augmenting the sustainability & ICT4D discourse in HCI. *Proceedings of the SIGCHI Conference on Human Factors in Computing Systems (CHI '12)* (New York, New York, USA, 2012).

[43] Walker, B., Holling, C., Carpenter, S. and Kinzig, A. 2004. Resilience, adaptability and transformability in social--ecological systems. *Ecology and society.* 9, 2:5 (2004).

[44] Water & Desertification: 2010. *http://archive.unu.edu/africa/activities/water.html.* Accessed: 2015-09-06.

[45] Wolf, A., Clarke, L. and Wileden, J. 1989. The AdaPIC tool set: Supporting interface control and analysis throughout the software development process. *IEEE Transactions on Software Engineering.* 15, 3 (1989).

Internet Media Upload Caching for Poorly-Connected Regions

Paul Schmitt
UC Santa Barbara
pschmitt@cs.ucsb.edu

Ramya Raghavendra
IBM Research
rraghav@us.ibm.com

Elizabeth Belding
UC Santa Barbara
ebelding@cs.ucsb.edu

ABSTRACT

Media uploads and downloads, even those on the order of a few hundred kilobytes, commonly fail when attempted over lossy, low-bandwidth, and high latency connections. These conditions, which are common for networks in rural, resource-poor areas, result in the inability for residents of these areas to fully participate in the modern Internet. We study traffic traces collected from two networks and find high locality of interest as well as poor performance for Internet media. We also find that users often abort uploads due to network performance. Given that media content produced by local users is often heavily consumed by local users, we propose VillageCache, a system which allows for appropriate local transformation and redistribution of media uploaded through an Internet cache. We build VillageCache and find it successfully delivers cached media, providing an orders of magnitude improvement in file transfer performance, bandwidth reduction, and the virtual elimination of video stalls in the face of poor network connectivity. Caches with upload capabilities placed at the edge of poorly-connected networks will enable users to produce and consume media-rich content while mitigating the constraints present in under-resourced networks.

Categories and Subject Descriptors

H.3.5 [**On-line Information Services**]: Web-based services

Keywords

World Wide Web; Internet Multimedia; Caching; Upload; Low Bandwidth

1. INTRODUCTION

The great majority of modern Internet content is built with the assumption of high-quality, always-on network connectivity. However, network infrastructure in developing regions typically lacks in the bandwidth available to users [1],

ACM DEV 2015, December 1–2, 2015, London, United Kingdom.
© 2015 ACM. ISBN 978-1-4503-3490-7/15/11 ...$15.00.
DOI: http://dx.doi.org/10.1145/2830629.2830636.

and often exhibits poor latency and loss characteristics. While great strides have been made to improve connectivity through ICTD research, the gap between what media-rich sites demand and what rural network infrastructures are able to provide remains, and in many cases is growing.

Without full participation on the Internet, cultures unique to developing regions are at risk of being forgotten [2]. Web services that encourage participatory culture, often characterized as "Web 2.0," are critical assets in the democratization of communication and provide a voice to people that previously went unheard. Traditionally, research in the ICTD space has focused on improving connectivity or the user experience for content *consumption*. This is often accomplished using content prefetching and predictive caching techniques; or requiring users to navigate through software platforms that alter the experience from the "native" versions of Internet sites. While these solutions help narrow the digital divide, the next logical step is to enable users to provide insight into their lives as content *producers* through mainstream sites, not heavily modified sites designed to avoid bandwidth consumption.

In recent years, web content providers have actively sought to improve the user experience for those connecting in developing regions. Google, for instance, has extensively grown their content delivery infrastructure by placing caches on local and regional ISP networks across the world [3]. However, despite the physical proximity to cached content, researchers have found that lack of peering and Internet exchange point (IXP) presence for some Internet service providers causes traffic between African clients and nearby content servers to take circuitous routes, with many routes detouring through European routers before returning to Africa [4]. Facebook has also recently pushed to make their service more available to users in developing regions by engineering their mobile app to use less bandwidth as they found that the poor network conditions in developing regions 'resulted in slow load times and constant crashes' [5]. The newly released 'Facebook Lite' [6] app only downloads high resolution copies of media if the user explicitly chooses to view a photo or video. The changes indeed make the Facebook app more efficient at consuming media in the face of poor network connectivity; however, uploading content remains an unsolved challenge. We strive to minimize bandwidth consumption for locally uploaded media by transforming and redistributing copies of local content at the network edge.

We perform in-depth, longitudinal analysis on network traces from two production networks in order to better understand network performance and user behavior in the context of media production and consumption. One network is in a village in Sub-Saharan Africa and the other is in a tribal community in the United States. We find that web media content represents a large percentage of overall traffic in terms of bytes and performance of associated traffic is poor (i.e. large uploads from the local network often fail or are canceled entirely by users due to poor network performance). We further find high locality of interest in media as content uploaded by local community members is heavily consumed by users in the same network. Our findings lead to our proposed solution for allowing uploaded content to be captured, transformed, and redelivered from an Internet cache placed at the access network edge.

Our network trace analysis findings inform our design of VillageCache, a system designed for placement at the network edge that captures locally uploaded media, makes the necessary transformations, and delivers it to local users in order to avoid unnecessary bandwidth consumption on the Internet gateway link. We build a prototype with the assumption that users in such regions have a relatively fast local network connection (e.g. a WiFi LAN) such that they are able to locally transfer large files at reasonable speeds. Unlike a traditional web cache, our proposal avoids the requirement for a download of the object in order to be cached by transforming locally-uploaded media and directly injecting them into the cache for subsequent requests. This is critical as even a single download of high resolution media content is often difficult or impossible in constrained networks.

Our paper makes the following contributions:

- We perform an extensive packet trace analysis from two production networks, leveraging multiple techniques to shed light on usage and performance across multiple layers of the network protocol stack.
- Through our analysis, we find poor media performance for users in the observed networks. Additionally, we observe that moderate and large uploads are rarely successful over a constrained link. We find high locality of interest in locally produced media. These findings provide key observations for our solution.
- We propose new HTTP headers to enable Internet caches to transform and store locally uploaded media for subsequent requests without requiring a single download from a web content server.
- We evaluate VillageCache in a lab environment that emulates realistic network properties. We show empirically that the system eases bandwidth usage and vastly improves the user quality of experience. Our solution allows users in poorly-connected networks to interact with modern Internet media content, which was previously impractical due to network conditions.

2. TRAFFIC ANALYSIS

We examine network packet captures gathered from two production networks: one in the village of Macha, Zambia, the other in a tribal community within the United States in order to gain insight into Internet performance and user media consumption.

Macha, Zambia: The Macha network traces we analyze represent a full calendar year, from April 2011 through March 2012. As is somewhat common for networks in developing regions, we have a data hole, in this case during August through October as the network was not opera-

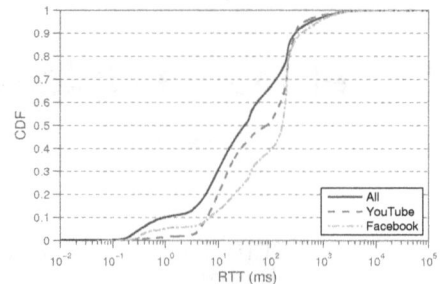

Figure 4: Observed RTT in Macha.

tional during that time. Internet access in Macha is available through a microwave terrestrial link shared over a local wireless network connecting approximately 300 community members. The Macha network is delivered using 802.11 devices acting as point-to-point links, hotspots, and layer-2 bridges. Public Internet access is gained through an Internet café. The bottleneck of the network is the shared Internet gateway link which has a committed speed of 2Mbps.

Tribal Digital Village (TDV): We also analyze six months of traffic collected in 2014 from the tribal digital village (TDV) network deployed in southern California[1]. The network currently consists of roughly 350 homes subscribing to either 2 Mbps or 3 Mbps service. The Internet backhaul link is 500 Mbps with 200 Mbps provisioned at the gateway location and the remaining 300 Mbps provisioned for subsequent hops. Microwave links provide the backbone to reach locations up to roughly 80 km away. Last-mile access is provided using 2.4 GHz and 5 GHz WiFi equipment.

2.1 Traffic characterization

We capture traffic using tcpdump at the networks' gateway links and analyze the packets using Tstat [7] and Bro [8] to profile real-world usage. We first investigate TCP performance metrics for all traffic as well as traffic specifically related to YouTube and Facebook to profile usage of those services as they are the most popular services in terms of flows and bytes in the Macha network. Next, we explore the properties of Macha flows that are classified as 'user-interrupted.' Lastly, we characterize the user quality of experience (QoE) for observed YouTube video traffic. The focus of our analysis on the TDV network traffic is on Instagram media; Instagram is the most commonly accessed media type in this trace. Overall traffic performance analysis for this network is omitted for brevity. Our analysis motivates the design of VillageCache by revealing high locality of interest for locally-created media as well as poor network performance for consuming such media using the existing infrastructure.

2.1.1 TCP latency

We investigate latency in the Macha network, which dramatically affects TCP performance and packet loss. Our analysis considers average TCP round trip time (RTT), as calculated by Tstat, for each flow. As shown in Figure 4, both YouTube and Facebook traffic typically experience longer RTT values than other traffic. The mean RTT for all traffic is 159.0ms, while the mean RTTs for YouTube and Facebook flows are 173.7ms and 232.1ms, increases of 9.2% and 46.0%, respectively. This is likely due to the physical

---

[1] http://sctdv.net/

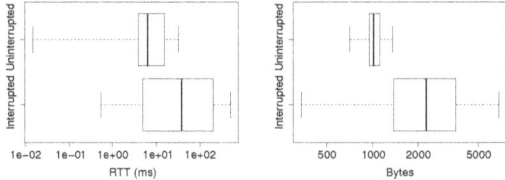

Figure 1: User-interrupted HTTP POSTs in Macha.

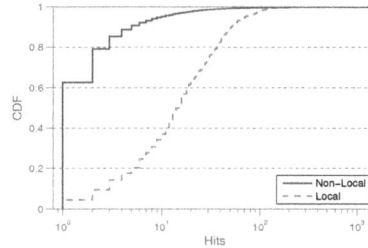

Figure 2: Local vs non-local Facebook image interactions in Macha.

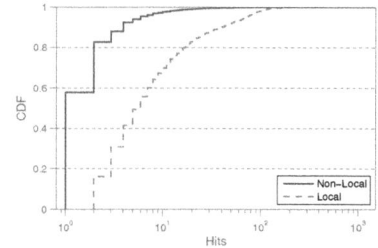

Figure 3: Local vs non-local Instagram media interactions in TDV network.

location of YouTube and Facebook content and circuitous routes to and from the rural ISP. Note that the relatively large number of reported RTT values less than 10ms are due to HTTP errors such as request timeout and malformed requests that were rejected by a local, non-caching Internet proxy, leading to LAN-speed RTT values.

2.1.2 Upload interruptions

To better understand how upstream bandwidth limits impact users' ability to contribute content to the Web, we analyze user behavior in regards to canceling flows using the metric presented in [9], where a flow is determined to be 'interrupted' if all of the following conditions hold: (1) A TCP RST is sent from the client to the server; (2) no TCP RST or FIN is sent from the server to the client; and (3) the time gap between the last data segment from the server and the actual flow end is less than or equal to the average RTT of the flow.

We focus on uploads by only investigating HTTP POST traffic; we compare RTT and bytes transferred between interrupted and uninterrupted HTTP upload flows. The Macha network traces include 9,324,212 POST flows, of which 61,232 were classified as interrupted. While this represents a small percentage of all POST flows, further analysis reveals these flows have significantly different characteristics, including bandwidth consumed, than uninterrupted flows. Figure 1(a) shows the measured TCP round trip time for interrupted flows is measurably different than flows that were allowed to complete. As shown, interrupted flows attain larger RTT values on the whole. The median for interrupted flows is 38.27ms while the median for uninterrupted flows is 6.23ms. Also of note is the difference in the upper quartile values between the two classifications. 25% of interrupted flows were longer than 200.99ms, while the longest 25% of uninterrupted flows were longer than 15.39ms. These results lead us to conclude that RTT plays a significant role in whether the user will cancel an upload or allow it to finish.

Figure 1(b) shows a box plot for bytes transferred over interrupted and uninterrupted sessions. We find that interrupted flows tend to have included more bytes than uninterrupted flows, though with a wider variance. Generally, we see that poor network connectivity, such as what we have witnessed in the Macha network, results in user frustration (and ultimately the user canceling a session) during large transfers. These discoveries motivate a system in which large file transfers are avoided across the constrained gateway link.

2.1.3 Facebook media locality

We analyze the locality of interest for Facebook media to discover potential benefits of localizing uploaded content.

We parse the traces to find the FBIDs for locally-uploaded Facebook images. To map FBIDs to Facebook uploads we employ a heuristic, where we search for image POSTs followed closely by an image GET, which includes the FBID, as the Facebook client downloads the image in order for the user to add metadata such as tags or friend identification. Using this information we are able to build a table of all Facebook image downloads for the year and determine whether those images were locally-created.

We examine the number of downloads per image for both local and non-local images. We define 'Local' as media that was uploaded by a local user and 'Non-Local' as media observed in the trace that did not originate in the local network. As shown in Figure 2, locally-generated images have a considerably higher hit-rate than those coming from external sources. We observe a mean hit-rate of 23.279 for local images, while non-local images are hit an average of 3.813 times. This high locality of content bolsters the argument for caching locally produced content at the network edge. The users most likely to download media are neighbors and friends of the user that uploaded the content.

2.1.4 Tribal Instagram traffic

We also investigate Instagram traffic on the TDV network in order to illustrate locality of interest. Prior work has shown Instagram to be the most popular service in the TDV network [10]. Additionally, other services such as Facebook and Google have recently moved to SSL encrypted sessions, making detailed header analysis in this trace impossible.

Similar to our Facebook analysis, we find ID values for all Instagram media (classified as public) uploaded during the observation period and compare IDs for subsequent downloads of content. Figure 3 shows the number of hits for locally-created media versus non-local media. As with our previous results for Facebook, we observe much more interest in locally created content compared to non-local content.

Next, we look at 'lifetime' of local and non-local Instagram media. We define lifetime as the time delta between the first and last observations of a media object in the traces. Similar to the hits observed, Figure 5 shows locally-produced media experience much longer lifetimes compared to non-local media. This result further propels the argument for keeping uploaded media cached at the network edge, even in well-connected networks.

2.2 Potential cache benefits

We illustrate the potential benefits of localizing content by observing the bandwidth burden and latency caused by the web services we target.

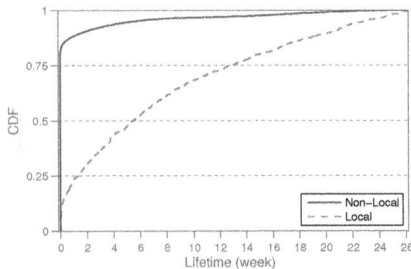

Figure 5: Lifetime for Instagram media in TDV network.

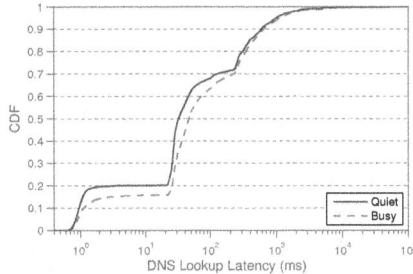

Figure 6: Macha DNS latency comparison.

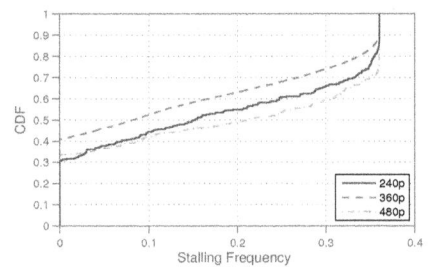

Figure 7: Macha YouTube QoE.

	Flows	GB	% Flows	% Bytes
YouTube	48,223	46.224	1.65%	36.00%
Facebook	571,530	9.156	19.61%	7.13%
Twitter	17,802	0.214	0.61%	0.17%
'Other' POST	202,857	1.375	6.96%	1.07%
'Other' GET	2,074,009	71.441	71.16%	55.64%

Table 1: Macha network traffic characteristics.

2.2.1 Service-specific network load

We analyze all web traffic to explore the bandwidth usage in the Macha network and find that the top two services in terms of bytes consumed are YouTube and Facebook, with a long-tail distribution of other Internet sites. As shown in Table 1, roughly 43% of all HTTP bytes are associated to either YouTube or Facebook, with YouTube leading all web sites with around 36% of all bytes. The table also shows Twitter statistics as Twitter is a representative example of the sites falling in the long-tail. Of note is the relatively small number of flows associated with YouTube traffic, yet the large percentage of bytes associated with the service. This makes video traffic an obvious target for a localization since those flows represent very large per flow byte transfers. Facebook traffic exhibits the opposite behavior, with many flows and comparatively fewer bytes. Further analysis revealed this was mainly due to lightweight Facebook IM traffic and a chatty web API. We believe Facebook videos and images remain valuable targets for VillageCache as they represent heavy bandwidth burdens on the network given their size and the overall popularity of the service.

2.2.2 Effect of YouTube and Facebook traffic on overall network performance

Large TCP flows impact other flows' attainable throughput. We investigate the impact of YouTube and Facebook media TCP flows on the overall network performance. We focus on one month of traffic, April 2011, and categorize time intervals into two types: intervals during which YouTube or Facebook flows were present, and intervals with no such traffic. Using the discovered time intervals we categorize DNS flows. 'Quiet' flows are DNS queries that began during times when there were no YouTube or Facebook flows. Conversely, 'Busy' flows are DNS flows whose first frame was detected during YouTube or Facebook activity. Over the course of one month, we detect roughly 1.2M 'Busy' DNS flows and 800k 'Quiet' DNS flows.

We consider DNS lookup latency, which we define as the time between an original client request and a server answer, including valid as well as error responses. This approach is similar to previous work [11]. Since DNS traffic uses UDP as the transport protocol, latency measurements more accu-

rately illustrate network conditions such as queuing delay as messages are encapsulated in a single packet and sessions are connectionless. DNS lookup latency is also a critical network metric as DNS performance strongly impacts client web traffic performance; each HTTP object must be resolved from a human-readable URL to an IP address. Figure 6 is a CDF plot of the DNS latencies observed. From the figure, we can estimate that the local network includes a DNS server corresponding to latency values of roughly 1ms. We can also observe the first-hop DNS server which corresponds to latencies from 20ms to up to around 200ms. Longer latency values are likely the result of DNS cache misses at the first-hop. In this case the performance of Busy and Quiet flows converge as congestion represents a relatively small portion of the overall lookup latency. We observe that the presence of YouTube or Facebook flows appears to have a detrimental effect on network performance when using either the local or first-hop server. DNS lookups performed during 'Busy' times experience a median increase of roughly 20ms compared to DNS lookups made during 'Quiet' times. Given the UDP transport used by DNS traffic, we can posit that the differences are evidence of network congestion.

2.2.3 YouTube QoE

We observe the performance of YouTube in the Macha network to illustrate the poor quality of experience for users due to the constrained link. Prior work [12] has shown that the most important factor in quality of experience for YouTube videos is the phenomenon of video stalls.

We examine the videos detected in the trace files with regards to the frequency of stalling events. YouTube videos are encoded with variable rate codecs; however, we categorize the videos by resolution and use the corresponding average bit rate for comparison. Over the course of the year, Tstat identifies 51,232 requests for videos encoded at 360p (default) resolution, 1,857 240p requests, and 1,529 480p requests. Hoßfeld et al. [13] finds that stalling frequency can be estimated for YouTube videos using the following equation, where x equals the V (video bit rate) divided by B (flow bandwidth):

$$F(x) = -1.09e^{-1.18x} + 0.36$$

The resulting stalling frequency value is defined as the ratio of the number of stalls and the duration of the video. Using this value we can estimate the maximum number of stalls that will occur given a video duration. Figure 7 shows a CDF of the stalling frequency values for videos observed in the traces. We see that videos encoded with all three resolutions perform rather poorly in the observed network. For example, the median stalling frequency for 240p videos

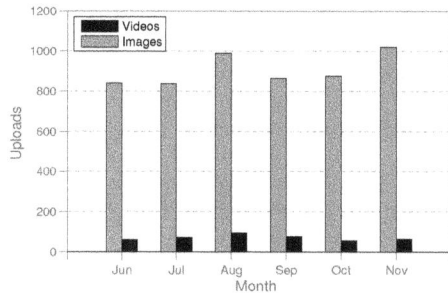

Figure 8: TDV network Instagram uploads.

encoded at 256kbps is roughly 0.2, given which the model estimates a maximum of 12 stalls per 60 seconds of video. Overall, we observe that the QoE for YouTube video in the Macha network is quite poor and as such the network provides one example of an environment that would benefit from localizing the media.

2.2.4 Instagram object duration

An important consideration for Internet caches is the duration that an object must be cached. We examine user interaction with Instagram media in the tribal network traces to find the time deltas between interactions on each media object. We assume a cache will use a least recently used scheme (LRU). Through our analysis we find that the time between hits is less than two weeks roughly 90% of the time with a median of less than one day. These results suggest that a caching system could be effective while retaining only a few weeks of content.

2.2.5 Instagram media storage

We compute the storage that would be required to cache locally-produced Instagram media observed in the TDV network traces. Figure 8 shows the number of images and videos uploaded each month in the tribal network. We see that uploads are rather steady across the observation period. We use the Instagram API to download all locally uploaded media objects to discover the total bytes uploaded for each month. We observe a monthly mean of 369.06 MB over the six month observation period. Given these findings, we believe that a cache deployed in networks similar to the observed networks would have attainable storage requirements.

3. VILLAGECACHE DESIGN

Our traffic analysis findings lead to the conclusion that a repository for locally uploaded media content at the network edge that can redeliver local content to mobile users without consuming Internet bandwidth would significantly ease congestion on the gateway link and offer improved performance. This particularly applies to Facebook and YouTube traffic as their associated traffic represents a large proportion of the bandwidth consumed in our Macha traffic analysis. Our design assumes that targeted networks are able to support fast local transfers and the Internet gateway is the bottleneck link. We envision the upload enabled cache will be placed at the Internet gateway, similar to our point of traffic collection in the observed networks, as such a location would typically allow for coverage of an entire rural community. Figure 9 gives an overview of the VillageCache system components.

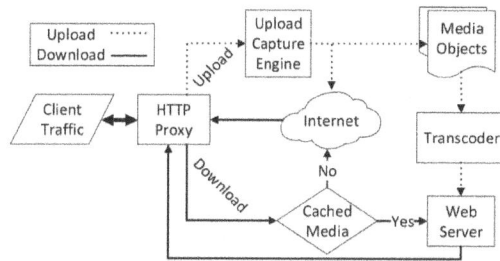

Figure 9: System architecture.

3.1 Upload capture engine

User uploads can be captured using multiple methods, depending on the desired user experience and level of acceptable intrusion. We explore possible directions for upload capture and discuss tradeoffs for each. All solutions result in a functionally equivalent system in which copies of uploaded media are kept locally and transformed in order to be transparently served back to users in subsequent requests.

3.1.1 Transparent upload scraper

The most desirable upload caching system is one that affords users the 'native' experience using web services. Ideally, the presence or absence of an upload cache is completely invisible to the user. Thus, we developed a transparent upload scraper mechanism. We chain a Squid proxy cache with a second proxy server running Tinyproxy on the same machine in order to transparently scrape file uploads. Only HTTP POST requests are forwarded to Tinyproxy while Squid services all other HTTP requests. We modify the Tinyproxy source to check the POST URL and content. If the POST is a Facebook or YouTube media upload, Tinyproxy saves the bytes contained in the POST request to a local file.

The transparent scraping method must include caveats including privacy and compatibility. First, as web services move toward SSL-encrypted traffic we must operate as an SSL man-in-the-middle using the Squid's ssl-bump mechanism explained further in section 3.3.2. This obviously raises privacy concerns as our proxy would have access to users' encrypted upload traffic. In terms of performance, transparent scraping does nothing to improve network performance during the initial upload. User uploads remain constrained by the Internet gateway link. Lastly, we build the scraper assuming HTTP sessions with the web services include an object identifier at the end of the upload in order to properly name the object in the local cache. This relies on the targeted web services to include such information in HTTP session traffic.

3.1.2 Custom local media upload portal

Improved performance can be attained if we are willing to sacrifice the native web service experience for user uploads. Since large file uploads during times of bandwidth saturation result in long sessions and frustration for all, we allow users intending to upload media to YouTube or Facebook to explicitly *time-shift* their transfers by uploading to a custom local portal. In order to time-shift uploads, we require user authorization to work on their behalf using OAuth. We gain access to user OAuth tokens through a local upload portal page in which users log in to their respective YouTube or

45

Facebook accounts and authorize the system. Users can upload video or images to the local page at LAN speeds as they avoid the gateway link. OAuth offers increased security versus locally saving user credentials, as the server only retains OAuth tokens and not clear-text credentials.

Upload time-shifting is accomplished by scripts that run during typically low bandwidth usage times such as late at night. The scripts use YouTube and Facebook API calls, along with the stored user OAuth tokens, to upload files without requiring any user interaction. We have targeted YouTube and Facebook for the initial design; however, similar techniques could be applied to any web service that uses OAuth authentication and an upload API.

The custom portal solution offers desirable performance and avoids bandwidth saturation via local transfers and time-shifting. However, users are required to explicitly participate through a non-native platform. Additionally, time-shifting results in a delay before the uploaded media are available via the web service. While these tradeoffs are substantial, we believe the solution may be acceptable in highly constrained networks or those prone to disconnection.

3.1.3 Custom HTTP POST request/response

Given the inherent privacy and future compatibility drawbacks of our transparent scrape mechanism, we submit a simple, powerful solution to allow for locally-uploaded media to be captured and appropriately transformed at the network edge for subsequent requests. We propose the introduction of optional HTTP headers associated with POST request / response pairs. Modern Internet proxy caches (e.g. Squid) are readily capable of performing specialized operations for specific HTTP requests and headers, making our solution feasible.

The POST request must specify that some part of the request is potentially cache-able media to signify to the cache that the bytes contained should be kept in memory until the server response is received. The corresponding POST response includes flags that indicate whether the media should in fact be cached, and specifies transformations that must be performed on the object, such as name, file type (e.g. jpg, png, mp4, etc), resolution, along with traditional cache headers such as timeout. Using this information, the cache system can convert the object to the appropriate format in order to enable subsequent cache hits. Such a system essentially mimics the media transformations that are done by the web services. Our proposed HTTP headers include:

POST Request
- **media-upload-cache:** Boolean indicating object is cache-able and should be temporarily kept by edge device.
- **media-upload-range:** Byte range of the cacheable object.

POST Response
- **media-upload-no-cache:** If present, discard object without placing in cache.
- **media-upload-resolution:** Resolution(s) to target with transcoded media.
- **media-upload-codec:** Codec(s) to transcode media.
- **media-upload-mime-type:** IANA MIME type for cacheable objects.
- **media-upload-name:** String to name object when placed in cache.

This solution is powerful because web services can change their media API without notice. A general solution is not possible without cooperation from the service. Since we argue for *optional* HTTP headers, service providers not interested in enabling upload caching can simply not employ the headers in their POST mechanisms. Services that do have an interest in improving user experience in poorly-connected networks can simply add the appropriate POST request and response semantics to their service.

3.2 Transcoder

We transcode uploaded media to multiple formats on the cache server in order to serve a broad range of client requests. We use the open-source tools ffmpeg and imagemagick to convert the original videos and images to formats with the same resolutions and codecs that web services use which are readily available [14]. This means we do not have a bit-for-bit copy of media objects, rather we create equivalent local objects to what is served by the web services. In the case of YouTube sessions, the client player requests the specific video format using the 'itag' value present in the HTTP request. We examine this value and provide the corresponding version of the video back into the HTTP/HTTPS session from the local server. As formats offered by YouTube evolve, we anticipate that ffmpeg will maintain the ability to produce files using the same codecs and container formats. Facebook images are converted to both WebP and JPEG formats of multiple sizes while videos are converted to MP4.

3.3 HTTP proxy

In order to redirect HTTP traffic to local resources when appropriate, we require a proxy that allows for analysis and modification of HTTP requests. For the prototype, we use Squid 2.7 running in transparent mode to provide both proxying and caching services to the local network. In order to function properly, the system must be placed at a location in the network hierarchy where all traffic destined for and returning from the targeted Internet services will pass through. This can be accomplished in a number of ways, including the use of firewall rules, or by placing the proxy inline with the gateway traffic. We chose Squid because it is widely deployed, well documented, and straightforward to alter in the case of necessary future changes. Lastly, Squid allows for HTTPS traffic proxying and redirection with the ssl-bump extension, a feature not widely available in other proxies.

3.3.1 Redirection to local media copies

Squid allows for HTTP redirection where a listener process examines HTTP requests and chooses whether or not to modify them. We leverage this functionality by building a custom redirector that determines whether or not a request is for cached media. In the case of Facebook images and videos, the 'FBID' contained withing the query string is used. YouTube requests are parsed to find the 'ID' of the requested video. The redirector searches the local web server to check whether there is a local copy available in the appropriate format for the requested file. If there is a local copy the URL request is altered to use the local web server; otherwise the URL request is passed on to the remote server unmodified.

It is important to note that the redirection engine only redirects image and video file requests and nothing else. A typical Facebook or YouTube HTTP session includes many requests for all of the objects on the page, including HTML, thumbnails, CSS, etc. These other objects are still retrieved from Internet servers rather than any local cache. While this consumes bandwidth, these objects are small in comparison to media content. Importantly, this behavior allows our solution to maintain content privacy settings for both services. For example, if a user does not have permission to access a YouTube video, the HTTP request does not include the video ID in the HTTP header. Instead, the request is of an image showing the user that they do not have the appropriate permissions to access that file. This functionality remains when our system is used, thus preserving YouTube's privacy settings.

3.3.2 HTTPS proxying

Many online services, including YouTube and Facebook, have recently moved toward SSL-encrypted HTTPS rather than unencrypted HTTP. This trend toward encrypted connections will continue and we anticipate that eventually most, if not all, Internet traffic will utilize HTTPS. To that end, we use the ssl-bump extension for Squid in which the proxy intercepts HTTPS sessions and examines them in a manner similar to unencrypted traffic. In order to make this work, clients are dealt certificates from our proxy machine as the server dynamically generates certificates for clients as connections are created. It is important to note that this technique is required for our prototype system only and not meant for a production environment. We feel this feature is valuable despite the potential increased visibility to users. If desired, ssl-bump can be disabled altogether by changing a single line in the Squid configuration file.

3.4 Web server

In order for local redirection to function, we must store media files locally and make them available via a web server. As shown in Figure 9, the web server delivers local content back to the proxy during browsing sessions. We use the Apache web server as it allows for streaming modules for various video formats and is widely deployed. Also, as streaming formats continue to evolve it is likely that Apache will remain an early target for compatibility.

4. EVALUATION

We construct VillageCache in a lab environment to assess its performance and the efficacy of localizing content distribution at the network edge. We use a server running Debian Linux 7.0 with Squid and connect to the Internet through the server with various mobile clients including Android tablets and phones via 802.11g/n WiFi. We place a machine upstream from the cache server in order to emulate the Macha network using *netem* and *tc* to throttle the link bandwidth as well as introduce latency similar to what we observed in Section 2.1.

4.1 File transfer time

We first explore file transfer times. We emulate a bottleneck 2Mbps link with an average RTT of 134ms that is uniformly distributed with a maximum variation of 20ms. We execute all file transfers 10 times with no competing background traffic and compare mean completion times.

The main goal of our system is to provide users in resource-poor networks the opportunity to fully participate in the modern Internet by improving media content performance. We compare HTTP GET times for various file sizes in two network scenarios to better illustrate the vast performance penalty when connecting via a constrained link. The first scenario consists of a client connected to cached resources via a local WiFi LAN. In the second, client traffic must go through the bottleneck link with parameters derived from prior packet analysis, as described above. We use varying file sizes up to 2GB. As expected, Table 2 shows that locally-stored web objects in poorly-connected networks are transferred in a fraction of the time it would take over a constrained link. Moreover, even moderate size file transfers across the constrained link take longer to complete than we can reasonably expect users to wait. Lastly, Internet cafés in developing regions often charge for Internet access based on time online rather than bytes used. In such situations it is clearly beneficial to localize media wherever possible.

4.2 YouTube

We evaluate the quality of experience for locally cached YouTube videos. These experiments were completed before a change in the HTTP object naming scheme utilized by YouTube. The current operation of YouTube makes object caching impossible, which led us to proposing the use of optional HTTP headers. Nevertheless, we present our experimental results to show the clear potential for caching such large media.

In our experiment automated browsers watch six 5-minute YouTube videos with different resolutions and video codecs passing through a constrained link. We vary the number of concurrent clients between 1 and 6. For each examined resolution (240p, 360p, and 480p) we run 10 sequences of 1 client, then two concurrent clients, and so forth up to six concurrent clients. The total is 210 videos viewed for each resolution with the performance analyzed in aggregate. We additionally run the experiment for 360p videos with 1Mbps UDP background traffic on the bottleneck link to examine the effectiveness of VillageCache during times of congestion.

As shown in Figure 10, the stalling frequency for each of the transfers is extremely low, particularly in comparison with Figure 7, resulting in stall-free playback for locally connected users. These results illustrate the dramatic improvement of the user experience when consuming files stored at the network edge rather than those stored in distant data centers.

4.2.1 Bandwidth savings

Bandwidth is a scarce and valuable commodity in poorly-connected networks. Our proposed system eases the heavy burden of media by avoiding the costliest transfer during a session, the media file itself. We compare the bandwidth consumed on the Internet gateway link by a client connecting without the use of VillageCache versus that consumed by a cache-enabled client using proxy logs to show requested files and the corresponding response size in bytes. As shown in Figure 11, the bandwidth savings witnessed for cached videos is strikingly large.

These savings are what we would expect from a typical web object cache. However, a system such as ours includes additional benefits that are particularly critical to poorly-connected networks. First, cached locally uploaded videos *never* need to be downloaded from the web as they are immediately placed into the cache at the time of upload. Typi-

Size (MB)	Local LAN (s)*	2Mbps Link (s)†
1	0.31	30.68
5	1.12	126.33
25	5.47	641.28
100	20.44	1,525.13
500	109.88	5,806.40
1,000	226.96	11,514.54
2,000	576.11	21,973.54

* Performance with cache
† Performance without cache

Table 2: Average file download times.

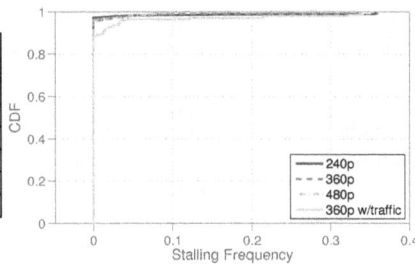

Figure 10: Cached YouTube QoE analysis.

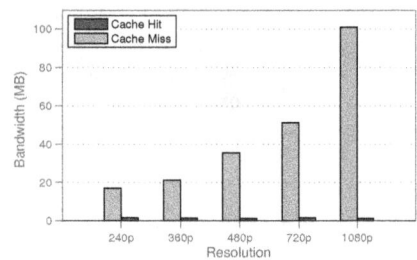

Figure 11: Cached video bandwidth savings.

cal web caches require the object to be downloaded from the source *at least once* to be properly associated with the corresponding web resource. As we see with the file transfer time measurements (Table 2) and user interruption of flows (Figure 1) behind a constrained link, even one large file transfer may be prohibitive for some networks. Our proposal allows users in these networks to participate in media-heavy web services, which was previously rendered impossible due to poor network conditions. Second, we have shown that users heavily consume locally uploaded media. This creates a multiplying effect for bandwidth saved in our evaluation; the actual bandwidth saved is much higher since local media will be disproportionately downloaded more often than non-local media.

5. RELATED WORK

In recent years there has been much research in the improvement of Internet experience and information dissemination for users in networks with poor connectivity [15, 16, 17, 18]. Caching techniques are often explored when confronted with a constrained link. Common approaches such as prefetching and aggressive caching can be built into browser plug-ins [15]. These types of systems help improve performance on individual computers. Our system proposal, on the other hand, is engineered with the cache placed in the network hierarchy where it can serve the entire community rather than individual machines. RuralCafe [19] is designed to allow for web searching over intermittent links in developing regions. TEK [20] also focuses on enabling web search from poorly connected networks using email. We have somewhat similar goals; however, we target a different context in media upload and consumption rather than web search.

Cloudlets [21] have been proposed to reduce delay, particularly for mobile clients. However, it is assumed that the cloudlet computer or cluster is well-connected to the Internet. We approach the problem assuming poor connectivity to the Internet from the local network.

Our work is informed by VillageShare [22], where content locality and time-shifted uploads in a rural African network are explored. We leverage the fact that content produced in poorly-connected networks is heavily consumed by users within them. However, where VillageShare was conceived as a custom local filesharing application, our vision is to make common, unmodified applications work in the absence of strong network connectivity. In our design, interactions are indistinguishable with sessions where content comes directly from the Internet service from the user perspective. This behavior is intentional and based on the notion put forth by Wyche [23], aiming for "ICT interventions grounded in

users' existing practices rather than introducing new and unfamiliar ones."

Lastly, Google and Facebook have recently proposed high-profile projects whose aim is to provide Internet connectivity to people in the world's most remote places using technologies such as balloons or drones. Our work is complementary and still beneficial in such environments as caches help most with constrained (e.g. high latency, low bandwidth, high loss, etc) links to the Internet, a likely result of such projects. Connecting the most remote places on Earth will require a multi-pronged approach; localizing content where appropriate is one of many potential avenues for exploration.

6. DISCUSSION AND CONCLUSION

In this paper we have presented analysis of media consumption in two real-world networks to demonstrate the potential for localizing Internet media content in poorly-connected networks. Our study concludes that users access media-rich sites even with poor connectivity but are discouraged from interacting with media content by network conditions. Using our findings we propose a simple solution to cache locally uploaded media at the network edge so as to avoid the requirement for even a single download for the object to be available to other local network users. We evaluate a system prototype of VillageCache in a lab environment and show that such a cache can drastically improve the user quality of experience when accessing local content as well as ease the load on the Internet gateway link.

Aside from improving the end user experience, our proposal is mutually beneficial for the content providers as it offloads low-bandwidth, slow-moving flows from their data centers. As more service providers look to gain users in the most remote places, alternative content distribution techniques are likely to be a major consideration.

Network-level localization of Internet media lends itself to multiple avenues of future research. Given the nature of poorly-connected networks, a delay-tolerant implementation of the system should be explored. An eventual consistency model could be implemented where local upload requests made during times of congestion could be time-shifted and uploaded to the cloud at a later hour when there is less traffic. Web services typically allow for OAuth authentication for API calls, allowing for a middlebox to gather local uploads and move them into the cloud on behalf of the users in a secure manner. Such a solution would alleviate the issues surrounding the initial content upload that we observed in Section 2.1.

Another interesting area for exploration is peering between locally-deployed caches. Network-level localization is convenient for system design, however different distribution models could be investigated leveraging social network analysis across multiple local installations. 'Similar' networks could then pre-share content amongst themselves in order to preemptively localize content that is likely to be locally requested. A final example, continuing with the idea of multiple deployed systems in a region, is a mobile app that could act as a data mule for copying local files to other local systems when the user migrates between them.

It is critical to enable full participation on the Internet by all users, particularly those whose cultures are at risk of marginalization. To that end, we hope network-level localization of locally-produced content provides a model that enhances user quality of experience while minimizing reliance on constrained Internet gateway links. In order to provide content to people in the most distant reaches of the world, services must rethink content placement and distribution strategies. Allowing decentralization can enable usage from networks that previously could not support full Internet participation.

7. ACKNOWLEDGMENTS

This work was funded through NSF Network Science and Engineering (NetSE) Award CNS-1064821 and the U.S. Army Research Laboratory and the U.K. Ministry of Defence under Agreement Number W911NF-06-3-0001. We would like to thank our partners in Tribal Digital Village for assisting us with traffic collection. We thank Barath Raghavan for comments and assistance in improving the manuscript.

8. REFERENCES

[1] E. Brewer, M. Demmer, M. Ho, R. Honicky, J. Pal, M. Plauche, and S. Surana, "The challenges of technology research for developing regions," *IEEE Pervasive Computing*, vol. 5, no. 2, pp. 15–23, 2006.

[2] N. M. Dauenhauer and R. Dauenhauer, "Technical, emotional, and ideological issues in reversing language shift: Examples from southeast alaska," *Endangered languages: Current issues and future prospects*, pp. 57–98, 1998.

[3] M. Calder, X. Fan, Z. Hu, E. Katz-Bassett, J. Heidemann, and R. Govindan, "Mapping the expansion of Google's serving infrastructure," in *IMC '13*, (Barcelona, Spain), 2013.

[4] A. Gupta, M. Calder, N. Feamster, M. Chetty, E. Calandro, and E. Katz-Bassett, "Peering at the internet's frontier: A first look at ISP interconnectivity in Africa," in *Passive and Active Measurement*, (Los Angeles, CA), 2014.

[5] K. Burnham, "Facebook overhauls android app for emerging countries." http://www.informationweek.com/software/social/facebook-overhauls-android-app-for-emerging-countries/d/d-id/1278740, 2014. [Online; posted 20-June-2014].

[6] V. Shankar, "Announcing Facebook lite." http://newsroom.fb.com/news/2015/06/announcing-facebook-lite/, 2015. [Online; posted 4-June-2015].

[7] M. Mellia, A. Carpani, and R. L. Cigno, "Measuring IP and TCP behavior on a edge node," in *Globecom '02*, (Taipei, Taiwan), 2002.

[8] V. Paxson, "Bro: A system for detecting network intruders in real-time," *Computer Networks*, vol. 31, pp. 2435–2463, Dec. 1999.

[9] D. Rossi, M. Mellia, and C. Casetti, "User patience and the web: a hands-on investigation," in *Globecom '03*, (San Francisco, CA), 2003.

[10] M. Vigil, M. Rantanen, and E. Belding, "A first look at tribal web traffic," in *WWW '15*, (Florence, Italy), 2015.

[11] J. Jung, E. Sit, H. Balakrishnan, and R. Morris, "DNS performance and the effectiveness of caching," *IEEE/ACM Transactions on Networking*, vol. 10, pp. 589–603, Oct. 2002.

[12] T. Hoßfeld, M. Seufert, M. Hirth, T. Zinner, P. Tran-Gia, and R. Schatz, "Quantification of YouTube QoE via crowdsourcing," in *ISM 2011*, (Dana Point, CA), 2011.

[13] T. Hoßfeld, R. Schatz, T. Zinner, M. Seufert, and P. Tran-Gia, "Transport protocol influences on youtube videostreaming QoE," *University of Würzburg, Institute of Computer Science, Tech. Rep*, 2011.

[14] Wikipedia, "Youtube — wikipedia, the free encyclopedia." https://en.wikipedia.org/wiki/YouTube#Quality_and_formats, 2015. [Online; accessed 19-September-2015].

[15] J. Chen, D. Hutchful, W. Thies, and L. Subramanian, "Analyzing and accelerating web access in a school in peri-urban india," in *WWW '11*, (Hyderabad, India), 2011.

[16] J. Chen, R. Power, L. Subramanian, and J. Ledlie, "Design and implementation of contextual information portals," in *WWW '11*, (Hyderabad, India), 2011.

[17] M. Chetty, D. Haslem, A. Baird, U. Ofoha, B. Sumner, and R. Grinter, "Why is my Internet slow?: making network speeds visible," in *CHI 2011*, (Vancouver, Canada), 2011.

[18] S. Isaacman and M. Martonosi, "The c-link system for collaborative web usage: A real-world deployment in rural Nicaragua," in *NSDR 2009*, (Big Sky, MT), 2009.

[19] J. Chen, L. Subramanian, and J. Li, "Ruralcafe: web search in the rural developing world," in *WWW '09*, (Madrid, Spain), 2009.

[20] W. Thies, J. Prevost, T. Mahtab, G. Cuevas, S. Shakhshir, A. Artola, B. Vo, Y. Litvak, S. Chan, S. Henderson, *et al.*, "Searching the world wide web in low-connectivity communities," in *WWW '02*, (Honolulu, Hawaii), 2002.

[21] M. Satyanarayanan, P. Bahl, R. Caceres, and N. Davies, "The case for vm-based cloudlets in mobile computing," *IEEE Pervasive Computing*, vol. 8, no. 4, pp. 14–23, 2009.

[22] D. L. Johnson, V. Pejovic, E. M. Belding, and G. van Stam, "VillageShare: Facilitating content generation and sharing in rural networks," in *ACM DEV 2012*, (Atlanta, GA), 2012.

[23] S. P. Wyche, A. Forte, and S. Yardi Schoenebeck, "Hustling online: understanding consolidated facebook use in an informal settlement in Nairobi," in *CHI 2013*, (Paris, France), 2013.

Low-power Low-cost Wireless Sensors for Real-time Plant Stress Detection

Mattia Zeni[*] , Elizabeth Ondula, Reagan Mbitiru[†] , Agnes Nyambura[‡] , Lianna Samuel,
Kala Fleming, Komminist Weldemariam
IBM Research – Africa
Nairobi, Kenya
{mzeni,eondula,rmbitiru,anyambur,lsamuel,kalaflem,k.weldemariam}@ke.ibm.com

ABSTRACT

Farm yields and crop quality are closely linked to environmental exposures during growth. Stresses can occur when too much or too little water is delivered. These nuances of farm production are often overlooked by the typical small scale farmer in sub-Saharan Africa. The result is that small scale farms, on average, underproduce by more than forty percent. In this paper, we describe the development of a small scale precision farming approach where fast soil moisture sensing via wireless sensor networks provides a low-cost, low-power option to reduce the potential for water induced plant stresses and increase yields. The solution is particularly suited to resource constrained environments with no access to grid power and poor network connectivity. By monitoring water intake by plants, we demonstrate the potential for fast data collection from wireless soil moisture sensors in the farm. Finally, we show that the developed wireless sensor nodes can run for more than five years with limited human intervention.

CCS Concepts

•Hardware → Sensors and actuators; Sensor applications and deployments; Sensor devices and platforms; Wireless devices; Wireless integrated network sensors;

Keywords

Developing Countries, Wireless Sensor Networks, Energy Efficient, Smart Farms, Moisture Sensor, Agriculture, Plant Stress Detection

---

*Mattia (mattia.zeni@disi.unitn.it) is a PhD student at the University of Trento, Italy.

†Reagan (rmugo@andrew.cmu.edu) is a graduate student at CMU Rwanda.

‡Agnes (anjoroge@andrew.cmu.edu) is a graduate student at CMU Rwanda.

ACM DEV 2015, December 1–2, 2015, London, United Kingdom

© 2015 ACM. ISBN 978-1-4503-3490-7/15/11. . . $15.00

DOI: http://dx.doi.org/10.1145/2830629.2830641

1. INTRODUCTION

Millions of small scale farmers across sub-Saharan Africa with average land holdings of less than 5 hectares account for almost 80% of the food supply [17, 24]. Most of these farms are rain-fed and have to contend with increasingly unreliable rainfall [18]. Although a range irrigation methods and a variety of farm inputs such as fertilizers and pesticides have been adopted by these farmers to ensure maximum yields, it is estimated that they still incur losses on the order of 30 - 40% [19].

With the rise of mobile applications and social media platforms, creative adaptations have been tailored to deliver small scale farmers with more information on market prices, modern farming practices, crop diseases, pesticides and fertilizers [1, 2, 3, 4, 13, 16]. In general, these delivery platforms have attempted to reduce information asymetries and increase farmer awareness on techniques to better manage and take control of the various factors affecting farm productivity. However, as farmers continue to incur losses, it is evident that more effort will be required to adapt mobile and other technologies to deliver more tangible outcomes for farmers.

Various environmental factors can induce stress and affect the growth and development of plants [22, 11] impacting both quality and quantity. To better understand the nuances of plant growth, sensors have been used to monitor different parameters in a range of precision agriculture applications. These involve the use of a variety of sensors on a farm such as temperature, humidity, soil moisture, leaf wetness, among others, which are networked and interfaced to a communications module where data is sent to a backend for processing and analytics.

Advances in wireless communication techniques, sensing and networking have made wireless sensor networks a key enabler in delivering context-aware applications which can then provide insights into the crop status [20, 25]. In addition to the conventional challenges in sensor network design (power efficiency, fault tolerance and self-organization) [23, 12, 21], low node density which has an implication on power, cost and reliability is a key challenge that needs to be addressed as one considers the design for development of wireless sensor network applications. For small scale farmers in sub-Saharan Africa, wireless sensor networks are generally not accessible, affordable or sustainable although the information and ease of management that such systems could provide would be useful for boosting farm output [15]. This drives the need to implement a minimal sensor set that can provide a base information set that informs on the conditions of the farm and crop reliably.

Soil moisture determinations are a critical component of this base information set required to boost crop growth. While soil moisture sensors are typically used to determine the soil water balance, they can also be used to provide real-time/near-realtime insights on plant stress [14]. We define plant stress as the state in which a plant either receives inadequate amounts of water necessary for it to produce optimum yield or where the plant receives too much water so that the water logged soil is unable to provide adequate oxygen levels to the plant for optimum metabolism. The use of a soil moisture sensor to detect plant stress levels in addition to soil water balance would reduce the number of additional sensors (such as leaf wetness, soil temperature, relative humidity, etc) required to provide updates on plant health, effectively reduce the cost of implementing precision agriculture in a small scale farm setting.

To address these requirements in a manner that makes sense in the sub-Saharan African context, we focus on the design and implementation of a low-cost, low-power wireless sensor network to detect plant stress using a farm located in Kangundo, Machakos in Kenya. We present this as a frugal approach to introduce small-scale precision farming for sub-Saharan Africa. We show the potential for fast data collection from wireless soil moisture sensors in the farm to monitor water intake by plants during their entire growth and development period. Our research team is composed of two water and agriculture experts, two hardware/sensor engineers, two programmers and a computer scientist.

We describe the use case scenario in Section 2. Section 3 describes the design requirements based on the specific use case and the lab trials carried out on the equipment to help determine the deployment conditions. Section 4 presents the characteristics of our custom designed low-power wireless sensor nodes. In Section 5 we describe the experiences in deploying the sensor nodes in an actual farm in Kenya. Section 6 presents the performance evaluation of such a system. Finally we conclude and outline future work.

2. USE CASE

In the implementation of this study, a farm located on one acre in Kangundo, Machakos County Kenya was selected. The area receives moderate rainfall in 2 seasons of the year (March - May, October - December). During the remainder of the year, the region receives modest to little rainfall, increasing the need for well timed irrigation to reduce the potential for plant stress. The soil on the farm has significant amounts of silt, which reduced the capacity to retain water. This characteristic is a likely contributor to plant stress during dry periods, and ultimately low crop yields.

The farm is subdivided into four plots on which different kinds of vegetables are grown to supply the local market. It has a shallow well for irrigation during the dry seasons. Water from the well is transferred to a 24,000 litre ground level tank using a solar pump. Water from this tank is then pumped into an elevated 5,000 litre tank which then feeds a drip irrigation network.

3. DESIGN REQUIREMENTS

In this section, we describe the requirements of a wireless soil moisture sensor network to collect soil moisture data for crop stress analysis. More specifically, the design of the low-cost low-power sensor nodes for real-time plant stress detection presented in this paper has been driven from the specific use case described in Section 2. The use case allowed us to elicit the requirements, divided into 4 main areas: data collection, sensing, connectivity and power efficiency requirements.

In what follows, we discuss these requirements in detail.

3.1 Data collection requirements

Soil moisture readings were required at frequent intervals to capture changes in the soil water balance and variations in plant water uptake patterns that might be driven by the stress levels [14]. The frequency of data collection was also influenced by the following factors:

- **Weather patterns in the region:** Sporadic rainfall in area meant that soil moisture readings had to be quite frequent to observe transient changes in soil moisture levels.
- **Soil's water retention characteristics:** Since the soil had significant amounts of silt, water retention was poor, further increasing the need to have frequent soil moisture level readings.
- **Topography changes:** With significant parts of the farm having varying elevations, a lot of rainfall was lost as surface runoff or quickly moved downstream through the soil. Significant rapid movement of water through the soil further necessitated frequent data capture of the soil moisture readings.
- **Power consumption of sensor nodes:** To increase the longevity of the batteries mounted on each of the sensor nodes, data collection was required at intervals that would not adversely increase power consumption. This way, sensor nodes mounted in the field could function for a longer time with minimal human involvement.

To better understand the data collection requirements, we used an experimental setup where bush beans were placed sequentially in two rectangular planters. Planter 1 contained Sensor 1, Sensor 2 and Sensor 3 and Planter 2 contained Sensor 4, Sensor 5 and Sensor 6. Each sensor was buried 4 cm below the surface of the soil, slightly off-center of the width of the planter and spaced 6 inches apart. Five bush bean seeds (Starke Ayres. Gauteng, South Africa) were planted next to each of the sensors and each test site was numbered, so that there was no confusion in the watering schedules for each site. The watering schedule was different in each planter and was devised to not only examine the water uptake of the beans as they grew but to also demonstrate how over irrigation in one region may affect neighboring plants. For example Sensor 1 and Sensor 3 were the furthest apart. In each region, the beans were watered every morning according to the following irrigation schedule which matched the sensor arrangement: Planter 1 –41, 0, 17–mL and Planter 2 – 97, 67, 9 – mL.

The soil moisture levels detected by the sensors were then plotted for comparison between the beans in each planter as shown in Figure 1. From the plot, it is noticeable that from the start of the experiment the sensor planted next to the bush beans that were not being watered (Sensor 2) showed a much lower soil water content than the sensors in the surrounding soil. Similar observations were made for Planter 2.

From these experiments and other considerations such as weather patterns at the farm, it was determined that the best frequency with which to sense and transmit soil moisture values with the lowest power consumption by the nodes was every 10 seconds.

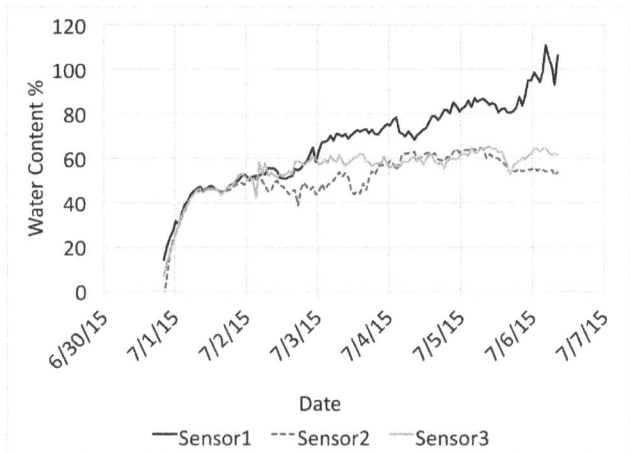

Figure 1: Soil moisture variation in Regions 1 - 3 for a period of 1 week.

3.2 Sensing Requirements

The soil moisture sensors record the percentage of moisture in the soil. The lower this value is, the greater the surface tension and the more energy it takes for a plant to extract water. The specific requirements that the soil moisture sensors have to fulfill were to provide reliable and accurate soil moisture readings, have low power consumption, be cost-effective, be easy and fast to deploy and easily available in the market to ease maintenance.

Based on the experimental sensing depth and distance measurements determined between the nodes, it was determined that each of the sensors on the farm should be inserted to a depth of $4cm$ and spaced 20 meters apart from each other.

3.3 Connectivity Requirements

Our needs in terms of connectivity are driven by the necessity to let each low-power low-cost sensor node communicate and upload data in real-time to the solar powered gateway. This gateway is then used to send data to the backend system for insights extraction. In such a scenario, the specific connectivity requirements include that reliable transmissions be sent across a maximum distance of 90 meters under different weather conditions. It is also required that fast and easy deployment using wireless technology be used in order to encourage adoption and lower the costs as well as cost-effective and very power-efficient transmission technologies be implemented to allow months or years of continuous sensing and transmission. Reliable transmission solutions with built-in acknowledgments were also required to improve data transmission reliability. A simple network configuration was also important so that repeater nodes were not required thus minimizing battery consumption while allowing devices to be added or removed from the network without manual reconfiguration. It is also necessary to have simultaneous transmission between multiple nodes and the gateway.

In order to keep the current consumption as low as possible we decided to keep the communication completely asynchronous (i.e. data was transmitted as soon as it was received by the nodes). In this way we don't need additional overhead packets to be exchanged between the nodes and the gateway.

3.4 Power efficiency requirements

One of the key requirements for this research study is to develop a low-power solution that requires little or no human intervention. Important power considerations included that the sensor nodes were able to run for months or even years without recharge of their battery and that data be sent in real-time to the back-end server to provide real time insights.

We therefore determined that with a capacity of up to $2348mAh$ found in a standard AA battery [5] that we should be able to run the device for a period of time of 4 years (35040 hours) or even more. We require an average current consumption for the entire board of $67\mu Ah$ as calculated in Equation 1:

$$ I = \frac{battery capacity}{uptime} = \frac{2348}{35040} = 67\mu Ah \qquad (1) $$

Given the low power requirements and a lack of existing low-power solutions, we needed to design our own custom boards and apply power optimization techniques. Such optimization techniques require careful consideration for the periods of data collection and submission by the sensors.

In the following sections, we discuss in detail the implementation and deployment of the four requirements discussed in this section.

4. LOW-POWER SENSOR NODE

In an initial stage we evaluated the possibility of building the sensor nodes for real time plant stress detection using Arduino Uno boards [7]. Arduino is an open-source electronics platform based on easy-to-use hardware and software. The reasons that brought us to this decision were the easy and fast development that this board allows and its low cost. Note that the cost of a ready to use Arduino Uno board is 20 Euros. However, due to the very strict constraints we had to follow, this solution was unfeasible. In fact, the Arduino Uno board consumes too much energy for our low power configuration. As reported by an independent source [6], the board without sensors and radio consumes up to $50mAh$ in wake mode. For this reason we had to design our own hardware and software as illustrated in Sections 4.1 and 4.2.

4.1 Hardware

The Arduino Uno is a good starting point for the sensor nodes we want to build. However, with such the strict requirements we had to satisfy, we needed to create our own custom hardware with state of the art technologies to increase battery life. We decided to use the same MCU the Arduino has, the ATmega328P-PU[1] micro controller and remove all the unnecessary components in order to obtain an higher energy efficiency. Moreover, our custom board is much cheaper than the original Arduino board, requiring

---

[1]http://www.atmel.com/Images/doc8161.pdf

less than $10Euros$ to be built. The board schematic developed is illustrated in Figure 2. It is composed of the power supply circuit, the ATmega328P-PU micro controller, the nRF24L01+ radio module and the gypsum moisture sensor.

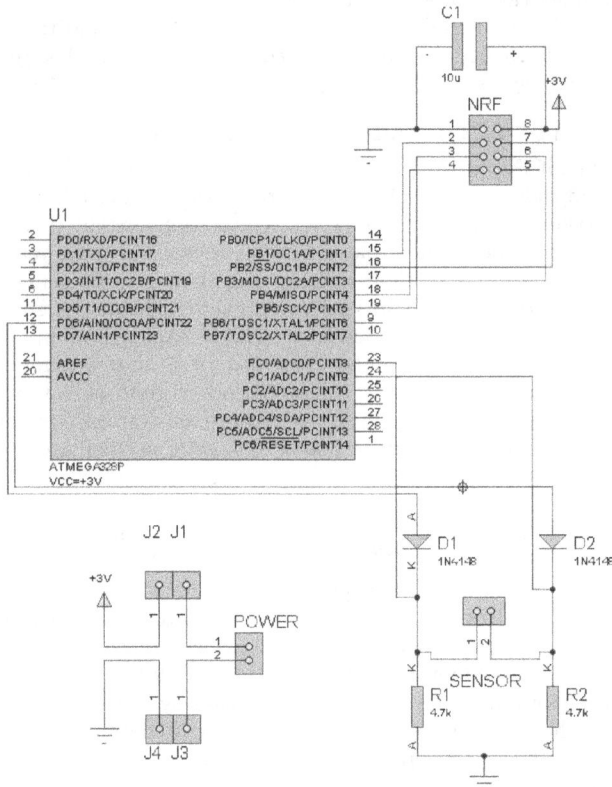

Figure 2: Custom ATmega328P-PU based board for plant stress detection.

4.1.1 Power Supply

In designing a very power efficient wireless sensor node, we decided to use 2 cheap and largely available Duracell AA Alkaline-Manganese Dioxide batteries configured in series as the power source. Usually the output voltage of the batteries drops while discharging. To stabilize the power supply, DC-DC converter components are used in electronic circuits to maintain a constant voltage level to be fed to the circuit for the entire life of the batteries. In our board we removed the converter and powered the circuit directly from the batteries. The main reason for this choice is that these converters have an efficiency that ranges from 50% for standard linear regulators up to 96% for switching ones. Even in the best situation, using the best switching converter technology, we have a 4% loss. This can be a considerable energy loss for our use case scenario in which with an expected life time of 4 years, 4% of the total energy can power the circuit for additional 2 months. The drawback of not using a DC-DC converter is that we don't have a stable voltage to power the circuit for the entire life of the batteries. In fact, as the battery performance chart in Figure 3 shows, for very low current values below $0.1mA$ such as in our situation, the voltage of the Duracell AA Alkaline-Manganese Dioxide batteries varies from an initial value of $1.6V$ when fully charged down to $0.97V$ when fully discharged. For our 2 battery series configuration this translates in a voltage range of $3.2V$ down to $1.94V$. To overcome this limitation and be able to

exploit 100% of the energy stored in the batteries, we carefully chose and set up the other components in the circuit to work in this range, as explained in the next Sections. The characteristics of the power source for our custom sensor node is set to voltage and capacity values $1.94V - 3.2V$ @ $0.1Ah$ and $2348mAh$ respectively.

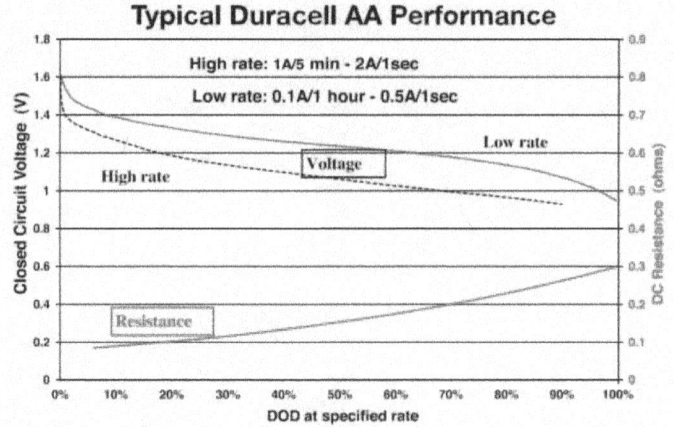

Figure 3: Duracell AA Alkaline-Manganese Dioxide Battery performance chart.

4.1.2 ATmega328P-PU Micro controller

The Atmel ATmega328P-PU micro controller is a high-performance 8-bit AVR RISC-based microcontroller that combines 32KB ISP flash memory with read-while-write capabilities. It is equipped with 1KB EEPROM, 2KB SRAM, 23 general purpose I/O lines, three flexible timer/counters with compare modes, a byte-oriented 2-wire serial interface, SPI serial port, 6-channel 10-bit A/D converter and five software selectable power saving modes.

In order to let this component work in the most efficient way, we used it in a specific configuration according to its specifications from the datasheet [8]. This micro controller can operate between $1.8 - 5.5V$, fitting our specifications about the input voltage of $1.94 - 3.2V$. In order to let the ATmega328P-PU work in this range, the clock has to be set at no more than 4Mhz, as illustrated in Figure 4. We decided to use a 1Mhz clock speed using the internal oscillator and resulting in a theoretical total consumption of only $0.2mA$ in active mode. In this configuration, we don't need the external oscillator and the two capacitors attached to it. The complete setup for the micro controller used in our custom sensor nodes is illustrated in Table 1 and the theoretical values for current consumption are provided.

Table 1: ATmega328P-PU set up and theoretical consumption values.

	Value
Voltage	1.94V - 3.2V
Frequency	1Mhz
I in Active Mode	0.2mA
I in Sleep Mode	0.1μA

4.1.3 Moisture Sensor

The type of soil moisture sensors that were considered are:

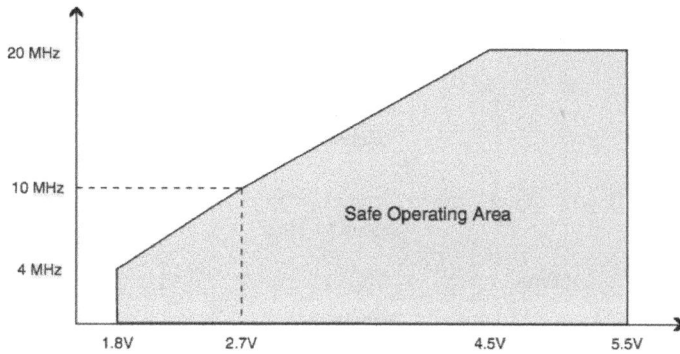

Figure 4: Maximum Frequency vs. VCC curve for ATmega328 micro controller.

- **Tensiometers**: can measure the soil moisture tension and have the advantage of being inexpensive and easy to install.
- **Electrical Resistance Blocks**: also known as Gypsum blocks, these are simple devices with two electrodes embedded in a block of gypsum. When blocks are buried in soil, water moves into or out of the block thanks to its porosity depending on the moisture level, changing the resistance between the two electrodes. Like tensiometers, gypsum blocks are cheap and easy to install.
- **Di-electric Sensors**: measure the di-electric constant of soil, a characteristic that changes with soil moisture. The main disadvantage is that these sensors are expensive.

For this paper we decided to adopt gypsum soil moisture sensors manufactured by Delmhorst (NY, USA). These sensors were chosen because although they are relatively inexpensive, have low maintenance requirements and absorb water at the same rate as plants thus providing relatively accurate measurements of soil moisture. Soil moisture readings recorded by the soil moisture sensors were converted to soil moisture content as a percentage using the formula $\frac{Mass of Water(g)}{Mass of Dry Soil(g)}$.

The gypsum block used for this paper is a simple electronic component whose resistance varies based on the moisture of the soil. To be able to read values out of it, we designed a very low power circuit that converts the internal resistance of the block into a voltage value, that is then read by the ADC module in the ATmega328P-PU micro controller. The circuit, that consists in a particular voltage divider, can be seen in Figure 2 and is composed of two branches with one 1N4148 diode and one $4.7KOhm$ resistor per branch, making it a very cheap solution. The branches are necessary since we use alternating electric polarities and therefore help to avoid electro-chemical effects interfering with the measurements.

This solution is very energy efficient because the $5V$ input used to power the circuit and measure the moisture value is generated by two output digital pins on the micro controller and is kept for an average of $17ms$ at $1.050mA$ for each measured value. The current value is calculated using the first Ohm Law as shown in Equation 2, where $V = 5$ is the supply voltage, $4.7KOhm$ is the reference resistance and $60ohm$ is the lowest resistance value for the gypsum sensor:

$$I = \frac{V}{R} = \frac{5}{4700 + 60} = 1.050mA \qquad (2)$$

Table 2: Circuit for moisture values collection characteristics.

	Value
Input V	1.9 to 3.6V
I consumption	1.050mA
Sensing timing	17ms

4.1.4 Radio

Among all the available spectrum for transmitting data using radio signals, we decided to focus on the 2.4GHz ISM frequency, because it is an internationally reserved band for the use of radio frequency energy for ISM (Industrial, Scientific and Medical) purposes and does not require a license. In particular, we decided to use the Nordic nRF24L01+, an ultra low power RF transceiver for the 2.4GHz ISM band. It integrates a complete RF transceiver, RF synthesizer, and baseband logic supporting a high-speed SPI interface for the application controller. The chip is both very efficient in terms of battery consumption and at the same time very cheap. An extract of its characteristics, together with the theoretical current consumption are presented in Table 3. As can be seen, the input voltage range fits perfectly with our power supply configuration, allowing to transmit the collected data until the battery is completely drained. From our tests we discovered that a $10\mu F$ capacitor between Vcc and $Ground$ is needed in order to stabilize the input power.

Table 3: nFR24L01+ characteristics.

	Value
Input Voltage	1.9 to 3.6V
Available transfer rates	250kbps, 1Mbps and 2Mbps
Available transfer power	0, -6, -12, and -18dBm
Operating Frequency	2.4GHz ISM band operation
Sleep mode I consumption	900nA
Tx I consumption	11.3mA at 0dBm
Tx timing	33ms at 250Kbps

4.2 Implementation

With the strict energy requirements we had for this paper, building ultra low power hardware was not enough to reach our goal. We needed to develop efficient software that relies on the ATmega328P-PU sleeping modes to spare energy when not necessary. In fact, without any special optimizations in the software and with the values of consumption for the hardware reported in Tables 1, 2 and 3, with a total capacity of $2348mAh$ for our battery configuration, the total uptime in hours for the sensor node can be calculated with Equation 3:

$$uptime = \frac{battery capacity}{I} = \frac{2348}{0.2 + 1.050 + 11.3} = 187h \qquad (3)$$

This value of ~ 187 hours of up time is very far from the desired value of several months or even years. To improve efficiency, a particular strategy to run the micro controller has to be followed. This and other optimization strategies in the network configuration and the sensing modes allows us to reach our goal of years of battery life, as explained in details in the following subsections.

4.2.1 Micro Controller Life Cycle

The battery life value calculated in Equation 3 assumes that the system is always active, collecting and sending data continuously. However, according to the requirements described in Section 3, we need to collect moisture values every 9.950 seconds using only few milliseconds of transmission as explained in Section 4.1.3. At such a sensing and data collection and transmission frequency, power consumption values can be further improved if we are able to deactivate the micro controller and the radio when not needed. This can be obtained by setting sleep modes available in the ATmega328P-PU. A sleep mode is a particular low power state in which the micro controller is not performing any operation, and the majority of its components are deactivated. When an external interrupt is triggered or after a predefined period of time, the chip re-activates itself to perform its main program and then goes back to sleep, continuously doing this in a loop. For our specific use case, this process is showed in Figure 5. We have 2 different power modes for the micro controller:

- **Low Power Mode**: the micro controller stays in this mode for most of the time. We decided to use a specific arduino software library to activate this low power mode on the MCU during the sleep cycles. This low power library is called the Rocket Scream Low Power Library [10]. According to the specifications, a standard Arduino board using the Power Down mode (LowPower.powerdown()) theoretically consumes $1.7\mu A$. This very low value is obtained by powering off all the components of the micro controller: WDT, ADC, BOD, the timers, and the communication peripherals.
- **Active Mode**: in this mode the micro controller is performing operations, the sensor is collecting data and the radio is transmitting them to the gateway.
  - **Sensing**: in this stage, the micro controller collects sensor data from the dedicated circuit as explained in Section 4.2.2. This phase lasts for an average of $17ms$.
  - **Transmitting**: once the sensor value has been collected, it needs to be send to the gateway. The transmission stage initializes the radio, sends the data over wifi and puts the radio back in sleep mode in an average time of $33ms$.

Table 4 shows a detailed overview about timing and theoretical energy consumption for the 5 power modes of the micro controller workflow.

Table 4: Micro controller workflow specifications: duration and theoretical current consumption for each component in each mode.

Description	Duration	Current	Capacity
Low Power Mode			
Micro Controller	$9.950s$	$1.7\mu A$	$0.00169mAh$
Radio	$9.967s$	$0.9nA$	$0.00089mAh$
Active Mode			
Micro Controller	$50ms$	$0.2mA$	$0.001mAh$
Moisture Sensor	$17ms$	$1.050mA$	$0.001785mAh$
Radio TX	$33ms$	$11.3mA$	$0.037mAh$
Total			$0.04214mAh$

With the micro controller executing the workflow illustrated in Figure 5, and according the new consumption val-

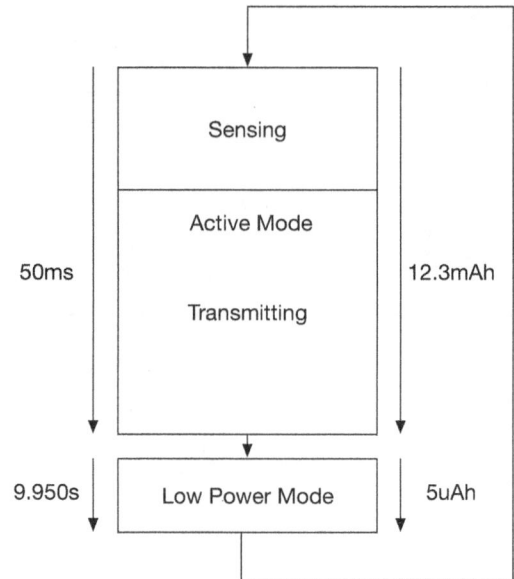

Figure 5: Micro-controller workflow. The micro controller is designed to have 5 main states.

ues, we can recalculate the expected battery life of Equation 3 with Equation 4:

$$uptime = \frac{batterycapacity}{I} = \frac{2348}{0.04266mA} = 55035h \quad (4)$$

The result of $55035h$ corresponds to a theoretical battery life of 6.28 years.

All the values presented in this Section about current consumption are theoretical and calculated according to the specifications in each device's datasheet. Section 6 presents the actual current consumption and battery life measurements we measured from our real life deployment of the sensor nodes in the Kangundo farm.

4.2.2 Sensor Reading

According to the data collection strategy specified in Section 4.1.3, and in particular how frequently data is collected from the sensor, we developed software that moisture sensor readings. Every 10 seconds, the sensor is activated through the digital outputs of the micro controller, current flows from the pins through the circuit and the sensor and the corresponding value is read on the analog inputs and converted to an analog value between 200 and 10000 ohms (with respect to the values presented in the datasheet that range from 60 to 35000 ohms [9]). The principle of operation consists of a voltage divider that uses two resistors in series in a circuit to create a calculable voltage value that depends on the moisture level. As described in Section 4.1.3 we use two branches in order to reduce interference therefore obtaining more accurate values. We also evaluated the possibility of collecting multiple readings per measurement, and transmitting the average measurements. However, this procedure requires additional time that increases depending on the number of times we perform a reading. Since the objective of this paper is to obtain the highest possible energy efficiency for these sensor nodes and since the gypsum sensors are accurate enough for our purposes, we decided to discard this option.

4.2.3 Wireless Communication

According to the requirements specified in Section 3 for the specific use case we want to follow, the wireless communication has been configured as described below.

The nRF24L01+ transceiver has several configurable parameters that can be tuned for the specific applications. In particular, its most configurable parameters that impact the energy efficiency of the communication are: transmission speed, transmission power, payload size, activation of acknowledgments.

The transceiver has 3 different transmission speeds: $250Kbps$, $1Mbps$ and $2Mbps$. According to the datasheet, the higher the speed the less reliable is the communication. In our specific use case since we required to transmit a limited amount of packets of a limited size, we focused more on reliability thus avoiding the necessity of retransmissions that require more energy. For this reason, we chose the lowest yet most reliable communication (with fewer retransmissions) speed of $250Kbps$.

The nRF24L01+ has 4 different transmission power levels: $0dBm$, $-6dBm$, $-12dBm$ and $-18dBm$. Since we required relatively long range communication of up to 90 meters, we measured the packet loss at receiving side for each of the power levels we decided to chose the highest one, $0dBm$. There were only slight disparities in power consumption while transmitting at the different power levels. Packet loss values at different distances from the transmitter for the chosen transmission power are showed in Figure 7.

To be able to send the moisture value to the gateway we decided to adopt a simple packet structure as shown in Table 5. We split the total payload of $4bytes$ into two fields: $2bytes$ for the moisture value and $2bytes$ for the address of the transmitting device. Since we had multiple devices communicating asynchronously, we needed a way to recognize the sender of the packet at the receiver side. Both these payload values are integers numbers.

Table 5: nRF24L01+ packet structure.

Header	Payload (address | value) {4bytes}

The transceivers were configured to use ACKs and the maximum number of retries for transmitted packets was set at 15 with $250\mu s$ between the retransmissions. No adverse effects due to interference were detected while determining the packet loss.

5. SYSTEM DEPLOYMENT

Once the system requirements were determined and the required hardware and software developed as defined in Section 2, the system was deployed on the Kenyan farm. The final objective was to collect moisture level measurements near the plants in order to generate insights about their stress level to help the farmer better schedule farming activities in the farm in a more productive way. These moisture values are collected using a network of low cost low power sensors spread across the farm, that have to operate autonomously without any human intervention for long periods of time. once the soil moisture readings are obtained, they are sent to a remote server for real time analysis and the generated insights are sent back to the farmers on their smart-phones.

This system was deployed in a typical Kenyan farm, many of which provide almost 80% of the total food supply in Kenya. These farms are characterized by small acreage, typically less than 5 hectares, are located in remote areas, are not connected to the power grid and usually have limited connectivity options, mostly only GSM/GPRS.

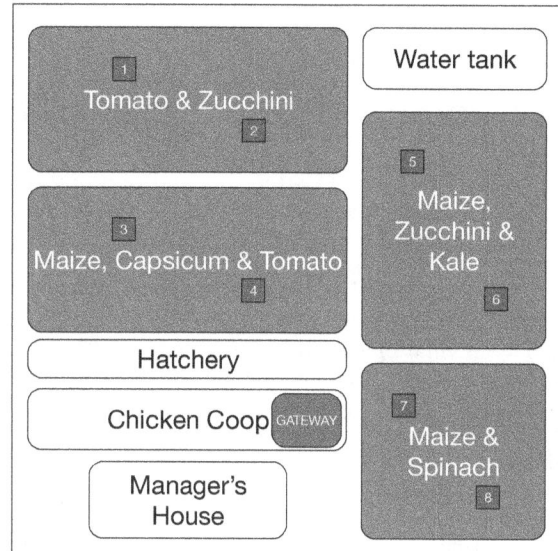

Figure 6: Map of the Kangundo Farm and sensors location.

The soil in the Kangundo farm in which the tests have been performed is composed of: clay 55.35%, sand 35.25% and silt 9.40%. Figure 6 presents the layout of the farm. Based on data obtained from our lab experiments, we placed 8 moisture sensors (in red in the Figure 6) equally spaced out in the 4 available plots (in green in the Figure 6). These 8 sensors are low cost sensor nodes with wireless connection capabilities and are very power efficient. Each sensor collects data about the soil moisture values that are sent in real time to the back end server for insights extraction. The only available connectivity available in the farm is through GPRS. However, providing GPRS connectivity to each of the sensor nodes was not feasible since this would have led to very high power energy requirements which would have required a technician to go to the farm every 20 days to change the batteries in each node. For this reason we decided to provide these nodes with a low-power local wireless connection to a central gateway that would be able to receive data from the sensors.

All the data is collected at fixed time intervals by the central solar powered gateway (blue in the Figure 6) that has less energy consumption constraints. This is because the central solar powered gateway is constantly powered by a battery pack and a photo voltaic panel installed with a GPRS modem on it. It consists of a Raspberry Pi[2] that is equipped with a nRF24l01+ transceiver and a USB 3G modem. Once all the data have been collected from the nodes on a regular basis, it encapsulates them in a single packet and sends it to the back-end system using the GPRS modem. Every node is placed at a distance between 10 and 90 meters in the line of sight from the gateway. The communication is kept asynchronous and unidirectional from the sensor nodes to the gateway in order to consume less power and for the same reason we decided to have a simple network topology,

---

[2]https://www.raspberrypi.org

avoiding multiple data hops or other techniques used often to increase the communication range.

Note however that in our current experiment, we assumed that within 10 seconds interval the moisture level could change. However, this assumption may not be realistic in ideal farming setting. Thus, we plan to experiment an instrumentation based approach to possibly determine the optimal intervals in real time.

6. EVALUATION

In this Section we show the results of the tests performed on the system in terms of battery life and network performances. We compare these results with the theoretical values in order to show how our system behaves.

6.1 Power Consumption and Battery Life

In order to evaluate the performances of the system and to predict the final lifetime of the battery powered wireless sensor nodes we performed an energy consumption test on each component in the sensor nodes for each of the power modes. The results collected with an oscilloscope are showed in Table 6.

Table 6: Micro controller workflow specifications: duration and real current consumption for each component in each mode.

Description	Duration	Current	Capacity
Low Power Mode			
Micro Controller	$9.950s$	$4\mu A$	$0.00398mAh$
Radio	$9.967s$	$1\mu A$	$0.00099mAh$
Active Mode			
Micro Controller	$50ms$	$1.2mA$	$0.0061mAh$
Moisture Sensor	$17ms$	$0.746mA$	$0.0012mAh$
Radio TX	$33ms$	$9.3mA$	$0.030mAh$
Total			$0.04303mAh$

According to Table 6, the micro controller in Low Power Mode has an average current consumption of $4\mu A$. While performing operations, its consumption is $1.22mA$. The sensor while collecting data consumes an average of $0.746mA$ and the radio device consumes $1\mu A$ while in low power mode and $9.3mA$ while transmitting.

With these measured current consumption values from real life deployment tests, and assuming a 10% losses to the battery capacity due to self-discharging and temperature variations, we can calculate the final battery life using Equation 5:

$$uptime = \frac{battery capacity}{I} = \frac{2348}{0.04303mA} = 49104h \quad (5)$$

We obtained a battery life value which is 89.22% of the theoretical value obtained in Equation 4 accounting for the losses of a real use case scenario. On average, this corresponds to $43\mu Ah$, which is below the actual threshold computed in the requirements section from Equation 1. With our solution, our custom low-cost low-power sensor nodes can collected data and send them in real time for analysis without any human intervention for more than 5.6 years.

6.2 Network Performance

Based on our laboratory experiments, it was determined that soil moisture sensor readings had to be transmitted every 10s at which point it would take 33ms for the nRF24L01+

transceiver to sense the channel and successfully transmit a signal. Measurements were made to determine the packet loss using these parameters between the transmitter and receiver to determine how far sensors on the farm could be placed without significant data loss. Data packets loss was capped at 18.03% for a distance of 90 meters which was the maximum distance a sensor and the gateway node. This was sufficient enough to extrapolate desired soil moisture values.

The obtained packet loss measurements for various distances are shown in Figure 7.

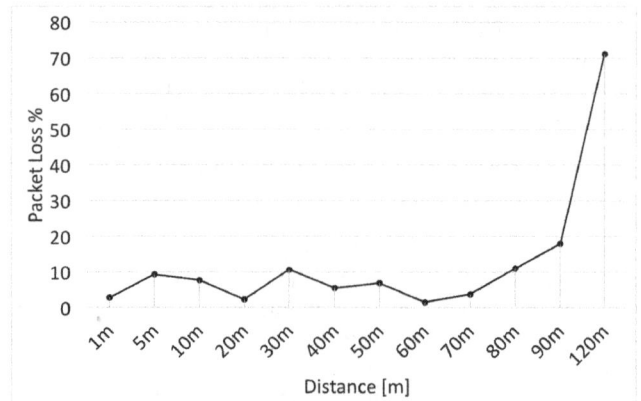

Figure 7: Packet loss measurements: A plot showing packet loss at various distances between transmitters/sensors and receivers on the farm.

The nRF24L01+ transceivers were configured with a high power setting to transmit at 0dBm. Even with this setting, power consumption for an entire sensor node was still low anticipated to discharge its respective AA batteries in approximately 5 years. A high power transmission setting was selected for the transceiver nodes to keep the number of sensors used to a minimum and to reduce the observed packet loss observed at lower transmission powers.

7. CONCLUSIONS AND FUTURE WORK

In this paper, we demonstrated by conducting a pilot that it is feasible to develop and deploy low-cost, low-power sensor networks for real time plant stress monitoring on small scale farms in sub-Saharan Africa, even though most of these farms are not connected to the electrical grid and have limited internet connectivity options. Our solution demonstrates that the cheap custom nodes we developed can be used to monitor soil moisture levels and to send this data in real-time to a back-end server for analysis with very little power consumption. Our evaluation showed that each of the nodes had an expected battery life of 5.6 years with two standard AA batteries.

We also showed that farmers using this low cost, low power sensor network could regularly receive real time updates on the soil moisture levels and modify their irrigation strategies to improve yields. More work is required to quantify the increase in yields for farmers over the short and long term. The extended life time for each of the sensor nodes will result in less maintenance and costs since battery recharging is not required thus leading to a reduction of the total deployment costs.

As future work, we plan to develop and deploy an intelligent data collection and transmission system. In this way, we hope to transmit changes in soil moisture levels only when they occur, therefore significantly reducing the power consumed by the various sensor nodes while increasing the life time of the devices.

8. ACKNOWLEDGMENTS

The authors would like to thank the anonymous reviewers who gave many useful suggestions and comments on early version this paper. The research reported in this paper was done while M. Zeni (mattia.zeni@disi.unitn.it), R. Mbitiru (rmugo@andrew.cmu.edu) and A. Nyambura (anjoroge@andrew.cmu.edu) were with the IBM Research Africa as research interns.

9. REFERENCES

[1] Esoko: Platform for connecting to Farmers. https://esoko.com.

[2] FarmerConnect: Personalized Extension Service. http://farmerconnect.org.

[3] iCow: Agricultural Information Service. http://www.icow.co.ke.

[4] MFarm: Market Prices. http://www.mfarm.co.ke.

[5] 1.5v aa duracell alkaline battery tests. http://rightbattery.com/118-1-5v-aa-duracell-alkaline-battery-tests/, Accessed August 2015.

[6] Arduino power consumption normal & sleep. http://gadgetmakersblog.com/arduino-power-consumption/, Accessed August 2015.

[7] Arduino uno. https://www.arduino.cc/en/Main/arduinoBoardUno, Accessed August 2015.

[8] Atmel avr 8-bit and 32-bit microcontrollers. http://goo.gl/A13nmd, Accessed August 2015.

[9] Model ks-d1 - owner's manual. http://www.delmhorst.com/Documents/PDFs/Operating-Instructions/KS-D1.pdf, Accessed August 2015.

[10] Rocket scream - lightweight low power arduino library. http://www.rocketscream.com/blog/2011/07/04/lightweight-low-power-arduino-library/, Accessed August 2015.

[11] S. A. Anjum, X.-y. Xie, L.-c. Wang, M. F. Saleem, C. Man, and W. Lei. Morphological, physiological and biochemical responses of plants to drought stress. *African Journal of Agricultural Research*, 6(9):2026–2032, 2011.

[12] A. Cano, E. Lopez-Baeza, J. Anon, C. Reig, and C. Millán-Scheiding. Wireless sensor network for soil moisture applications. In *Sensor Technologies and Applications, 2007. SensorComm 2007. International Conference on*, pages 508–513. IEEE, 2007.

[13] A. Crandall and J. Kieti. Startup business models and challenges for east african magriculture innovations. In *IST-Africa Conference and Exhibition (IST-Africa), 2013*, pages 1–10. IEEE, 2013.

[14] C. Hedley, J. Ekanayake, and P. Roudier. Wireless soil moisture sensor networks for precision irrigation scheduling. In *Workshop abstracts, advanced nutrient management: Gains from the past-goals for the future*, page 85, 2012.

[15] A. H. Kabashi and J. Elmirghani. A technical framework for designing wireless sensor networks for agricultural monitoring in developing regions. In *Next Generation Mobile Applications, Services and Technologies, 2008. NGMAST'08. The Second International Conference on*, pages 395–401. IEEE, 2008.

[16] B. G. Leib, J. D. Jabro, and G. R. Matthews. Field evaluation and performance comparison of soil moisture sensors. *Soil Science*, 168(6):396–408, 2003.

[17] S. Y. Lisar, R. Motafakkerazad, M. M. Hossain, and I. M. Rahman. *Water stress in plants: causes, effects and responses.* 2012.

[18] C. Müller, W. Cramer, W. L. Hare, and H. Lotze-Campen. Climate change risks for african agriculture. *Proceedings of the National Academy of Sciences*, 108(11):4313–4315, 2011.

[19] N. J. Papanastassiou. . crop-environment interactions in sub-saharan africa.

[20] K. Römer and F. Mattern. The design space of wireless sensor networks. *Wireless Communications, IEEE*, 11(6):54–61, 2004.

[21] Z. Ruirui, C. Liping, G. Jianhua, M. Zhijun, and X. Gang. An energy-efficient wireless sensor network used for farmland soil moisture monitoring. In *Wireless Sensor Network, 2010. IET-WSN. IET International Conference on*, pages 2–6. IET, 2010.

[22] H.-B. Shao, L.-Y. Chu, C. A. Jaleel, and C.-X. Zhao. Water-deficit stress-induced anatomical changes in higher plants. *Comptes rendus biologies*, 331(3):215–225, 2008.

[23] T. Wark, P. Corke, P. Sikka, L. Klingbeil, Y. Guo, C. Crossman, P. Valencia, D. Swain, and G. Bishop-Hurley. Transforming agriculture through pervasive wireless sensor networks. *Pervasive Computing, IEEE*, 6(2):50–57, 2007.

[24] S. Wiggins. Can the smallholder model deliver poverty reduction and food security. 2009.

[25] X. Wu and M. Liu. In-situ soil moisture sensing: measurement scheduling and estimation using compressive sensing. In *Proceedings of the 11th international conference on Information Processing in Sensor Networks*, pages 1–12. ACM, 2012.

Leveraging Smartphones to Monitor Attendance in Public Facilities

Ali Inam, *Technology for People Initiative*

Murtaza Taj, *Lahore University of Management Sciences*

Sohaib Khan, *Lahore University of Management Sciences*

Umar Nadeem, Independent Researcher

Zahra Mansoor, Independent Researcher

Zubair Khurshid Bhatti, *The World Bank, Islamabad Office*

Contact: ali.inam@tpilums.org

Attendance monitoring through smart phones aims to address the problem of absenteeism in public schools, health facilities and other services that pose a challenge of monitoring. The premise of this intervention is based on finding a cost and process efficient technological system that would accurately monitor attendance, thereby providing an alternative quality check and balance system, which will lead to an increase in the overall productivity of public institutions across the country.

We deployed an automatic attendance monitoring system based on a unique facial recognition system in the field where we provided smartphones to staff members of public schools and health facilities of Sheikhupura and Gujranwala to capture photos for recording attendance. Technological impediments faced while finding a cost effective voice and finger print recognition solution were recorded before deployment. We show that using smartphones for attendance monitoring is feasible for creating a strong deterrent against absenteeism. However, there are several social, cultural and technological impediments that have to be given adequate consideration during any rollout of such technology.

ACM Categories & Descriptors: H.5.m Image Processing and Computer Vision: Miscellaneous

Keywords: Attendance monitoring; facial recognition; performance management

DOI: http://dx.doi.org/10.1145/2830629.2830632

Bap re Bap! Driving Experiences through Multimodal Unruly Traffic on Bumpy Roads

Nova Ahmed, Lamia Iftekhar,
Silvia Ahmed, Ridwan Rahman,
Tanveer Reza, Sarah Shoilee
North South University
Dhaka, Banlgadesh
nova.ahmed@northsouth.edu

Charisma F. Choudhury
University of Leeds
Leeds, UK
C.F.Choudhury@leeds.ac.uk

ABSTRACT

Congestion, lack of compliance to traffic laws, multimodal traffic, opportunistic decision making and poor road conditions are few of the key challenges faced by drivers in a developing country's metropolitan city such as, Dhaka, Bangladesh. The driver's experience is affected by such road conditions which in turn shapes up their driving behavior and thus affects the traffic conditions which has been studied using sensor enabled tools as well as qualitative methods from a developing country's context.

Categories and Subject Descriptors

H5.m [**Information Interfaces and presentation**]: Miscellaneous

General Terms

Human Factors, Experimentation, Measurement

Keywords

Developing Country; Measurement of Driver Experiences; Multimodal Traffic; Dhaka Traffic

1. INTRODUCTION

Bap re Bap! is a commonly used expression in Bengali which closely matches to the expression *Oh my goodness!* to illustrate the driver experiences in Dhaka, Bangladesh, a city of more than 14 million people, severe traffic congestion and poor road conditions.

Our challenges had many dimensions as depicted in Figure 1-(a) and (b). From the traffic viewpoint, we have multimodal traffic (*heterogeneous*)- vehicles with various speeds. Various vehicle driversdiffer in their education level and knowledge on traffic rules [5] as well as roadside safety. The fact that traffic rules are very often violated, both by the

ACM DEV 2015, December 1–2, 2015, London, United Kingdom.
ACM 978-1-4503-3490-7/15/12.
DOI:http://dx.doi.org/10.1145/2830629.2835214 .

Figure 1: Traffic in Dhaka (a) Severe Congestion [3] (b) Excavated Road [1].

drivers and the pedestrians, make the situation more complex. Moreover, heavy traffic situation exacerbates due to the poor road conditions across the city [6]. The combination of these factors puts the driver in a unique position and we want to portray the driver experiences. We define **Driving Experience** [1]. A bad driving experience can have a profound effect on his/her level of aggressiveness as well aslong lasting effects on health and well-being [4]. Most research work related to vehicle drivers have been done predominantly in the context of drivers in the developed nations. Driving in a developing country is a highly different experience [5] and our goal is to formally study the driving experience from the perspective of drivers in the developing nations, starting with Dhaka.

We have studied the driving experiences using sensor based automated methods as well as qualitative methods that bring out the feelings related queries from drivers. Our discussions gave us a direction on the factors that affect the drivers the most. These measures could hep in formulating targeted interventions to enhance driving experience. To the best of our knowledge, our work is the first instrumented vehicle study in Bangladesh, and very likely, in South Asia.

2. SENSOR-BASED STUDY

Our sensor-based study involved most of our resources in terms of design, development, deployment and testing of sensor-enabled systems that may support a driver. *Sensing*

---

[1]Here 'driving experience' is not to be confused with the concept of *how long a driver has been driving* (measured by years or by mileage).

Uneven Roads: The custom built sensors have been built using Arduino connected to a MPU-6050 Accelerometer to capture the motion in X, Y, Z direction as can be seen in Figure 2-(b). An illustration of various road trips is shown in Figure fig:hardbk-(a). It can be observed that the X and Y-axes data do not vary a lot through various road conditions while Z axis shows visible changes through bumpy roads. *Sensing Hard Brake:* The brake sensor is used with inexpensive and available ultrasonic sensors attached beneath the brake pedal; a hard brake is detected by the ratio of the distance from the pedal to the floor and the time length during which the pedal has been pressed, calibrated to provide readings in centimeters and time is recorded using Arduinoas seen in Figure 2- (b) and (c). *Measuring Experience through Facial Expressions:* We have used a video recorder program that is able to record the driver expressions as well as the surrounding road conditions using two cameras in an advanced mobile phone as can be seen in Figure 2-(d). This is an intrusive technique as the driver is aware of the sensing mechanism.

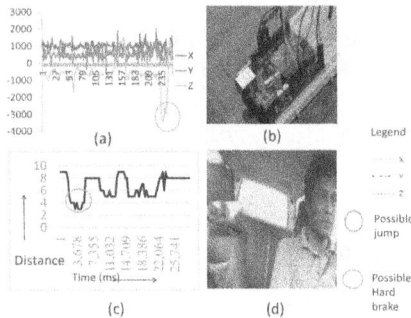

Figure 2: Sensors used in study (a) Road jumping mesurement (b)Hard BrakeSensor (c)Measuring hard brake (d) Video Sensing.

It is interesting to note that the sensors are able to reflect the information of the road conditions. However, the user experience varies a lot from person to person and requires some level of communication involving human interaction.

3. QUALITATIVE STUDY

Our qualitative study involved 28 drivers sharing their experiences in a semi-formal and informal setup. The informal setup was needed to talk to the rickshaw pullers who preferred liberty to speak in a free format and often changed topics at their own will . We offered a choice of TK 100 (less than 1 GBP) or phone credit of equivalent value to all our participants. We asked for car drivers using snowball sampling [2] and the study expanded by word of mouth for private car drivers. We approached rickshaw pullers and commercial drivers directly on roads and through known links. Our summary of study is presented in Table 1[2].

4. CONCLUSIONS

Driving experience plays a very important role on the traffic behavior and road safety. The experience can be crucial if the traffic situation itself is challenging. We have

---

[2]The numbers in the right two columns of Table 1 will not add up to the total counts in the leftmost column as some drivers mentioned multiple factors

Table 1: Summary of Qualitative Study

	Action during Unexpected Events	What Irritates you
commercial drivers (total: 8)	• hard brake (7) • sometimes hard brakes do not help (1)	• bumpy roads (1) • traffic jam (1) • long driving hours (8) • hunger (1) • comments from backseat (8)
private drivers (total: 8)	• hard brake (5) • slowdown (2) • yell (1) • understand human behavior (1)	• traffic jam (1) • very tired (1) • full stomach (1) • behavior of bus drivers(3) • parents advising how to drive (1) • phone calls (1)
rickshaw pullers (total: 10)	• do not want to brake. Move to side instead (10)	• When braking is needed (all) • hunger (all) • long hours of duty (all)

explored ways to find out about driver's experiences and identified factors that govern driving experience in an urban scenario with chaotic multimodal traffic in the context of Dhaka, Bangladesh. We have conducted instrumented vehicle study, unprecedented in the context of Bangladesh and supplemented it with qualitative studies. An extended study in this area can significantly improve the safety aspects and overall well-being of the drivers.

5. REFERENCES

[1] http://www.dhakatribune.com/sites/default/files/imagecache/870x488_article_high/article/2014/06/02/back-20140601-zakir-0278.jpg. Last Accessed on July 2015.

[2] Patrick Biernacki and Dan Waldorf. Snowball sampling: Problems and techniques of chain referral sampling. *Sociological methods & research*, 10(2):141–163, 1981.

[3] Ragib Dhar. http://www.dhakatribune.com/sites/default/files/imagecache/870x488_article_high/article/2013/07/15/4-20130712-Rajib-Dhar-0119.jpg. Last Accessed on July 2015.

[4] E. Gulian, A. I. Glendon, G. Matthews, D. R. Davies, and L. M. Debney. The stress of driving: A diary study. *Work and Stress*, 4:7–16, 1990.

[5] Md Mozahidul Islam and Charisma F Choudhury. A violation behavior model for non-motorized vehicle drivers in heterogeneous traffic streams. In *Transportation Research Board 91st Annual Meeting*, number 12-3192, 2012.

[6] Khaled Mahmud, Khonika Gope, and Syed Mustafizur Rahman Chowdhury. Possible causes & solutions of traffic jam and their impact on the economy of dhaka city. *Journal of Management and Sustainability*, 2(2):p112, 2012.

An Investigation into ICT-Addressable Causes of Maternal Mortality in Pakistan

Amna Batool
Department of Computer Science
Information Technology University
Lahore, Pakistan
ab133@itu.edu.pk

Samia Razaq
Department of Computer Science
Information Technology University
Lahore, Pakistan
samia.razaq@itu.edu.pk

Kentaro Toyama
School of Information
University of Michigan
Ann Arbor, Michigan, United States
toyama@umich.edu

ABSTRACT

Maternal mortality is still a threat for developing countries, and this continues to be true in Pakistan. Though there are global efforts to address maternal health issues using Information and Communication Technologies (ICTs), studies have not considered this question from the perspective of both medical practitioners and pregnant mothers. Through semi-structured interviews of health personnel and expecting women, we identify some ICT-addressable causes of maternal mortality. We conclude that using ICTs to deliver relevant and timely information with regards to hospital/clinic visits, medication, and some pre-natal practices could benefit mothers if it is conducted in collaboration with a trusted healthcare facility.

1. INTRODUCTION

Globally, approximately 800 women die each day due to complications related to pregnancy. 99% of these deaths occur in developing countries. Pakistan, with around 30,000 deaths annually, is amongst the top 3 countries in South Asia with the highest maternal mortality [1].

The medical causes of maternal mortality are well-known: hemorrhage, anemia, obstructed labor, sepsis, eclampsia, and severe bleeding. Apart from the medical causes, however, there are other indirect determinants like poverty, low literacy, lack of information and inadequate health services that also play a major role, particularly in rural areas, in increasing maternal mortality.

Using semi-structured interviews with medical personnel and pregnant mothers, we try to investigate the causes of maternal mortality in Pakistan that could be addressed by an ICT-based information system.

2. RELATED WORK

Around the world, information and communication technologies (ICTs) are increasingly being used to address causes of maternal mortality. Sending reminders to expecting mothers for supplement adherence is an effective way to improve maternal health keeping in view the huge mobile penetration around the globe [2]. Similarly, counseling expecting mothers by promoting maternal health using mobile technology also verifies the effectiveness of ICTs in maternal health domain [3]. Facilitating health workers by providing them user friendly interfaces for better labor monitoring is also helpful in labor rooms in developing countries [5].

Unfortunately, Pakistan contributes nothing in these ICT-based interventions to reduce maternal mortality. Our work focuses on understanding the causes of maternal mortality that can be addressed through ICT-based interventions.

ACM DEV 2015, December 01-02, 2015, London, United Kingdom
ACM 978-1-4503-3490-7/15/11.
http://dx.doi.org/10.1145/2830629.2835215

3. METHODOLOGY

We conducted a qualitative field study consisting of semi-structured interviews with various health personnel as well as expecting mothers to learn about maternal health in Pakistan. All interviews were conducted in Urdu and responses were recorded on paper.

3.1 Health Personnel Interviews

Eighteen interviews were conducted with medical personnel from all levels of Pakistan's health delivery system. The interview protocol focused on three topics: how hospital personnel perceived the current maternal health situation in Pakistan; what they perceived as the key determinants of maternal mortality; and what, if anything, could be addressed with an ICT-based intervention.

The interviewees were chosen from five sites ranging from tertiary care hospitals to primary care centers: 2 senior gynecologists and associate professors in public medical universities, 3 gynecologists from two public hospitals, 8 medical officers (MOs) from a public hospital, 1 Lady Health Visitor (LHV; this is a formal title), 1 Lady Health Supervisor (LHS), 2 Lady Health Workers (LHWs) and 1 midwife from a Rural Health Center (RHC) and a Basic Health Unit (BHU). Each interview took between 20-60 minutes.

3.2 Interviews with Expecting Mothers

We also conducted semi-structured interviews with 93 expecting mothers when they visited a hospital. The site of these interviews was the antenatal Out Patient Department (OPD) of the Lady Willingdon Hospital, a public obstetrics and gynecological hospital serving underprivileged communities in Lahore. The interviews were undertaken over the period of a month between July and August, 2014. Most of the interviews were short – between 5 to 7 minutes – because we could not impose too much on the women. Our questions focused on their literacy level, their gravidity (the number of previous pregnancies) and parity (the number of previous births), their preference for home/hospital birth, their current source of antenatal care information and the communication technologies they have access to.

The results below are based on a preliminary, informal analysis of all interview notes. No formal coding was performed.

4. FINDINGS

Below, we report on the overall status of mothers visiting the hospital as well as the major themes that arose in the interviews.

4.1 Status of Mothers

Almost half of the women interviewed were illiterate or semi-literate. Most of the pregnant mothers were in their third trimester (79 %) and had visited the same hospital twice before on average. Some were in their 2nd trimester (19%), and a very small number (2%) were in their first trimester. The majority of the women mentioned their mothers-in-law, mothers, and/or relatives (60%) as their source of antenatal care information. Some (12%) rely on LHWs for pregnancy-related information. About a quarter (28%)

had no source of pregnancy-related information. More than half of the women (54%) we interviewed, said that they had their previous delivery at a hospital and they prefer hospital births, particularly the low-cost public hospitals. Most of the women had access to cell phones: their own mobile phone (25%), their husband's (20%), or a phone shared by the whole family (30%). The women were used to both voice and text (57%), though some used only voice (40%), and a very small number relied only on texts (3%).

These findings suggest that women with hospital-birth experiences prefer the hospital, but that many women receive little information about hospital births thus relying on secondary sources for information, or wait until the second half of their pregnancy to make a visit.

4.2 Misinformation or Lack of Information

One theme which occurs repeatedly is a general lack of basic knowledge about health and pregnancy among low-income mothers in Pakistan. They are unaware of the value of routine checkups during pregnancy; iron supplements; pre-natal supplements; ultrasound appointments; high-risk indicators; or even the value of hospital births. This unawareness is noted by medical personnel and is confirmed by pregnant mothers, often through their recitation of misinformation.

A male gynecologist at a public hospital noted the following about his patients:

"There is no concept of routine health checkups in Pakistan... They don't know that they can be deficient in blood because of their menstrual cycles if they don't get proper iron intake. They are not aware that they should meet the iron deficiency before they get pregnant again."

A gynecologist from a public hospital said this of ultrasound:

"I see many patients who think that ultrasound rays are harmful for their fetus, hence they never get an ultrasound."

One mother – surprisingly, a PhD candidate in a public university in Lahore – confirmed:

"I have heard that ultrasound rays are harmful for the fetus. Hence I have not performed this test yet. Although I am doing research on brain cancer but when it comes to oneself, you become suspicious of things like that."

The consequences of this ignorance can be devastating. One 7-month pregnant mother was admitted to the hospital for abortion because of fetal abnormalities which were revealed to her only at the 7th month when she performed her first ultrasound. According to doctors:

"It would have been much less painful, both physically and emotionally, if she had performed an ultrasound at an earlier stage."

A senior gynecologist at a public medical college said,

"Expecting women are unaware of all the high-risk indications in pregnancy, in case of which they should visit the hospital and consult a doctor. If we can make them aware of what these high risk indications are and how they have to tackle these situations, we can surely make some difference."

4.3 Reliance on Non-Medical Advice

Another prominent theme is the reliance on advice from people without medical training, including traditional midwives ("*daai*") and relatives, particularly mothers-in-law.

A senior gynecologist mentioned that she often saw sepsis cases caused by midwives' mismanagement.

"I have seen midwives who have kept one big nail of their little finger to cut the baby's cord; this is the level of hygiene of these midwives... They have unsterilized surgical equipment

and all they use to sterilize it is Dettol [an over-the-counter disinfectant]."

Other medical personnel note that mothers-in-law play a powerful role in determining what mothers do:

"They have their mothers-in-law who don't allow them to come to hospital unless they have complications."

Pregnant mothers, in fact, do not control the decision about hospital visits on their own. During one visit, a mother said:

"Don't put next week's date for test, I want to get all my tests done today as I am not sure if my family would allow me to come again next week."

Mothers say mothers-in-law provide folk advice such as...

"We have given birth to children without any doctors or hospitals in our time and our kids turned out to be OK. So there is no need to go to hospital for regular checkups."

Mothers with little say in family planning, have to follow their husbands' and mother-in-law's wishes. One mother, expecting for the second time in a year, with low hemoglobin was asked by the doctor why she did not wait longer. She said,

"My husband had to go out of country and my mother-in-law wanted me to be pregnant again before he left."

4.4 Other Problems

Other themes that emerged in the interviews include the frequency of pica (a disorder in which mothers eat coal, soil, raw rice, and other non-foods); self-medication with bad pharmaceuticals; and lack of immunization against tetanus.

5. DISCUSSION AND CONCLUSION

While the root causes of maternal mortality in Pakistan are complex, one of the mediating causes is that women lack key knowledge that could help reduce threats to their health. This suggests that ICTs that deliver relevant and timely information could be of benefit to mothers. But as is increasingly understood in ICT-for-development research, even where lack of information is a problem, it is very rarely the only obstacle.

Following amplification theory [4], we therefore propose that among the information problems we have identified, it is the ones that hospitals and clinics themselves can influence that are amenable to further improvement with ICT. Based on our interviews, these are:

- Making timely antenatal care visits to the hospital/clinic
- Taking supplements and getting vaccinated
- Adhering to a healthy diet and healthy life style

Other issues, such as reliance on a medically unsanctioned midwife or eliminating the bad influence of family members are problems beyond the existing medical system (though they could be addressed through ICTs working with other organizations).

6. REFERENCES

[1] Y. P. Khan, S. Z. Bhutta, S. Munim and Z. A. Bhutta, "Maternal health and survival in Pakistan: issues and options," *J Obstet Gynaecol Can,* vol. 31, no. 10, pp. 920-929, 2009.

[2] N. Pai, P. Supe, S. Kore, Y. S. Nandanwar, H. A, E. Cutrell, W. Thies, "Using automated voice calls to improve adherence to iron supplements during pregnancy: a pilot study," in *6th Int'l Conf. on Info. & Comm. Technologies and Development,* 2013.

[3] D. Ramachandran, V. Goswami and J. Canny, "Research and reality: using mobile messages to promote maternal health in rural India," in *Proc. 4th ACM/IEEE International Conference on Information and Communication Technologies and Development,* 2010.

[4] K. Toyama, Geek Heresy: Rescuing Social Change from the Cult of Technology, PublicAffairs, 2015.

[5] H. Underwood, "PartoPen: enhancing the partograph with digital pen technology," in *CHI'12 Extended Abstracts on Human Factors in Computing Systems,* 2012.

RFTrack: TVWS Spectrum Measurements using Android Phones

Marco Rainone
Solvitech
Italy
mrainone@libero.it

Marco Zennaro
ICTP
Italy
mzennaro@ictp.it

Ermanno Pietrosemoli
ICTP
Italy
ermanno@ictp.it

ABSTRACT

Despite successful trials in several Developing Countries, TVWS has not gained the amount of attention that it deserves. One of the reasons is the lack of awareness by both the general public and the spectrum regulators about the abundance of idle spectrum. Traditionally, spectrum measurements required expensive instruments and considerable operator's expertise. This has changed with the emergence of low cost spectrum analyzers that are also easier to operate. In this paper we present an Android application called RFTrack that measures spectrum using a low-cost spectrum analyzer and geo-tags the data using the phone's GPS. Data is stored in the internal memory. Once an Internet connection is available, the program sends data to a server that presents the results in an easy-to-understand way. After having performed some measurement campaigns with this set up, we believe that this is a useful tool to demonstrate the existence of significant swats of of underutilized spectrum, especially in rural areas of developing countries.

1. TVWS IN DEVELOPING COUNTRIES

In telecommunications, white spaces refer to frequencies allocated to a broadcasting service but currently not used locally. They offer superior propagation characteristics and are very often idle due to low population density (it makes no business case for broadcasters to cover sparsely populated areas). Existing deployments in Developing Countries are based on temporary licenses [1].

2. SPECTRUM MEASUREMENTS

Spectrum measurements have been performed in many countries, both industrialized and developing. The general consensus is that large parts of the spectrum are empty, especially in rural areas [2]. One of the issues faced by engineers in developing countries is the cost of measurement tools (spectrum analyzers with GPS and memory). Another issue is visualization of spectrum usage, once the measurements have been carried out. Specialized equipment to mea-

ACM DEV 2015, December 1–2, 2015, London, United Kingdom.
ACM 978-1-4503-3490-7/15/11.
DOI: http://dx.doi.org/10.1145/2830629.2835216 .

Figure 1: RFTrack measuring spectrum occupancy at the Galapagos Islands

sure and visualize spectrum usage cost more than 10 kUSD. Citizen groups that want to apply for the unused spectrum to extend connectivity to rural areas face the same issues.

3. RFTRACK

RFTrack is an Android application that reads data from a low cost RF Explorer spectrum analyzer, geo-tags the measurements and saves them in the internal phone memory. Measurements are saved every 150 msec in an sqlite database. Once an Internet connection is available, measurements can be sent to an email address that then triggers the processing and visualization phase. The Android app and the server software are based on open source component. Figure 1 shows an Android phone connected to an RF Explorer spectrum analyzer, carrying out measurements in Ecuador.

4. SETUP

The first step to carry out a measurements campaign is to connect the RF Explorer SA to the Android phone via a suitable cable (one that has a mini USB connector on one side and a micro USB connector on the other side). Once the SA is connected, the RFTrack application is automatically launched. The user can choose the frequency range or leave the default value (300 to 900 MHz) selected. The measurement campaign starts immediately. Every ten measurement a beep is produced as a reminder that the phone is correctly acquiring data. Once the campaign is over, users can send the data to an email address of their choice and analyze data

Figure 2: Options presented to the user

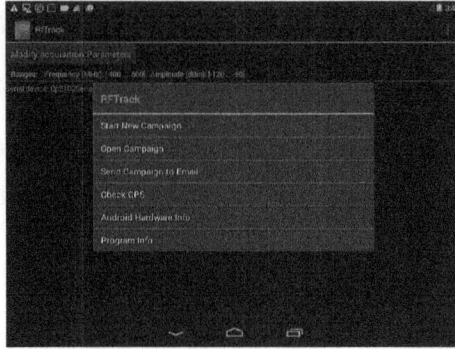

Figure 3: Data privacy options

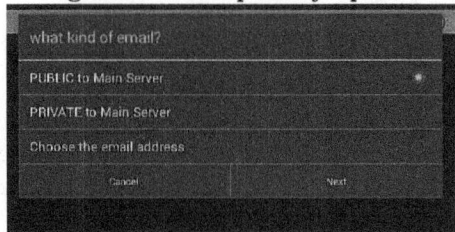

Figure 4: Heatmap of spectrum measurements in Mozambique

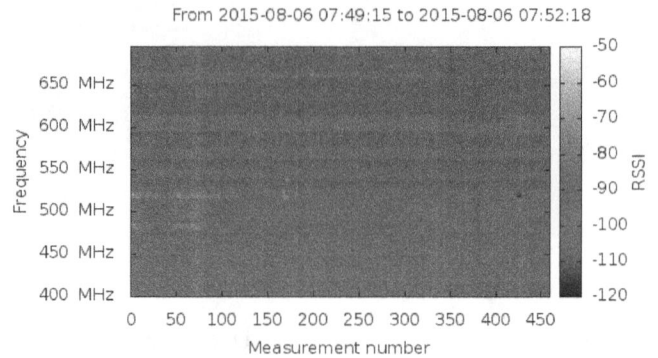

Figure 5: Percentage of measurements at a certain frequency that are under the threshold value of -100 dB, in Mozambique

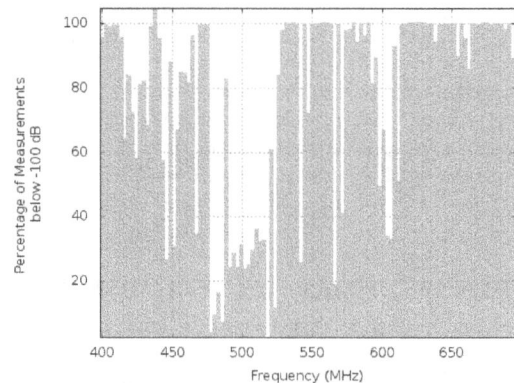

independently or to a predefined address configured for the automatic processing and subsequent visualization. We decided to use email to minimize the transfer time. Figure 2 shows the basic UI of RFTrack. The user can start a new measurement campaign, open an existing campaign (to add measurements to an existing one), send the measurements via email and perform some hardware tests. Figure 3 shows the options presented to the user in terms of data privacy. Data can be published openly (sent to a default address), published privately (the measurement campaign is not visualized on the main site) or data can be sent to a specific address to be later analyzed.

5. DATABASE

The latest version of RFTrack uses an sqlite database to store data. In the database we store name and info of the measurements campaign, the type of antenna used (omni or directional), latitude, longitude, altitude (meters above the see level), speed (in m/s), estimated measurement accuracy and time as provided by the GPS. If it is not possible to detect the position through the network or the GPS, the user can manually enter longitude, latitude and altitude.

6. RESULTS

We used RFTrack to measure spectrum usage in Mozambique, Ecuador and Morocco. Figure 4 shows a heatmap where the X axis shows the measurements, Y axis shows the frequencies and the color represents the measured signal level. Figure 5 shows the number of measurement at a specific frequency that are under a certain threshold.This is particularly useful since the choice of the threshold is quite significant in deciding if a particular channel is being used or not. These graphs are automatically produced by the server once the measurements are sent.

7. CONCLUSIONS

We presented RFTrack, an Android app to measure spectrum occupancy using a low cost spectrum analyzer. Users can accept default values for maximum simplicity or choose particular frequency bands and minimum/maximum amplitude levels for greater measurement control. The preliminary results show that spectrum measurements can be easily carried out and that visualizations are easy to understand. We thank the Shuttleworth Foundation for supporting this project.

8. REFERENCES

[1] M.T.Masonta et al., Television White Space (TVWS) Access Framework for Developing Regions, in proceedings of IEEE AFRICON 2013, Mauritius, 9-12 September 2013

[2] T.Brown et al., A Survey of TV White Space Measurements, in proceeding of Africomm2014, Uganda, 24-25 November 2014

Summarization Search: A New Search Abstraction for Mobile Devices

Sunandan Chakraborty
New York University
sunandan@cs.nyu.edu

Zohaib Jabbar
New York University Abu Dhabi
zohaib.jabbar@nyu.edu

Lakshminarayanan Subramanian
New York University
lakshmi@cs.nyu.edu

1. INTRODUCTION

Mobile users in developing regions are known to have a relatively poor web experience [7] due to three fundamentally limiting factors: limited network bandwidth, high cost of connectivity and high latency. Several measurement studies have demonstrated web page load times in the order of several seconds to a few minutes [4] triggered due to poor network connectivity and high end-to-end latencies for even simple DNS lookups. Several prior efforts have proposed important optimizations at different network layers including the design of new transport protocols [10], new caching protocols [5] [7] [8] , middlebox strategies [11],delay tolerant network solutions [8] and rethinking the design of the applications to operate in such extreme environments [6] [9] [1] [7] [2].

In this paper, we propose *summarization search* as a new search abstraction for mobile users in developing regions built around the goal of minimizing the need for interaction and exploration involved in a standard web search task. The summarization search engine is implemented as an additional layer above a standard search engine model. Hence, it uses the state-of-the-art ranking, indexing and retrieval as offered by standard search engines. The contribution of this paper is not in these standard procedures of web search but presenting the results in a novel way which potentially can improve the experience of searching the web from mobile devices. This abstraction is specifically designed for *focused* search queries, where the search action of the user relates to a specific information need. The goal is to provide a user with her information needs within a single round of interaction. Given a query, our summarization search service interacts with conventional search services (like Google, Bing etc.), analyzes the contents of the top search result pages and provides a condensed and summarized search response to the user, highlighting the essential parts – with respect to the query – from the target documents. In essence, the users can find their appropriate search result in at most one or two clicks, one for the search and one for choosing the result page.

ACM DEV 2015, December 1–2, 2015, London, United Kingdom.
ACM 978-1-4503-3490-7/15/12.
DOI: http://dx.doi.org/10.1145/2830629.2835217.

We evaluated the summarization search interface using a set of 400 queries from users using Mechanical Turk crowdsourcing platform and asked the users to rate the summarized search results. The users were asked to rate the results in a scale of 5 (1 is high and 5 is low), where around 85% of the queries received an average rating of 1 or 2. The user study also showed that in 55% of the cases the users found the information in the summarized search result page, without the need for further browsing. This demonstrates the effectiveness of the summarization search, where in more than half the cases users can obtain the information with just one operation of submitting the query. Although many of the commercial search engines can do the same for very specific types of queries, our system is capable of performing this for generic web search queries.

2. METHODOLOGY

The summarization engine uses the Google Search API to download the the top 64 (configurable) search result pages. The key goal of the summarization engine is to perform detailed text analysis of all the result pages to prepare a condensed summary page across all the search result pages. Text Summarization is a process of creating a concise version of a larger text preserving the main theme of the original text. There are different ways of summarizing a text. Two popular methods used in the NLP literature are Extraction based summarization and abstraction based summarization [3]. Our text summarization uses the extraction based summary approach which involves creating the summary by using exact sentences from the original text. Unlike the standard task the extraction in our case is driven by the query terms, highlighting the portion of the documents which have high relevance with respect to the query terms. Our extraction based summarization algorithm has two steps: (a) identification of key terms in a document w.r.t. the query terms; (b) identification of key portions of a documents using the key terms identified in the previous step.

To identify important key terms in a document we use a natural language parser to parse each sentence. This step breaks down each sentence into noun phrases, verb phrases and prepositional phrases etc. The noun phrases are the most informative parts of the sentences and the verbs – which depict the actions – have relevance too. A popular measure to determine importance of a term is the term frequency-inverted document frequency (TF-IDF). We computed IDF of the noun and verb phrases as the web probability of them using the Microsoft Ngram Web Service [1]. Let $P_{web}(t_i)$ represent this measure for the phrase t_i. High value of the web probability represents the popularity of the phrase. This means it has relatively less importance in this context because it tends to appear very frequently in any large English corpus of text. $P_{corpus}(t_i)$ is the normalized frequency of t_i. This score is similar to TF-IDF but in this case all the documents is a focus set of documents resulting from a query. Hence, many important terms might have high document frequency and using TF-IDF weights will lower their scores. The algorithm for summarizing the search results is presented below.

Algorithm 1 Summarization Search

---

procedure SUMMARIZE(query = q, document= d)
   for each $t_i \in V$ **do**
      compute $Imp(t_i) = P_{corpus}(t_i)/P_{web}(t_i)$
      compute $Imp_{norm}(t_i) = \frac{Imp(t_i)}{\sum_i Imp(t_i)}$
   end for
   for each $s_j \in d$ **do**
      compute $Score(s_j) = \sum_{t_i \in s_j, V} w_t \times Imp_{norm}(t_i) + \sum_{t_q \in s_j, Q} w_q \times Imp_{norm}(t_q)$
   end for
   $S \leftarrow sort([\forall s_j \in d], key = Score(s_j), order = Desc)$
   $summ\_score \leftarrow 0$
   $summary \leftarrow empty\_list$
   for $s_j \in S$ **do**
      if $\Delta summ\_score_{k-1:k} \leq \epsilon$ **then**
         break
      else
         $summ\_score \leftarrow summ\_score + Score(s_j)$
         $summary.append(s_j)$
      end if
   end for
   $summary \leftarrow sort([\forall s_j \in summary], key = j, order = Asc)$
      ▷ j = sequence no. of the sentence in document d
   return summary
end procedure

---

3. EVALUATION

We performed a user study to both generate queries and evaluate the summarization search interface for those queries. In the first round of the user study, users were asked to submit queries which they are more likely to submit from mobile devices instead of desktop/laptop computers. In the second phase we engaged 30 users to evaluate the results from these queries. The goal was to evaluate the quality of the summarized search results. The user study was done using the Amazon Mechanical Turk platform and the chosen users were all Mechanical Turk Masters. Masters are workers who have demonstrated high accuracies in previous tasks and this ensured better quality in the user responses.

We asked the users to judge the summarized search responses based on the given query and rate the quality using a score between 1(highest) and 5(lowest). Every query was rated by all the 30 users. We computed the mean and mode of the scores of each query rated by all the users. Figure 1 shows the histograms of frequency distributions of mean and mode scores for all the queries. Around 45% of the queries received an average rating between 1 and 2 and more than 80% of the queries received positive ratings from the users.

---

[1] research.microsoft.com/en-us/collaboration/focus/cs/web-ngram.aspx

Figure 1: Histograms of ratings per query for all users – mean (left) and mode (right) rating per query

Table 1: Average ratings per query per user for different types of queries

Type of query	Average rating
Rating-type	2.25
Information-type	1.72
Location-type	2.32

Figure 1(right) shows that more than half (52%) of the queries received a score of 1 from majority of the users (i.e. mode score of 1). We also evaluated the performance for different types of queries in this study. We manually classified the queries into 3 sets – location-specific, ratings-type and information-type. Location specific queries are those where users asked about points of interests in (or *near*) a location (e.g. find the nearest movie theater in *location* etc.) Examples of rating type query is 'top restaurants'. Finally, information type queries are those where users looked for specific information (e.g. "fastest land vehicle"). Table 1 summarizes the relative performance across these categories. The results show that the performance was best for information-type queries and worst for location-types. A probable explanation is that information-type had very specific answers and we did not use any location services which might have resulted in some erroneous results.

4. REFERENCES

[1] Chen, J. and Subramanian, L. and Li, J. RuralCafe: web search in the rural developing world. WWW. 2009
[2] Teevan, J. and Ramage, D. and Morris, M. Ringel. # TwitterSearch: a comparison of microblog search and web search. WSDM. 2011
[3] Radev, D. R., Hovy, E., and McKeown, K. (2002). Introduction to the special issue on summarization. Computational Linguistics., 28(4)
[4] Y. Zaki, J. Chen, T. Pötsch, T. Ahmad, and L. Subramanian. Dissecting web latency in ghana. In *IMC 2014*.
[5] J. Chen and L. Subramanian. Interactive web caching for slow or intermittent networks. In *DEV 2013*.
[6] D. Iland and E. Belding. Emergenet: robust, rapidly deployable cellular networks. *Communications Magazine, IEEE*, 52(12), 2014.
[7] A. Balasubramanian, N. Balasubramanian, S. J. Huston, D. Metzler, D. J. Wetherall. Findall: A local search engine for mobile phones. *CoNEXT 2012*.
[8] S. Isaacman and M. Martonosi. The c-link system for collaborative web usage: A real-world deployment in rural nicaragua. In *NSDR 2009*.
[9] W. Thies, J. Prevost, T. Mahtab, G. T. Cuevas, S. Shakhshir, A. Artola, B.D. Vo, Y. Litvak, S. Chan, S. Henderson, M. Halsey, L. Levison, and S. Amarasinghe Searching the World Wide Web in Low-Connectivity Communities. In *WWW*, 2002.
[10] Y. Zaki, T. Potsch, J. Chen, L. Subramanian, C. Gorg Adaptive Congestion Control for Unpredictable Cellular Networks. *SIGCOMM 2015*.
[11] A. Balasubramanian, B. Levine, A. Venkataramani. DTN Routing as a Resource Allocation Problem. ACM Sigcomm, August 2007

Octopus: A Zero-Cost Architecture for Stream Network Monitoring

Andrés Arcia-Moret
Computer Laboratory
University of Cambridge, UK
andres.arcia@cl.cam.ac.uk

Jesús Gómez
RESIDE
University of Los Andes
Venezuela
jagomez@ula.ve

Arjuna Sathiaseelan
Computer Laboratory
University of Cambridge, UK
arjuna.sathiaseelan@cl.cam.ac.uk

Categories and Subject Descriptors

C.4 [**Computer Systems Organization**]: Performance of Systems—*Measurement techniques*

Keywords

wireless networks monitoring; stream computing; low-cost networking

1. INTRODUCTION

Considering the growing demand and popularity of Do-It-Yourself (DIY) networks, low-cost devices managed by the people, for the people and the ease of deployment of localised/decentralised Internet services, it is mandatory for such networks to have an efficient low cost monitoring platform. Appropriate monitoring is crucial to ensure availability, responsiveness and users' Quality of Experience (QoE). This is specially relevant for the developing world where Community Networks (CN) are increasing in popularity and complexity [1].

CN have the capability to grow into complex arrays of interconnected nodes with different link layer technologies (wireless being more common), along with data flowing from and to not just standard Internet services but also local services: local institutional repositories, local mail servers, community clouds[2]. Furthermore, CN users can deploy their own services catered to the local population with almost no restrictions.

Keeping track of the various network metrics in real time and to compute relevant analytics, require stream processing capabilities. Regular characteristics such as congestion, packet losses, routing inefficiencies, latency or bandwidth usage are difficult to understand and deploy from the perspective of well-known (and resource hungry) applications. It is also well-known that substantial improvements can be achieved on service performance if the monitoring information is available to the system administrator in real time.

We propose a system that focuses on the ease of data visualisation and the use of commodity hardware allowing lay

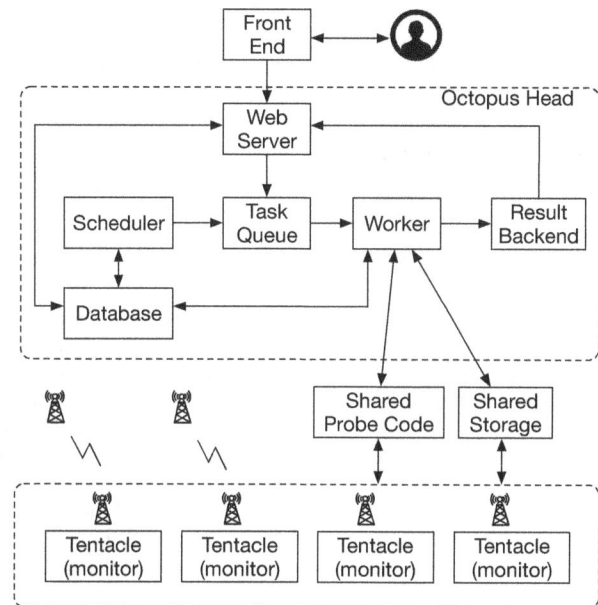

Figure 1: Octopus monitor architecture

people to understand the rough behaviour of their networks. Effective data visualization can also help in communicating system performance through the use of various graphical (and intuitive) elements[1], allowing administrators to easily discover patterns and draw conclusions on system performance.

Current emerging approaches for on-demand computation such as stream computing[2] are part of our motivation, as it plays an important role in small data applications. Moreover, it addresses the problem of requesting live information that otherwise should be handled in batches. In our specific case, a stream computing approach allows the monitoring-user (with enough capabilities) to schedule the visualisation of results whenever the CPU usage (of the service holder) is low, thus assuring appropriate use of low-cost resources.

2. OCTOPUS

Octopus Monitor (OM)[3] is a service to provide low-cost network monitoring solutions and data visualization to make

---

[1] http://www.highcharts.com
[2] https://en.wikipedia.org/wiki/Stream_(computing)
[3] Available at: http://150.185.138.59/octopusmonitor

analysis about the state of art network set-ups. Fig. 1 summarizes the architecture of OM, a stream processing oriented monitoring system that consists of the following: (a) *A central monitor entity* (the Octopus Head, OH) that controls the monitoring of different independent link and service monitors. **Octopus Head** is the entry point of the web app, it allows the interaction with users of type: **Admin** who is able to create tests and visualizations as well as manage other users, **Monitoring Users** that own monitors and are gathering data and viewing results and, **Unauthenticated users** that are able to view the home page, register and view the results shared by monitoring users. Heavy io/processor bound tasks are delegated to a distributed processing system. (b) *Distributed monitoring elements* referred as the *tentacles*. **Tentacles** are remote network monitors deployed by the monitoring users, as previously mentioned, tentacles execute periodic tests according to a schedule defined by Admin. Within tentacles, a monitoring-user specify the links that are to be monitored and the parametrized tests. A tentacle is able to load test modules and schedule them for execution on run time; tests can be executed simultaneously and exceptions are independently handled so that eventual problems go unnoticed by other concurrent tests.

In addition, the Octopus also has (c) A data repository (most likely in the cloud) that conveniently stores traces and offers the possibility of increasing the granularity of observations, (d) A code repository to store the logic of probes, (e) Using the stream processing principle for retrieving pertinent information at the right time with a pertinent (appropriate) use of limited resources and (f) Use of caches to store previous expensive (heavy io/processor bound) visualizations.

Distributed Task Processing As the OH has to be offloaded of long running tasks, we use a distributed task processing system where one or more workers execute asynchronous tasks, and so we use task distribution system and a task queue manager (i.e., Celery/Redis). Other companion components correspond to: a **Database** for storing processed traces in compact format, user preferences and monitoring configurations. It also serves the test integration framework and the scheduler. **File Cache** to speed up previously calculated plots and avoid repetition of intensive tasks. **Static Media Server** for ready-to-consume files stored in the file cache that rarely change. Serving these files through the main web server is known to be grossly inefficient, and can overload the server unnecessarily.

On network monitoring characteristics. There is a wealth of innovative solutions and web applications that provide different approaches for network monitoring and benchmarking[4]. Although all of them offer roughly the same standard monitoring metrics for networks from an end-to-end perspective, none of them offer an architecture for distributed continuous monitoring within a DIY network, taking into account low-cost hardware. Metrics such as RTT, per hop RTT, packet losses, throughput, etc. are common on active projects on network monitoring and could be independently implemented in Octopus.

Automating network probes. New probes can be part of Octopus monitoring workflow in two stages: development and deployment. At development stage, the monitoring-user defines probes, tests and visualizations; then the monitoring-

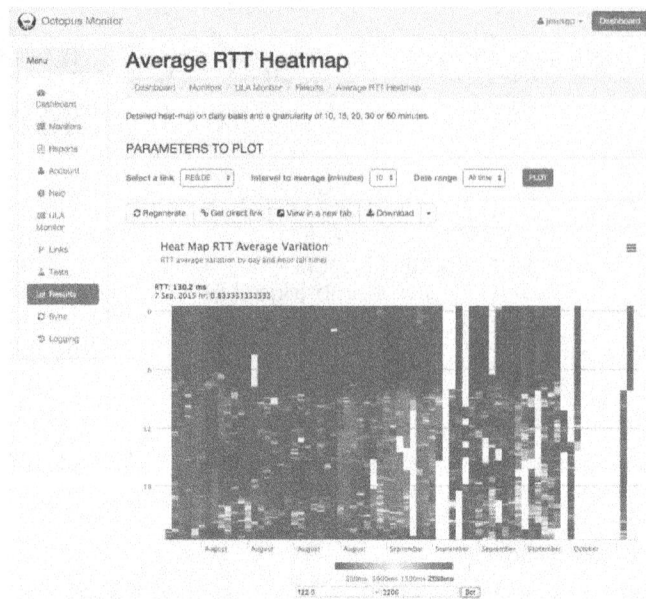

Figure 2: Screen shot of Octopus, monitoring a University of Los Andes independent user service.

user pushes the probe code into the code-repository. In order to easily deploy and integrate new probes, a simple pull from the code-repository on the OH and OT suffices.

Finally, in Fig. 2 shows a screen shot of the Octopus up-and-running prototype. It shows a 2.5 month monitoring of a web-server summarizing, in a heatmap, RTTs in 10 min chunks.

3. CONCLUSIONS

We have developed Octopus, a prototype for low-cost network monitoring that is easily scalable and highly configurable. We can incorporate new probes and tests through a simple strategy. Octopus allows monitoring of DIY and CN for independent users. Currently we are deploying Octopus in various CNs in developing countries.

4. ACKNOWLEDGEMENTS

The research leading to these results has received funding from the European Union's (EU) Horizon 2020 research and innovation programme under grant agreement No. 644663. Action full title: architectuRe for an Internet For Everybody, Action Acronym: RIFE. We would also like to thank Juan Tirado for comments on an earlier draft.

5. REFERENCES

[1] J. Saldana, A. Arcia-Moret, B. Braem, E. Pietrosemoli, A. Sathiaseelan, M. Zennaro. Alternative Network Deployments. Taxonomy, characterization, technologies and architectures. IRTF, 2015.

[2] R. Baig, R. Rocaa, F. Freitag, L. Navarro. guifi.net, A Crowdsourced Network Infrastructure Held in Common. In Computer Networks, 2015.

---

[4]http://netalyzr.icsi.berkeley.edu/, http://projectbismark.net/

Designing for a Rural Online Learning Community

Aditya Vishwanath
Georgia Institute of Technology
Atlanta, Georgia
avishwanath6@gatech.edu

Neha Kumar
Georgia Institute of Technology
Atlanta, Georgia
neha.kumar@gatech.edu

ABSTRACT
As mobile technologies and internet connectivity fast penetrate rural, low-resource settings, there is tremendous potential for them to enable accessible and large-scale learning environments. We present findings from a needs assessment exercise conducted at after-school classrooms in three villages in Tamil Nadu (India). Using a tablet application as a design probe and iterating on its design through a six-week qualitative study, along with interviews with different stakeholders, led us to an enriched understanding of how the application of mobile technologies could contribute towards the design for a rural, online learning community. We conclude with our plan for future work to this end.

Categories and Subject Descriptors
H.5.0 [Information Interfaces and Presentation]: General

Keywords ICTD; HCI; learning; India

1. INTRODUCTION
As mobile technologies and internet connectivity become more affordable, they are increasingly being brought into formal and informal learning environments to leverage the role they might play towards engaging children and targeting learning outcomes. In 2004, Wang et al. contributed a methodology for centralized packaging of content appropriate for rural schools [7]. In 2009, Kam et al. explored the potential of mobile phones for language learning, targeting children in rural India [5, 6]. More recently, Cross' research has studied the potential of technology to target more effective learning outcomes [1, 2]. Our research builds on this work by contributing a study that introduces (and iterates on) a tablet application to assess the responsiveness of students and the receptiveness of tutors to this technology, both as a diagnostic tool and learning aid. Based on our findings, we make a case for our future work – an educational intervention that entails the design for a rural, online learning community.

2. METHODOLOGY
We conducted our needs assessment exercise in three learning environments (after-school classrooms) situated in the villages of Uthiramerur, Vadanallur, and Kulathakarai in the Kancheepuram district of Tamil Nadu (India). We obtained access to these classrooms through our collaboration with a local NGO that has been implementing learning projects in the state since 1996. We held interviews with 5 classroom tutors and 5 NGO staff, interacted with all 60 students (evenly distributed from third to sixth grades), and conducted participant observation over a period of six weeks. The goal was to understand the students' interaction with learning technologies introduced by their tutors in class. We used TFL – a mobile application developed by the NGO – as a design probe [3]. TFL was shown to the students in the after-school classrooms on a US$70 Android device. Students in two of three classrooms were taught how to use the device and application at the start of the study. In the third classroom, the application was introduced after two weeks to offer a point of comparison. Students engaged with the device on a one-to-one basis. We solicited feedback from students and factored it into the design through iterations every two weeks.

3. LEARNING MATH ON TABLETS
TFL was designed by the NGO to present third to sixth graders with math problems, the content of which was determined in collaboration with local tutors (employed by the NGO). The user interface (UI) was designed to be minimal for first-time tablet users (all students were well-versed with basic/feature mobile phones but not computers or the internet). The first prototype of the app had a home screen with four test options – *Addition*, *Subtraction*, *Multiplication*, *Division* – and a *Summary* tab. If a student selected one of the four topics, she/he would be prompted to type out her/his name and then be presented with eight/nine problems on that topic, with increasing difficulty. Each screen had one problem on the selected topic on top, a number pad below, and a large rectangular box for rough work. There were two additional buttons, one for *backspace* and one for *next question*. Students received immediate feedback, with applause for a correct response and a squeak otherwise. By selecting the Summary button on the home screen, the tutors were able to view (and edit/delete) the names and responses of students who had taken the above tests. Tutors used these summaries to assess areas that needed attention for each student.

4. UNDERSTANDING CONTEXT
We now describe lessons we learned from our needs assessment exercise and motivate our future work in this space.

4.1 'Appropriate' Technology
The UI of the app was designed to be minimal in order to avoid any confusion/fear on the students' part, especially since most of them had never used a tablet before. We did not find the students confused by the design in any way. They also adapted quickly to minor application updates such as changing the rough work area to occupy more screen space in lieu of less space for the number pad. Our takeaway was that tablet applications, designed appropriately, could be a suitable technological medium for these children to interact with and learn on. Tutors also showed no hesitation in using and experimenting with a new platform. Since English was the medium of instruction at each of these schools (even though conversations largely took place in Tamil), there were no linguistic barriers to be concerned about either.

ACM DEV 2015, December 01-02, 2015, London, United Kingdom
ACM 978-1-4503-3490-7/15/11.
http://dx.doi.org/10.1145/2830629.2835219

4.2 More Avenues for Exploration

The comfort level of tutors became apparent when we found that they had downloaded free third-party educational content from the Google Play store. One of the tutors mentioned that she had heard from someone about a good English learning application on the Play store, so she downloaded it and gave it to students to play with. Other tools downloaded by the tutors included apps that taught students how to count large sets of objects and conduct household science experiments. Students also displayed an interest to use the tablet to do their homework. The tablet thus came to be used more as a learning and practice tool, as against its original purpose to facilitate aptitude testing and skill-set analysis. We view this as significant, revealing the potential of such applications for teaching *and* learning in rural Indian settings.

4.3 Opportunities for Personalized Learning

Tutors utilized the app data to maintain an official record of each student's individual progress, and began to assign content that was appropriate for each child. Each student's progress was independent of the rest of the class's progress. Over six weeks, tutors prepared a comprehensive record of the required math focus areas for each student, and gave the student appropriate math problems for practice in class and as homework. Students thus received a personalized curriculum and engaged in self-paced learning of math for six weeks.

Opportunities for personalized learning are particularly relevant here because the students are from different grades. Tutors are cognizant of each student's grade and background and therefore appreciated being able to test whether the different students' performances were satisfactory. Sixth graders did ask for more challenging problems and we will factor this in for future work.

4.4 Improved Learning Outcomes

None of the students had been exposed to a tablet prior to this study. As mentioned, one classroom of students was not given the tablet for the first two weeks. Midway into our study, at the end of three weeks, we found that students in the classrooms that were provided with a tablet practiced more math than the students who did not have the tablet, all else unchanged, and the students in the former group were able to verbally convey the procedures to carry out three digit multiplications with more confidence than the students in the latter group.

The tutors told us that after the introduction of the tablet in the classroom, students engaged themselves in more group discussions on difficult math problems, and voiced their opinion to the class more often than before the tablet was introduced. There were multiple instances of self-organized learning, where students sat in a circle around the tablet, and tried to collaborate and solve a difficult math question, or a technical glitch in the software, with varying success levels. The NGO's hope was that with this model of learning, the increase in classroom engagement would reduce dropout rates, which remains a serious concern.

5. FUTURE WORK

Given our lessons from the six-week study, we propose a holistic model to incorporate mobile technologies into a larger online learning environment. Our model is centered on the design of a rural, online, learning community with participation from students, tutors, NGO staff, and curriculum designers. We will continue work with the same NGO and classrooms to ensure that our lessons remain applicable. This NGO has been operating after-school classrooms in 35 villages in the vicinity, including the three we studied. The tutors voiced the intent of connecting students across these classrooms to a centralized database of educational content that is both engaging for students and valuable for tutors. The NGO is keen to support this intent.

At the core of this social learning environment will be a forum for questions, ideas, announcements, and general threads of interest. The content would – by design – be open-source and comprised of a repository of books, texts, videos and other supporting educational material, such as curricula and testing guides. Tutors would have the ability to curate the content so that it is within the broad guidelines of being meaningful, updated, and inclusive. The platform will allow for hosting video sessions, where students and tutors may participate in discussions and collaborations. Tutors will organize and lead lecture sessions and review discussions in such a space. Students will be able to use this space for team projects, personal discussions, and interactions with students from other schools and/or social backgrounds.

From a technical standpoint, the platform must have the capability to support large volumes of data and large numbers of users in the presence of low data transfer speeds and low rendering capacities of browsers and machines. The platform must also exist as a real-time communication system, with cloud storage. We note that 3G connectivity was available consistently across these villages although it may not be reliable enough for video sessions. We will start with sharing text and audio content. Tasks requiring larger bandwidth will be postponed until better connectivity is available – potentially via "small-scale cellular networks" [4].

A curriculum with an online platform for communication and collaboration as a central component can facilitate partial self-organized learning along with supervised learning, especially in after-school learning spaces. An online platform could grant users a large resource and the ability to experiment with new strategies backed by scientific data. This model provides a support system for a student to fall back on and derive additional support from outside the classroom. Students may use this community as a tool to aid them in academic as well as co-curricular development such as moral skills, leisure reading, and exposure to new hobbies, ideas, and innovations. We hope that provision of meaningful content will overcome the constraints imposed by poor infrastructure to address existing gaps in formal and informal learning environments, thereby overcoming the last mile challenge in offering effective education.

6. REFERENCES

[1] Cross, A., et al. "VidWiki: Enabling the crowd to improve the legibility of online educational videos." *(CSCW '14)*.

[2] Cross, A., et al. "TypeRighting: combining the benefits of handwriting and typeface in online educational videos." *(CHI '13)*

[3] Gaver, B., Dunne, T., and Pacenti, E. "Design: cultural probes." *Interactions* 6.1 (1999): 21-29.

[4] Heimerl, K., et al. "Local, sustainable, small-scale cellular networks." *(ICTD '13)*

[5] Kam, M., et al. "Designing digital games for rural children: a study of traditional village games in India." *(CHI '09)*

[6] Kumar, A., et al. "An exploratory study of unsupervised mobile learning in rural India." *(CHI '10)*

[7] Wang, R., et al. "The Digital Study Hall." Computer Science Department, Princeton University, Tech. Rep. TR-723-05 (2005).

Text for a Ride, in Uganda[+]

Silvia Figueira, Michael Brew, Bryant Larsen,
Pratyusha Joginipally,
Sowmya Chandrashekarappa
Frugal Innovation Lab, Santa Clara University
Santa Clara, California, USA
1-408-554-4105
sfigueira@scu.edu

Ty Van Herweg
Fulbright Scholar, Wakabi
Uganda
ty.vanherweg@gmail.com

ABSTRACT

Cellular phones have been enabling people to connect everywhere. Through social networks or applications that provide important services, people in communities around the world have been using cellular phones to solve important problems. Considering this ubiquitous availability of cellular phones, we have developed an SMS-based system to connect boda-boda drivers with people that need transportation in remote rural areas in Uganda. Our system is being tested in the field and will be used in the near future by Wakabi, a local social enterprise.

Categories and Subject Descriptors

K.4 [Computers and Society]: Social Issues, Organizational Impacts

General Terms

Design, Economics, Human Factors

Keywords

SMS-Based System, Transportation in Rural Africa

1. INTRODUCTION

In Uganda, 85% of the population lives in rural areas [1] and many people do not have the means to transport either themselves or their goods to where they need to go. Farmers need to move their produce, business people may need to work in big cities, and non-governmental and charity organizations need to ship their supplies to those in need. These objectives should not be impeded by the lack of access to transportation.

In Uganda, there are currently fleets of hire-able motorcyclists that will ferry people and goods between remote villages and big cities, but connecting drivers and riders is a difficult process that decreases the potential effectiveness of the entire system. The service relies on word of mouth and does not provide a unified interface for riders to request drivers, leaving many villagers helpless. On the other hand, drivers spend much of their time waiting around for potential customers because they generally only have access to a limited pool of clientele.

To solve that problem, we have developed a system to connect drivers with riders. As shown in Figure 1, our mobile solution allows people needing rides to connect with drivers who are in

ACM DEV 2015, December 01-02, 2015, London, United Kingdom
ACM 978-1-4503-3490-7/15/11.
http://dx.doi.org/10.1145/2830629.2835220.

need of clients via SMS. Users send a text message with their location to a predefined number. A motorcyclist registered with our service then receives the message if he or she is in a nearby location and responds by either accepting or rejecting the request. If accepted, the rider's phone number is sent to the driver so that a meeting location can be established. These drivers pay a monthly fee to be registered with our service while collecting their fare directly from the riders.

Note that, to compensate for the lack of access to GPS information in the phones used in rural areas in Uganda, our system provides a numbered list of regions from which both drivers and riders select a number to determine their location. Given that, the proximity between drivers and riders may not be precise, but this is a small inconvenience considering the service provided by our system.

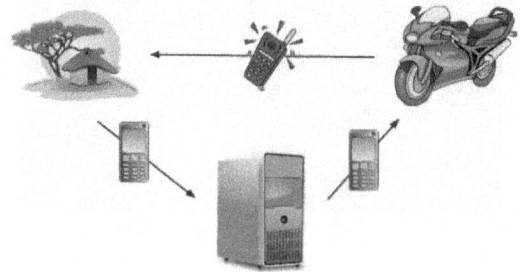

Figure 1. Conceptual model for our SMS-based ride system.

A system that connects people who have transportation needs with available motorcyclists through SMS will open the door for many of those that were previously bound by their lack of transportation. Drivers will receive SMS messages whenever someone needs a ride, decreasing their idle time and, consequently, increasing their profit. With the possibility of attaching trailers to the motorcycles, large quantities of goods can also be moved on demand. We are not giving the people of Uganda new modes of transportation, but we are connecting drivers and riders so that they cooperatively help one another.

Our system is being deployed and tested in a rural community in Uganda, and the initial feedback was positive. By using SMS and cloud services, deployment was simple and our system has the chance to scale throughout rural Uganda.

2. FEASIBILITY STUDY

Before starting this project, we researched the feasibility of such a tool, and the findings were promising. In [2], Kalba provides an insightful article about how the use of "Mobile Money" has expanded within Africa in the past six years. His analysis shows that services offered through mobile technology have been well received by the African population. Our conclusion was that, if users are comfortable trusting SMS to handle their banking transactions, they will similarly trust SMS to handle their transportation needs as well.

In [3], the authors present the findings of a survey asking Ugandans if they would support an SMS-based service that relays personal medical information. The majority of participants said they would use such a service, while 90% said they were unconcerned about unintended disclosure. These results gave us confidence to build an SMS service specifically to the Ugandan market.

In addition, in [4] the authors include survey results concerning boda demographics. The majority of drivers are young males between 16 and 30 years of age, and many reported that they feel it is impossible for them to eventually own the actual motorcycles they use. Hopefully with the use of our system, they will have more customers, thereby increasing their income.

3. THE SYSTEM

Our system contains two main modules, the front-end, which interacts with the administrator, and the back-end, which interacts with the drivers and riders. The front-end entails a web portal, as shown in Figure 2, which enables the administrator to manage the system, add drivers, check their status and evaluations, and so on.

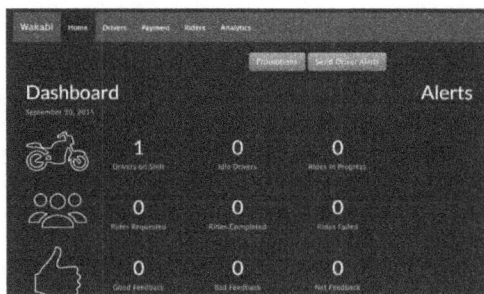

Figure 2. Web portal.

The back-end entails the SMS communication with the drivers and riders. When the drivers are available, they check in and make their location available through SMS. When a rider wants a ride, he/she communicates his/her location and receives a phone number for a nearby driver, all through SMS. The driver and rider talk on the phone and arrange the pick up. After the ride, the driver makes himself available again, by sending the new location to the system. The rider is then asked to evaluate the driver.

Drivers pay the system for a number of rides, and drivers with pre-paid rides are chosen in a round-robin fashion when a ride from their location is requested.

4. DEVELOPMENT

To work in rural Uganda, where people do have cellular phones, but access to data and/or smartphones is limited, our system had to be SMS-based. Also, to simplify the deployment process, our processing and data had to be handled by a commercial cloud service. In addition, when developing applications to be deployed in other countries, it is important to rely on technologies and services that are available anywhere in the world. For this reason, our system was developed based on the technologies shown in Figure 3 and described below.

We chose to use third-party service Twilio to handle all the SMS routing because it had already been deployed and proven to

work in different locations, enabling us to deploy easily in another country.

To host our back-end processing and data, we used Heroku. Using a commercial cloud service enabled an easy deployment in Uganda. Also, it will allow for quick and easy scaling, as well as guaranteed uptime and customer support.

Node.JS was the framework used in the server. Node.JS offers a variety of modules, which are easy to install and integrate. It will allow for easy scaling, while the availability of node modules helped speed up development.

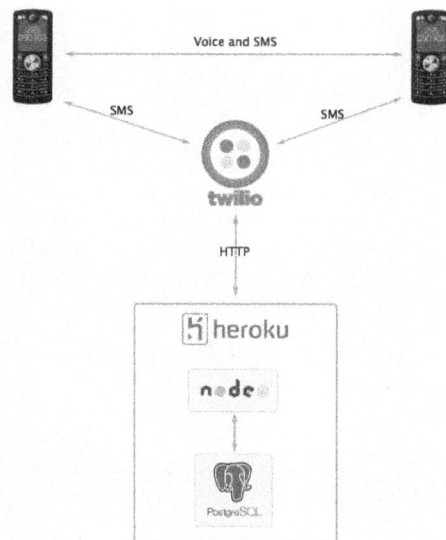

Figure 3. Technologies used.

5. CONCLUSION

Developing an SMS-based system to help connect drivers and riders in remote locations will solve several problems such as the transportation of goods to buyers. Solving these problems will help local businesses to flourish and remote communities to develop.

6. REFERENCES

[1] Rural Population. *The World Bank*. DOI - http://data.worldbank.org/indicator/SP.RUR.TOTL.ZS.

[2] Kalba, K. Africa's Mobile Money Story. *Intermedia*, 41 (5), 26-29.

[3] Siedner, M.J., Haberer, J.E., Bosco Bwana, M., Ware, N.C., and Bangsberg, D.R. High acceptability for cell phone text messages to improve communication of laboratory results with HIV-infected patients in rural Uganda: a cross-sectional survey study. *BMC Medical Informatics & Decision Making*, 12 (1), 56-62.

[4] Kisaalita, W.S. and Sentongo-Kibalama, J. Delivery of urban transport in developing countries: the case for the motorcycle taxi service (bodaboda) operators of Kampala. *Development Southern Africa*, 24 (2), 345-357.

· This work has been supported in part by a gift from Vodafone Americas Foundation.

Improving Flight Accuracy for Aerial Wildlife Surveys in Sub-Saharan Africa

Howard Frederick[1], Edward Kohi[2], Jay Lorenzo[3], Michael Coyote[3], Ted Schmitt[3] and Kirk Larsen[3]

[1]Independent consultant, Arusha, Tanzania; simbamangu@gmail.com
[2]TAWIRI, Arusha, Tanzania; edward.kohi@yahoo.co.uk
[3]Vulcan Inc., Seattle, WA; {jayl, michaelc, teds, kirkl}@vulcan.com

ABSTRACT

Aerial surveys are vital to assessing animal populations as part of an effort to understand ecosystem health, a primary component of social and economic development in rural regions of Africa. This paper describes the design, deployment and preliminary performance results of a mobile application that provides visual real-time feedback to assist cockpit crews conducting aerial surveys.

Categories and Subject Descriptors

H.5.2 [**User Interfaces**]: Graphical user interfaces (GUI); J.7 [**Computers In Other Systems**]: Real time

Keywords

Flight Data Logger; Transect; Aerial Survey

1. INTRODUCTION

Healthy ecosystems, including thriving wildlife populations, are a major component of social and economic development across many regions in rural Africa. The monitoring of wildlife populations, including the use of aerial surveys, is essential to healthy ecosystems as it informs wildlife management planning, identifies poaching hotspots, and tracks ecological trends.

A common method of aerial survey called a systematic reconnaissance flight, or transect sample count, is conducted by flying carefully defined lines in a given region, counting the animals observed within the strips visible from each side of the aircraft and then extrapolating to estimate the total population [1]. The lines, called transects, must be flown within a precise altitude, speed and course to minimize the extrapolation errors and to enable comparison with previous results where possible.

Maintaining altitude and course is difficult since multiple instruments typically need to be referenced simultaneously by the pilot (e.g. altimeter, GPS and airspeed). Consistency in flying performance is important not only for general safety but also for providing a consistent platform for observation, and minimizing biases. The software and hardware package described in this paper was designed to reduce the burden on the pilot by integrating altimeter, speed and GPS into a single console with a graphical indicator and altitude deviation.

The software further simplifies the management of flying individual transects by allowing a flight plan of transects to be pre-loaded, as well as logging flight data automatically instead of by the manual recording on paper by a Front Seat Observer (FSO) or surveyor.

This paper describes the design and usage of an Android-based survey assistance device we call the Flightlogger, developed as part of the Great Elephant Census project [2] (GEC), which makes improvements in these areas:

(i) *Flight accuracy.* Provide an in-flight management system that helps the pilot navigate to and maintain course on individual transects through a real-time integrated display of altitude, speed and location.

(ii) *Cognitive load reduction.* Automate the collection of flight data such as transect start/stops and altitude readings enabling the FSO to focus upon collecting other data.

(iii) *Flight data error reduction.* Provide a pre-flight system that loads a full flight plan (e.g. transects for a given region and day) via GPX files and provide a post-flight system that downloads the recorded flight data.

Additional requirements were to create a unit with a cost below $500 USD, that was ruggedized for rural African environments. It required intuitive UI controls to minimize the amount of training needed, and had to be easily installable in a wide variety of survey aircraft.

2. DESIGN AND IMPLEMENTATION

The Flightlogger system is based on a 7" Android tablet, which acquires altitude readings from a laser altimeter mounted externally on the survey aircraft. The tablet is mounted to the aircraft dashboard using a small flight case containing a 3D-printed tablet mount, supplemental battery for all-day flying and a serial to USB converter which interfaces with the USB port on the tablet.

The system includes a set of distributed services that are responsible for sampling and validating incoming data from sensor and altimeter input, and assembling it into time sensitive samples. It then broadcasts that data every second for use by the logging and user facing components of the system.

One goal of this design was to allow the tablet to be detached from the system and carried by the survey team for

ACM DEV 2015, December 1–2, 2015, London, United Kingdom.
ACM 978-1-4503-3490-7/15/11.
DOI: http://dx.doi.org/10.1145/2830629.2835221.

preflight setup and post-flight analysis. During flight planning, surveyors plot the routes and transects for the survey on laptops or workstations, save the routes using the GPX interchange format, and transfer them to the tablet via USB. The device is then reattached to the flight case, which initializes and displays a set of status lights. The purpose of these lights is to give a visual representation of altimeter, GPS and battery health. These status lights provide a means of alerting the survey team to possible issues that may arise both preflight and during the flight.

To choose a transect to survey, the user selects from a list of routes that are displayed on the tablet. Once a route is selected, the device displays the distance to the first transect, and provides a means to start logging flight data. Data is logged every second, which relieves the FSO from manually recording altitude samples and transect waypoints.

The flight interface mimics a standard Instrument Landing System (ILS) cockpit display, leveraging the pilot training that goes into interpreting the graphical altitude and course markers on an ILS display. When flying a specified transect, deviation from the target course is shown with one marker (vertical), while deviation from the target altitude is shown by another (horizontal; in combination the two show a crosshair). If the aircraft goes outside of the expected range (in altitude or course) then the markers change color as an additional visual cue. To increase flight accuracy, altimeter readings obtained while flying over trees and other natural features, are averaged within a 5 second window.

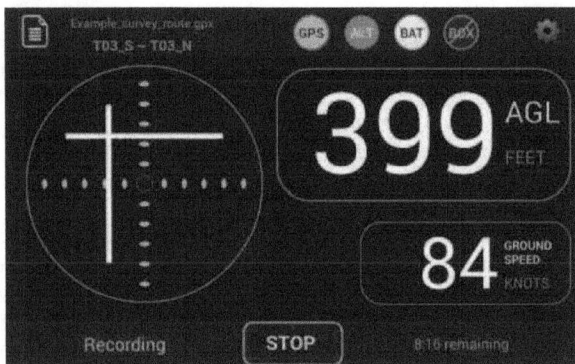

Figure 1: Flightlogger main interface

Post flight, the tablet provides a means to summarize the transects flown, generating both GPX- and CSV-formatted reports of the data collected. The survey teams can then download the reports for further analysis by attaching the tablet to their laptop.

3. EVALUATION

As our work has been in support of the ongoing GEC it has been difficult to obtain experimentally significant measurements of the impact of Flightlogger over the course of the census because repeat survey flights are not pragmatic.

We have however, been able to make comparisons using similar aircraft and pilots in the field, which we believe is representative of the results that have been achieved to date.

We examine three survey flights flown in similar terrain in sub-Saharan Africa, evaluating differences between planes and pilots. We compare the deviation from desired survey height (AGL) for three flights in Figure 2.

Surveys flown with the Flightlogger display smaller deviations than those flown with a traditional radar altimeter system, and a smaller range of deviations, indicating that flight performance is improved.

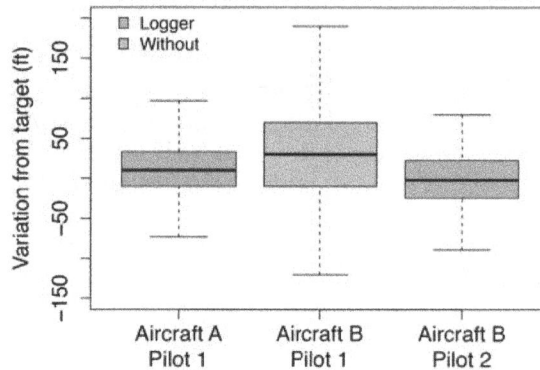

Figure 2: Transect accuracy with and without the flight data logger, with boxplots showing deviations from target heights.

Not easily captured in statistics is the improved workflow in the cockpit, as the front seat observer is relieved of numerous data capture tasks, reducing cognitive load.

The GEC has flown 18 of 21 countries planned to date. The Flightlogger system has been used by eight crews surveying in Kenya, Tanzania, Mozambique, Zimbabwe, Botswana, Zambia, and the Western trans boundary countries, representing a majority of overall elephant populations.

4. CONCLUSIONS

The Flightogger has provided a focused technical intervention that has been shown to increase the productivity of aerial surveys supporting the GEC, at least as shown by preliminary and anecdotal results.

Acceptance of the Flightlogger has been favorable. We initially anticipated building 10 units for the GEC, but have sent 19 to date, with further requests indicating positive adoption. Future work will include evaluating this project with more data and in more detail, and to look at end to end system problems of the GEC.

5. ACKNOWLEDGEMENTS

We are indebted to Falk Grossman and Dr. Mike Chase for their support and feedback. We are grateful to the Paul G. Allen Family Foundation for the funding of the Great Elephant Census. Our thanks go to the GEC PI team at Vulcan, especially Dr. Kathleen Gobush, Lauren Kickham and Joel Masselink.

6. REFERENCES

[1] CRAIG, G. C. Aerial Survey Standards for the MIKE Programme. Version 2.0. https://www.cites.org/common/prog/mike/survey/aerial_standards.pdf, 2012. Accessed: 2015-10-07.

[2] The Great Elephant Census: Project Description. http://www.greatelephantcensus.com/the-census/, 2014. Accessed: 2015-10-07.

Enabling Compliance of Environmental Conditions

Utkarsh Dwivedi*
IBM Research India, New Delhi
utkdwive@in.ibm.com

Anirban Dasgupta
IIT Gandhinagar
anirbandg@iitgn.ac.in

ABSTRACT

Industrial projects in India have to agree to specific sets of environmental conditions in order to function. Lack of compliance with these conditions results both in irreversible damage to the local environment as well as conflicts among the industry and the local community. Our aim is to provide a system that raises general awareness in the local community about the environmental conditions in vogue among the nearby industries so that compliance violations can be reported early on. We outline work in progress to mine the text of the clearance conditions and build a searchable mapping system that can answer various queries about these conditions.

1. INTRODUCTION

Over the last few decades, India has seen a rapid growth in industrial development. The number of new industrial projects that are being setup each year has in fact been accelerating. The challenge, therefore, is to maintain the quality of different environmental indicators while reconciling the economic and social needs. The mechanism to measure and check the effect of environmental impact is controlled by different government regulatory agencies– the Ministry of Environmental Affairs etc. For each new industrial site or infrastructure expansion, the appropriate authorities issue an Environmental Impact Assessment, following which the project can be cleared. The concerns raised by the regulatory authorities, local citizenry and civic bodies (e.g. village or city administration) are codified in terms of "Environmental Clearance" (EC) documents. These documents form a legal contract that the corresponding industry has to abide by. Ensuring compliance to the conditions stated in the EC is the obvious next step needed to maintain the environmental status quo. Currently, such compliance checks are done by the same regulatory authorities, who are severely resource constrained. As a result, compliance to these conditions is a severe issue. A recent report by the organization Namati, in collaboration with local organizations in Mundra, [3] details rather extensively the inadequacy of compliance in most industrial projects there and its effect on the local fishing and other communities. Citizen complaints to the PCBs are an important mechanism to trigger compliance monitoring and enforcement. As per the OECD report [1], in Maharashtra, between April 2004 and March 2005, citizens filed 761 complaints with respect to air, water, solid waste and noise pollution. However, citizen complaints can be not productive (or not useful in a legal proceeding) if they are unrelated to the exact clearance conditions. Thus a potential solution to the compliance issue could be found if the larger community could be made aware of the environmental issues and the various restrictions that have been imposed on the industries functioning in their locality.

In order to both encourage citizen complaints by spreading awareness of the clearance conditions in effect, and to ensure that such complaints are actually related to environmental clearance conditions, it would thus be useful if we could make the documents accessible to as broad a population as possible.

2. PROBLEM AND TOOLS

The Ministry of Environmental Affairs (MoEF) does an admirable job of keeping the EC documents in the public domain. However, there are still a number of barriers for a general user in comprehending and utilizing the information stored in these EC documents. These are the following:

- EC documents are available publically, but they are not easily searchable, and extracting any information from them requires significant amount of effort.

- The technical language of these documents inhibits an easy comprehension of what the conditions are. For each industrial site, there is actually a collection of documents, with addendums to the original. Each such document contains a collection of clearance conditions.

- The user is typically not able to get a global view of the clearance conditions associated with a particular region or location.

3. SOLUTION

We collected the EC documents and identified their locations using a regular expression based strategy. Next, we applied text mining tools, namely Latent Dirichlet Allocation (LDA) based modeling of the collected clearance conditions from all documents. This identifies the latent topic for each clearance conditions, and can then be used to cluster conditions as well as identify similar conditions to a given one.

3.1 Collecting and preprocessing the data

Environmental clearances are available at the MoEF website http://environmentalclearances.nic.in (13614 clearances granted till July, 2014) which are html, pdf or scanned pdfs, we worked with html files. An EC document contains a file number, addresses of the MoEF and concerned company, subject with location and name of project. It begins with an introduction to the project, and conditions of the clearance if granted, subdivided to general and specific conditions. This text suffered from irregularities in following a common notation for clearances, file number formats. We programmatically downloaded html files, scraped them, and violations were extracted using REGEX. We extracted the file number for indexing, location of a project and the clearance conditions. Then the data was stripped of stopwords, and stemmed to build a vocabulary. Finally, we made a corpus of 24 manually chosen and 600 scraped EC docs, yielding 700 and 8500 clearance conditions respectively. Now we had to make sense of this text, we used 20 EC's, a subset of this corpus for further analysis.

ACM DEV 2015, December 01-02, 2015, London, United Kingdom
ACM 978-1-4503-3490-7/15/11.
http://dx.doi.org/10.1145/2830629.2835223

* - work done as a visiting scholar from IIT Guwahati at IIT Gandhinagar

4. USING LDA FOR CLUSTERING

We used Latent Dirichlet Allocation technique for making sense of the compliance conditions, using online batch based approximation, which is faster than a full corpus based approach [2]. This allows us to introduce structure to this unstructured data, helping us cluster it and define similarity. We use the open source Python implementation provided by the authors.

5. RESULTS

We found best parameters for LDA empirically and implemented the recommended TFIDF inspired term score i.e. Hellinger distance grouping for the sense of similarity between two documents. These results are for a 13 topic running of LDA over a corpus of 700 violations from 24 clearance documents.

5.1 Document Similarity

To allow us to determine the efficacy of the treatment of these conditions by LDA, we made the corpus searchable using an open source searching and indexing library, Whoosh in Python. When a query of a particular clearance would be entered, two of the most conditions would be returned using the TFIDF inspired similarity score [2]. Below is an example of a query and its response. The following is an example of a query document:

"Separate funds shall be allocated for implementation of environmental protection measures long with item-wise break-up."

For the above query document, we found the following two nearest documents to it using the Hellinger distance over the topic vectors:

"Special package with implementation schedule for free potable drinking water supply in the nearby villages and schools shall be undertaken in a time bound manner."

"A special scheme for upliftment of SC & ST population in the study area shall be formulated and implemented in a time bound manner..."

Thus we can see, some associations can be made using this LDA topic models– we are working to further improve this clustering. We are also working to setup a search index using keywords e.g. 'forest', 'encroachment' etc. allowing an easier way to explore these documents.

5.2 Clustering and keywords

We then clustered conditions using these topic distribution vectors, using K-means method with K determined empirically as K = 10. We extracted top 10 keywords in these cluster of clearance conditions using TFIDF. Figure 1 shows term distributions over for a topic. Figure 2 shows top words of some clusters that made most sense.

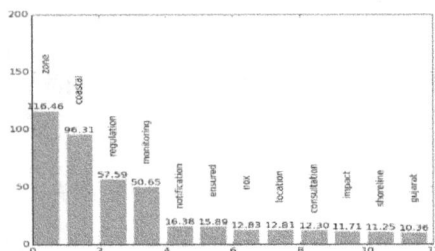

Figure 1: Term Distribution of a Topic

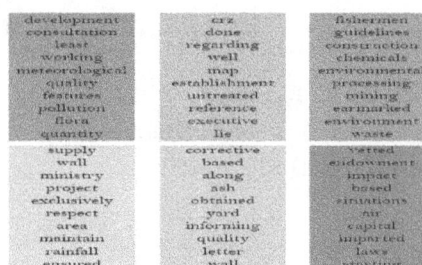

Figure 2: TFIDF ranked word descriptors for topic clusters

6. LOCATION MAPPING

For making a geographic sense of these documents we made use of the subject line and a record of all clearances. Figure 3 shows the results over a map of Gujarat. Currently one can hover over the marker to view the file number of the corresponding environmental clearance, presenting an overview of the dataset.

Figure 3: Automatic location mapping results

7. CONCLUSION

This project is work-in-progress and we are currently working on developing better indexing and visualization methods for the EC documents. We plan to use MTurk to transcribe scanned pdfs and construct a rich repository of the regulatory information in India. On the other hand, in collaboration with Namati, we have also built a Ushahidi based web platform (http://env-compliance.in) to collect the compliance related complaints by the local environmental activists. We are currently working to integrate the compliance report collecting portal with the document analysis and visualization site and build a one-stop portal where interested users can analyze existing environmental compliance conditions as well as upload reports and evidences for violations of these. We plan to conduct a qualitative assessment of this system, to see if relevant search results are being returned, and if one can make associations with the compliance condition and the triggering activity.

8. REFERENCES

[1] Environmental Compliance and Enforcement in India: Rapid Assessment.
http://www.oecd.org/environment/outreach/37838061.pdf.

[2] Matthew Hoffman, Francis R Bach, and David M Blei. Online learning for latent dirichlet allocation. In advances in neural information processing systems, pages 856–864, 2010.

[3] Namati, Mundra Hitrakshak Manch (Forum for the Protection of Rights in Mundra), Machimar Adhikar Sangharsh Sangathan (MASS), Ujjas Mahila Sangathan. Closing the enforcement gap:Findings of a community-led ground truthing of environmental violations in Mundra.
http://www.namati.org/wpcontent/uploads/2013/ 10/Kutch-proofed-0.1-merged.pdf

From sustainable Community Networks to sustainable Community Clouds

Roger Baig
Fundació Guifi.net
Gurb, Catalonia
roger.baig@guifi.net

Felix Freitag
UPC
Barcelona, Spain
felix@ac.upc.edu

Agustí Moll
Routek, SL
Barcelona, Catalonia
agusti@routek.net

Leandro Navarro
UPC
Barcelona, Spain
leandro@ac.upc.edu

Roger Pueyo
Routek, SL
Barcelona, Catalonia
rogerpueyo@routek.net

Ramon Roca
Fundació Guifi.net
Gurb, Catalonia
ramon.roca@guifi.net

Categories and Subject Descriptors

C.2 [**Computer-Communication Networks**]: Community Networks; J.m [**Computer Applications**]: Miscellaneous—*Community Clouds*

Keywords

Community networks, community clouds, sustainability.

1. INTRODUCTION

The advent of community networks has shown that citizens can take action not only at the technical level to expand the Internet but also at the governance level. What started as isolated and uncoordinated efforts to, mainly, bring connectivity to undeserved areas (using hacked WiFi devices – the so called Wireless communities) has evolved into self-organised groups offering effective tools to empower people to self-satisfy their telecommunication needs under sustainable alternative models to the dominant one in the global Internet.

Inspired by the success of community networks we propose the community network cloud (community cloud) as an instrument to fight the threat posed by the concentration of vast amount of data in few multinational corporations (privacy, vendor lock-in, etc.) and to make the use of the community network infrastructure more efficient. We argue that a cloud formed by community-owned local computing and communication resources able to provide services of local interest, can emerge and be sustainable if the appropriate tools and mechanisms are in place to coordinate the collective action in an effective manner. Our studies [1] on guifi.net[1] unveiled a comprehensive model for deploying and operating network infrastructure as a common-pool resource [2] with the required governance tools fully operational. Stimulated by our findings on the guifi.net model for network infrastructure we elaborated a proposal and a work plan to develop community clouds. Here we present the principles of our proposal, its state of development, the results already achieved, the next steps and the conclusions drawn.

2. COMMUNITY CLOUD AS A COMMON-POOL RESOURCE

The fundamental principles of guifi.net, which revolve around i) the openness of access (usage) of the infrastructure, and ii) the openness of participation (construction, operation, governance) in the development of the infrastructure and its community, also apply to the community cloud, defined to be fully inclusive. The application of these fundamental principles result in a community cloud resource and service infrastructure which is a *collective good*, *socially produced*, and governed as a *common-pool resource*.

3. DEVELOPMENT

The development of the community cloud and its implementation in guifi is an iterative process. The phases are:

- Phase 1: Identification of local, specific end-user needs that can be satisfied applying knowledge, experience with research, development and deployment of a small pilot and evaluation of initial impact.

- Phase 2: Learning from the previous cycle, with co-design and co-development of new solutions, larger pilot, evaluation of impact, and analysis of initial innovation as template models, and probably expansion to a few external pilots, transposing the models and solutions already developed.

- Phase 3: Consolidation, refinement, generalisation, transposition, formalisation of sustainable, scalable innovation processes, and therefore enabling and supporting replication to many other communities.

4. CURRENT STATUS AND IMPACT

We are currently completing the first phase of development. Our key software component is *Cloudy*, a Debian-based GNU/Linux distribution for low-consumption devices

---

[1]The largest community network to the best of our knowledge with 30,000 working nodes, 55,000 kms of links.

ACM DEV 2015, December 01-02, 2015, London, United Kingdom
ACM 978-1-4503-3490-7/15/11.
http://dx.doi.org/10.1145/2830629.2835222.

(e.g. RaspberryPi) to be attached to the community network, including a set of software components covering infrastructure, platform and application services adapted to the characteristics of the community network infrastructure (low availability, unstable links, limited throughput, etc.). Computing resources come as virtual machines (containers). The central platform component is a service announcement and discovery[2] which uses the Serf gossip protocol for exchanging information about services available. Platform components include basic tools for building community networks (DNS naming, network monitoring, Web proxy), as well as many end-user oriented services (group and private (encrypted) distributed storage, live and on-demand video, etc.).

The status of deployment of the community cloud infrastructure is measured by the number of instances deployed and services provided. The values are obtained through a publicly available Cloudy instance [3]. Figure 1 shows the evolution of the number of these numbers along the forth week of September 2015 from the perspective of this public instance. Obviously, the number of cloudy instances is the highest followed the number of Serf instances[4]. More interesting is to observe the distribution of the rest of services. Two groups can be clearly identified. The first, with an average around one third of the cloudy instances seen, and the second with only two or three instances in average. The first group is composed by all the traditional guifi.net services (DNS, Proxy, and Graph server) and, interestingly, a distributed mass storage service (Syncthing). The second group (PeerStreamer and OWP) includes less attractive services for the community[5].

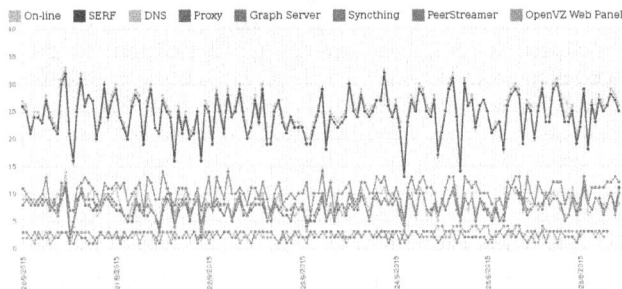

Figure 1: Number of Cloudy instances and services in the community cloud during one week.

In terms of social participation, the number of subscribers of the users mailing list (47) is an evidence of the interest of the guifi.net community and number of subscribers of the development mailing list (23) shows that this interest goes beyond the mere consumption. In the last annual face-to-face guifi.net community meeting the discussion showed interest in several key aspects: infrastructure, with many participants willing to deploy Cloudy nodes as part of a second phase of expansion to duplicate the number of nodes; software, with a discussion of improvements of Cloudy and the development of new components with additional support for

---

[2]DADS, Distributed announcement and discovery of services
[3]`http://demo.cloudy.community` User, Password: *guest*
[4]Serf is active by default, so in steady state these two numbers should match. The remaining services must be manually activated, therefore not running in all instances.
[5]Both were introduced during the development of Cloudy.

new services; services, with ideas for new services, migration of existing guifi.net services to Cloudy for better availability and quality of use, maintenance and integration of these services; governance, with an initial discussion about models and limits of contribution, consumption, compensation, and specifically the balance between individuals and professional resource and service providers.

Regarding economic activity, one SME is already developing a tailored solution for remote encrypted mass storage using Cloudy as a platform and we are aware of others which are also considering to port some of their services to it.

5. FUTURE WORK

We have identified the balance between the efforts spent in deploying, operating and governing the network infrastructure, which brings practical experience and sustainability to the infrastructure, and the efforts spent in developing the definition, organisation and governance of the framework, which guarantees the feasibility and scalability of the whole ecosystem, as one of the of the keys to success. Now that we have an effective tool for deploying the community cloud (Cloudy and its integrated services) and a significant number of Cloudy instances already in place and growing organically, we will focus our efforts in improving the framework by i) defining its boundaries and developing a license to protect the cloud ecosystem; ii) defining the rules for appropriation and contribution of resources and services, and the economic compensation system to enable and harmonise any economic activity; iii) identifying the best practises as templates for innovation in service development and provision using the guifi.net community cloud.

6. CONCLUSIONS

Community network clouds have a disruptive potential with local cloud resource and service infrastructures open for access (usage), and open for participation (construction, operation, governance), organised and governed as common-pool resources. This model originates and translates from the mature guifi.net network infrastructure model. The successful uptake of our Cloudy software reveals the user interest, acceptance and positive impact of our proposal. Ongoing challenges are in supporting the growth of the community cloud in terms of contribution of additional computing resources, development and operation of additional services, further definition of the framework for participation, definition of best practises, and a detailed evaluation of the socio-economic impact of this cloud commons.

7. ACKNOWLEDGMENTS

This work was supported by several projects: the European Commission FP7 FIRE CONFINE (FP7-288535), CLOMMUNITY (FP7-317879), H2020 RIFE (H2020-644663), and the Spanish government (TIN2013-47245-C2-1-R).

8. REFERENCES

[1] R. Baig, R. Roca, L. Navarro, and F. Freitag. guifi.net, a crowdsourced network infrastructure held in common. *Elsevier. Computer Networks - In-press*, September 2015.
[2] E. Ostrom. *Governing the commons: the evolution of institutions for collective action.* Cambridge University Press, Nov. 1990.

Growing DEV, Building Community, Making a Difference

Edward Cutrell
Microsoft Research
Bangalore, India
cutrell@microsoft.com
http://research.microsoft.com/~cutrell

ABSTRACT

In 2010 the first edition of ACM DEV was held at Royal Holloway, University of London. The conference was co-located with the ICTD conference, but the idea was to facilitate a more technical conversation between researchers about the state of the art in exploring how ICTs can be used for social and economic development. Since then, we've enjoyed six ACM DEV meetings around the world, published almost 200 papers, and seen students attend their first conference and later return as PIs.

Coincidentally, 2010 was also the same year I took over management of the amazing TEM group at Microsoft Research India and began working full time in ICT4D. One could say that DEV and I have grown up together in the field; I've been to every DEV and have even had the responsibility of organizing it. It's possible we've even matured a little! Lately I've been thinking a lot about what makes research in this area special: Why do people want to work in this space and what can we hope to accomplish together? Since our journeys in this area have been so close, I thought I might be in an interesting position to step back and ask a few questions for DEV as a group:

1) Who is "DEV" and how do we grow our community to thrive in the years ahead? Who do we want to be?

2) What do we want from our conference and community? Sure, it's a place for publishing work, but what else could or should it be?

3) What is our mission? I believe that ICT4D research offers us the opportunity to apply our expertise in technical research to solve very real problems being faced by people who are frequently marginalized or vulnerable and usually ignored by tech. To the extent that the DEV community buys into this notion, how do we progress from publishing ideas to on-the-ground impact?

ACM DEV is six years old and it's still evolving and changing. This is a perfect time to pause and consider what we want it to be both for the future of our community and for the benefit of the people we are working with and for.

Categories and Subject Descriptors
H.5.m. Information interfaces and presentation (e.g., HCI): Miscellaneous.

Keywords
ICTD; Global Development; Accessibility

ACM DEV 2015, December 1–2, 2015, London, United Kingdom.
ACM 978-1-4503-3490-7/15/12.
DOI: http://dx.doi.org/10.1145/2830629.2830652

BIO

I am a Senior Researcher at Microsoft Research India, where I manage the Technology for Emerging Markets group (TEM). I also hold an affiliate faculty appointment in the Information School at the University of Washington and the Department of Software Information Systems at UNC Charlotte. I received my BA in Psychology and Cognitive Science from Rice University. I went on to study Cognitive Neuropsychology at the University of Oregon where I received my PhD. I have been working in the field of Human-Computer Interaction (HCI) since 2000.

My research concerns the exploration and measurement of human interactions with information technology. Over the years, I have worked on a broad range of HCI topics, including input technologies, visual perception and graphics, intelligent notifications and disruptions, and interfaces for search and personal information management. My current research focuses on Information and Communication Technologies for Development (ICTD). I work with a multidisciplinary team to study, design, build, and evaluate technologies and systems that are useful for people living in underserved rural and urban communities. The goal of this work is to understand how people in the world's poor and developing communities interact with information technologies, and to invent new ways for technology to meet their needs and aspirations.

iPeer: A Sociotechnical Systems Approach for Helping Veterans with Civilian Reintegration

Rizwana Rizia[1], Zeno Franco[2], Katinka Hooyer[2], Nadiyah Johnson[1], A B M Kowser Patwary[1],
Golam Mushih Tanimul Ahsan[1], Bob Curry[3], Mark Flower[3], Sheikh Iqbal Ahamed[1]

[1]Marquette University
Ubicomp Lab, WI, USA
{rizwana.rizia, nadiyah.johnson,
abm.patwary,
golammushihtanimul.ahsan,
sheikh.ahamed}@marquette.edu

[2]Medical College of Wisconsin
Milwaukee, WI, USA
zfranco@mcw.edu,
katinka.hooijer@gmail.com

[3]Dryhootch of America
Milwaukee, WI, USA
bob@dryhootch.org,
mark@dryhootch.org

ABSTRACT

The challenges of civilian reintegration can adversely impact the life of veterans. Research shows that peer-mentorship can be very effective for mental health problems. Dryhootch (DH), a veteran-led community organization, has successfully implemented a peer-mentor program for veterans going through civilian reintegration. This article proposes iPeer, a mobile-based augment for the DH peer-mentor program. iPeer tracks the status of the veterans in real-time and presents the status report to veteran mentors (VM) who also went through similar experiences. The participating veterans are assessed semiweekly on their social functioning and risk taking behaviors through surveys. Our major contributions include, (1) proposing a mobile social-computing support for remote and after-hour access of socio-interactive care for veterans going through civilian reintegration, (2) identifying four key issues that need to be addressed when designing such a sociotechnical system for veterans and (3) presenting qualitative evidence about the impact of the technology-augmented process on target-users' experience.

Author Keywords

Veteran mental healthcare; mobile computing; symptom monitoring; electronic peer-mentorship; socio-technical systems; collaboration systems;

ACM Classification Keywords

H.5.m. Information interfaces and presentation (e.g., HCI): Miscellaneous.

INTRODUCTION

Veterans are more likely than ordinary people to suffer from mental illness because they were exposed to traumatic situations during their combat deployment [5]. Approximately 1.7 million troops have deployed as part of Operation Enduring Freedom (OEF) and Operation Iraqi Freedom (OIF). Consensus estimates suggest that around 18.5% of OEF/OIF veterans will be diagnosed with post-traumatic stress disorder (PTSD) [7]. Moreover, many campuses have recently seen a significant increase in the registration of OEF/OIF veterans. Those veterans may suffer from impaired cognitive skills, problems with concentration, difficulty managing assignments, approaching instructors. Therefore, there is a need for services that may help them deal with their limitations [14].

DH is a small non-profit organization independent of any government veteran serving institutions e.g. the Department of Veteran Affairs (VA). DH provides an informal network of peer support to assist veterans reintegrating into civilian life. Each member of DH is a veteran who has dealt with civilian reintegration [8]. Although DH services are open to veterans from all eras, the organization has recently developed an interest in extending its existing peer mentor program to younger student veterans (OEF/OIF veterans). The majority of OEF/OIF veterans are younger than 29 and have specific needs (e. g. after-hours availability of social support services). They are interested in using modern communication mediums (e. g. social media, smartphone apps etc.) [23]. Additionally, many of the reintegration problems reported by veterans such as occupational issues and anger control occur in the "real world" , and are not addressed adequately through hospital based outpatient therapy alone [16]. Furthermore, given the severe consequences of reintegration problems faced by OEF/OIF veterans [12], DH has been focusing on redesigning its successful peer mentor program for digital delivery based on the identified needs of this population.

This article presents an expansion of the DH veteran peer-mentor program, to provide broader access for OEF/OIF veterans specifically on collegiate campuses. The expansion includes - (1) *the development of a mobile phone based peer-mentor support program – iPeer*, (2) *collecting real-time social functioning and risk taking behavioral data from veterans by providing semiweekly surveys via iPeer*, (3) *A report based on the survey results is presented to the*

ACM DEV 2015, December 01-02, 2015, London, United Kingdom
© 2015 ACM. ISBN 978-1-4503-3490-7/15/11…$15.00
DOI: http://dx.doi.org/10.1145/2830629.2830643

VM, thus helping the VM to remotely track his/her mentee's status during civilian reintegration.

Since iPeer project was initiated for student veterans, the paper begins with a description of the civilian reintegration problem faced by this population. The need assessment is presented next. Subsequently, we present the related works. The prototype of iPeer was developed following a collaborative design approach. The stages of this collaborative design, its outcomes and usability findings are described in the subsequent sections. Finally a discussion on the research limitations and conclusion with future works are presented.

VETERANS AND CIVILIAN REINTEGRATION PROBLEM

During the collaborative design phase, the research team visited the DH centers twice a month. During those visits we had an opportunity to talk with more veterans. Once one of them said, "the civilian reintegration problems faced by student veterans are more severe". We asked him to describe more. He went on saying,

"From the day you enter bootcamp until the day you leave the service, all you ever do is to find ways to conquer any obstacles that may lead you to loose. You are trained physically to overcome that obstacle, we do exactly what the leadership guys tell us to do, follow their instructions. Now when we come to classroom atmosphere, we have to use this (pointing to his head, indicating intelligence) to succeed, which we are not used to. Coming back to classroom after service, where we used to succeed for years, we are now put in a situation which we cannot conquer. We are not used to losing, we are used to winning. When you tell us to go in classroom where we have to maintain a C average, where we can see others who are even younger than us are getting A's, we feel stupid. We cannot go back, we are trapped here. We just feel like we have wasted five years of our life. That's when we start getting dark, start drinking".

Many OEF/OIF veterans have enrolled in colleges using their GI-Bill benefits [14]. A study reported that mental health, substance abuse, financial and relationship related problems are more severe among younger veterans than older veterans [40]. According to a study 93% of the student veterans reported difficulties in college campus settings (e. g. difficulty in relating to younger non-veteran classmates, lack of necessary skills for basic course work and difficulty in concentrating in the classroom [20]). Additionally, maladaptive responses to war experiences are often reflected in their behaviors. During our visits to the DH center, we asked one veteran mentor to describe his experience when he enrolled in college after deployment. He described his experience as,

"During the Afghanistan war I saw streets crowded with people. But just before attacks people start to rush into their homes and the streets become empty. At this moment we have to be very alert and conscious. This experience keeps coming back at college campus where corridors are full of students before class starts. But just when the class starts people rush into the classroom and we go back into a very alert state. I remember sitting back in the classroom and one day I counted all the tiles in the ceiling [in order to not react]. ".

A study revealed that 96% of veterans who received VA services expressed interest in obtaining assistance with civilian reintegration [16]. Systematic guidance is needed to ensure mental wellness of reintegrative veterans [17]. Government agencies do not have sufficient reach into all the veteran communities [18]. Furthermore, health promotion plans often emphasize individually focused behavior change strategies and neglects environmental foundation of health [4]. An individual's behaviors are often result of environmental influences. As a result there is an increasing focus on community-based prevention models for healthcare [25].

NEED ASSESSMENT

Methodology

DH has a partnership with several institutions for over five years. The DH community-academic partnership for veteran health includes faculty from the Milwaukee VA Medical Center, the Medical College of Wisconsin, the University of Wisconsin-Milwaukee and the Marquette University. DH and its partners identified the improvement areas for their peer-mentor program through formal and informal meetings among veterans, community engagement specialists (CES) and social scientists (SS).

Areas of Improvement

In order to meet the specific needs of student veterans DH began to seek technology-augmented approaches. At this point they also began to identify the existing limitations of their paper-based peer mentor program. Two main improvement areas are, (1) Service efficiency and (2) Service continuation [see Figure 1].

Service Efficiency

Paper-based behavioral surveys are at the core of this improvement area. This approach requires VMs to visit their mentees to acquire survey data, which works well for older veterans (e.g. Cold War and Vietnam Service periods, most of whom are retired and have flexible schedules). VMs need to evaluate the survey responses using their judgment. The process is inefficient at times because VMs also struggle with cognitive problems such as attention, concentration etc. [14]. Moreover, when the number of mentees exceeds 20, it becomes strenuous for the VMs to manage their face-to-face meetings. This often requires setting up appointments, traveling to multiple locations and adjustments to work/school schedule, etc. Another limitation is recall-bias. The self-reported survey responses of the mentees are often biased by memory-recall [24].

Reintegrating veterans often struggle with problems such as information processing, sequencing, short-term-memory, slower thinking etc. [14]. Thus, recalling incidents are often mixed with ambiguity. The paper-based approach also makes data management difficult by storing survey responses in filing cabinets. If left unlocked, it may result in disclosure of confidential information. Additionally, data analysis for research purposes is challenging, although the VMs recognize that the longitudinal data could provide useful information about impending problems with their veterans. Furthermore, data from the paper-based approach is not rapidly transformed into meaningful information. Several of the VMs expressed that a visual summary of the data from the weekly assessments might help them to easily identify at risk veterans.

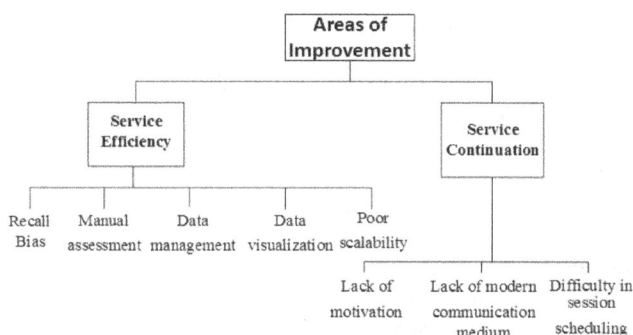

Figure 1. Improvement areas.

Service Continuation

Many of the OEF/OIF veterans have low motivation to seek out services that are purely mental health oriented. Their needs are focused on reintegration in college, rebuilding relationships and maintaining employments [18]. They are considerably less likely to visit VMs due to this instrumental focus, a problem not encountered with the older veterans served by DH. Additionally, veterans with social anxiety, which is common during the reintegration period, may prefer computer over human interaction [14]. One veteran expressed that he would not participate in the study until the app was ready because he did not want to interact with people. Moreover, the mobile-based solution have been noted by DH as a needed tool to better manage after-hour access to DH services.

RELATED WORKS

The two key regions of related literature are, (1) mobile applications available for veteran mental healthcare and (2) the effectiveness of peer-mentorship for mental health problems.

mHealth for Veterans

In order to support veterans and caregivers, the VA has released a series of secure mHealth applications to expand clinical care beyond the traditional office visits [26]. *PTSD Coach* is an app developed by the VAs' National Center for PTSD [27]. It helps users diagnosed with PTSD to manage

their symptoms. *PE Coach* is another app developed by the the VA. This app is used by the professionals who provides Prolonged Exposure (PE) psychotherapy sessions to PTSD patients [15]. Similar to *PTSD Coach, eCBT Trauma* helps users with PTSD assess their symptoms, graph their symptoms over time and email a caregiver [28]. *PTSD Support* is another app that helps veterans and their families to become more knowledgeable about PTSD [29]. *PTSD Eraser* is an app that facilitates meditation techniques to cope with PTSD. *Breathe 2 Relax, T-2 Mood Tracker* are other apps that help PTSD symptom management [30]. There are other mental healthcare apps that are not PTSD specific. For example, *Online Care* lets veterans and therapists to have online consultation. *Care4Caregiver* is designed for caregivers to manage their stress level. *CBT-i Coach* is developed to support Cognitive Behavioral Therapy (CBT). *PFA Mobile* is an app for families of survivors to provide psychological first aid (PFA) [26]. Although research suggests mobile-based VA services can reduce healthcare cost and increase self-management ability [21], currently there are no evidence that shows effectiveness of those apps. Nonetheless, reports disclose that veterans and caregivers show interest in mHealth [22].

Peer-Mentor Program for Mental Health Care

"Traditional definitions of mentoring can be summarized as a dyadic relationship in which the mentor, the senior person in age or experience, provides guidance and support to the less experienced person" – Ensher et al. [31]. Davidson, et al., suggest that people who are fighting with mental health problems can benefit from those who overcame similar problems successfully. Their research also suggests that peer programs can offer a person hope for a better life [32]. The importance of mutual support groups was presented in some research studies to improve the quality of life of people experiencing adversities [33]. Another research shows the effectiveness of electronic mentorship for young populations with special needs. E-mentoring provides a way to communicate while maintaining their disabilities less visible. Internet, email and online discussion groups are able to overcome barriers of time and distance. Thus, making e-mentoring more effective [6].

Discussion on the Related Works

The mobile apps developed by the VA primarily focus on diagnosable mental health conditions which differentiate them from the iPeer project. iPeer's predominant focus is the psychosocial process of civilian reintegration. The other apps focus on "*treatment*" while iPeer focus on "*prevention*" by addressing readjustment problems before they spiral out of control and become psychiatric issues. This is important because while relatively few veterans (15-20%) will be diagnosable [7] with PTSD, most will face some adversity as they transition back to civilian life [16]. This actually supports our first contribution which identifies iPeer as a support network for the period of civilian reintegration.

POS REP is an app for veterans which also focuses on preventing mental health problems rather than treating conditions [9]. While both iPeer and *POS REP* share the same objective, there are differences between them: *(1) POS REP does not track the veteran's progress or status through the process of reintegration, iPeer does this through behavioral data collection, (2) POS REP connects with veterans only in the perimeter range, but iPeer assigns a dedicated trained VM support.* iPeer takes a unique sociotechnical systems [10] approach for mental healthcare by providing, *(1) the first mHealth app that uses EMA-based peer-mentor support to help veteran reintegration, (2) the first after-hour mobile peer-mentor support for younger veterans on collegiate campuses and (3) comfort of use for student veterans.*

IPEER DESIGN AND DEVELOPMENT

We went through a yearlong design process to implement the system that addresses the findings of the need assessment section and also is faithful to the essence of this human driven process. In this section we will describe the design process and its outcomes.

Methodological Complications

Initially CESs and SSs met DH veterans formally and informally to gather requirements [1]. The requirements were translated to the technology team by the CESs. This became a continuous and unbounded process. The high level requirements were, *(1) Veterans should receive surveys on their mobile devices on a regular basis, (2) User interface should display accessible peer contact buttons, (3) The app should enable VMs to add mentees and (4) The app should enable VMs to review the survey responses of their mentees on their mobile devices.* The details of the user interface were left up to the technology team. They developed an alpha version (AV) of the system which consisted of two separate apps that run on smartphones. "iPeerMentor" and "iPeerVeteran" are respectively the apps for the VMs and mentees. A server shares and stores data among VMs, mentees and researchers.

Before the deployment of the AV, several system usability workshops were conducted among the VMs, researchers and the development team. The development team installed the app on the phones of the VMs. They were asked to comment on the application. Some of the positive feedbacks were, *"I am now able to see panel of mentees"* – says one VM. *"I like the call/text option, it's now easy to contact with my mentee. I don't need to find his contact information"* – says another VM. *"The snapshot of mentee status is really great. I can now just enter in the app and access all my mentees' status"* – expressed one VM. *"The mentee app gave easy access to survey questionnaire"* – another VM on the mentee app. Finally the AV was deployed among the VMs and their mentees on the University of Wisconsin Milwaukee. However, the deployment failed with a series of complaints reported from both veterans and VMs. Reasons for this failure were,

software limitations and the low frustration tolerance and anxiety typical to veterans [14].

Several veterans reported that the app was *"not working at all"*. For example, many mentees reported that they were not comfortable with the survey process. They were answering a lot of questions and lacked motivation to finish the surveys. The veterans were missing the comfort of face-to-face peer-mentorship. A process that should, to some extent, mimic human interaction was needed in this system. This revealed that there was a communication gap. Initially, DH VMs overestimated the usability of the AV because they did not have a plan to actualize the functionality of the app. The AV was an opportunity for several teams to take some steps toward understanding the problem space and start thinking collaboratively. It also showed that DH's idea of the app was conceptual, rather than requirements driven. They needed to visualize the project to a certain extent. As a result the need for *Community Collaborative Design* came apparent. Figure 2 summarizes the failure of the AV.

Method

We went through an iterative process where each phase improved the design and development of the prototype that was tested by VMs [11]. The participation of the VMs ensured input of the target-users' experience with DH [19]. Therefore, the *Community Collaborative Design Process* dovetails with the shift in design methodology from an object perspective to a human needs perspective [13].

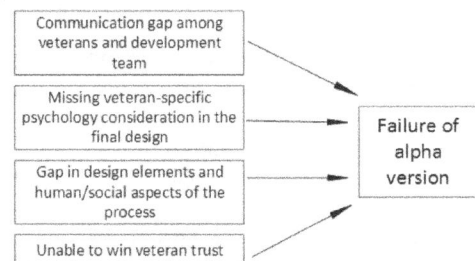

Figure 2. Summary of AV failure.

Partners of the Community Collaborative Design
DH, Medical College of Wisconsin (MCW), the University of Wisconsin-Milwaukee (UWM) and the Marquette University (MU) have brought unique expertise in the design process. MCW brought expertise in community-engagement processes. The CESs from MCW had post-doctoral training in *Community Based Participatory Research*. They also had experience with community-academic partnerships for health. The CESs worked as translators between the veterans, VMs and the technology team [1]. UWM contributed the veteran population and MU developed the mHealth application.

The iterative design process
VMs, CESs and the technology team had weekly tech meeting to review the app. VMs and researchers tested and provided feedback. The day following the tech meeting the CESs and VMs evaluated the app. Each meeting generated

user interface recommendations based on the VMs' cultural experiences. The result of this design assessment was then presented in the following tech meeting. The VMs suggested feature modifications which led to the next level of development [see Figure 3].

Figure 3. a) VMs trying the app on their phone, b) VM presenting their design suggestions

System Components
In this section we will describe the two client modules, *(1) iPeerVeteran and (2) iPeerMentor.*

iPeerVeteran Module
The mentees receive semi-weekly surveys. The survey is available during, Monday-Tuesday and Friday-Saturday. VMs identified that the beginning and end of the week, are important for capturing data. They wanted to know how their mentees were doing at the beginning of the school/work week and at the transition point to the weekend when some crises are more likely to occur (e.g. drinking, etc.). The home screen has two "check-in" options for each of the time-slots [see Figure 5(a)]. The mentees get access to the available survey after selecting the corresponding "check-in" button. Red text on the "check-in" button indicates a missed survey. The "contact mentor" menu item gives the mentees call or text options.

iPeerMentor Module
The home screen holds a list of all the mentees managed by the mentor. Each mentee on the list is represented with three items. (1) A photo of the mentee, (2) two icons representative of the survey responses for the ongoing week and (3) a graph that illustrates the survey responses over several weeks [see Figure 4]. The icons representing survey responses for the ongoing week are, (1) a red-thumbs-down, (2) a green-thumbs-up or (3) a red-cross-mark. The red-thumbs-down indicates undesirable answers, a green-thumbs-up represents positive answers and a red-cross-mark indicates that the survey was not taken. Mentors use easy-to-locate buttons to text, email or call mentees.

VETERANS' RESPONSES AND FEEDBACK

Methodologies
Table 1 presents a summary of the methods and participants involved in the design research and app usability study.

Discussion with the collaborative design participants
We received useful feedbacks from the VMs participating in the collaborative design. The conversations were audio recorded with permission from the VMs.

Focus group
Before the deployment of iPeer we organized a focus group among DH, SSs, CESs and technology team at one of DH service centers. Invitations were sent to ten mentees and five VMs. The session started with one of the developers giving a presentation about the app. Afterwards the veterans were grouped into mentor-mentee dyads and were assisted by developers to review the app. The second focus group took place on the University of Wisconsin-Milwaukee veteran service center. There were total 7 OEF/OIF veteran mentees present during this focus group. We received some feedback that addressed the key issues behind the design of the iPeer system

One-to-One Interview
Following the focus group we had a one-to-one interview with a gulf war era veteran. He was 53 years old and has been a VM for one year.

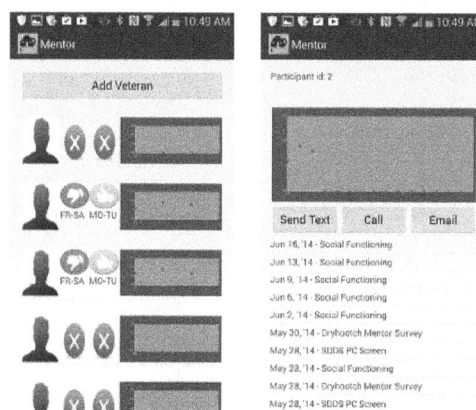

Figure 4. a) List of mentees with their status summary, b) details of an individual status on iPeerMentor

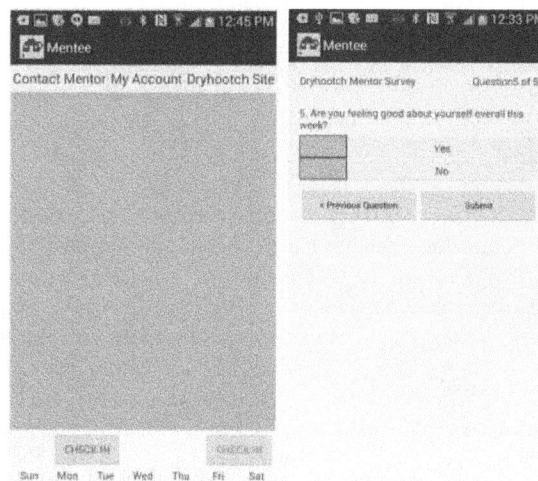

Figure 5. a) Check-in process in the mentee app, b) survey screen opened after selecting check-in

Table 1: Methods of design research and app usability study

Method	Focus Area	No. Of Veterans Participants	Military Service Period	Data Accumulation Process
Community collaborative design in technology lab	System requirements	10 Veteran Peer-mentor	OEF/OIF, cold War	Weekly meeting and interviews over an 18 month period
First focus group in a Dryhootch center	Interface usability	15 Veteran mentors and mentees	Vietnam, OEF/OIF, cold War	Close room audio and video recording, conversational session, simulation of mentoring session
One-to-One interview (Follow up first focus group)	Importance of technology mediated peer-mentoring	1 Veteran mentor	Gulf war	Notes on conversation
Second focus group in a university veteran service center	Interface usability	7 Student veterans	OEF/OIF veterans only	Audio record conversations and notes on responses on usability

Responses from the Collaborative Design Participants

A VM said, "*I feel very relaxed now, as I don't have to find time for appointments ... I can see their survey responses through my mobile-device ...*". This reveals the fact that iPeer would significantly reduce the load on mentors allowing them to manage approximately 20 veterans. Currently, VMs cannot rapidly refer to baseline scores to see how their veterans are doing over broader time periods (0, 6, 12 week). "*My mentee may not be doing well this week for some reason ... I need to see if this is just momentary or consistent. I need something that I can have a glance and know her overall status*" – says one VM. The graphical display [see Figure 5] gives the mentor a representation of their veterans' status over a range of time.

Discussion on Feedback from Focus Group

During the focus group several veterans expressed their doubt about the effectiveness of the mobile-based peer-mentoring. One senior veteran said – "*I prefer face-to-face peer-mentoring. I cannot trust a device*". Again another veteran responded – "*But this might work for younger veterans. They share everything publicly*". Another veteran added – "*Facebook is used extensively by OEF/OIF veterans, often these FB groups for veterans never involve face-to-face contact*". However, it was also noted that the app will work well for introverted veterans. One of the VMs noted that he needs to commute to reach his mentees and felt that the app would facilitate better communication. It was also noted that the app may assist VMs to organize large collection of mentee information. Yet most of them agreed that some form of visual and voice interaction is necessary. The discussion session ended with a survey question – "*How many of you ... feel like this technology can augment the Dryhootch peer mentor program vs. How many feel like the peer mentor program can only be done face to face?*". Unanimously, the veterans at the close of the session (15 individuals) felt that the technology could augment the existing social process. However, they also noted that the technology should not replace social interaction.

Response from the One-to-One Interview

The main objective of this session was to gain perspective about the augmented-technology from an older veteran. His response on peer-mentoring preference was:

"*I prefer face-to-face approach. Peer to peer support is personal, with younger guys ... they already know each other, they are on Facebook, they know what they ate that day ... they share everything, but the 35-60 year olds are more people persons. And the over 60 are dinosaurs. Veterans feel more connected when you talk to them face to face, it's about trust. They become more comfortable with me after 3 or 4 meetings ... we can talk about more personal stuff ... It's like any relationship.*"

We asked him if he sees this app, in any way, helpful to the face-to-face relationship. He said:

"*The app will help monitor on a more regular basis. At a glance we can know who's having issues ... because people isolate when they have issues, so it will be vital, especially if a person is suicidal, to know right away what that persons state is. For example, I've had the experience where people have texted me that all hope is lost and I've been in a loud place or not heard the beep go off and noticed it 20 minutes later.*"

The above comment enables us to see how the mobile augmented service reduces the mentors' workload. Then he went on saying:

"I'm realizing how vital my phone is to me ... the vets I'm assisting. Other vets call us to say they are on the verge of drinking ... or doing what's getting them in trouble. If we have the app we can get to them quicker. And we need their address in there. Then that's where face to face comes in. We need that face to face, especially in crisis mode."

The above comment expresses how iPeer helps in improving the mentors' level of communication with their mentees. In addition he added:

"The app will be great for alerts. We could end up with 300 or 400 people that we only see once every six months, that's hard to keep track of. We get a thumbs down and we know, hey I have to pay attention to this guy ..."

From the above comment we recognize how the data visualization feature helps in improving the mentors' awareness about their mentees' status.

DISCUSSION

A number of themes developed from our analysis of the collaborative design. We present these as four key issues that need to be addressed when designing and evaluating a sociotechnical system for veteran mental healthcare. Our derived issues are, *(1) Find an indirect route without psychiatric label, (2) Understand the jargon of the social system, (3) Understand the psychology of the veteran community and (4) Establish trust among the veteran community and researchers.*

Find an indirect route without psychiatric label
During the collaborative design meeting we discussed the significance of labeling an app as a psychiatric intervention. One of the veteran mentor expressed his opinion,

"We are always being labeled. We look for ways to stay out of labeling. That's the VA stance. We go in there, we are told that we have PTSD and need to make psychiatric appointments and that's when we stop going there. Staying away from labeling would help the mentees to adopt the service".

One of the important lesson that came out from the second focus group is, the apps released by VA are too focused on psychiatric symptoms. Almost all of the veterans (total 7) expressed that they are not likely to use a system that is too focused on treating psychological conditions. They would like to have the option to make certain features inactive. This is the reason the VA apps are not very appealing to the veterans. Current literature only shows psychiatric treatment specific interventions for veterans. iPeer does not have any feature that directly addresses psychiatric treatment. For example, the survey questions for the AV were all evidence-based and validated from standard psychometric scale [2], e. g., "The possibility of drinking

heavily at a social function". Several mentees reported that they were not comfortable with this type of questions and as a result the question format was redesigned by the researchers, e. g. "How stressful has this week been?". The lesson here is, **veterans are more comfortable with services that are labeled without a psychiatric focus.**

Understand the jargon of the social system
One of the senior VMs summarized the peer-mentor process as, *"Well, I check-in with my mentees, they check-in with me. I see how they are doing and connect with them if they need it".* The "check-in" approach [see Figure 5(a)] formed a sociotechnical system by augmenting the social aspect of the process [10]. The "check-in" process was elicited in discussions with VMs about what wasn't working with the AV. One of the VMs asked, *"Can you develop a relationship through technology?".* They did not want the veterans to feel like they are filling in surveys for research. The "check-ins" are analogous to the business process of peer mentorship when it is not augmented by technology [34]. Additionally, veterans use the word "check-in" in the DH peer-mentor program. As a result using the word "check-in" to access surveys makes them feel more like they are providing the information to the peer mentor. Also, during the second focus group the OEF/OIF veterans expressed that they would like to see NCOs (Non-Commissioned Officers) or other trusted roles available at all times to answer requests to connect. NCO is a term to describe a military rank between enlisted personnel and officers. They are generally well respected by soldiers, while officers may not be. The lesson learned is, **incorporate the social aspect of the process by using jargons sensitive to the veterans.**

Understand the psychology of the veteran community
A VM using an older Android device said, *"I deal with anxiety and my hands sweat. Touch screen does not work for me. I want to use a phone with keypad".* The AV failed on her phone due to backward compatibility issues. The app frustrated her. This shows how veteran specific mental conditions can impact a seemingly successful release. Consensus among veterans and researchers is a necessity. Arranging the "check-ins" on specific week days is an example that addresses veteran specific psychological needs [see Figure 5(a)]. A VM mentioned, *"In military services, we have a very structured life. We are always instructed what to do by the seniors.".* The placing of the "check-ins" on weekly calendar dates directs veterans to complete the surveys [16]. The lesson is, **as veterans are the primary user of this system, their specific psychological and cultural needs, capabilities and limitations should be analyzed as high priority for designing system features.**

Establish trust among the veteran community and researchers
VMs believed that trust among veterans and those who interact with veterans is important. He expressed, *"I believe in government conspiracy ... They only care as long as we are fit for deployment. I and many others find it very hard*

to trust anyone. They may exploit our private information". Research suggest that community-academic partnership may enhance public trust [3]. Furthermore, collaborative design process itself may help in limiting the effect of their specific behavioral issues. For example, veterans are known to suffer from low frustration tolerance [14]. After the AV deployment, several veterans were frustrated with the app and considered the project a failure. As soon as the collaborative design started, the VMs could see how the app was evolving. During the weekly design meeting the technology team showed the VMs and the researchers how to use iPeer. They went through iPeer for 15-20 minutes under the supervision of the developers. This instant training had the benefit of developing trust among the veterans and reducing their frustration. They were able to see that their thoughts were valued and that they were assisting in building up the system in a way they want it to work. Also, during the second focus group the OEF/OIF veteran mentees also expressed their interest in periodically answering questions about app improvement suggestions. This clearly demonstrates their interest in actively participating in the app design process. When they see that their opinions are valued they are more likely to be engaged with system. This is an example of improved patience. Our derived lesson here is, **facilitate active participation of the veteran community in decision-making to increase trust and reduce the effects of veteran specific behavioral issues for a long term project.**

CONCLUSION

In this paper we presented the development of a mobile-based veteran peer-support system called iPeer through collaborative design. We also outlined the initial findings of this ethnographic and design-based research. The ethnographic part of our research shows improvements of the DH's peer-mentor service. However, it actually represents a part of the app usability. The app is currently ready for deployment with features to support the peer-mentor service. It will be deployed among the veterans on UWM campus and we will conduct formal data analysis to demonstrate its wide range implications. Even though student veterans were the primary focus of iPeer, DH is interested in making it applicable to other populations. The goal is to modify the system in later deployments with modules for specific sub populations of veterans, while using the iPeer framework as the foundational platform.

ACKNOWLEDGMENTS
This project was funded by Healthier Wisconsin Partnership Program (HWPP), and is conducted as part of the Dryhootch Community-Academic Partnership for Veteran Health. We thank all the veterans from UWM campus for helping us move forward with the project by providing their valuable time and feedback.

REFERENCES

[1] McNall, M., Reed, C. S., Brown, R., & Allen, A. (2009). Brokering community–university engagement. *Innovative Higher Education*, Volume 33, Issue 5, Pages 317-331.

[2] Blais, A.-R and Weber, E. U. The Domain-Specific Risk Taking Scale for Adult Populations: Item selection and preliminary psychometric properties. Defence R&D Canada, Technical Report, December 2009.

[3] Christopher, S., Watts, V., McCormick, A. K. H. G., & Young, S. (2008). Building and maintaining trust in a community-based participatory research partnership. American Journal of Public Health, 98(8), 1398.

[4] Stokols, D. Translating Social Ecological Theory into Guidelines for Community Health Promotion. *American Journal of Health Promotion*, 1996, Volume 10, Issue 4, Page 282-298.

[5] Hartl, T. L., Rosen, C., Drescher, K., Lee, T. T. and Gusman F. Predicting High-Risk Behaviors in Veterans With Posttraumatic Stress Disorder. *The Journal of Nervous & Mental Disease*, July 2005, vol. 193, Issue 7, Pages 464-472.

[6] Shpigelman, C., Weiss, P. L. and Reiter, S. E-Mentoring for All. *Journal of Computers in Human Behavior*, July 2009, Volume 25, Issue 4, Pages 919-928.

[7] Burnam, M. A., Meredith, L. S., Tanielian, T. and Jaycox L. H. Mental Health Care For Iraq And Afghanistan War Veterans. *Journal of Health Affairs*, June 2009, Volume 28, Issue 3, Pages 771-782.

[8] http://dryhootch.org/

[9] http://pos-rep.com/

[10] Appelbaum, S. H. Socio-technical systems theory: an intervention strategy for organizational development. *Journal of Management Decision*, 1997, volume 35, Issue 6, Pages 452-463

[11] Maier, A. Complete Beginner's Guide to Design Research, June 2010. Retrieved on 12 March [Online] Available: http://www.uxbooth.com/articles/complete-beginners-guide-to-design-research/

[12] Resnik, L., Bradford, D. W., Glynn, S. M., Jette, A. M. Hernandez, C. J. and Wills, S. Issues in defining and measuring veteran community reintegration. *Proceedings of the Working Group on Community Reintegration, VA Rehabilitation Outcomes Conference*, 2012, Volume 49, Pages 87 – 100.

[13] Christiaans, H. and Diehl, J. THE NECESSITY OF DESIGN RESEARCH INTO CULTURAL ASPECTS. *Proceedings International Association of Societies of Design Research, Hong Kong Polytechnic University*, 2007.

[14] Church. T. E. Returning Veterans on Campus with War Related Injuries and the Long Road Back Home. *Journal of Postsecondary Education and Disability*, 2009, Version 22, Issue 1, Pages 43-52.

[15] PTSD Support App – Mobile Health Marketplace. *The leading directory of mobile health apps and devices*, n. p., n. d. [Online].Available: http://www.mobilehealthmarketplace.com/listings/pe-coach-ptsd-support-app/

[16] Sayer, N. A., Noorbaloochi, S., Frazier, P., Carlson, K., Gravely, A. and Murdoch M. Reintegration Problems and

Treatment Interests Among Iraq and Afghanistan Combat Veterans Receiving VA Medical Care. *Journal of Psychiatric Services*, 2010, Volume 61, Pages 589-97.

[17] Demers, A. When Veterans Return: The Role of Community in Reintegration. *Journal of Loss and Trauma: International Perspectives on Stress & Coping,* 2011, Volume 16, Issue 2, Pages 160 – 179.

[18] Harrell, M. C. and Berglass, N. Well After Service: Veteran Reintegration and American Communities. *Report for Center for a New American Security (CNAS),* 2012.

[19] Collins, A., Joseph, D. and Bielaczyc, K. Design Research: Theoretical and Methodological Issues. *Journal of the Learning Sciences*, 2004 Volume 13, Issue 1, Pages 15- 42.

[20] Plach, H. L., and Sells, C. H.. "Occupational performance needs of young veterans." *American journal of occupational therapy*, 2013, Volume 67, Issue 1, Pages 73-81.

[21] Darkins, A., Ryan, P., Kobb, R., Foster, L., Edmonson, E., Wakefield, B., and Lancaster, A. E. Care Coordination/Home Telehealth: The Systematic Implementation of Health Informatics, Home Telehealth, and Disease Management to Support the Care of Veteran Patients with Chronic Conditions. *Telemedicine and e-Health*. December 2008, Volume 14, Issue 10, Pages 1118-1126.

[22] Bresnick, J. VA pilot brings together mHealth and EHRs for better care. December 2013. Retrieved on 21st July 2014. [Online]. Available: http://ehrintelligence.com/2013/12/10/va-pilot-brings-together-mhealth-and-ehrs-for-better-care/

[23] Brown, T. T. and DeBakey, M. E. Societal Culture and the New Veteran. *INTERNATIONAL JOURNAL OF SCHOLARLY ACADEMIC INTELLECTUAL DIVERSITY*, 2009, Volume 11, Issue 1.

[24] Shiffman, S., Stone, A. A. and Hufford, M. R. Ecological Momentary Assessment. *Annual Review of Clinical Psychology*, November 2007, Volume 4, Pages 1-32.

[25] McLeroy, K. R., Norton, B. L., Kegler, M. C., Burdine, J. N. and Sumaya, C. V. Community-Based Interventions. *Am J Public Health*, 2003, Volume 93, Issue 4, Pages 529 – 533

[26] Pai, A. "15 apps from the Department of Veterans Affairs" 11 Nov 2013. MobiHealthnews. Retrieved on Retrieved on

12 March 2014 [Online]. Available:http://mobihealthnews.com/27237/15-apps-from-the-department-of-veterans-affairs/

[27] Support for PTSD: PTSD app at Real Warriors. n. p., n. d. [Online]. Available: http://www.realwarriors.net/active/treatment/ptsdcoach.php

[28] Grohol, J. M. (2010). MindApps Releases eCBT Trauma. Psych Central. Retrieved on March 12, 2014, [Online]. Available http://psychcentral.com/blog/archives/2010/02/16/mindapps-releases-ecbt-trauma/

[29] "PTSD Support by Mobile Roadie" PTSD Support on the App Store on iTunes. 04 Dec 2013 . Apple App Store. Retrieved on 12 March 2014 [Online]. Available: https://itunes.apple.com/us/app/ptsd-support/id379160810?mt=8

[30] Stein, Traci. "Free Apps for Relaxation, De-Stressing & PTS" 18 March 2013 . healthjourneys. Retrieved on 12 March 2014 [Online]. Available: http://www.belleruthnaparstek.com/update-from-belleruth/a-spate-of-free-apps-for-relaxation-de-stressing-pts.html

[31] Ensher, E. A., Thomas, C. and Murphy, S. E. Comparison of traditional, step-ahead, and peer mentoring on protégés' support, satisfaction, and perceptions of career success: A social exchange perspective. *Journal of Business and Psychology*, 2001, Volume 15, Issue 3, Pages 419-438.

[32] Davidson, L., Chinman, M., Kloos, B., Weingarten, R., Stayner, D. and Tebes, J. K. Peer Support Among Individuals With Severe Mental Illness: A Review of the Evidence. *The Journal of Clinical Psychology: Science and Practice*, June 1999, Volume 6, Issue 2, pages 165–187.

[33] Borkman, T. Self-help groups at the turning point: Emerging egalitarian alliances with the formal health care system? *American Journal of Community Psychology*, 1990, Volume 18, Issue 2, Pages 321-332.

[34] Sutcliffe, A. Applying small group theory to analysis and design of CSCW systems. *Proceedings of the 2005 workshop on Human and social factors of software engineering*, 2005, Pages 1-6.

Suhrid: A Collaborative Mobile Phone Interface for Low Literate People

Syed Ishtiaque Ahmed[1], Maruf Hasan Zaber[2], Mehrab Bin Morshed[2], Md.Habibullah Bin Ismail[2],
Dan Cosley[1], Steven J. Jackson[1]

[1]Department of Information Science, Cornell University, Ithaca, NY, USA 14850
[2]Department of Computer Science and Engineering, BUET, Dhaka, Bangladesh 1000
{sa738, drc44, sjj54}@cornell.edu, {maruf.zaber.09, mehrab.morshed, bahar61119}@gmail.com

ABSTRACT

The design of accessible mobile phone interfaces for low literate people usually assumes an individual model of use, and are often limited by the low technical expertise and/or cognitive ability of users in marginal communities of developing countries. Drawing on previous ICTD scholarship around shared and intermediated use of technology and our own ethnographic field study, we introduce a collaborative model of use in the design of *Suhrid*, a mobile phone interface that helps low literate users perform common phone tasks by receiving remote help from higher-literacy members of their community. The results of our six week long deployment of Suhrid among 10 low literate rickshaw pullers in Dhaka, Bangladesh, indicate the potential of collaborative use models to help low-literate people more effectively use mobile phones while strengthening bonds between them and the people in their community who provide help.

Categories and Subject Descriptors

H.5.2 [**User Interfaces**]: Interaction styles

General Terms

Human Factors

Keywords

Collaborative Interface; Low Literate User; Gift Economy

1. INTRODUCTION

Making technologies accessible to low-literate users is a long-standing challenge for ICTD researchers and practitioners. The rapid growth of mobile phone penetration in the developing world in the last two decades has driven important change across many aspects of life, from education and health to political participation and the informal economy. However, low literacy has limited these impacts, especially among poor and marginal populations; therefore helping low-literate users reap the benefits of mobile devices is an increasingly important question in ICTD research.

Previous work in this area has attempted to overcome this problem by using non-textual interfaces that incorporate graphic

ACM DEV 2015, December 01 - 02, 2015, London, United Kingdom
Copyright is held by the owner/author(s). Publication rights licensed to ACM.
ACM 978-1-4503-3490-7/15/11$15.00
DOI: http://dx.doi.org/10.1145/2830629.2830640

and audio based commands and content. While these efforts have shown benefit, they also face important limits, including the need for additional computational support from the device, which may not be available in low-resource environments, and the technical and cognitive abilities of users interacting with icons and audio commands. As a result, the design of an effective phone interface for low-literate people remains an ongoing challenge.

Our work is built around a shift in perspective about the use of 'personal' devices like mobile phones from an individual model to a more communal model, in which users figure not as atomized individuals, but as nodes within wider social networks that can be drawn on to overcome barriers that literacy poses to technology use. Prior studies in ICTD have shown that technology use in developing and low-resource contexts is frequently collective or distributed in nature, with the use of technologies like mobile phones shared among the user's family, friends, and other community members [4, 27]. Intermediate use of technologies is similarly prevalent; several studies have shown that low literate people often take help from digitally literate people close to them for operating their own mobile phones [23, 28].

At the center of intermediate use lies the practice of 'help' by able members of the community. We see an opportunity to leverage this practice through a community-sourced model that connects low-literate users to higher-literacy remote peers in their immediate network to both accomplish tasks and strengthen social bonds. In this paper, we present a design intervention that exploits the social values and practices of a community of rickshaw pullers in Dhaka and their intermediate use of technologies to provide low-literate members access to their basic mobile phone operations. Our previous ethnography on the same garage informed us of the intermediate use of mobile phones among this community. Based on that and an additional focus group study, we designed, developed, and deployed *Suhrid*, a phone application that allows the rickshaw pullers to remotely get help from their garage owner for placing phone calls and saving contacts. A six-week field deployment of Suhrid with 10 rickshaw pullers showed that it effectively helped low-literate users make better use of their phones. More generally, we argue that Suhrid shows the potential of designs that leverage shared and intermediate use in contexts where such use is common.

2. RELATED WORK

Literacy has long posed important challenges to mobile phone use among poor and marginal populations. In their 2006 paper, Chipchase et al. documented various ways illiterate people used mobile phones [7]. Their study showed that some functions (e.g., turning the phone on or off, accepting incoming calls) were easy for the users, while other functions (e.g., sending text messages, finding contacts from the contact list) were more difficult. Furthermore, understanding and responding to basic information about the phone (e.g., remaining battery power, network connectivity, incoming text messages) was often challenging. These problems often led to confusion, mistakes, embarrassment, and non-use. A number of mobile handset vendors worked to address these problems by providing audio and visual clues for battery alerts, network connectivity, text messages, and so on [32]. However, problems related to operations like finding contacts from the address book and placing calls remain.

2.1 Designing for Individual Phone Use

A common design response to problems of literacy is to develop interfaces that use less text in order to reduce literacy requirements. For instance, icon-based interfaces have been used to support low-literate or illiterate populations of Indian village women [9], domestic laborers [20], and farmers [21], while audio interfaces have been developed for low-literate Pakistani health workers [30] and Indian farmers [25]. Color has also been used with some success to help low-literate users with address books [31] and phone contact lists [14]. A more detailed review of such design work can be found in Medhi [17].

These approaches face a number of practical challenges. For icon-based interfaces, removing text doesn't necessarily remove usability problems. Besides the difficulty of finding icons that make sense to low-literate users across a range of social and cultural contexts, hierarchical presentation of icons may fail due to cognitive challenges stemming from unfamiliarity or misrecognition of hierarchical orderings of information [18]. For audio interfaces, the users still need to remember the audio commands and their hierarchy. Such speech interfaces are also more error-prone than touch or graphical interfaces [25].

A common characteristic across each of the abovementioned design strategies was the assumption that a single user would use the device. This assumption leads to designs focused on communicating with that single user through graphical signals or audio clues; such designs depend on the individual user's memory and skills.

2.2 Communal Model of Technology Use

Individual use is not the only use model; a growing body of ICTD work has demonstrated that social use is common in low-resource contexts. For example, Burrell's ethnography in Ghana revealed how technologies like land-phones, computers, and televisions were shared among the members of a community [4]. Rangaswamy et al. found a similar sort of shared model of technology use in Mumbai slums [27, 28].

In the case of phones, the devices are not only shared between people, but also often used with the help of others, especially in the case of low-literate individuals. Parikh and Ghosh have discovered that low-literate Indian women take help from field workers to communicate with microcredit providers [23, 24]. Sambasivan et al. have reported the practice of helping in informal setting for operating mobile phones in India [29]. Kumar et al. have pointed to the network of actors beyond individual users supporting the consumption of mobile phone services in India [15]. Our previous work has shown how illiterate rickshaw-pullers in Dhaka, Bangladesh depend on literate social peers to support and access basic mobile phone operations [1].

This communal model extends to the systems of maintenance and repair by which devices and wider infrastructures are sustained in low-income environments. Work by Jackson et al. [12, 13] and Houston [11] with mobile phone repairers in Namibia,

Bangladesh, and Uganda has shown the significance and extent of the local and global networks of materials and knowledge that sustain mobile phone use in many developing countries.

These studies connect in turn to ideas from Mauss' classic anthropological work *The Gift*, which has shown the centrality of networks and rituals of gift-giving and mutual support as a central feature of social life across a wide range of cultural contexts [16]. Drawing on Mauss, we argue that the essence of gift embedded in technical help produces and reciprocates honor, respect, and trust among the members of a community. This spirit is often hidden under the layers of official technical support infrastructures in the developed Western world, revealed only once those supports fall short [26]. Without such infrastructure, that spirit is more visible in developing countries through the shared and intermediate practices around technologies. Thus, asking for help in these contexts may be less of a burden or something to be avoided and more an integral part of community practice that allows people to provide gifts and thus strengthen bonds. Collectively, these sources have led us to think differently about the site and nature of mobile phone 'use', forming the starting point for the collaborative use model that underpins our design intervention.

In addition to collaborative use, we are also committed to collaborative design with specific target communities, both practically and ethically. A body of ICTD literature has pointed out the limitations of designing technologies in developing countries due to the lack of material infrastructures and resources [6], and the challenges of setting up new ones [10]. Here, involving the existing social infrastructure and community practices may transfer some responsibilities from technologies to the communities. Further, working closely with communities can lead to new design opportunities; Bellotti et al. have argued that designs that leverage the altruistic nature of human behavior should not only facilitate an extended access to different services through a shared economy model, but also create fields for newer technologies [2]. However, long-term engagement with local communities through ethnographic techniques is required to understand the social infrastructure, cultural values, and community practices. This sort of long-term engagement points to another central challenge of ICTD research, which has a long history of short term research projects that have often failed to respect (and thus, meet) the needs of specific contexts [8].

3. RESEARCH CONTEXT

Our current study was done with a community of rickshaw pullers in Dhaka, Bangladesh whom we studied through a six-month ethnography [1]. Here, we review key elements of the context from that study to help situate the current work.

We conducted our study in Kamrangirchar, a small area in Old Dhaka with many rickshaw garages. Usually the owners of the rickshaw garages buy the rickshaws and rent those to the rickshaw pullers on a half- or whole-day basis; the particular garage that we studied had 73 rickshaws, and Dhaka has a huge number of people (almost all male) who earn their living through rickshaw-pulling. This livelihood is not a wealthy one: after paying rent to the garage owner the daily income of a rickshaw puller in a day ranged from 300 Taka ($3.80[1]) to 800 Taka ($10), and this is in the lower tier of the society.

---

[1] 1 Taka is equivalent to approximately 1.2 US cents.

On average, the rickshaw pullers are also in a lower educational range in society. Most of the rickshaw pullers dropped out of primary school, while the rest never went to a school; often this was because they had to help support their families [22]. None of them could read or write a complete sentence in any language. They were familiar with Bangla and English digits, but they could not read numbers when two or more digits were put together. Thus, these rickshaw drivers are a largely low literate population.

Still, the use of mobile phones is very common among the rickshaw pullers, mirroring general trends of increased phone use among lower income residents of Dhaka over the last five years [5]. Our previous study revealed that all of the rickshaw pullers had their own mobile phones. Most of those mobile phones were Java-enabled China-made devices costing between 2,000 Taka ($25) to 10,000 Taka ($120). Many of them bought their mobile phones from second-hand markets or mobile repair shops at a savings of about the 50% of the original prices. The rickshaw pullers reported that they would spend around 20-30 Taka (25-35 cents) per day using their phone.

Basic functions such as making calls and saving contacts were not easy for the rickshaw pullers because reading and writing contact names and numbers requires literacy skills, and although they tried workarounds described in the design goals section below, these often led to frustration. In practice, they would often get help from their garage owner. Although the garage owner was not educated in formal schools, he had basic literacy skills, and as a tech-savvy person, owned several models of smartphones and had used a variety of other phones. His literacy and technical knowledge, combined with the social and economic connections between him and the pullers, led the garage owner to be a primary support for the pullers in using their phones [1]. He also arranged for electric power supply, outlets, and phone adapters in the garage so that the rickshaw pullers could recharge their phones while resting.

We chose this particular rickshaw puller community because of the fit with our condition of low-literacy, the use of phones, the social structure of help giving, and our convenience to reach and study them. All the members of our team who worked in the field were affiliated with a local university close to the garage. All of them were born and brought up in Bangladesh, and speak Bangla like the rickshaw pullers.

4. *Suhrid*

We turn now to the design of Suhrid (Bangla for 'a good friend'), an application to support the low-literate rickshaw pullers in getting help from their social connections for two basic operations on their mobile phones: 1) placing a phone call to a contact and 2) saving a contact. We first discuss the major design goals and constraints that arose from prior work and our own interactions with the garage owner and pullers, then how the design and implementation of Suhrid supports them.

4.1 Focus Group and Design Goals

We conducted four focus group discussions at the garage in the evening, when the rickshaw pullers were usually back from their work. The number and identity of participants were not the same in each discussion; rickshaw pullers who were present in the garage at those times and were interested in discussing joined, leaving in the middle if they had work to do. However, there were almost always at least six pullers present in these discussions, along with the garage owner. We discussed with the rickshaw

Figure 1. A focus group discussion at the rickshaw garage. The garage owner (wearing a cap) participated with seven other rickshaw pullers in that session. (The picture is taken and shared with proper permission of the people in the picture. The faces are blurred for anonymity)

pullers questions around the length, purpose, and patterns of their mobile phone use. Participants were not paid for their participation in this round of the study; however, food and drink were supplied during our discussions. The discussions were audio recorded with their permission, and later transcribed in Bangla and translated into English. Two members of our team coded the discussions independently; their findings were matched in a group discussion among the team and the main themes were extracted.

All of our rickshaw puller participants reported that the two main tasks that they did with their mobile phones were placing and receiving phone calls. They shared their difficulties in finding a contact from their contact list. They said they often tried to memorize the contact numbers by face, sometimes they tried to remember the position of a contact in their list, and so on. These processes often did not work well, and they ended up choosing the wrong person to call. Then they became embarrassed after talking to the wrong receiver, and sometimes they decided not to place a phone call to avoid this embarrassment. They also wasted money when they placed phone calls to wrong numbers.

The rickshaw pullers also reported that they often struggled to find ways to save a new contact on their phone. Sometimes they used punctuation symbols to remember the contact associated with a given number (e.g., "# is for *Mr. Choudhuri*; ## is for *Mr. Mitra*"), but then later forgot. They also found it difficult to save a number from their dialed, received, or missed call lists. They said they usually took help from their garage owner for these tasks. The garage owner also agreed that he often helped them for these. However, they informed us how they struggled when they were away from their garage. All the participants opined that a mobile phone application that could help the rickshaw pullers to remotely get that help from the garage owner would help them.

An immediate design challenge was the functionality of the mobile phones that our participants were using. Since most of them were not using smartphones, and they used a variety of devices, it was difficult for us to design a single interface. However, one of the rickshaw pullers suggested that many of them were thinking to buy smartphones soon. The rest agreed, sharing their experiences of using smartphones owned by friends or relatives. We shared that designing on a smartphone would be easier for us. We showed our own smartphones to them, and briefly gave them an idea about the interface. They all expressed

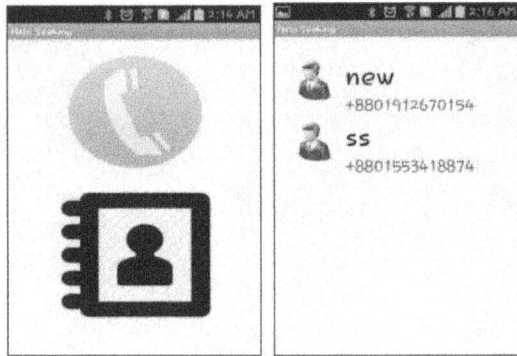

Figure 2. The first version of UI for low-literate rickshaw pullers. (Left) The interface for selecting if they wanted to place a call or save a contact. (Right) The list of helpers. In both cases the goal was to minimize the number of elements on the screen and the need for literacy skills.

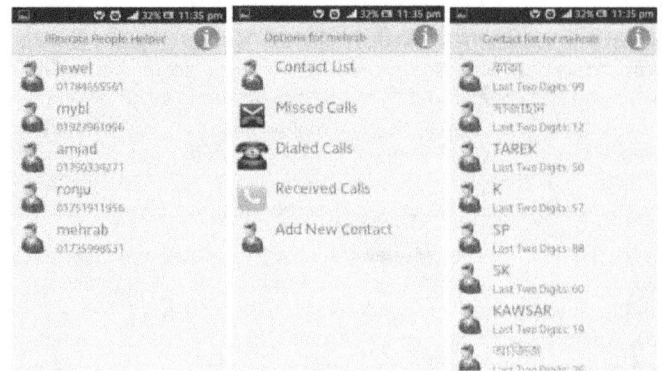

Figure 3. Three screenshots of the helper side interface. On the left, the list of seekers subscribed to this helper. In the middle, the contact list, lists of missed, dialed, and received calls, and an option to add a new contact to the contact list. On the right, the contact list of one of the seekers, showing only the last two digits of the phone number to address privacy concerns.

their excitement about having an application for them in a smartphone. We asked them if smartphones would be affordable for them. They showed us the costs of some of the Java enabled phones that they were using, and some cheap Chinese-branded smartphones in the market, and argued that the differences would be minimal. They further argued that the better quality of the pictures and video on a smartphone would rationalize the additional cost they would bear. Based on their recommendation, we decided to design an Android phone application for helping the rickshaw pullers reach their helpers when they were away from them.

4.2 Interfaces

Suhrid has two interfaces: one for the low-literate users ("seekers") and one for the help providers ("helpers"). Based on our findings, we emphasized the two basic phone operations that the rickshaw pullers needed the most: placing calls and saving contacts. Both our own work and previous studies show that low-literate people often get confused with too many icons in the interface [18]. Hence, on the seeker's side, Suhrid starts with an interface with only two icons (Figure 2, left). The top icon was for sending a request to place a call and the bottom icon was for sending a request to save a contact. The rickshaw pullers chose the icons during our group discussions. After choosing one of these two icons, the next screen appears with the list of helpers (Figure 2, right). We used comic fonts in that interface to give that an informal and friendly look. Touching a helper's name would place a call from the seeker's phone to that helper's phone through Suhrid.

On the helper's side, Suhrid displayed the list of seekers subscribed to that helper (Figure 3, left). On choosing any seeker, Suhrid would show a list with five entries: a) contact list, b) missed calls, c) dialed numbers, d) received calls, and e) an option to add a new contact to the contact list (Figure 3, middle). If the helper chose any of these, he could see the corresponding list. However, our previous study showed that some rickshaw pullers were concerned about the privacy of their contacts [1]. It also reported that the rickshaw pullers would often remember the contacts by the last three digits of their phone numbers. So, we left the last two digits visible to facilitate referencing the correct phone numbers between the seekers and the helpers, but hid the

rest of the number to increase the pullers' confidence that the numbers would be private (Figure 3, right).

4.3 Functions

4.3.1 Seeking help

We found in our field study that rickshaw pullers would only get help from the people they knew. The garage owner was also interested in helping the rickshaw pullers because he knew them. Hence, we chose a system that paired people who knew each other (versus an anonymous crowdsourcing model). In Suhrid, the pairing up could be done by adding a helper on the seeker's interface and adding a seeker in the helper's interface. Since this task needed some competency with the mobile phone, we assumed that the helper would do this task when they were co-present with a seeker they agreed to pair up with.

For seeking help, the low-literate user needed to open Suhrid on their mobile phone, select whether to place a call or save a contact, and choose the helper from the list. If it was the first time the seeker was calling the helper through this application, then the list of incoming, outgoing, and missed calls, and the contact list would be sent from the seeker's phone to the helper's phone. If it was not the first time, then the system only sent changes of these lists since the last time they contacted that helper.

4.3.2 Placing calls

If the seeker requested help for placing a call to somebody from their contact list or from dialed, received, or missed call logs, then the helper could easily find that on his interface and find the appropriate name. The helper would choose that contact and the application would send that number to the seeker's phone. The seeker's application would receive the number and place a phone call from his phone after getting a confirmation from the seeker. This way, the low-literate people could place a phone call to anybody they wanted.

4.3.3 Saving contacts

If the seeker asked help for saving a contact to their contact list that could also be done in a similar way. The seeker could request to save a number from their dialed, missed, or received calls' lists, or could just tell the helper a phone number to save with a particular name. The helper could find the number in one of the lists, or just simply type it on the software screen. After getting the number, the helper could save the contact with the appropriate name into their local copy of the helper's contact list. Suhrid would then send a message from the helper's phone to the seeker's, which the software would intercept and use to update the contact list on the seeker's phone. This way, the new contact would be saved in both phones.

4.4 Implementation
The application was built for Android-based smartphones using Java. To avoid the need for an Internet connection, communication between the mobile phones was done through text messages. For example, when the seeker's phone needed to send the contact list to the helper's phone, the application on the seeker's phone would compose a formatted text message putting the contacts' names and mobile phone numbers one after another. This message was often long, and the system needed to break the message down to several text messages for sending. On the helper's phone, the application would receive these messages one after another, and re-construct one single message. Then the application would parse that message to extract each contact and make a contact list for the seeker in the helper's phone.

5. USABILITY EVALUATION
After developing Suhrid, we conducted one laboratory study and two field level user studies to understand the usability of this application. We made necessary changes to Suhrid based on our findings in these studies.

5.1 Laboratory Study
We invited the rickshaw pullers and the garage owner to visit our university in order to introduce them to our system formally and to see if they had any difficulties in using it in the lab. The session was two hours long, and each of them was paid 800 Taka ($10), which was equivalent to a puller's earnings for their whole day and also satisfied the garage owner. There were three reasons behind this session. First, we had enough smartphones in our laboratory so everyone could use one. Second, they were interested to see the laboratory and how we work. Third, we believed that this session helped us develop a better relationship with our participants.

A total of 12 rickshaw pullers and the garage owner came to visit our laboratory. We also invited four undergraduate students to help in this session. The demonstration session was conducted in Bangla and lasted for three hours. We first lectured them about the use of a smart phone and then we showed them its basic features. To provide them first-hand experiences we divided our participants into four groups, each consisting of three rickshaw pullers and one undergraduate. Each group was given a smartphone to play with and the undergraduate, who was an expert smart phone user, helped them.

First we briefed them how to use the "touch" action to operate the smartphones. Participants picked up the basic operations (touching instead of pressing buttons, turning a phone on or off, etc.) very quickly. We then demonstrated Suhrid. After that interactive session, the participants were allowed to practice the use of our application. To mimic the real-life scenario, their helper, i.e., the garage owner, was taken to another room so that he could not verbally communicate with the participants, but could communicate with them through our application.

All 12 rickshaw puller participants were told to ask the garage owner through Suhrid for help in placing a phone call and saving a contact. Five of them could perform both of the tasks in the first

attempt without any help. The average time they took to place a call was 40 seconds, and the average time for saving a contact was 1 minute. Four of them forgot the process, so our team members helped them remember. Three of these four participants could complete both of these tasks after the reminder. The remaining person needed instruction one more time. The other three participants performed the calling task twice; apparently they misunderstood our instructions. However, when we explained the task again, they could perform both tasks in the first attempt.

After the tasks, we asked them about their general impression about Suhrid. All of them expressed their excitement around it. They said the reason why some of them had initial difficulties was because both smartphones and the application were new to them. We then asked the garage owner about his experience. He said that he enjoyed the whole process, and praised the software.

5.2 Field Level User Study, First Round
Although the rickshaw pullers and the garage owner performed satisfactorily in the lab, and expressed their satisfaction in using the application, we wanted to understand if that would be reflected in the context they spend most of their time. So, the next week, we conducted a field level user study at their garage with 10 of the 12 participants who attended our demonstration session. We tried to replicate a similar situation of help-seeking there. We made sure that the garage owner/helper couldn't communicate verbally with the participants and that other rickshaw pullers present in the garage did not help them either. As before, we paid each participant the average income of a whole day.

5.2.1 Call Generation
Each participant was asked to generate three phone calls to numbers saved in their phonebook. Three of them hesitated in the beginning as they thought they might break the expensive smart phones by their inexperienced use. However, when we assured them that no such thing would happen, they started using the smartphone. Five rickshaw pullers succeeded in all three trials. The other five made mistakes in the first trial, but succeeded in the second two trials.

The first trial of call generation took on average 45-50 seconds including the time to press the call button, select the helper, talk to the helper over the voice call, and receive the response from the helper's application. Both the participants and we considered this time much longer than the usual time one takes to place a phone call to somebody. According to our observations and their feedback, inexperience with touchscreens, lack of confidence, and confusion of the "save" icon with the "call" icon were the main reasons for this delay. The average time for successful call generation was eventually reduced to 30-35 seconds in the next two trials, which the rickshaw pullers considered good enough.

5.2.2 Contact Saving
Next, we asked each of our participants to save a random contact number or any unsaved contact number from their call history using Suhrid. Like before each of them attempted the test thrice. This time, their confidence using the touch screen seemed to have improved. However, only three of them were successful in all three attempts. Two participants failed in all three attempts. After the test they explained that the low success rate in contrast to the call test was mainly due to their confusion with the two icons in the interface, struggling with differentiating the functions of two graphical objects, one for 'calling' and the other for 'saving a contact'. This observation matches with Medhi et al.'s claim

about the weakness of low-literate people in handling the cognitive load associated with graphics [17, 19].

5.3 Field Level User Study, Second Round

In our next round of design, we responded to these problems by removing the initial interface for choosing a service on the seeker's UI. Upon opening the app, the list of helpers would appear immediately (Figure 2, right). On selecting the helper, a call would be generated to the selected helper. The seeker would then tell the helper whether he was trying to call somebody or save a contact. The helper then would use the appropriate lists through Suhrid (Figure 3, middle) to find the number. Upon selecting the number, Suhrid would offer the helper an option for either making a phone call or saving that number in the contact list. We made the necessary changes in the application according to this design, and then conducted another round of field level user study at the rickshaw garage in Kamrangirchar two weeks after the first round.

We used the same 10 participants, setup, payment, and task that we did in the first round. Eight out of 10 participants were successful in all three attempts on both tasks this time. The other two failed in in one attempt each. One of them ran out of credit in the middle of the process while the other one asked the helper to help him call to a number that had not actually been saved in his phonebook. In one case the helper mistakenly saved a different number from the call log, so we repeated that test and the rickshaw puller succeeded. The overall remarks of the participants were overwhelmingly positive. One participant commented,

"Just one click and some other person does the job from another place! I don't have to do anything!! It will be a great help for me if I use this phone. Not only for me, but also for every low literate and illiterate people will be happy to use this application."

6. DEPLOYMENT

After the success in the second round of field usability testing, we decided Suhrid was ready for a real deployment to understand better how Suhrid would help this rickshaw puller community. The rickshaw puller participants were chosen based on their interest to participate in our study, which lasted six weeks. Ten smartphones were given to the pullers and two other phones were given to the garage owner and his brother who would work as the helpers. All participants kept the smartphone as compensation. The garage owner and the rickshaw pullers recommended the owner's brother as a second helper. He would often come to the garage and help them in operating their mobile phones the same way the garage owner did, and was willing to participate in the deployment and able to operate Suhrid. So, in the helpers' list on Suhrid, each of the rickshaw pullers had the number of the garage owner at the top followed by the number of his brother.

The lists also had a third number. We were curious about whether people would take help from strangers when their normal helpers weren't available, in the way that some crowdsourcing applications such as *VizWiz* [3] enable people to get help from strangers. To do this, we recruited two freelance workers, students of a local university from outside the rickshaw puller community. After talking to both the rickshaw pullers and the freelance workers, it was decided that the rickshaw pullers would pay 2 Taka (3 cents) each time they asked the freelancers for help. The rickshaw pullers were clearly informed that they would have to pay when they would seek help from these freelancers. Each freelancer was assigned to be the third and final helper for half of the rickshaw pullers.

To evaluate Suhrid, we collected three main sources of data. First, we collected usage data through a text message Suhrid sent each time a rickshaw puller asked for help that included the seeker, helper, and the time. We received permission from our participants to collect these data. Second, at the end of six weeks, we went to the garage and interviewed each of our participants about their experiences throughout the deployment period. These interviews were audio recorded with the participant's permission and conducted in Bangla. The average length of the interviews was 30 minutes and participants were given 200 Taka ($2.5) each as compensation. Finally, we invited the rickshaw pullers to our university guest room one more time. This was both a focus group discussion and a formal conclusion of the study. All of the participants were paid 800 Taka ($10) for this two-hour session. We did not invite the garage owner and his friend this time to allow the rickshaw pullers to express their experiences freely. Instead, we had a separate group discussion with the garage owner and his brother at the garage.

In both of the focus group discussions we asked them about their experiences of using Suhrid. Those questions included if they had any difficulties in using Suhrid, in which situations they used Suhrid, if they got help whenever they needed, what their experiences were around the freelance workers, why their usage of Suhrid declined over time, and if they had any other issues with Suhrid. The transcription, translation, coding, and resolution processes were the same in this round as before.

6.1 Results

The interviews and focus group discussions revealed a number of important aspects around the use of Suhrid. Participants described the ease of using the software, its value and availability, and the appreciation it gave them for the giving of help between them. They also expressed concerns about privacy and reluctance to take help from the freelance workers, as well as the gradual decline of their usage of Suhrid over time.

6.1.1 Ease

All seekers were satisfied with the ease of using Suhrid. One of them said,

"This software is very easy to use. I didn't find any difficulty while using it. See? Here is the icon I had to press to call the Mahajan. And if the Mahajan is not available I press the second number." [Mahajan means the 'The big person'. Here he referred to the garage owner. The second number was his brother's.]

The helpers also found Suhrid easy to use. The garage owner said,

"When you first gave me the software I understood the full functionality. Here is the list and I can select any of them and see the list of the missed call, received call and their phone book. .... It's very easy to use."

6.1.2 Availability

Suhrid also provided the seekers valuable services and help, sometimes at critical times. As one participant said,

"I was at the hospital for a checkup of my father and I needed to call a doctor. Another person saved the number, I remembered the name by which he saved it but couldn't find it. It was an emergency. I called the Mahajan and asked him to dial the number for me. He did and I talked with the doctor."

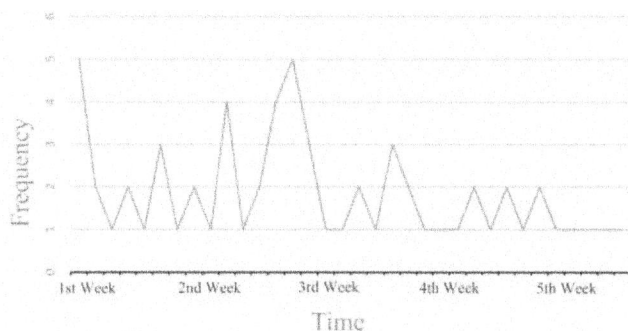

Figure 4. Daily usage of Suhrid during field deployment. Use of Suhrid was higher in the first few weeks, then declined.

The seekers shared how Suhrid helped them by making the helper available in the contexts they needed. One participant said,

"Normally when I get out of home to go to Mahajan I forget by the time for which reason I went there. So, most of the time that doesn't help me. But with this software I can easily call him and ask him to save a contact for me. Sometimes it takes time but work gets done."

Seekers almost always got help from their helpers, first trying to get help from their garage owner, then the owner's brother. In only five cases, they could not get help from either of them. In three such cases, they took help from the freelance workers. In the remaining two cases, they stopped trying.

6.1.3 Reluctance to Take Help from Freelancers
The seekers expressed their lack of interest in receiving help from the freelance workers. All of them said that they did not need to call the freelancers because they had almost always got help from their garage owner. Also, they reiterated that help should come from people they knew. One of them said, *"I don't feel comfortable asking help to somebody I do not know."* Once he said that, the rest of the participants agreed, saying, *"yes"*. One seeker who took help from one of our freelance workers said,

"Although I took help from him, I never asked him how he was doing. It was only regarding help. I only called him for help nothing else. He was always my last option for help."

6.1.4 Improving Communal Bonds
In contrast to their experience with freelancers, both the seekers and the helpers reported that using Suhrid with people they knew strengthened their community feelings. The concentration of help requests on the garage owner and the brother was not a concern to them; both reported that they had enjoyed their task. We asked them if the number of incoming helping requests ever bothered them. The garage owner said that he always had his mobile phone with him, and the time and efforts it needed to help one was not overwhelming to him. However, he also mentioned that he could not respond to couple of calls as he was busy in saying prayers.

All of the rickshaw pullers reported that the availability of their garage owner all the time helped them realize how much care the garage owner had for them. One rickshaw puller said, *"Now I realize how caring he (the garage owner) is. You cannot help somebody like this if you do not care for them a lot."* The garage owner said that the relationship between him and the rickshaw pullers improved because of Suhrid because now they were taking help even after leaving the garage. He said, *"It is great to come*

closer, and to make them understand how a well-wisher should be. Now they know better how much I care for them. You can see the added respect in their words these days."

6.1.5 Gradual Decline of Usage
Despite the value people drew from using Suhrid, its use declined over time. In total, it was used 63 times over the span of six weeks (Figure 4). The number of requests sought for placing a call was much higher (41) than for saving a number (22). Among the 63 requests, the garage owner received 46, his brother received 14, and the freelancers received 3.

Participants informed us that usage declined because initially they had to take more help to save the new contacts, so the number of requests was high. Also, they often call the same numbers, which they learned to call themselves after taking help once or twice. Then they would only take help whenever they had to call a new number or a save a new contact. Furthermore, they still often took help from the garage owner in person when both were in the garage together; Suhrid was mainly useful when the puller and owner were not in the same place.

6.1.6 Concerns
The seekers also shared several concerns around Suhrid. One of them complained that our software damaged his mobile balance. He said,

"I had 50 taka in my mobile when I called Mahajan but when I finished talking to him, I noticed after some time that my balance is zero. I was confused." (500 Taka is approx. $6)

Later, we discovered he had not turned off his mobile phone after calling, and that caused a big deduction from his balance. Another seeker wondered about the privacy of the contacts saying,

"I didn't understand how the garage owner was able to call my wife through my phone. And how did he save contact numbers in my phone remotely? Was the number saved in his phone too?"

We explained to him why it would not be possible for the garage owner either to know the phone number or to place a call to his wife. He seemed to be satisfied with our explanation.

7. DISCUSSION
The design, development, and deployment of Suhrid generate a number of immediate lessons for better designing a UI for low-literate people, and some larger lessons pertinent to problems of design in the context of developing countries.

First, our study supports previous findings around the struggle of low-literate users with hierarchical presentation of information on graphical interfaces [18]. The confusion that arose in the first field study with the selection interface went away with the removal of that screen, suggesting the value of minimizing hierarchy in the interface. The fact that the rickshaw pullers struggled with even two icons on the selection screen, but were able to sequentially navigate through the list of three helpers, may indicate that low-literate users might be better at memorizing the relative positions of contacts than the interpretation of symbolic icons.

Second, our study suggests that privacy management is important in designing shared-use interfaces. Contact information can be confidential and the privacy associated with different parts of contact information is dependent on the users' interpretation. The fact that rickshaw pullers used the last three digits of phone numbers to identify contacts had to be respected in our design:

showing only two digits balanced the needs for communicating between helpers and seekers while respecting seekers' perceptions of privacy. A related sensitivity concerned asking for help from people outside the community. We found our participants preferred to get help from another person in their own community over somebody from outside. This particular finding may suggest limits to more generic crowd-sourced solutions, and encourage future researchers to weigh local sensitivities before advancing crowd-based responses to local use challenges in such contexts.

Third, like many other technologies for developing countries, Suhrid demonstrates how cost influences design choices. The community, according to their cost-benefit analysis, rationalized the choices of the Android platform and text-based communication. The credit in the balance that was spent for a typical use of Suhrid, including both the call itself and the text messages sent in the background, was around 70 to 90 paisa, or about one US cent, for the seeker and 30 to 40 paisa for the helper. Although we reimbursed participants in the end for all the text messages Suhrid generated during the deployment, in general participants would need to pay for Suhrid themselves. Thus, we asked our participants if this expenditure would be heavy for them. They all considered this expenditure justified for the service. One participant said,

"A rickshaw puller is not as poor as you think. I usually spend 500-600 Taka for my mobile phone every month. And I would be happy to spend 1-2 Taka if I could get my purpose served with remote collaboration." (500-600 Taka is approx. $6-$7, and 1-2 Taka is approx. 2 to 3 cents)

Fourth, we observed that the low-literate rickshaw pullers started learning the contacts while taking help from Suhrid. While explaining the gradual decline of the usage, they mentioned how they could recognize the old contacts from their memory and they only needed help for the new contacts. They said they could recognize the faces of the contact names or numbers. This finding suggests that such a help system might also eventually educate and empower individual users over time. This gradual decline in help-seeking also suggests that their cost for using Suhrid would likely decline over time as well.

Beyond the lessons for immediate design, our study indicates a number of bigger concerns for ICTD. First, our study showed that extending the reach of help strengthened the relationship between the rickshaw pullers and the garage owner. The garage owner expressed his satisfaction to be able to come closer to the rickshaw pullers because of Suhrid. Likewise, the rickshaw pullers praised the garage owner for helping them in important times through Suhrid. Thus, beyond its immediately instrumental effects in extending effective use among low-literate populations, Suhrid performed a secondary but no less important role in strengthening and reinforcing local social relations, notably relations of respect and trust between the garage owner and rickshaw pullers. This finding echoes in modest form Mauss' classic finding around the importance of mutual aid and gift giving as a central and indeed constitutive moment of social life [16]. If the goal of ICTD work is to empower and support not only users but also the wider networks and communities of which they are a part, design options that leverage and extend core features and principles of sociality itself ought to figure more prominently in the field.

Second, our study demonstrates the importance of anchoring design interventions in longer-term programs of ethnography and community engagement. Unlike emphasizing scaling up 'one size fits all' technologies, we ground our designs in the values, norms, and practices of a particular community through our engaged field work. This helped us address many nuances of design that would be otherwise difficult to find out. For example, decisions like using the Android platform, remote help, revealing only two digits of phone numbers, or communicating through text messages came out of the users' values and practice.

Third, our deep engagement with the community helped relax the power differences between the designers and users, and opened up opportunities for designing technologies with their participation. The rickshaw pullers often discussed with us other problems of their life, along with a range of ideas towards solutions. For example, some rickshaw pullers joined a co-operative society where they needed to pay regularly, and they needed help to determine and remember saving from their everyday income. We are now working with them towards technology solutions that may help with this goal. While such long-term and locally responsive models of community engagement may limit the 'scaling up' of single technologies to wider social and cultural contexts, they suggest new opportunities to design multiple, appropriate technologies for the same community—opportunities that may extend the depth, impact, and responsibility of ICTD work. They also demonstrate the kind of long-term commitment to places and individuals that may serve as a partial antidote to the kinds of "research tourism" [8] long identified and criticized in ICTD work.

8. CONCLUSION
In this paper, we have described the design, development and deployment of our community sourced mobile phone interface for a low literate rickshaw puller community in Dhaka. Building on our ongoing ethnographic work, Suhrid seeks to leverage and extend existing distributed practices of technology use to overcome literacy-based barriers to mobile phone use within our target population. We involved the members of the community in each step of our design process, and conducted two rounds of field level user studies to refine our design. Finally, we deployed Suhrid for 6 weeks and conducted a post-deployment user study through interviews and focus group discussions to understand its successes and limitations. Our study generates a number of lessons the use of icons, privacy, and cost-benefit negotiation in designing such collaborative interfaces in developing countries. Furthermore, we present our arguments supporting the potential of gift-based design and long-term engagement in ICTD works.

9. ACKNOWLEDGEMENT
We thank the garage owner, and the rickshaw drivers, and the freelance workers for their support during this study. We thank the Department of Computer Science and Engineering (CSE) of Bangladesh University of Engineering and Technology (BUET) for providing us laboratory facilities. We also thank International Fulbright Science and Technology Fellowship and Intel Science and Technology Center for Social Computing (ISTC*SC) for supporting this research.

10. REFERENCES
[1]   Ahmed, S.I., Jackson, S.J., Zaber, M., Morshed, M.B., Ismail, M.H.B. and Afrose, S. 2013. Ecologies of Use and Design: Individual and Social Uses of Mobile Phones Within Low-Literate Rickshaw-Puller Communities in Urban Bangladesh. In *Proc. DEV-4*, 14:1–14:10.

[2] Bellotti, VM. et al. 2014. Towards community-centered support for peer-to-peer service exchange: rethinking the timebanking metaphor. In *Proc. CHI'14*, ACM, 2975–2984.

[3] Bigham, JP. et al. 2010. VizWiz: nearly real-time answers to visual questions. In *Proc. UIST'10*, ACM, 333–342.

[4] Burrell, J. 2010. Evaluating Shared Access: social equality and the circulation of mobile phones in rural Uganda. *Journal of Computer Mediated Communication*. 15, 2 (2010), 230–250.

[5] Chen, G. and Rasmussen, S. 2014. *bKash Bangladesh : A Fast Start for Mobile Financial Services*. World Bank.

[6] Chen, J. 2015. Computing within Limits and ICTD. In *Proc. LIMITS'15*.

[7] Chipchase, J. 2006. How do you manage your contacts if you can't read or write? *Interactions*. 13, 6 (2006), 16–17.

[8] Dearden, A. 2013. See no evil?: ethics in an interventionist ICTD. *Information Technologies & International Development* 9, 2, 1-17.

[9] Ghosh, K., Parikh, T.S. and Chavan, A.L. 2003. Design considerations for a financial management system for rural, semi-literate users. In *Proc CHI EA'03*, ACM. 824–825.

[10] Heimerl, K., Hasan, S., Ali, K., Parikh, T. and Brewer, E. 2015. A Longitudinal Study of Local, Sustainable, Small-Scale Cellular Networks. *Information Technologies & International Development*. 11, 1, 1-19.

[11] Houston, L. 2014. Inventive Infrastructure: An Exploration of Mobile Phone. PhD Thesis, Lancaster University.

[12] Jackson, S.J., Ahmed, S.I. and Rifat, M.R. 2014. Learning, innovation, and sustainability among mobile phone repairers in Dhaka, Bangladesh. In *Proc. DIS'14*, 905–914.

[13] Jackson, S.J., Pompe, A. and Krieshok, G. 2012. Things fall apart: maintenance, repair, and technology for education initiatives in rural Namibia. In *Proc. iConference'11*, 107–116.

[14] Joshi, A., Welankar, N., Kanitkar, K. and Sheikh, R. 2008. Rangoli: a visual phonebook for low-literate users. In *Proceedings of the 10th International conference on Human computer interaction with mobile devices and services*, 217–223.

[15] Kumar, N. and Parikh, T. 2013. Mobiles, music, and materiality. In *Proc. CHI'13*, 2863–2872.

[16] Mauss, M. 1954. *The gift: Forms and functions of exchange in archaic societies*. IG Cunnison. London: Cohen and West.

[17] Medhi, I. 2015. User Interface Design for Low-Literate and Novice Users: Past, Present and Future. *Foundations and Trends in Human-Computer Interaction*. 8, 1, 1-72.

[18] Medhi, I., Lakhmanan, M., Toyama, K. and Cutrell, E. 2013. Some evidence for the impact of limited education on hierarchical user interface navigation. In *Proc. CHI'13*, 2813–2822.

[19] Medhi, I., Prasad, A. and Toyama, K. 2007. Optimal audio-visual representations for illiterate users of computers. In *Proc. WWW'07*, 873–882.

[20] Medhi, I., Sagar, A. and Toyama, K. 2006. Text-free user interfaces for illiterate and semi-literate users. In *Proc. ICTD'06*, 72–82.

[21] Medhi-Thies, I., Ferreira, P., Gupta, N., O'Neill, J. and Cutrell, E. 2015. KrishiPustak: A Social Networking System for Low-Literate Farmers. In *Proc. CSCW'15*, 1670–1681.

[22] Meheri, T. 2012. *Rickshaw Cycle Drivers in Dhaka: Assessing Working Conditions and Livelihoods*. Erasmus University.

[23] Parikh, T.S. and Ghosh, K. 2006. Understanding and designing for intermediated information tasks in India. *IEEE Pervasive Computing*. 5, 2, 32–39.

[24] Parikh, T.S., Ghosh, K. and Chavan, A.L. 2003. Design studies for a financial management system for micro-credit groups in rural India. In *ACM SIGCAPH Computers and the Physically Handicapped*, 15–22.

[25] Patel, N., Chittamuru, D., Jain, A., Dave, P. and Parikh, T. 2010. Avaaj Otalo: a field study of an interactive voice forum for small farmers in rural India. In Proc. CHI'10, 733–742.

[26] Poole, E.S., Chetty, M., Morgan, T., Grinter, R.E. and Edwards, W.K. 2009. Computer help at home: methods and motivations for informal technical support. In *Proc CHI'09*, 739–748.

[27] Rangaswamy, N. and Nair, S. 2010. The mobile phone store ecology in a Mumbai slum community: Hybrid networks for enterprise. *Information Technologies and International Development*. 2, 3, 51-65.

[28] Rangaswamy, N. and Sambasivan, N. 2011. Cutting Chai, Jugaad, and Here Pheri: towards UbiComp for a global community. *Personal and Ubiquitous Computing*. 15, 6, 553–564.

[29] Sambasivan, N., Cutrell, E., Toyama, K. and Nardi, B. 2010. Intermediated technology use in developing communities. In *Proc. CHI'10*, 2583–2592.

[30] Sherwani, J., Ali, N., Mirza, S., Fatma, A., Memon, Y., Karim, M., Tongia, R. and Rosenfeld, R. 2007. HealthLine: Speech-based access to health information by low-literate users. In *Proc. ICTD'07*, 1–9.

[31] Wiedenbeck, S. 1999. The use of icons and labels in an end user application program: an empirical study of learning and retention. *Behaviour & Information Technology*. 18, 2, 68–82.

[32] *Global Accessibility Reporting Initiative (GARI): Mobile Handset/Device Accessibility Report*. Available at: http://www.gari.info/

ICTs in Rural Education: Let the Game Begin

Adèle Botha
CSIR Meraka
UNISA School of Computing
PO Box 395
Pretoria, 0001 South Africa
+27 12 841 3265
abotha@csir.co.za

Marlien Herselman
CSIR Meraka
UNISA School of Computing
PO Box 395
Pretoria, 0001 South Africa
+27 12 841 3081
mherselman@csir.co.za

ABSTRACT

Over a period of three years, 255 teachers at 26 schools in Cofimvaba, which lies in the very rural Nciba district of the Eastern Cape Province, South Africa, have been using mobile tablets in their classrooms to support teaching and learning. The purpose of this paper is to describe the novel gamification approach to Teacher Professional Development in a unique context where schools are deprived of resources but still managed to successfully integrate mobile tablets in their classroom practices. These practices have changed the way teachers teach towards a pedagogy that is more suited to the information age. The success of this TPD model lies in the application of lessons learnt from literature, selected game elements, rewards based on demonstrated competencies, flexibility, innovation, creativity and co-creation. All of the teachers[1] who took part in the project, achieved the 13compulsory badges, which is noteworthy. This implies that all participating teachers applied all the ICT integration skills demonstrated in the ICT for Rural Education (ITC4RED) TPD course at least once in their classroom, and were able to collect evidence to support that they have gained the necessary competencies.

Categories and Subject Descriptors

H.1.2 [User/Machine Systems] Human factors

General Terms

Documentation, Performance, Design, Human Factors,

Keywords

Gamification, Mlearning, Resource Constrained, Teacher Professional Development, Rewards, Mobile Technology.

1. INTRODUCTION AND BACKGROUND

Educators believe that technology has great potential to improve education [1], improve student learning and change classroom practice. Technology has the capacity to support powerful and

---

[1] Two headmasters withdrew and a number of teachers had to stop due to medical reasons.

ACM DEV 2015, December 1-2, 2015, London, United Kingdom.
© 2015 ACM. ISBN 978-1-4503-3490-7/15/11...$15.00.
DOI: http://dx.doi.org/10.1145/2830629.2830646

sophisticated learning environments and is often seen as the golden key in facilitating technology-enhanced, student-centered teaching environments [2]. Hardman [3] also indicates that ICTs have the ability to act as a catalyst to transform pedagogical practices in classrooms. However many ICT for Education initiatives in South Africa and the rest of the developing world have resulted in failure [4-6]. Teachers in rural areas are willing to use technology to support teaching and learning, but find the pedagogy a challenge. They are often not confident enough to integrate the technology into their teaching activities [4, 6]. In those cases where ICT initiatives in schools do include some kind of training component, the focus is often on computer literacy and related keyboard skills, rather than how to use the technology as a tool for teaching and learning [6].

This paper will focus on an intervention which is coined as the Information Communication and Technology for Rural Education Development (ICT4RED) initiative. It was a large-scale longitudinal pilot (over 3 years) that explored the use of tablets in 26 deep rural schools in the Nciba district of Cofimvaba in the Eastern Cape Province of South Africa.

The macro-economic perspective of the area is one of few commercial opportunities, high unemployment, low incomes, a shrinking population of economically active people and a growing number of school-going youth. This area is regarded as a resource constrained environment. A resource constrained environment for the purpose of this paper, is best described by Anderson, et al. [7] as an environments where there is low-income communities and low bandwidth. These environments provide unique constraints (e.g., cultures where people are unfamiliar with or afraid of technology, environments where power and network connectivity are scarce and expensive).

The pilot extends to include 3 senior secondary schools (Grades 10 to 12) and 23 junior and primary secondary schools (Grades R to 9) [8]. The challenge was to introduce technology (in this case tablets and other supporting ICT hardware and infrastructure) in ways that would enhance teaching and learning, support sustainability beyond the project and ensure true integration into existing education processes, whilst managing very real logistical and infrastructure problems. This is a challenge that can be seen as significant in ICT in Education initiatives in rural areas.

This initiative was part of the Technology for Rural Education Development (TECH4RED) research programme which aimed to contribute to the improvement of rural education via technology-led innovation. It was initiated by the Department of Science and Technology (DST) in collaboration with the Department of Basic Education (DBE), the Eastern Cape Department of Education (ECDoE) and the Department of Rural Development and Land Reform (DRDLR) in South Africa. TECH4RED applied a range of technology-intensive interventions, including initiatives in ICT, nutrition, health, water, sanitation and energy to determine the extent to which the programme will enable positive contributions at all levels and spheres of influence in the school system [9]. It is envisaged that the learning from this programme could enable evidence-based policy development within the government of South Africa. ICT4RED was thus part of TECH4RED and focused only on how technology can support teaching and learning [10].

ICT4RED, aimed to investigate the application and deployment of tablets, supported by other technologies (which include school infrastructure, network connectivity, e-textbooks and other electronic resources) to 26 schools in a rural school district [10]. In order to do this 12 components were selected which were identified as playing a role in ICT for development projects in South Africa, especially in resource constrained environments [11]. The discussion of these are beyond the scope of this paper but are well expounded on in Herselman and Botha [10]. For the purpose of this paper only the Teacher Professional Development (TPD) component will be interrogated. The TPD aimed to meet teachers where they were with reference to their teaching and technology proficiency, and to scaffold their development incrementally in order for their classroom practice to reflect a 21st century teaching and learning engagement as modelled on the EPG [12] emergent pedagogy.

2. CHALLENGES FACING TEACHERS WHO EMPLOY TECHNOLOGY IN THEIR CLASSROOMS IN SOUTH AFRICA

Challenges facing teaching and learning in South Africa include[13]: the apartheid legacy of unequal education infrastructure; high levels of poverty in communities; weak quality of learning and teaching; lack of accountability across the system; corruption and inefficiencies in the system; ineffective leadership and managements; on-going changes in the curriculum; and ineffective implementation of the language policy. Some goals for *The Action Plan 2014 of the Department of Basic Education in South Africa* [14] include ensuring an environment that inspires learners to want to come to school to learn and teachers to teach, increasing learner access to a wide range of media, including computers, which enrich their education, improving the average performance across all grades, increasing the number of learners who have mastered the minimum mathematics competencies, and increasing the number of learners to pass physical science [14]. However, there are significant inequalities with regard to ICT skills and access in South Africa among learners and teachers who are already disadvantaged due to a range of social imbalances [15].

ICT can potentially help address challenges such as inadequate resources and under-qualified educators [3], yet it is in resource constrained environments that educators are having most difficulty in integrating the use of ICTs into teaching and learning.

By addressing the ICT needs for educators in these communities, the prospects for both education and the community at large may be improved. The impact of a developing context is evident in findings that suggest that schools in under-resourced areas could not afford in-house technical support and were then reliant on external support arrangements, which was often deemed insufficient [16]. Furthermore, it was reported that most educators have inadequate ICT and pedagogical competencies for effective

integration of ICT into their work. Learners from disadvantaged backgrounds often have low technical skills, and because most of them do not have computers at home they have no opportunity to practice and hone skills what are introduced in lessons. Consequently, educators spend large amounts of time dealing with the functional use of technology, instead of teaching the subject content [16].

3. METHODOLOGY APPLIED

In developing the ICT4RED TPD course [17], a design science methodology was applied. Design Science research focuses on creation and the purpose of design is "to change existing situations into preferred ones" [18]. Design science addresses *wicked problems* in Information Systems and is fundamentally a problem-solving paradigm. Wicked problems as explained by Hevner and Chatterjee [18] relate to the ill-defined environmental contexts, creativity and teamwork to produce effective solutions. There are compelling arguments to accept the educational exploitation of ICT within resource constrained environments such as the Cofimvaba school district as a wicked problem. The overarching research on the implementation of ICT in rural education was grounded in the philosophy of pragmatism applied a deductive reasoning approach.

The ICT4RED engagement with the schools extended over 3 years, with an initial pilot study at 1 school in 2012. In 2013 the engagement was scaled to 11 other schools and in 2014 to the remaining 14 schools. In total therefore the endeavor reached 26 schools. It incorporated 6 500 learners, 255 teachers and 32 district officials. The ICT4RED initiative envisaged the development of appropriate contextual frameworks, models, guidelines and tools to inform other similar initiatives where appropriate. The discussion of each of these artifacts and their full monitoring and evaluation activities within the ICT4RED initiative is beyond the scope of the paper but interested parties can access the relevant narrative [19]. This paper is concerned with the ICT4RED TPD and aims to describe the novel gamification approach to Teacher Professional Development in a unique context where schools are deprived of resources but still managed to successfully integrate mobile tablets in their classroom practices.

The following section will outline the design decisions made and detail the operationalisation of these decisions within the rural disconnected environment.

4. ICT4RED TPD COURSE DESIGN AND IMPLEMENTATION

Grant [20] argues that TPD is a practical endeavor and further implies that the process goes *beyond* training as an acquisition of skills to include the development of new insights into pedagogy and reflection by teachers on their teaching practice.

A working definition of the ICT4RED TPD was adopted and is presented below:

The ICT4RED Teacher Professional Development is a supported process to guide the development of relevant teacher knowledge and proficiency to enable classroom practice to portray a 21st century technology enhanced teaching and learning engagement.

Mindful of the ICT4RED initiative's overarching objective of investigating the application and deployment of new and existing technologies at schools, the classroom interactions in the participating schools had to change in a way that would accommodate the introduction and use of these technologies. The change in classroom practice to accommodate the introduction and use of new and existing technologies at schools, as directive, was to be operationalized through the introduction and integration of Tablet technology (section 4.2) and a Teacher Professional Development course.

The ICT4RED TPD course narrative is one of changing classroom practice to portray more of an "emerging pedagogy for the information age" and less of a "traditional pedagogy" as discussed by Voogt [21, 22]. This implied that the change was towards greater learner centered activities, greater collaboration and creativity. In addition the classroom practice would move towards a greater integration of subject content and evaluation would be less teacher directed and formative in nature.

The course takes around a year to complete as each of the modules should ideally be separated by approximately 3 weeks teaching time to allow teachers to implement the module strategy and collect the relevant evidence in their own classes. The 10 modules and their teaching strategy and content focus are given below:

Table 1: ICT4RED TPD course outline

Module	Compulsory Badges
	ICT4RED badge. Committing yourself
Module 1	Jigsaw strategy and getting to know your tablet.
Module 2	Storytelling as a strategy and my technology journey
Module 3	Roleplay as a teaching strategy and navigating issues that arise when implimenting ICT in my school.
Module 4	Learning stations as a teaching strategy and creating digital content. What types of content are there.
Module 5	Mind mapping strategy and implementing an acceptable user's policy in your class.
Module 6	Flipped classroom as a teaching strategy creating lesson plans for ICT integration.
Module 7	Game-Based Learning strategies and creating educational video's . Copyright, plagiarism, Creative Commons.
Module 8	Field trips as a teaching strategy. Gallery walk as a teaching strategy. Taking my classroom into the world through a scavenger hunt.
Module 9	Gallery Walks as a teaching strategy. Digital Identities, Phishing, Online safety Cyberbullying, Personal Learning networks Professional Learning communities
Module 10	Reflecting on the journey. How to present

The ICT4RED TPD course endeavored to build a toolbox of skills, technology and competencies that would empower teachers to integrate technology meaningfully into their classroom practice in order to portray a 21st century engagement. Each module in the curriculum is *about* relevant content *through* a teaching strategy *using* technology to facilitate the teaching and learning interaction. In addition teachers would be exposed to:

- best practice in group work;
- different assessment strategies;
- concept of a reflective practitioner; and
- concepts regarding online learning and additional resources.
The toolbox would consist of the following.

4.1.1 Teaching strategies
Nine teaching strategies were identified as relevant. The criteria for strategy selection was that it needed to work well in classrooms with or without technology, that it had to be learner centered and that teachers would be able to adapt it across the learning spectrum to all levels of teaching and all subjects.

4.1.2 Content
Relevant content that would enable the teachers to confidently engage in the information age and which could support the current curriculum applied in South African classrooms, were selected. This content did not focus on subject content as the course would not be limited to a specific subject or phase. Teachers would become co-creators in the sense that they had to merge the prescribed *how* (with tablet technology using teaching strategies) and the *what* (their subject content).

4.1.3 Technology skills, competencies and hardware
These were relevant skills and competencies to enable teachers to confidently use the technology to enhance the teaching and learning interaction. The technology hardware would consist of a device, the enabling environment and hardware attachments that would facilitate the teaching and learning interaction. This would include access to a projector, Mobikits[2], charging stations, a content server etc. Consideration had to be given to the constraints of the environment and the cost (both monetary and opportunity costs).

As a result, a number of ICT4RD TDP Course design decisions were made. These are outlined and their implementation described below. Section 5 outlines some relevant preliminary results[3] and section 6 discusses the implications of the findings.

4.2 Technology used
Android Tablets were chosen as the technology that would support the teachers. As all educators had access to a mobile device, it was felt that the barrier to proficiency would be significantly reduced in this way. Android devices were selected due to the open nature of the operating system and the large quantity of free apps that are available. A specific tablet selection process was developed to determine which Android tablet will suit the constrained environment and context the best. The discussion of this tool is beyond the scope of this paper.

4.3 Connectivity
The TPD course was designed in such a way that it did not require any internet connectivity. Although consensus was that this was not the most desirable way to structure the course it was pragmatic. Initially all of the schools were disconnected and there was very limited infrastructure that would support sufficient connectivity. An internet like experience was catered for through a local Wi-Fi hotspot and content server. Opportunities to connect to the internet were incorporated in various ways through challenges that were articulated as 4 of the 5 challenge badges. These internet based challenge badges were an email, twitter, app evaluation and blog collaboration badge.

4.4 Gamification
Gamification as a design strategy was implemented. Educational Gamification can be viewed as the design strategy of using game

---

[2] A Mobikit is a mobile container as big as a suitcase that provides secure storage and charging for, and includes 15 seven inch preloaded Android devices, which can be used in the classrooms with learners.

[3] Final results are due to be released end 2015.

design elements in educational contexts to support teaching and learning goals [23]. Fundamentally Educational Gamification has to be about learning and learning gains and should be grounded in best practice pedagogical principles [23]. The game elements outlined by Costello and Edmonds [24] for play, derived from a survey of play theories, were adopted . Although the distinction between play and games are given by various authors [25-27], Costello and Edmond's framework accommodate the hedonistic attributes that was considered desirable [26]. In addition Deterding, et al. [25] argue that in practice, gamified applications often give rise to playful behaviors. Costello and Edmonds [24] elements are: creation; exploration; discovery; difficulty; competition; danger; captivation; sensation; sympathy; simulation; fantasy; camaraderie, and subversion. These elements were then purposefully designed into the facilitation of the TPD sessions. Not all elements were designed to be present in each of the sessions but rather an appropriate combination was strived for in accordance with Juul and Deterding et al. [25, 28].

The ICT4RED TPD course presentation would in addition incorporate principles identified and adapted from Stott and Neustaedter [29] as: Freedom to fail, rapid feedback, progression and storytelling.

4.4.1 Freedom to fail
The ICT4RED TPD adopted badges as interim goals. These were clearly articulated as a set of 13 compulsory and 5 optional goals. Each of these goals is operationalized as a badge. Teachers had multiple opportunities to achieve skills and competencies to enable the achievement of a specific badge.

Figure 1: Badges linked to the Narrative

4.4.2 Rapid feedback
The course was structured so that the teachers receive feedback on each goal as a set of skills and competencies that they attempt and submit proof of for accreditation by a badge. The successions of badges guide them on a learning path and they receive feedback from inbuilt sequencing so that there are multiple small units of accomplishment. Originally it was envisaged that Mozilla open badges would be used, but as the teachers lacked a digital presence and had no emails, this did not materialize.

4.4.3 Progression
The course was structured to scaffold the attainment of technology, content and pedagogical proficiency as (Figure 1 & 2):

- Appropriate technology knowledge related to an Android Tablet and its use to support the teaching and 21st Century learning engagement, The participants were assumed to be novices and scaffolded to progress from, being able to use the tablet as a personal device (I can work with a tablet), to

use as professional device (I can teach with a tablet), and cumulating in the use of a tablet as a collaborative tool (I can work through the tablet).

- Content knowledge and skills related towards being, participating, teaching and learning in a digital world.
- The pedagogical knowledge that was limited to teaching strategies that would successfully outline the integration of technology into a 21st Century learning environment. The choice of strategies was done on its robustness and replicability. Knowledge on own practice was encouraged through reflection on practice towards reflective practitioners.

Figure 2: ICT4RED TPD Course learning path

As such, the teacher is nudged into becoming an online participant, contributor and learner and encouraged to position them to become lifelong learners and contributors in the digital world.

4.4.4 Storytelling
The narrative is articulated as a learning path that is operationalized through the attainment of 13 compulsory badges that represent the 13 compulsory learning goals of the curriculum.

4.5 Co-creation
The TPD would cover a broad spectrum of teachers and, per se, could not be subject or phase specific. The teacher, as content and context expert, had to become a co-creator in the process. The opportunity was facilitated as follows:

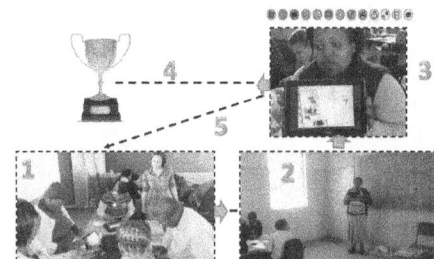

Figure 3: Implementation of the TPD course

In step 1, the learning strategy, skills and other competencies are simulated during the TPD session. This provides an opportunity to experience the strategy, learn about a topic and gain technology skills. Subsequent to the TPD session, in step 2, the participating teachers have about 3 weeks to apply the teaching strategy using technology in their own class. They adapt their own practice to incorporate the curriculum theme into the teaching strategy while evaluating their technology affordances. They become co-creators of the implementation, and training trickled over into classroom practice. Teachers are then required to record evidence as outlined in each badge criteria. In step 3, an external badge evaluator evaluates the evidence provided by the teacher and either award the badge or gives meaningful input on possible improvements. In this case the teacher can resubmit at any given time. If there are still modules left, another TPD session will be done and the process repeats (step 5). If all the modules have been presented the participating teacher has the opportunity to graduate and earn their device, should they have achieved the minimum criteria (step 6) as described in the following subsection.

4.6 Earn as you learn

Resulting from the adoption of Gamification, rewards were incorporated. The needed technology hardware would be provided *in use* and not *in case*. This was operationalized through a concept that was called *earn as you learn*. It implied that the need for technology hardware would first be created and then be met. The use of the technology hardware was implicitly linked to various goals articulated as badges that teachers had to earn and achieve in order to progress along a defined learning path (Figure 3). Sets of badges were then linked to particular technology hardware endowments for teachers and schools as outlined in Table 2 and Table 3.

Table 2: Badges linked to technology rewards for teachers

Total badges earned.	Tablet accessory.
Commitment badge	Tablet cover
N = 4	SD card
N = (4 already earned) +5	Earphones
N = (4+5 already earned) +2	Tablet pen
All compulsory badges earned N= (4+5+2 already earned) +1	Tablet

The following diagram of the learning path gives an indication of the estimated timeframe when the schools would become eligible to receive the various technology hardware endowments.

Figure 4: Indication of technology earning for participating schools. (1) Projector, (2) Mobikit (3) additional Mobikits, internet connection and/or 1:1 tablet rollout to learners.

Criteria for participating schools to receive a particular technology endowment are given in the table below.

Table 3: Individual School technology endowment criteria

School achievement linked to technology endowment.
Criteria: 80% of 5 badges per participant. For the school to earn a projector the ideal would be: Each teacher tried a minimum of 4 new teaching strategies. This is a total of 5 badges per teacher. We expect the school to have achieved 80 % of this total. So for a school with 10 people on the course, it would imply that they can earn a total of 50 badges. 80% of this is 40 badges. To give the school some incentive, this implies that the total needs to be 80% of 5 badges per participant. If teachers do more badges, they will achieve the total sooner. If not all teachers are doing the compulsory badges which will be achieved much later in the intervention. This gives incentive for champions to take the lead and have a sence of ownership as regards the earned technology.   **Technology endowment**: Projector.
Criteria: 80% of 7 badges per participant. For the school to have Mobikits the ideal would be: Each teacher tried 5 new strategies. Teachers have started to create digital content by contributing to the Educational Content Creator Badge. This would imply that teachers have something to share with the learners. They have become contributors.   **Technology endowment**: Mobikit.
Criteria: 80% of 9 badges per participant. For the school to have tablets for learners, the ideal would be: Each teacher tried 8 new strategies, The Mobikit is actively being used. Teachers are creating digital content and are integrating the technology into the teaching and learning. Teachers and the institution are now ready to cope with the disruption of the technology.   **Technology endowment**: Additional Mobikit or Tablets to learners.

4.7 Simulations

The course was presented as an ideal case (physical simulation) of what classroom practice should portray for each of the modules. This implied that each teaching strategy and technology skill was experienced by the teachers before they were required to apply it in their own classrooms. As such, the *jigsaw teaching strategy* was introduced and modelled through the jigsaw teaching strategy, *storytelling teaching strategy* was presented through storytelling and so forth. In addition the course was presented at the teacher's school. The course training sessions were in effect demonstrating to them how to navigate their resource constrained environment when they implemented the technology and teaching strategy into their classroom practice. The presentation of the course and experience of the teachers attending the ICT4RED course was thus contextual, practical and relevant to the teacher's realities in their own school. On days when there was no electricity the facilitator demonstrated how this obstacle could be navigated when they were using the tablet in their own class.

This paper aimed to describe the novel gamification approach to Teacher Professional Development in a unique context where schools are deprived of resources but still managed to successfully integrate mobile tablets in their classroom practices. In the rest of the paper, evidence is presented to substantiate the claim that the technology was integrated successfully into classroom practice.

5. RESULTS

Design science research produces artifacts created by humans usually for a practical purpose. March and Smith [30] differentiate among four different types of artifacts: concepts, models, methods and instantiations. Thus the aim of the ICT4RED TPD component was to design and develop a TPD course for teachers as an artifact. Two important characteristics of design science artifacts addressed are relevance and novelty [31]. First, an artifact should be relevant, that is, resolve an important problem. Secondly, to differentiate Design Science Research from routine design, Hevner, et al. [32] suggest that Design Science Research should address either an unsolved problem in a unique and innovative way or a solved problem in a more effective or efficient way.

The ICT4RED TPD course could be considered innovative as it implemented game elements and implicitly scaffolded technology competencies while explicitly aligning with the professional activities of teaching, learning and classroom practice.

In each or the three iteration of implementation, a baseline teacher's survey was completed by all the participating teachers. Follow up questionnaires were administered on completion and interviews with teachers were done by the research team. Evidence was collected from the teachers towards the validation of each badge. In addition the teacher's electronic reflection notes were collected. The results outlined here are selected from the preliminary results [33] towards to substantiating the claim that the technology was integrated successfully into classroom practice of participating schools and teachers.

5.1 Teacher completion

During the three phases all the participating teachers achieved the minimum compulsory badges and thus earned their tablets.

The completion rate for participants was 100%. Of the 225 participating teachers and headmasters, all 225 achieved the minimum of 13 compulsory badges. There were 91 individuals who completed more than half of the optional badges to earn a merit graduation. A total of 3,998 badges were assessed according to criteria supplied by assessors who were not directly involved in the facilitation process and were verified by an external party for quality control [17]. All the participating schools achieved the criteria for earning all available technology endowments and received tablets for learners (see Table 3 for criteria).

The reward of a tablet on completion of the course was initially a large drawcard for the teachers. Some of the teachers were reluctant to start the course and commit themselves but after being ensured that they could withdraw at any stage agreed to give the process a chance. A running total badge tracking system was kept and teachers falling behind were able to be identified and assisted. There was a fair amount of interschool competition and teachers supported their colleagues in an attempt to outdo another neighboring school.

5.2 Teacher response

Teachers reacted positively to the intervention. The absenteeism across attendance for all modules were very low with a total

average absenteeism rate of 4% recorded. Attendance across all modules was significantly high and is considered to indicate that the teachers' engagement with the ICT4RED TPD course was affirmative. Attendance for the last five modules in 2014 were significantly lower than attendance in the first five modules – partly because a funeral coincided with the

Figure 5: Field trip (Module

module 7 and 8 training which was held on a Saturday, and partly because of an increase in the number of clashes with other Education Department engagements such as meetings, moderation and training since January 2014. The course modules were specifically aimed at making it fun as there was a fair amount of workshop fatigue evident as a result of changes in curriculum that had taken place in the last few years. Lecture types of interactions were purposefully avoided and active participation sought.

5.3 Classroom practice

Classroom practice reflected more of an *emerging pedagogy for the information age* as teachers' demonstrated increased proficiency in implementing the learner centered teaching strategies that formed part of the ICT4RED TPD course. All of the participating teachers earned the 13 compulsory badges and a fair amount of them did at least half of the challenge badges. This implies that they attended the training sessions, integrated their own subject content, presented the lesson and collected evidence to reach the interim goals articulated as badges. This was the case

at least once for each of the badges that the teachers earned. It implied that teachers were able to use the technology skills related to an Android Tablet and felt comfortable enough to integrate technology into their classroom practice using selected teaching skills.

Figure 6: Math lesson using Jigsaw strategy (Module 1)

Facilitators were from the local area and were available to help teachers to plan specific lessons around strategies and content. Informal communities of practice started to form and ideas were shared amongst teachers from different schools.

5.4 Teacher knowledge

As the teachers attended the ICT4RED TPD sessions they acquired knowledge towards being, participating, teaching and learning in a digital world. It can be noted that 90% of the teachers earned the email badge and 51% the blog collaborators badge. These two badges were not facilitated but were challenge badges and left to the teachers to do. Internet connectivity presented significant challenges, even attempts to provide internet connectivity at designated times were only marginally successful.

It was found that most of the teachers had someone else set up their email address and used local businesses supplying Wi-Fi to access the internet. It was a significant challenge for the teachers to manage the updating of the apps on the tablet as this would consume large amounts of their data. Facilitators held additional workshops to help the teachers to personalize their devices for maximum battery life and minimum data use.

5.5 Teacher confidence

Teachers demonstrated sufficient confidence to experiment with the use of software and hardware in their teaching practice. The participants were asked in the follow-up questionnaire if the use of ICT for teaching and learning had changed from the teacher's point of view and, if yes, what had changed. Most of the participants reported that it has changed. A significant smaller number of participating teachers indicated that they thought that there was some change or no change at all. This may be because

Figure 7: Teacher confidence in the use of the Technology increased

teachers were not utilizing the technology for teaching and learning outside of the ICT4RED course badging requirements. The changes that were reported included the use of videos, content from the content server and online assessment by pupils. Teachers reported a perceived change in pupils' attitude and attention in the classrooms. They indicated that learners were very eager to work with the tablets and absenteeism was down. When asked to rate how many teachers in a school changed their practice, the response varied from school to school. There seemed to be consensus that some change had occurred but the change was not perceived to be 100%. It can however be deduced that the ICT4RED course made an impact in most teachers' practice and that teachers have demonstrate proficiency in guiding and assisting learners to use technology to learn.

5.6 School change

From the interviews held with teachers it was evident that the participating schools had started changing the frequency with which they incorporated the technology into their teaching and learning practices and workflow. Teachers at all schools reported a change in pupil behavior as well as an interest in learning within at least half of the classrooms. The schools seemed to have established functioning ICT committees, with a significant number of female representatives in most schools. They mentioned that parents were supportive of the changes. Safety and

security issues and longer term sustainability of the project are some parental concerns that were reported by teachers. Despite many precautions taken there were some incidents of theft from individual teachers and from schools.

5.7 Administrative use

Although the initiative did not have a focus on using the Tablet technology for administrative purposes, about three quarters of the phase one and two schools reported that teachers (between 50% and 90% of staff) were in fact using their tablets for administrative tasks. The administrative functions included typing of examination papers, capturing of children's marks on the tablets, report writing, doing online exercises, assessments, sending and receiving emails from colleagues, doing mind maps and doing planning schedules.

5.8 District involvement

Teachers at schools reported a change in the way the district interacted with them after the initiative started in their school. The officials involved in e-learning and institutional development were singled out and were reportedly visiting schools more frequently. They were reportedly assisting teachers to plan lessons using specific curriculum content. In addition the teachers reported that the officials were providing moral support, boosting teachers' confidence and suggesting strategies on how to store the tablets to prevent theft.

6. DISCUSSION

Gamification as a design strategy proved to be very successful. In the first two iterations a multitude optional badges were catered for and left to the teacher to attempt when they wanted to. The second iteration saw a rework of the optional badges towards a more simplified criteria and a reduced number. In addition the challenge badges were strategically placed to provide challenges at appropriate times throughout the course. This format proved to be more successful.

The amount of time spent on collecting evidence from each teacher was vastly underestimated. The expectations from the teachers were that the badge evaluation and awards would take place before every TPD session. The backlog of uncollected badges forced the implementation team to incorporate a session in phase 2 dedicated to collecting badges. After this a team was formed to evaluate collect and track badges. In the third iteration district personnel were recruited to assist.

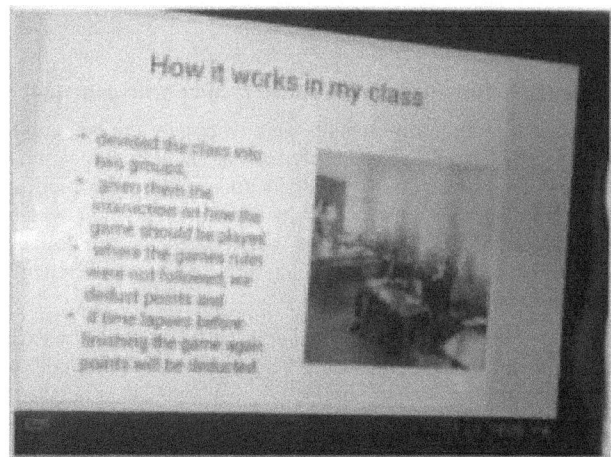

Figure 8: Evidence provided in order to attain a badge

The flow from training experience to classroom practice was facilitated by the interim goals, articulated by the badges. The badge goal, achievement, assessment and the conferring of the badges served a number of functions:

- It outlined clear transparent expectation;
- It provides an opportunity for the teacher to demonstrate individual proficiency;
- It acknowledges achieved competence;
- It allows teachers to individualize and appropriate learning into practice;
- It acts as a scaffolding environment for achieving the teacher development goal;
- It allows the initiative initiators to acknowledge individual growth;
- It acts as an early warning signal of teachers falling behind;
- It allows for timeous investment in further technology needs; and
- It allows for champions to surface and to be acknowledged.

Originally the thought was to award teachers with Mozilla Open Badges. This plan had to be abandoned as individuals without an email address and internet could not receive an electronic badge and the value of display was lost. As such stickers were used to symbolize the achievement.

The presentation of the course material went through a number of iterations. Initially the course material was planned to be given in an electronic format. Teachers however were adamant that they wanted printed material with lots of space to make notes. To mitigate this, A5 booklets in phase 2, and later A4 files in phase 3 were used. The file allowed teachers to add their own content and examples as needed.

How-to-tutorials were developed and incorporated into the ICT4RED TPD course modules so that teachers would have a reference for searching the needed technical skills. An icon was added to indicate the existence of a relevant tutorial.

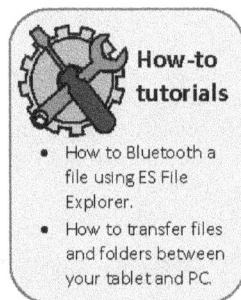

Figure 9: How-to tutorials added to aid participants[34]

In the third iteration, the schools were extremely remote, and the participating schools were much smaller than in the first two iterations. As such, three central locations were identified and where training took place. This centralized facilitation was not ideal but enabled the facilitators and teachers to cut down on travel time. In addition, the teaching strategies worked better for larger groups of participants.

Teachers teach the way they're taught. If a facilitator as an expert cannot model it, the chances are very good that it will not spill over into a novice's classroom practice. As such, it is advised to rather not include a skill, strategy or technology that an expert needs training on. It can be argued that when there are too may barriers to implementation, it will rarely become ingrained into novice teaching practice. Actions speak louder than words and there is very little that can replace the actual experience of ICT integration. This situation is exasperated when working with teachers in resource constrained areas that experience a challenging environment beyond the technology.

The interaction design of a TPD learning interaction should be a positive learning experience for the teacher to translate into a willingness to experiment in their own classroom. The well-structured incorporation of game elements were received exceptionally well. In addition teacher had to redefine their own understanding of teaching and learning and gain a familiarity with the foreign concept of learner centric teaching to fully appreciate its value for their own practice. In addition to becoming comfortable with learner centric teaching, teachers needed to understand how the activity of learning could look different from their conception of a silent classroom with learners not communicating. This was found to be a significant challenge for headmasters as well. The idea of controlled chaos had to be experienced and then facilitated.

Teachers are very hesitant to integrate technology into their teaching and learning if they have not mastered and integrated it into their personal life. As such the technology hardware that is introduced and promoted needs to be at least available and preferably retained by teachers to become comfortable with it in order to gain the competency and confidence level to implement it into classroom practice.

The bandwidth challenges in resource constrained areas are significant and are likely to be for the near future. An *internet-like* experience created by accessing a local content server containing cached content should not be disregarded. Considering ICT integration into education as only a connected internet endeavor is possibly an inappropriate view for resource constrained environments and tends to lead to a type of uptake paralysis whereby an either internet or nothing notion is prevalent. This results in a costly technology focus and unrealistic expectations that do not realize. Appropriate pedagogies and technologies for ICT integration should incorporate a disconnected or limited connectivity approach that pragmatically attempts to mitigate the realities of so many teachers and learners.

7. CONCLUSION

The teacher professional development interaction is costly and needs to be seen as an investment in more than just mastering a technology for the sake of it. Careful consideration needs to be given to content, strategy as well as technology use. Technology in and of itself will not influence classroom practice. Teachers have to implement it or at least allow it into their classroom. On a large district level, this needs to be a facilitated endeavor. Appropriate curriculum-aligned content is still a major challenge, especially for younger and small home language learners. There needs to be a push to get locally-contextualized content developed that is designed for mobile devices. The enormity of this undertaking can only be mitigated if each teachers become content contributors in their own right.

8. ACKNOWLEDGMENTS

Our thanks to funders and participants of the TEC4RED research programme and ICT4RED initiative and reviewers of the conference. Special mention to Jay Chen for the time and effort spent on assisting the final version of this paper.

The ICT4RED Teacher Professional Development Course was licensed under the Creative Commons Attribution-Non-commercial-Share Alike 3.0. and can be downloaded, changed and implemented free of licensing charges from http://www.ict4red.blogspot.com/p/about.html.

9. REFERENCES

[1] J. Keengwe, G. Onchwari, and P. Wachira, "Computer technology integration and student learning: Barriers and promise," *Journal of Science Education and Technology,* vol. 17, pp. 560-565, 2008.

[2] R. Hermans, J. Tondeur, J. van Braak, and M. Valcke, "The impact of primary school teachers' educational beliefs on the classroom use of computers," *Computers & Education,* vol. 51, pp. 1499-1509, 2008.

[3] J. Hardman, "An exploratory case study of computer use in a primary school mathematics classroom: new technology, new pedagogy?: research: information and communication technologies," *Perspectives in Education: Recearch on ICTs and Education in South Africa: Special Issue 4,* vol. 23, pp. p. 99-111, 2005.

[4] M. Ford and A. Botha, "A pragmatic framework for integrating ICT into education in South Africa," in *IST-Africa, 2010,* 2010, pp. 1-10.

[5] A. Byteway, S. Cox, C. Dumas, and I. van Zyl, "Educator discourses on ICT in education: A critical analysis Moira Bladergroen and Wallace Chigona University of Cape Town, South Africa," *International Journal of Education and Development using Information and Communication Technology,* vol. 8, pp. 107-119, 2012.

[6] E. Were, J. Rubagiza, and R. Sutherland, "Bridging the digital divide? Educational challenges and opportunities in Rwanda," *Development,* vol. 31, pp. 37-43, 2011.

[7] R. E. Anderson, R. J. Anderson, G. Borriello, and B. Kolko, "Designing technology for resource-constrained environments: Three approaches to a multidisciplinary capstone sequence," in *Frontiers in Education Conference (FIE), 2012,* 2012, pp. 1-6.

[8] R. Van Rensburg and U. Du Buisson, "Title," unpublished|.

[9] G. Bloch, *The toxic mix: What's wrong with South Africa's schools and how to fix it*: Tafelberg, 2009.

[10] M. Herselman and A. Botha, Eds., *Designing and implementing an Information Communication Technology for Rural Education Development (ICT4RED) initiative in a resource constrained environment: Nciba school district, Eastern Cape, South Africa (In Press).* Pretoria, South Africa: CSIR Meraka, 2014, p.^pp. Pages.

[11] M. Ford, "ICT4RED Implementation Framework," in *Designing and implementing an Information Communication Technology for Rural Education Development (ICT4RED) initiative in a resource constrained environment: Cofimvaba school district, Eastern Cape, South Africa,* M. Herselman and A. Botha, Eds., ed Pretoria, South Africa: CSIR, 2014.

[12] J. Voogt, "IT and curriculum processes: Dilemmas and challenges," in *International handbook of information technology in primary and secondary education.* vol. 20, J. Voogt and G. Knezek, Eds., ed New York: Springer, 2008, pp. 117-128.

[13] M. Prinsloo, *The context of public primary education*: Centre for Democratising Information, 2012.

[14] Department of Basic Education. (2012, June). *Action Plan 2014: Towards the realisation of schooling 2025.* Available: http://www.education.gov.za/LinkClick.aspx?fileticket=zpM1hJi8qDs=&tabid=418&mid=1211

[15] G. Gudmundsdottir, "When does ICT support education in South Africa? The importance of teachers' capabilities and the relevance

of language," *Information Technology for Development,* vol. 16, pp. 174-190, 2010.

[16] A. Chigona, W. Chigona, M. Kausa, and P. Kayongo, "An empirical survey on domestication of ICT in schools in disadvantaged communities in South Africa," *International Journal of Education and Development using ICT,* vol. 6, pp. 21-32, 2010.

[17] A. Botha, "Teacher Professional Development," in *Designing and implementing an Information Communication Technology for Rural Education Development (ICT4RED) initiative in a resource constrained environment: Cofimvaba school district, Eastern Cape, South Africa,* M. Herselman and A. Botha, Eds., ed Pretoria, South Africa: CSIR Meraka: Integrative Competency Area, 2014.

[18] A. R. Hevner and S. Chatterjee, *Design Science Research in Information Systems: Theory and Practice.* New York: Springer, 2010.

[19] ICT4RED. (2014, September). *ICT4RED publications.* Available: http://ict4red.blogspot.co.za/p/resouces.html

[20] C. M. Grant. (n.d.). *Professional development in a technological age: New definitions, old challenges, new resources.* Available: http://ra.terc.edu/publications/TERC_pubs/tech-infusion/prof_dev/prof_dev_frame.html

[21] J. Voogt and G. Knezek, "IT in primary and secondary education: emerging issues," in *International handbook of information technology in primary and secondary education.* vol. 20, J. Voogt and G. Knezek, Eds., ed New York: Springer, 2008.

[22] J. Voogt and L. Odenthal, "Met het oog op de toekomst. Een studie naar innovatief gebruik van ICT in het onderwijs," *With a view to the future: A study of innovative use of ICT in education).* Enschede, Netherlands: University of Twente, Faculty of Educational Science and Technology, 1999.

[23] A. Botha, M. Herselman, and M. Ford, "Gamification beyond badges," in *IST Africa,* Mauritius, 2014.

[24] B. Costello and E. Edmonds, "A study in play, pleasure and interaction design," in *Proceedings of the 2007 conference on Designing pleasurable products and interfaces,* 2007, pp. 76-91.

[25] S. Deterding, D. Dixon, R. Khaled, and L. Nacke, "From game design elements to gamefulness: defining gamification," in *Proceedings of the 15th International Academic MindTrek Conference: Envisioning Future Media Environments,* 2011, pp. 9-15.

[26] K. Huotari and J. Hamari, "Defining gamification: a service marketing perspective," in *Proceeding of the 16th International Academic MindTrek Conference,* 2012, pp. 17-22.

[27] J. McGonigal, *Reality is broken: Why games make us better and how they can change the world*: Penguin. com, 2011.

[28] J. Juul, "The game, the player, the world: looking for a heart of gameness," in *DIGRA Conf.,* 2003.

[29] A. Stott and C. Neustaedter, "Analysis of Gamification in Education," 2013.

[30] S. T. March and G. F. Smith, "Design and natural science research on information technology," *Decision Support Systems,* vol. 15, pp. 251-266, 1995.

[31] G. Geerts, "A Design Science Research Methodology and its Application to Accounting Information Systems Research," *International Journal of Accounting Information Systems,* 2011.

[32] A. R. Hevner, S. March, J. Park, and S. Ram, "Design science in information systems research," *Manage Information Systems Quarterly (MIS),* vol. 28, pp. 75-105, 2004.

[33] B. Williams, "Preliminary Evaluation of the ICT4RED Initiative - Preliminary Working Evaluation Report " CSIR Meraka, Pretoria, South Africa2013-2015.

[34] A. Botha and M. Verster, "ICT4RED Teacher Proffesional Development," ed. Pretoria, South Africa: CSIR, 2014.

A Usability Study of an Assistive Touch Voice Interface based Automated Teller Machine (ATM)

Sara Muneeb, *Information Technology University*
Mustafa Naseem, *Information Technology University*
Suleman Shahid, *Tilburg University/LUMS*
Contact: sm479@itu.edu.pk

Traditional ATM user interfaces are text heavy and are not designed for use by low and non-literate users. We surveyed 88 randomly selected ATM users, and found a high occurrence of PIN loss, confusion between touch screen and physical buttons, anxiety in case of anomalous machine behavior, and hesitation and fear of using an ATM among low and non-literate users. We then proposed and evaluated an assistive touch voice interface, that at the push of an on-screen "speaker" icon, read out in Urdu (the local language) the text written next to the icon. 25 literate and 25 non-literate users were recruited to test a traditional interface without the voice system, while 13 literate and 13 non-literate users were recalled to test the assisted voice based system. The results are presented in table 1.

Table 1. Usability Evaluation with and without voice system

Criterion	Usability Without voice system		Usability With voice system	
	Literate	Non-literate	Literate	Non-literate
Understanding via Observation Sheet				
Cash Withdrawal	6.64	2.6	8.53	7.30
Fund Transfer	4.56	0.88	8.61	7.38
Balance Inquiry	6.84	2.84	8.23	7.46
Time Taken in Seconds				
Cash Withdrawal	112.76	234.45	140.9	482.09
Fund Transfer	253.62	1201.5	362.09	535.11
Balance Inquiry	53.23	116.62	96.09	132.1
Error Rate in Percentage				
Cash Withdrawal	52%	92%	38%	84%
Fund Transfer	80%	100%	30%	84%
Balance Inquiry	56%	96%	61%	61%

The results show that an assistive voice icon helps low and non-literate users to make basic transactions such as cash withdrawal, fund transfer and balance inquiry at ATMs using traditional text-based interfaces.

ACM Categories & Descriptors: H.5.2 [User Interfaces]: Voice I/O
Keywords: Automated Teller Machine; HCI; Usability; Interaction Design; Voice Interface
DOI: http://dx.doi.org/10.1145/2830629.2830635

Classification Models for New Language Communities: Building Domain-Specific Message Categorization

Jessica Long, *Idibon*
Robert Munro, *Idibon*
Nicholas Gaylord, *Idibon*
Contact: jessica@idibon.com

U-Report is a social messaging tool developed by UNICEF that allows people in developing countries to respond to polls, report issues, and become agents of positive change within in their communities. This program, which has grown to serve over 15 countries in 3 years, is already outpacing the ability of UNICEF and its partners' human workforce to review incoming messages. Incoming messages vary in urgency, from greetings and appreciation to imminent public health and security risks. We present a procedure for automatically identifying and classifying urgent messages via bootstrapping human-labeled data to build semi-supervised classification models.

Semi-supervised classification is a well-known tool for text categorization. Yet in many domains it remains difficult to use because of need for human-labeled training data. We show how creating a feedback loop between human judgments and machine predictions both accelerates annotation and improves message classification accuracy. Using this labeled data, we train seven independent classifiers to identify messages related to specific topics of interest to UNICEF. We compare the classifiers' ability to identify important messages to a baseline where analysts are able to read a fixed number of messages per day. We note significant increases in f-score, ranging from 0.16 to 0.6, when switching from the naïve appproach to ours. We currently label thousands of messages per day for U-Report Nigeria in real time, and use small holdout sets to continue monitoring precision and recall. Future work will involve extending our language-agnostic text classification methods to build categorization models in additional non-English languages served by U-Report.

ACM Categories & Descriptors: I.2.7 [Artificial Intelligence]: Natural Language Processing
Keywords: Crowdsourcing; machine learning; multilingualism; natural language processing; classification; implementaiton
DOI: http://dx.doi.org/10.1145/2830629.2830633

The Price is Right?

Statistical evaluation of a crowd-sourced market information system in Liberia

Joshua E. Blumenstock
University of Washington
Information School
Seattle, WA
joshblum@uw.edu

Niall Keleher
University of Washington
Information School
Seattle, WA
nkeleher@uw.edu

ABSTRACT

Many critical policy decisions depend upon reliable and up-to-date information on market prices. Such data are used to construct consumer price indices, measure inflation, detect food insecurity, and influence macroeconomic policy. In developing countries, where many of these problems are most acute, reliable market price information can be hard to come by. Here, we evaluate data from Premise, a new technology for measuring price information using crowd-sourced data contributed by local citizens. Our evaluation focuses on Liberia, a country with a history of economic and political instability. Using data from Premise, which recently began data collection in Liberia, we analyze tens of thousands of individual price observations collected at hundreds of different locations in Monrovia. We illustrate how these data can be used to construct composite market price indices, and compare these constructed indices and prices for individual products to "ground truth" data from the Central Bank of Liberia and the United Nations World Food Programme. Our results indicate that the crowd-sourced price data correlates well with traditional price indices. However, we find statistically and economically significant deviations from traditional measures that require deeper investigation. We conclude by discussing how indices based on Premise data can be further improved with simple supervised learning methods that use traditional low-frequency data to calibrate and cross-validate the high-frequency Premise-based indices.

Categories and Subject Descriptors

J.4 [**Computer Applications**]: Social and Behavioral Sciences; G.3 [**Mathematics of Computing**]: Probability and Statistics

General Terms

Human Factors, Measurement, Economics, Algorithms

Keywords

Consumer price index; premise; crowd-sourcing; ICTD

1. INTRODUCTION AND MOTIVATION

The Consumer Price Index (CPI) is one of the most important economic statistics used by policymakers to determine macroeconomic policy and to evaluate the health of an economy [17]. It is the primary barometer for measuring inflation, which in turn impacts both fiscal and monetary policy; it is used to calculate purchasing power and determine exchange rates; it also directly impacts wages and welfare payments in both the private and public sector.

The CPI is intended to capture the overall cost of goods and services paid for by a typical individual at local markets. It requires two primary inputs: the "basket of goods" that is intended to be representative of a typical consumer; and the price for each of the goods in the basket. Prices of goods in the common basket are the focus of this paper.

In developed economies, consumer price data are typically obtained from a variety of sources, including supermarkets, service locations, and online retailers [4]. In the United States, for instance, "Bureau of Labor Statistics data collectors visit or call thousands of retail stores, service establishments, rental units, and doctors' offices, all over the United States, to obtain information on the prices of the thousands of items used to track and measure price changes in the CPI."[1] In developing economies, where most transactions are analog and the national statistical offices are more resource-constrained, there are fewer sources of accurate and up-to-date market price information [6, 15].

The lack of reliable and up-to-date price information is particularly problematic in fragile economies, where dependence on subsistence agriculture and the lack of insurance and other social safety nets can exacerbate the welfare impacts of weather shocks, political instability, and food insecurity as mediated through price changes. In Liberia and neighboring countries, for instance, food prices have been one of the primary instruments used in assessing the economic impacts of the recent Ebola outbreak [21, 11, 14].

Here, we investigate a new technology for collecting price information in developing countries, which relies on "crowd-sourced" observations collected by local citizens with mobile phones. We focus on Premise, a technology platform that allows for mobile-equipped citizens to capture and upload price information to a central service. This technology, described in greater detail in Section 3.1, is similar to a small number of related platforms that enable crowd-sourced data collection in developing countries. The mClerk [12] and txtEagle [7] platforms are the most directly comparable systems of

---

[1] http://stats.bls.gov/cpi/cpifaq.htm#Question_8, accessed July 2015

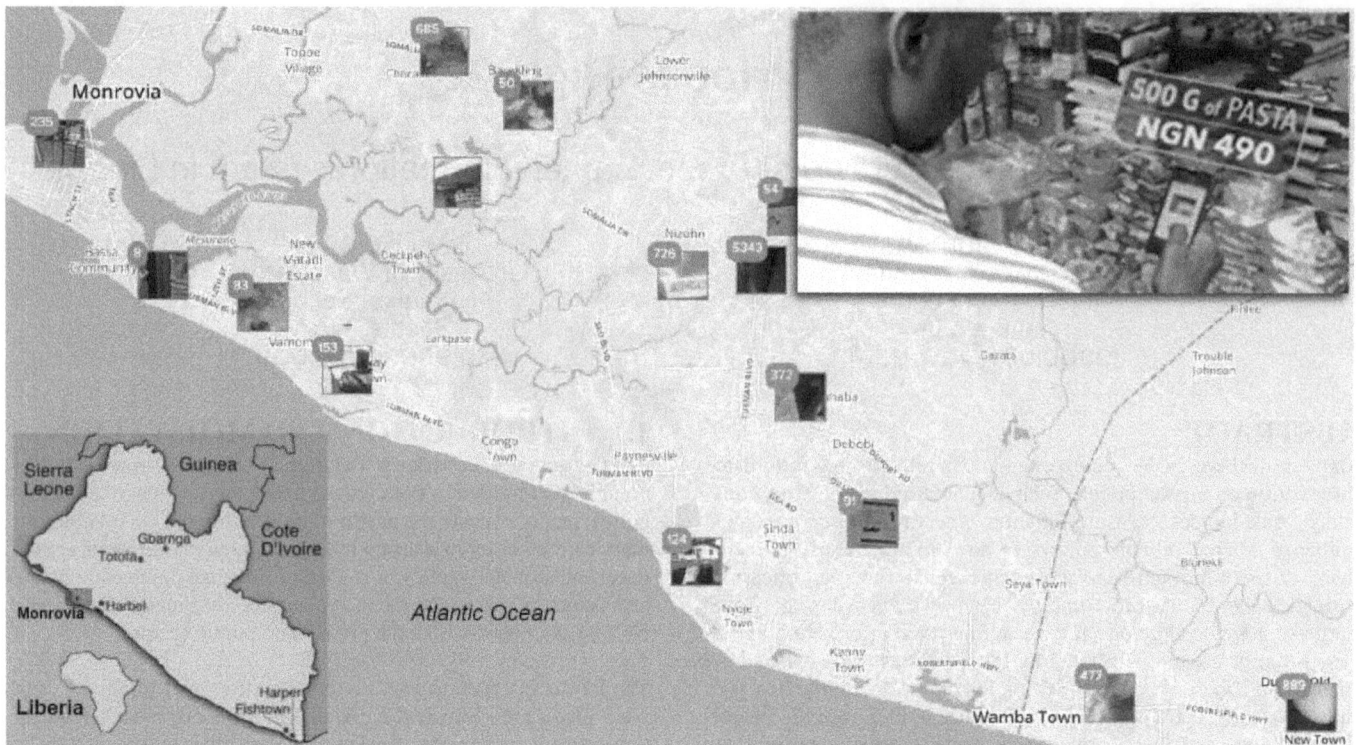

Figure 1: **Premise Data collection methodology.** Premise indexes and analyzes data captured by a global network of contributors. Bottom-left: Location of Liberia and its capital Monrovia. Main figure: Locations from which contributors have captured data. Numbers indicate the number of data points collected from each location over the past three months; square icons are actual images uploaded by contributors. Top-right: Schematic of data capture process in which a contributor uses a cameraphone to photograph the prices of pasta at a local market. These photos are sent to Premise and form the basis for the data we analyze.

which we are aware; both use mobile-based platforms to gather data from low-end mobile phones. More broadly, several examples of researchers sourcing data from the crowd exist. For instance, [19] study microblogging in response to a large earthquake in Haiti in 2010, and [1] describe several other emerging technological systems that facilitate participatory contribution in development areas including agriculture, rural development and natural resource management. In the closest study to our own, [13] conduct a feasibility study to explore the use of the Jana platform for collecting price data. While [13] demonstrate the potential of the platform, they focus on a description of the technological platform, rather than on evaluating the accuracy of the collected data in comparison to external sources of validation data.[2]

Different from prior work, our focus is not on the technological artifact or interface used to collect data; rather, we study the data generated by this platform, and statistically evaluate its potential for use as an index of inflation and related economic activity. The empirical analysis relies on data generated from the Premise network of contributors in Liberia, which has been collecting price information on 38 market goods in Monrovia since late 2014. We present the dataset and document several prominent features related to the stability and noise present in the raw data (Section 3.1), discuss corrections that improve the reliability of derivative metrics (Section

3.2), and describe a basic method for computing a consumer price index from the crowd-sourced data (Section 3.3). Section 4 compares these indices to alternative measures of inflation in Liberia.

This paper thus makes three primary contributions. First, we illustrate how crowd-sourced market data can be used to construct price indices, and characterize the statistical properties of these indices. Second, we carefully evaluate these indices by comparing them to traditional methods for measuring food insecurity. Finally, we discuss a simple supervised learning framework that can be used to improve the accuracy of high-resolution estimates through calibration and cross-validation with low-resolution sources of data.

2. BACKGROUND: CONSUMER PRICE IN-DICES IN LIBERIA

Following Liberia's long-entrenched civil war and post-conflict recovery, which ended in 2003, the country took several years to achieve political and economic stability. Between 2011 and 2014, consumer prices in Liberia followed a roughly linear trend with mean year-to-year inflation of approximately 9%. In the period following the Ebola Virus Disease epidemic, the country saw an uptick in the price index, with year-to-year inflation rising to a peak of 16.3% in September 2014. With the rise in consumer prices, concern over access to food was heightened. As of writing, the government and international agencies remained vigilant to the threat to food security that increased prices posed for Liberian households [14].

---

[2]A much more extensive literature, which we do not review here, explores the potential for data collection using mobile phones in developed economies [16]. A seperate literature discusses how mobile data can be used for population-based inferences of social and economic indicators [8, 10, 5].

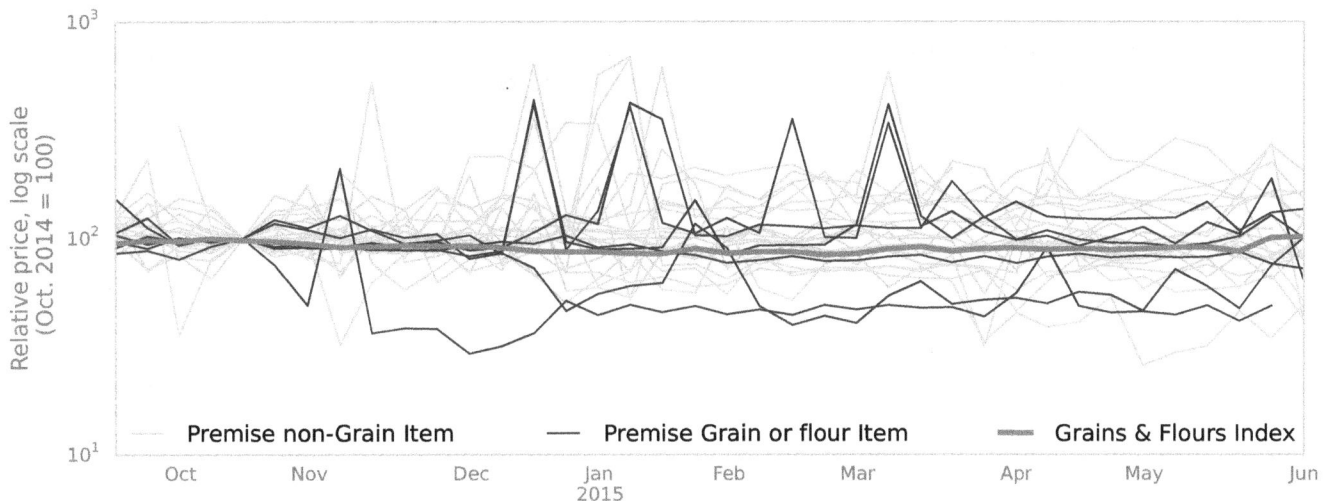

Figure 2: **Raw data captured by Premise contributors.** Data for 38 different products is captured by Premise contributors (light grey lines). Of these goods, 6 are in the "Grains and Flours" product group (dark blue lines), corresponding to bread, bulgur wheat, butter rice, cassava flour, fan-fan rice, and USA parboiled rice. Using the methods described in Section 3.3, these six product price-series are aggregated into a single sub-index for the product group (red line). Each series is normalized to a value of 100 on October 15, 2015.

Price data is historically accessible to a limited set of actors and on an infrequent basis. Official price data is collected by the Liberian government and analyzed by the Central Bank of Liberia in order to produce aggregate price indices on a monthly basis. Data collected by the United Nations World Food Programme (WFP) is typically collected for the purpose of monitoring food insecurity. However, data collected for food security monitoring covers a more limited set of consumption items and locations relative to the government statistics.

Price data plays an integral roll in the WFP's forecasts of food shortages, as food prices influence household spending decisions. As such, the WFP uses food prices as an indicator of the impact of economic shocks on households. Access to timely price data has been especially important during the 2014-15 Ebola epidemic in West Africa, where the combination of restricted economic activity, loss of life, and loss of sources of income have culminated in a threat to food security [21].

3. PREMISE DATA

3.1 Technology platform

Premise (www.premise.com) is a technology company based in San Francisco that offers a platform for capturing data from a distributed network of individual contributors.[3] The intent of the platform is to enable rapid and adaptive measurement of local economic and social infrastructure, using data collected by local citizens. Premise recruits individuals in urban and rural regions of developing countries to perform simple, structured tasks that capture information about their local community (Figure 1). Premise currently operates in 32 countries worldwide. A major focus of Premise's efforts to date has been on collecting price data from developing countries.

Premise contributors use photo-enabled phones to capture prices in local markets. Contributors are compensated in the local currency, and are trained in person prior to submitting data. Each day, contributors receive a list of *tasks* which detail the items for which price observations are needed. Contributors are typically paid a piece rate for each successfully completed task, for an amount "on the order of the price of an egg" for each data point captured.[4] Photos and price information submitted by the contributor go through a quality control screening process, described in more detail below.

Beginning in September 2014, Premise initiated data collection in Liberia in an effort to produce a Food Staples Price Index (FSPI) as well as other measures of economic and business activity. Premise data collection in Liberia launched in response to the 2014 Ebola Virus Disease epidemic in West Africa. The initial goal was to provide timely information about prices of key consumer goods. The initial focus has been in Monrovia, where Premise collects daily price observations for staple foods and non-food consumer items in all of Monrovia's major market areas (Figure 1). In the summer of 2015, Premise expanded data collection in rural markets of Liberia, beginning with the towns of Voinjama and Fish Town.

Premise currently receives approximately 600 price observations per week for a basket of 38 unique products, from a small network of independent contributors in Liberia.[5] As can be observed in Appendix Table A1, which presents summary statistics for the raw contributor data, there is a great deal of variation in the frequency at which each product is observed, the number of unique locations at which a product is captured, and the price level and variance for each product over time. As we describe in the following section, the number of errant observations also varies considerably by product.

---

[3]Contributors are analogous to enumerators or surveyors in traditional terminology for primary data collection.

[4]Based on private correspondence with Premise staff, July 2015.

[5]Data volumes in Liberia are low compared to other contries. For example, Premise contributors submit upwards of 15,000 observations per week for 150 items in Nigeria.

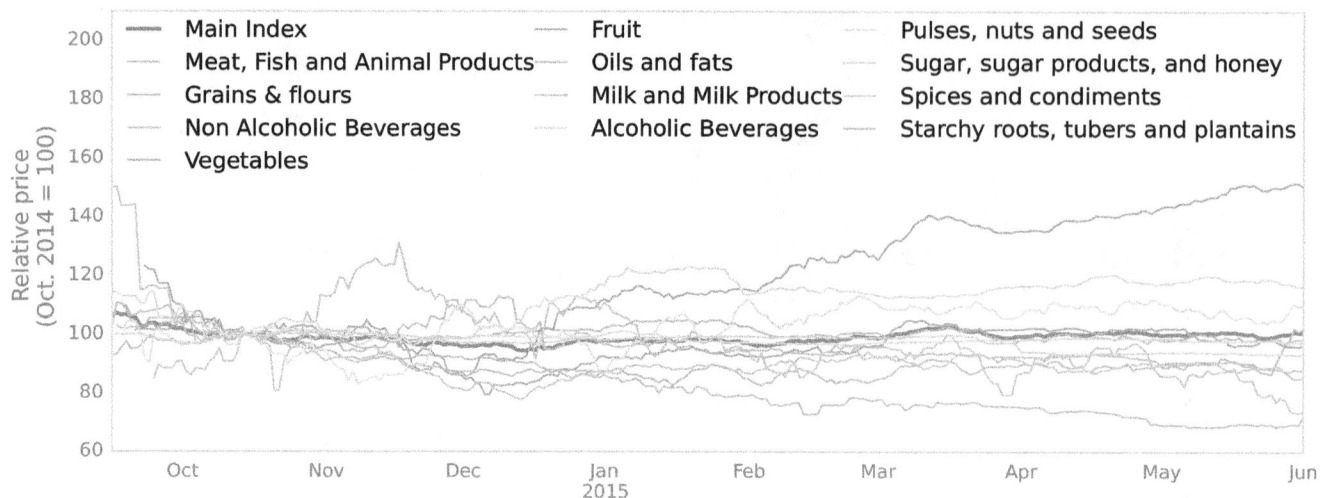

Figure 3: **Premise FSPI and sub-indices, as calculated from contributor data.** Following the procedure described in Section 3.3, sub-indices are computed for each of the 12 product groups listed in Table 1. Using the weights listed in the same table, the composite Food Staples Price Index, the Premise equivalent of a CPI, is calculated and shown as a thick red line.

3.2 Detecting outliers in crowd-sourced data

The raw data captured by Premise contributors in Liberia are illustrated in Figure 2. Here, we plot a separate time series for each of the 38 products as a semi-transparent grey line. Each of these lines represents the daily average price for that product, averaged across all observations taken on that day by all contributors in all locations. Highlighted in blue are the six time series corresponding to products in the "Grains and flours" category. In red is the composite sub-index, calculated using a procedure we will shortly describe.

As is evident in the product-level time series in Figure 2, the raw data collected by Premise contributors is subject to several sources of error. On some occasions there appear to be idiosyncratic spikes where a single product's price will change by as much as 200%; at others, these spikes appear to be correlated across products. Of primary concern is disentangling from actual changes in prices from measurement error. As has been documented in related work, there are many possible sources of such error, both accidental and deliberate [13, 3, 2]. These include input errors (for instance, a misplaced decimal point or a photograph of the floor), as well as outright fraud where a contributor intentionally falsifies data. Premise implements several measures to detect and prevent such deliberate fraud [18], but many of these are not publicly disclosed, and in practice affect a relatively small number of total captured data.

In follow-up work, we are developing more refined techniques for identifying and removing erroneous data, which may constitute as much as 20% of the total data captured on the Premise platform. Here, we describe a simple procedure that, based on manual verification, appears to catch a large share of these errors. Formally, we denote by P_{itlk} an observation recorded by individual i at time t in location l for item k. We define price outliers as those observations that deviate significantly from historical prices for a given product, i.e.,

$$|log(P_{itlk}) - log(\mu_{tlk})| > \lambda_k \sigma_{tlk} \qquad (1)$$

where $\mu_{tlk} = \frac{1}{Nn}\sum_i \sum_{s<t} P_{islk}$ is the average historical value for k at location l (assuming N individuals and n observations where $s < t$),

and σ_{tlk} is the corresponding standard deviation. When insufficient observations exist from which to derive reliable estimates of μ_{tlk} and σ_{tlk}, a "bootstrap" process is used to manually curate and reject anomalous observations. In this framework, λ_k is the key parameter which determines the stringency with which outliers will be identified.

Currently, Premise employs a common threshold across all products of $\lambda_k = \lambda \approx 3$. In ongoing work, we are exploring a supervised learning approach to determining a product-specific λ_k, which will allow for some products with greater expected variation over time to exhibit more intertemporal variability. We are also testing density-based techniques [9] and other alternative methods for outlier detection.

3.3 Computing CPI from crowd-sourced data

A primary objective of the Premise application is to convert the disaggregated price data collected by the network of contributors into more meaningful price indices, similar to the CPI, which can then be used to measure inflation and inform food policy decisionmaking. Here, we describe the process used to construct the Food Staples Price Index (FSPI), the Premise equivalent of the CPI, from the disaggregated data. Formally, our goal is to compute an aggregate CPI_{rm} for a region r in month m, from a large number of disaggregated price observations P_{itlk}.

Given the set of P_{itlk} with outliers removed, the FSPI CPI_{rm} is constructed using a process based loosely on the methods employed by the US Bureau of Labor Statistics [4]. Initially, the average daily price P_{Tlk} for item k at location l is constructed by taking the average of all $|T|$ observations collected on day T,

$$P_{Tlk} = \frac{1}{N|T|}\sum_{i \in l}\sum_{t \in T} P_{itlk} \qquad (2)$$

This value is still quite specific, as l can be as precise as a single storefront location, and k can be unique to an item SKU, such as the price of one bottle of Club Beer (a local beer), or the cost of a bucket of low-grade gari (a local flour). These item-day averages are next aggregated into product-day averages P_{TlK} by standardiz-

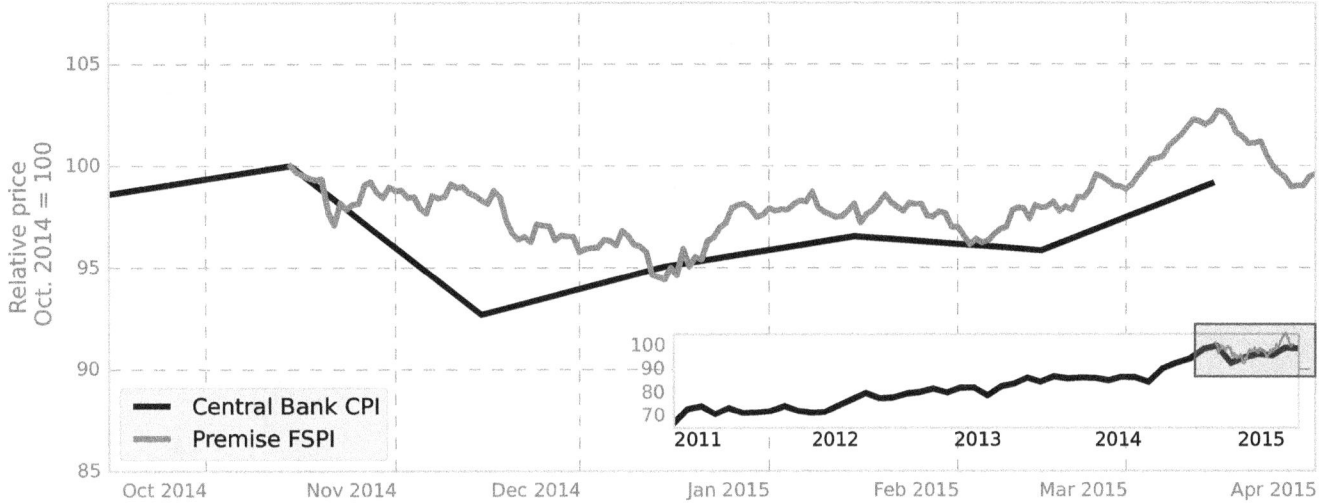

Figure 4: **Comparison of FSPI to Central Bank CPI.** Main figure shows the CPI calculated by the Central Bank of Liberia and the FSPI based on Premise data. Inset figure displays the Food and Non-Alcoholic Beverages relative price from May 2011 to April 2015.

ing units of measurement (e.g., pounds to grams) and taking the geometric mean of related products (e.g., beef briskets), i.e.,

$$P_{TlK} = \left(\prod_{k=1}^{K} P_{Tlk} \right)^{1/k} \qquad (3)$$

Product-day averages are similarly aggregated across all locations in a region and across all days in a time window to produce monthly estimates of the regional cost of a specific product. These product averages are further aggregated into product sub-groups (e.g., standard cut beef), product groups (e.g., beef), and sub-indices (e.g., meat). This aggregation uses weights that are determined based on the estimated expenditures of consumers on the various items. In Liberia, these weights are determined by a recent consumer expenditure survey [20].

In Liberia there are 12 *sub-indices*, which indicate the prices of the most common items in the country. The final step in constructing the FSPI is to combine the sub-indices into a single consumer price index that reflects the price level of a typical market basket of food staples. The weights w_k for each of the sub-indices used in constructing the Liberian FSPI are given in Table 1. Thus, the composite FSPI can be expressed as a weighted aggregate of the original contributor observations:

$$CPI_{rm} = \frac{1}{|r||m|} \sum_{l \in r} \sum_{T \in m} w_k P_{TlK} \qquad (4)$$

The FSPI for Liberia, computing using the above methodology, as well as the 12 sub-indices, is shown in Figure 3. To emphasize the fluctuations within a product category over time, each index is normalized so that the value on October 15, 2014 is set to 100.

4. EVALUATION RESULTS

The methods described above make it possible to construct a CPI-like metric, the FSPI, as well as several sub-indices of product-group prices, from the data captured by Premise contributors (Figure 3). In order to validate the relevance of these constructs, we take two approaches - one at the aggregate index level and another at the item level. We draw from two sources of data for the vali-

Index component	weight (%)
Alcoholic Beverages	1.2%
Fruit	9.2%
Grains and Flours	13.7%
Meat, Fish and Animal Products	16.8%
Milk and Milk Products	6.1%
Non Alcoholic Beverages	12.0%
Oils and Fats	3.0%
Pulses, Nuts and Seeds	2.9%
Spices and Condiments	8.0%
Starchy Roots and Tubers	11.4%
Sugar and Sugar Products	2.2%
Vegetables	13.4%

Table 1: **Weights used in constructing the FSPI.** The composite Food Staple Price Index is constructed as the weighted sum of 12 primary sub-indices, where the above weights are determined based on a recent household expenditure survey.

dation. The purpose of this comparison is to judge the consistency and reliability of Premise data vis-a-vis an economic indicator for the Liberian economy as well as a best-available option for policy-makers interested in food security as proxied by the price of individual goods. The data for the former comparison comes from the Central Bank of Liberia, while the item-level comparison is conducted with a primary source of data collected for the United Nations World Food Programme with the purpose of tracking threats to food security in Liberia.

4.1 Comparison data

4.1.1 Central Bank of Liberia

The Central Bank of Liberia releases headline consumer price index data from the 15th day of each month. National price level are based on monthly price surveys conducted by the Liberia Institute of Statistics and Geo-information Services (LISGIS). Price indices

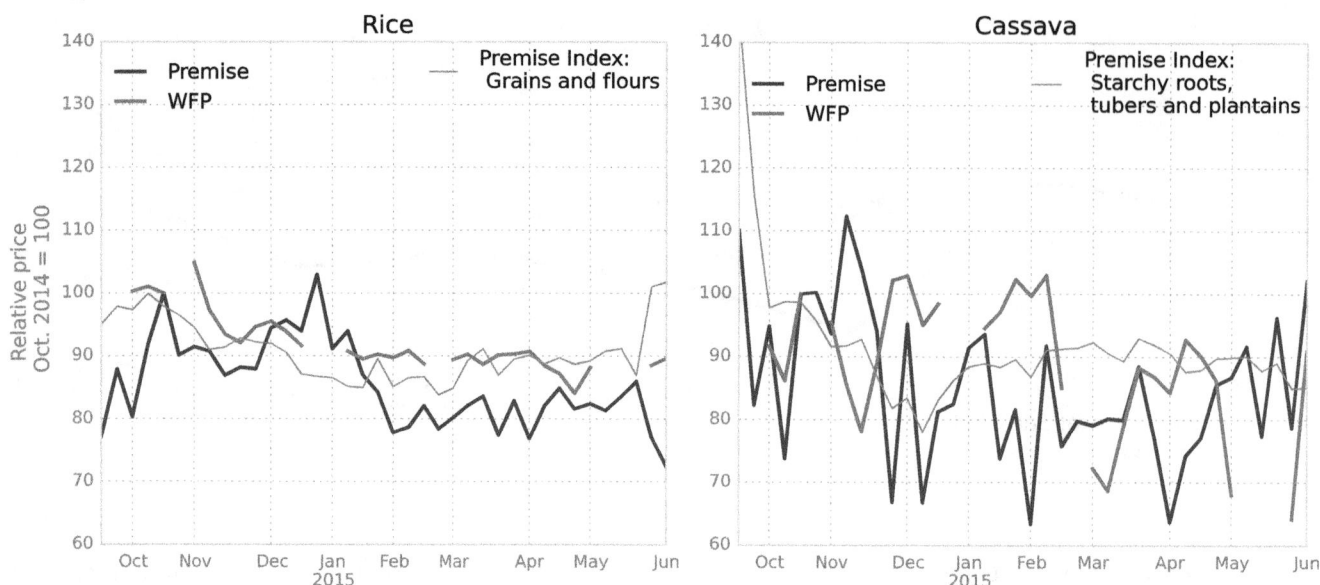

Figure 5: **Comparison of Premise and WFP Item Prices.** Average price data for two food items in Liberia. The blue lines represent the average weekly price data collected for rice (left) and cassava (right). The green lines indicate the corresponding price data for the same item, collected by the World Food Programme's Building Markets initiative. The red line indicates the composite sub-index from Premise data, constructed from all goods in the grains (left) and starchy roots (right) product categories. Each series is normalized to a value of 100 on the week of October 15, 2015.

are provided for the overall price level, food and non-alcoholic beverages (split by domestic and imported food), transportation, and imported fuel. The inset of Figure 4 displays the time series of the Food and Non-Alcoholic Beverages Index for Liberia between May 2011 and April 2015. To emphasize relative changes in prices, the index is normalized so that the value of the index in October 2014 is equal 100. The impact of the Ebola epidemic, which caused year-to-year price inflation to peak at 16% in September 2014, is evident in the figure. Note that the Central Bank index is intended to be nationally representative, but Premise data for this period is restricted to the capital city, Monrovia.[6]

4.1.2 World Food Programme

We additionally compare the product-level data captured by Premise contributors to data acquired from United Nations World Food Programme (WFP), which conducts regular data collection for key food prices in order to assess food security and identify price shocks that disproportionately affect poor households. We utilize data collected for the WFP on a key set of consumption goods in Liberia, which were initiated in part to monitor the impact of Ebola on price inflation. For the purpose of comparability with the Premise data, we restrict the WFP data to a subset of four goods: imported rice, cassava, palm oil and charcoal.[7] Figure 5 shows the time series of mean weekly price of both rice and cassava, as independently observed in Premise and WFP data.

4.2 Statistical comparison

---

[6]In July 2015, Premise initiated data collection in two rural markets, but these data were not available at the time this research conducted.

[7]The WFP data captured six products in total, including brown cowpeas and gari flour; however, the Premise data collection does not include these items.

Comparison to baselines

We compare the Premise data to both the Central Bank food and non-alcoholic beverages index and the WFP individual item prices for the period from September 2014 to April 2015. Effectively, we seek to quantify the differences in Figures 4 and 5. These results are presented in Table 2, which indicates the average per-month error (RMSE) as well as the correlation between datasets over time. Since the CPI data is collected at the monthly level while the Premise data exists in daily averages, we compare the two series by making monthly comparison of the CPI to the average Premise data over the preceding 30-day period (row 1), and also by linearly interpolating the CPI data between monthly observations and comparing at the daily level (row 2).

As is evident in Table 2, we find suggestive evidence of a correlation between the aggregate indices. Importantly, these correlations do not account for potential delays and offsets in the different series. For instance, if the Premise FSPI is a leading indicator of the CPI, or vice versa, such patterns would not be reflected in the results in Table 2. However, correlation of individual food item prices is weaker. Our analysis thus suggests two areas for further investigation. First, through a longer time series of indices, we will be able to test for a more robust lagged structure to the relationship between the Central Bank indicators and Premise indicators. Second, the variation in food item prices within and across sources suggest that methods for screening outliers and validating price data with multiple source may improve stability of official price data for individual products.

Modeling improvements

Our analysis thus far indicates a suggestive correlation between Premise data and the indices collected by the Liberian Central Bank. Moving forward, we believe a promising area for research lies in

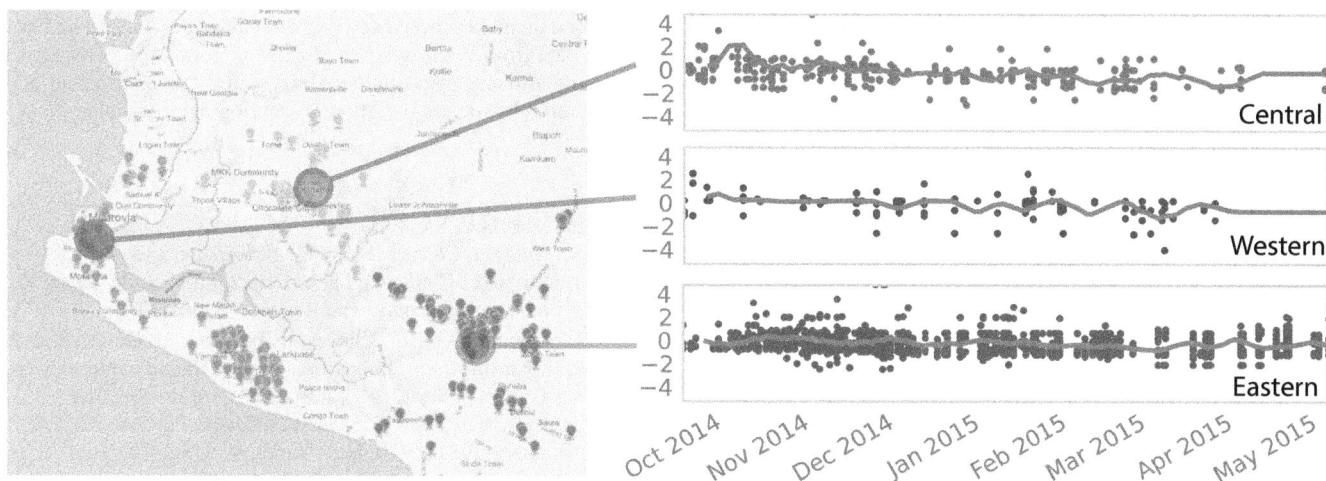

Figure 6: **Geospatially disaggregated time series.** Premise data include individual price data for 38 consumer goods from 310 unique locations in Monrovia, Liberia. Figure shows normalized prices for grain and flour products in the three geographic locations, with a red line to indicate the 10-day moving average across all observations from each sub-region. Sub-regions are identified using k-means clustering with five clusters specified using latitude and longitude of the observations submitted by the Premise contributor.

	Corr	RMSE	RMSE (% of mean)
A. Central Bank Food Price Index			
FSPI (Monthly Average)	0.64	2.97	3.58%
FSPI (Daily vs. Central Bank linear interpolation)	0.73	2.39	2.88%
B. Food Items (WFP, relative prices)			
Rice	0.54	8.94	9.77%
Cassava	0.03	16.27	18.71%
Charcoal	0.35	6.29	6.64%

Table 2: **Model performance.** Measures of model accuracy and error, comparing Premise data to data collected by the Liberian Central Bank and the World Food Programme.

using different sources of "ground truth" data to better calibrate the model used to construct the FSPI. To take a simple example, one might imagine using cross-validation to select the optimal parameters for outlier detection (in our case, the λ_k described in Section 3.2). This is a complicated task, however, as there are known issues with existing sources of price as CPI data, so it is important that any supervised learning approach not overfit the ground truth data. However, by calibrating with multiple sources of external data, collected through different processes and at different spatial and temporal resolution, we believe it should be possible to build more robust and accurate price indices.

5. DISCUSSION

While Premise data is correlated with the two traditional price measures we were able to obtain, there are statistical discrepancies that are not easily resolved.[8] While we largely treat the Central Bank of Liberia's CPI data as "ground truth" and assume that deviations observed in the Premise FSPI are errors, it is also conceivable that the Premise data might at times be accurate where Central Bank data is not. Indeed, the two sources of data, while comparable,

[8]One obvious source of these difference may be the differences in sampling frames used in data collection, for instance the fact that the Central Bank surveys the entire country's prices while Premise is thus far focused in Monrovia; as Premise expands to additional markets it will be possible to test this hypothesis.

have distinct advantages and disadvantages that we discuss briefly before concluding. Similarly, the WFP data relies upon the accuracy of reports from on-the-ground surveyors that are no less prone to errors than Premise contributors. In fact, real-time data quality controls can be put in place through Premise's technology that are often lacking or slow to implement through traditional price data collection methods.

5.1 Advantages of traditional price data

A primary advantage of traditional sources of price information is that they are familiar to most consumers of price data. Governments and international organizations have well-established mechanisms for collecting and processing price data, and a standard set of best practices exist for determining sample frames, deciding price frequencies, and integrating the resulting measures into macroeconomic decisionmaking. Centralized administration of these efforts further ensures that governments and international organizations play an integral role in the collection of critical economic data. Private sector efforts may be more subject to a different optimization problem, i.e. profit maximization.

There are also economies of scale in centralized data collection. Governments and international organizations conduct data collection, such as censuses, expenditure surveys and firm surveys, that are complimentary to price data. For example, expenditure surveys are integral to updating consumption basket estimates that feed into consumer price indices.

5.2 Advantages of Premise CPI

Relative to traditional models of price data collection, the Premise platform offers several distinct advantages. In particular, Premise data is highly granular, and can be sourced continuously in time and space, increasing the ability to track prices in real-time, in sub-regions of the country. In Figure 6, for instance, we show how the original data, collected from over 300 unique locations, can be aggregated to form sub-regional price indicators. For the figure, we cluster all of these locations geographically (using k-means on the market geocoordinates), then aggregate all data by cluster. The three time-series graphs on the right show the original price data in the grains and flour category, from each of these market clusters (the points on the graphs). The red line indicates the 10-day moving average, similar to the sub-index described earlier. While generally correlated, there is within-market volatility that is not clearly reflected in the Monrovia aggregate. Such patterns are not visible in most traditional sources of price data.

While our focus has been on price data collection, the crowd-sourcing framework can also be used to capture a much wider array of data types. Near-term possibilities include street mapping, collecting information on the availbility of public utiles, and mapping financial inclusion. The Premise platform for recruiting and compensating contributors makes it possible to quickly scale data collection efforts, and to target specific regions with less reliable data.

6. CONCLUSIONS

We describe and evaluate data from Premise, a platform for collecting crowd-sourced price information from networks of local contributors in developing countries. Our focus on the statistical properties of the Premise data, and on comparing Premise-based indices to more traditional measure of price inflation, reveals several promising areas for future work.

First, further quantitative work would benefit greatly from a longer panel of price data. While the Premise data contains tens of thousands of observations and is collected at extremely high frequency, the authoritative central bank data is collected only monthly. With only 9 months of overlapping data, it is difficult to make robust statistical comparisons.

Second, there is considerable scope for improvement in the techniques used to identify erroneous data, caused both by innocent error and intentional fraud. The outlier removal system we describe and implement appears to be reasonably effective, but is rather coarse and relies heavily on (possibly unjustified) intuition. Given a labeled training set, where the source of erroneous data points is known, it would be possible to develop more sophisticated methods tailored to specific products, locations, and contributors.

Finally, and perhaps most promising, we believe significant progress can still be made in developing methods for supervised learning that use authoritative data to improve the accuracy of estimates based on high-frequency data from Premise and related sources. Here, we made the simple point that inflation forecasts appear to improve when historical CPI data is supplemented with data from Premise. Analagous approaches could be used to increase the granularity of official CPI estimates (beyond the country-month), or to construct monthly Premise estimates that correspond more closely to official benchmarks. As before, the absence of a long panel of training data makes these exercises difficult in the immediate term, but as data from Premise's global network continues to stream in, it will open many opportunities for research that can impact how prices and inflation are measured in developing economies.

7. REFERENCES

[1] H. Ashley, J. Corbett, D. Jones, B. Garside, and G. Rambaldi. Change at hand: Web 2.0 for development. *Participatory Learning and Action*, 59(1):8–20, 2009.

[2] B. Birnbaum, G. Borriello, A. D. Flaxman, B. DeRenzi, and A. R. Karlin. Using Behavioral Data to Identify Interviewer Fabrication in Surveys. In *Proceedings of the SIGCHI Conference on Human Factors in Computing Systems*, CHI '13, pages 2911–2920, New York, NY, USA, 2013. ACM.

[3] B. Birnbaum, B. DeRenzi, A. D. Flaxman, and N. Lesh. Automated quality control for mobile data collection. In *Proceedings of the 2nd ACM Symposium on Computing for Development*, page 1. ACM, 2012.

[4] BLS. The Consumer Price Index. In *Bureau of Labor Statistics Handbook of Methods*, number 17. Dec. 2008.

[5] J. E. Blumenstock. Calling for Better Measurement: Estimating an Individual's Wealth and Well-Being from Mobile Phone Transaction Records. In *Proc. 20th ACM Conference on Knowledge Discovery and Mining (KDD '14), Workshop on Data Science for Social Good*, NY, 2014.

[6] A. Cavallo. Scraped Data and Sticky Prices. SSRN Scholarly Paper ID 1711999, Social Science Research Network, Rochester, NY, Apr. 2012.

[7] N. Eagle. txteagle: Mobile Crowdsourcing. In N. Aykin, editor, *Internationalization, Design and Global Development*, number 5623 in Lecture Notes in Computer Science, pages 447–456. Springer Berlin Heidelberg, 2009.

[8] N. Eagle, M. Macy, and R. Claxton. Network Diversity and Economic Development. *Science*, 328(5981):1029–1031, May 2010.

[9] M. Ester, H.-P. Kriegel, J. Sander, and X. Xu. A density-based algorithm for discovering clusters in large spatial databases with noise. In *Proc. 2nd ACM Conference on Knowledge Discovery and Mining*, volume 96, pages 226–231, 1996.

[10] V. Frias-Martinez, C. Soguero-Ruiz, E. Frias-Martinez, and M. Josephidou. Forecasting socioeconomic trends with cell phone records. In *Proceedings of the 3rd ACM Symposium on Computing for Development*, page 15. ACM, 2013.

[11] R. Glennerster and T. Suri. Economic Impacts of Ebola: Bulletin Four. *IGC Bulletin*, May 2015.

[12] A. Gupta, W. Thies, E. Cutrell, and R. Balakrishnan. mClerk: Enabling Mobile Crowdsourcing in Developing Regions. In *Proceedings of the SIGCHI Conference on Human Factors in Computing Systems*, CHI '12, pages 1843–1852, New York, NY, USA, 2012. ACM.

[13] N. Hamadeh, M. Rissanen, and M. Yamanaka. Crowd-sourced price data collection through mobile phones. In *New Techniques and Technologies for Statistics*, 2013.

[14] K. Himelein and J. G. Kastelic. The socio-economic impacts of Ebola in Liberia : results from a high frequency cell phone survey. Technical Report 96196, The World Bank, 2015.

[15] M. Jerven. *Poor numbers: how we are misled by African development statistics and what to do about it*. Cornell University Press, 2013.

[16] N. Lane, E. Miluzzo, H. Lu, D. Peebles, T. Choudhury, and A. Campbell. A survey of mobile phone sensing. *IEEE Communications Magazine*, 48(9):140–150, Sept. 2010.

[17] N. Mankiw. *Principles of Macroeconomics*. Cengage Learning, Jan. 2014.

[18] Premise. Premise Data Corporation: Food Staples Indexes, Nov. 2014.

[19] K. Starbird and L. Palen. "Voluntweeters": Self-organizing by Digital Volunteers in Times of Crisis. In *Proc. SIGCHI Conference on Human Factors in Computing Systems*, CHI '11, pages 1071–1080, New York, NY, USA, 2011. ACM.

[20] USAID. USAID Liberia Feed the Future Population Based Survey. Technical Report AID - OAA -C-11-00169, USAID, July 2013.

[21] World Food Programme. Ebola Response: from crisis to recovery. Technical report, World Food Programme, 2015.

Market good	# observations	# locations	Units	Min	Max	Mean	SD
Banana	819	201	piece	0.33	25	10.47	3.73
Beef Brisket (fresh, raw)	317	102	piece	5	200	42.42	37.30
Beer	718	177	cl	0	1833.33	11.56	74.65
Bitter Ball	476	130	kg	0	475	74.28	53.98
Bitter Kola	823	192	piece	0.91	35	13.96	4.7
Boiled Eggs	891	206	piece	1	25	13.24	2.54
Bread	1002	202	piece	5	500	72.35	48.49
Bulgur Wheat	830	168	kg	0.03	3187.5	49.91	116.3
Butter Rice	886	183	kg	0.68	7437.5	85.2	353.04
Cassava	749	165	piece	0.11	100	15.12	9.12
Cassava Flour	979	203	kg	0	4250	57.45	228.58
Cassava Leaf	377	109	piece	8.33	100	18.90	14.07
Charcoal	807	193	kg	2.4	1190	17.25	59.93
Chloride	842	199	liter	0	2000	152	88.76
Fan-fan Rice	839	170	kg	1	4250	68.77	147.18
Fuel (Diesel)	569	164	liter	10.57	1733.33	100.95	111.06
Instant Coffee	518	154	gram	0.01	10	2.72	2.63
Kidney Beans (dry)	805	175	kg	0.18	15937.5	203.45	869.62
Live Chicken (medium size)	361	81	piece	0	1300	615.95	244.02
Mayonnaise	613	168	ml	0.01	739.34	35.02	96.95
Onion	1098	214	piece	0.4	125	21.47	20.59
Orange	852	193	piece	2.5	125	16.57	11.29
Palm Butter	711	158	kg	3	2500	35.37	149.35
Palm Oil	997	198	liter	9.51	1800	110.71	80.40
Petrol (gas)	682	175	gallon	0.31	710	252.43	111.52
Plantain (Cooking Banana)	900	198	piece	0	250	20.37	11.26
Potato Greens	608	141	piece	0.5	35	14.2	4.74
Powdered Milk	846	197	gram	0	70	0.86	2.78
Salt	918	190	gram	0	4.25	0.09	0.23
Sardines (canned)	332	99	gram	0.04	4.25	1.55	1.53
Seasoning cube	434	108	gram	0	127.5	0.72	6.11
Smoked Fish	592	162	piece	0.52	550	70.24	81.93
Sugar	967	198	gram	0	8.75	0.12	0.54
Tomato	564	132	piece	0.08	500	22.07	33.62
USA Parboiled Rice	981	205	kg	5	6250	92.21	279.91
Vegetable Oil	1012	197	liter	1.35	580	130.4	41.09
Water (Bag)	1035	217	ml	0	5.71	0.02	0.18

Table A1: **Summary statistics of Premise contributor data.** Data collection in Liberia began in October, 2014, with products and market locations being gradually added since then. Significant variation between products in data quality and quantity.

Looking at Cities in Mexico with Crowds

Darshan Santani
Idiap Research Institute
EPFL, Lausanne, Switzerland
dsantani@idiap.ch

Salvador Ruiz-Correa
Center for Mobile Life
CNS-IPICYT, Mexico
src@cmls.pw

Daniel Gatica-Perez
Idiap Research Institute
EPFL, Lausanne, Switzerland
gatica@idiap.ch

ABSTRACT

Mobile and social technologies are providing new opportunities to document, characterize, and gather impressions of urban environments. In this paper, we present a study that examines urban perceptions of three cities in central Mexico (Guanajuato, Leon and Silao), which integrates a mobile crowdsourcing framework to collect geo-localized images of urban environments by a local youth community, and an online crowdsourcing platform (Amazon Mechanical Turk) to gather impressions of urban environments along twelve physical and psychological dimensions. Our study resulted in a collection of 7,000 geo-localized images containing outdoor scenes and views of each city's built environment, including touristic, historical, and residential neighbourhoods; and 156,000 individual judgments from MTurk. Statistical analyses show that outdoor environments can be reliably assessed with respect to most urban dimensions by the observers of crowdsourced images. Furthermore, a cross-city statistical analysis shows that outdoor urban places in Guanajuato (a touristic, cultural heritage site) are perceived as more quiet, picturesque and interesting compared to places in Leon and Silao, which are commercial and industrial hubs, respectively. In contrast Silao, is perceived to have lower accessibility than Leon. Finally, we investigate whether the perceptions of urban environments vary across different times of the day and found that places in the evening are perceived as less happy, pleasant and preserved, when compared to the same place in the morning. Through the use of collective action, participatory sensing and mobile crowdsourcing, our study engages citizens to understand socio-urban problems in their communities.

Categories and Subject Descriptors: H.4.m [Information Systems Applications]: Miscellaneous

Keywords: Mobile Crowdsourcing; Urban Perception; Outdoor Places; Collective Action; ICTD; Mexico

1. INTRODUCTION

Community awareness and action on urban problems are long-standing practices in developing countries [13]. The ability to reflect and act upon concerns defined by a community's interests and

ACM DEV 2015, December 01–02, 2015, London, United Kingdom .
Copyright is held by the owner/author(s). Publication rights licensed to ACM.
ACM ACM 978-1-4503-3490-7/15/11 ... $15.00.
DOI: http://dx.doi.org/10.1145/2830629.2830638.

values for its own benefit takes on special relevance in Latin America due to the local governments' inability to realize the full potential of both human and economic resources and a historically slow (when not absent) response by the authorities. Civic engagement and action with the local environment have educational, social, and economic aspects [11].

In this context, mobile and social technologies are providing new opportunities to document, characterize, map, and ultimately address urban problems in developing cities. Mobile crowdsourcing efforts for urban mapping and surveying conducted by citizens equipped with mobile phones (who generate reports, take pictures, or create maps) are emerging, often concentrated in informal settlements and other problematic regions [28, 1, 2, 36]. Other recent approaches are studying cities in the developed world, and use online crowdsourcing platforms to establish the feasibility of obtaining reliable estimates of urban impressions of physical and psychological constructs like safety, beauty, and quietness, elicited by images of the city taken at street level [30]. The possibility of obtaining crowdsourced perceptions of the socio-urban image of a city by non-residents is valuable for developing cities, specially when the cities have large flows of visitors (tourists, students or business people), as it could help to understand the choices that non-locals make regarding the use of the public space, or to identify misperceptions due to the lack of local context.

In research examining urban impressions in developed cities using online crowdsourcing, judgments have been elicited using images obtained from Google Street View (GSV) [30, 25, 17]. Even though GSV provides a scalable and automated way to collect images, it suffers from two limitations. First, the GSV image database is not exhaustive in spatial coverage in developing countries due to accessibility and safety issues. For instance, due to the way Google collects street views (via cameras mounted on top of a vehicle), GSV does not always contains images of narrow streets and winding alleys. In a recent study, we found in a small sample of images taken in this type of area that more than half of GSV images were either unavailable or erroneous within a mid-size touristic city in Mexico [28]. Second, GSV images fail to capture the temporal aspects of a city: only static views are available, and it can take years before images are updated. This does not facilitate studying the effect of time of the day in the perception of the urban environment, which is a key aspect as discussed in urban studies literature [23, 20]. In contrast, mobile crowdsourcing represents an opportunistic, just-in-time way of documenting urban changes over time.

In this paper, we present a study on urban perception on three cities in central Mexico, which integrates: (1) mobile crowdsourcing involving a local youth community to collect first-person perspective images depicting urban issues that are defined by the community itself, and (2) online crowdsourcing using Mechanical Turk

(MTurk), where US crowd-workers contribute their impressions on photos of the urban environment along twelve physical and psychological dimensions of a place. Our contributions are:

1. A mobile crowdsourcing framework involving over 70 local students that resulted in a data set of 7,000 geo-localized images collected in three cities in Guanajuato state (Guanajuato, Leon, and Silao), each one characterized by distinct geography, economic activity, and population (Section 3). The data set contains outdoor scenes and views of each city's built environment, including touristic, historical, and business sites, residential neighbourhoods, and areas with narrow streets and alleys.

2. An online crowdsourcing study on MTurk to gather impressions of crowd-workers along 12 physical and psychological labels including (*dangerous*, *dirty*, *interesting*, *happy*, *polluted*, etc.), based on 1,200 images (400 images per city) (Section 4). The studied dimensions include and extend those studied in recent literature. Statistical analyses on 144,000 individual judgments show that the outdoor scenes in the investigated cities can be reliably assessed by observers of crowdsourced images with respect to most urban dimensions.

3. A cross-city statistical analysis shows that outdoor urban places in Guanajuato city are perceived as more *quiet*, *picturesque* and *interesting* compared to places in Leon and Silao. In contrast, Silao is perceived to have higher accessibility than Guanajuato, but less accessibility than Leon. Overall, Guanajuato has the highest mean scores amongst all three cities on most positive labels and lowest scores on negative labels (Section 5.4). This finding is relevant as it could inform both citizens and authorities about significantly different perceptions that could lead to action.

4. As a way of showing the additional value of mobile crowdsourcing with respect to GSV-type surveying, we present a study about how the perceptions of urban environments vary across different times of the day using a small image sample and 12,000 individual judgments. The results show that places at evenings are perceived as less *happy*, *pleasant* and *preserved*, in comparison with mornings. We do not observe statistically significant differences in perception of *dangerous* between mornings and evenings for the studied places (Section 5.5).

Overall, our current work engages youth communities as actors of social change and contributes towards understanding sociourban problems in cities through the use of collective action, participatory sensing, and crowdsourcing technologies.

2. RELATED WORK

2.1 Systems for reporting urban issues

There are various existing systems that allow citizens to report urban issues. One in the developed world is FixMyStreet (FMS) [3], launched in the UK in 2007 [18], and later implemented in other countries (mainly in Europe) with varying degrees of success. FMS allows people to share and map text reports about problems; the system allows uploading images as an optional feature. SeeClick-Fix [4], was launched in the US in 2008. These systems have not generally been adopted in Latin America, among other reasons, because they require an authority committed to take ownership for the system and respond timely to the reports. A recent analysis of six years of FMS reports concludes that only 11% of them contain images, but also that image uploading is a significant indicator of the actual response of the authorities to the reports and the commitment of reporters to keep contributing [34]. These findings support our choice of mediating participation via geo-localized photo taking. On the other hand, in contrast to these systems, which by de-

sign promote individual participation [10], our work is community-oriented and puts community interests and action at the center.

In this sense, our work is closer to a number of open mapping initiatives in developing regions. Notable examples include the Kibera slum in Kenya [1], and various systems built around Ushahidi [5]. In Latin America, other examples include the work done to map informal settlements in Buenos Aires, Argentina [2], and in Rio de Janeiro, Brazil [12]. Another mapping effort is led in India by Humara Bachpan [36], an organization that conducts civic campaigns centred on "child clubs" to create maps of marginalized neighborhoods in India slums. Two differences between these initiatives and our work are (1) the engagement of communities of youth in both data collection and data appropriation exercises; and (2) the development of a methodology to produce crowdsourced assessments of the conditions of photographed urban places.

Finally, social media channels are being used to generate reports of urban-related concerns, sometimes containing photos. In Mexico, Twitter has been notably used for real-time, eyewitness reports of insecurity and drug-related crimes in towns and cities [22]. This is an attractive alternative, but it is limited to people who agree to join these services and accept corporate-driven terms of use.

2.2 Crowdsourced urban perception

In the field of architecture and urban planning, many of the studies about visual perceptions of built environments have used qualitative research methods including interviews, visual preference surveys [31, 23] and observation of the built environment using either actual or simulated images [19]. However, most of these studies are either conducted in controlled laboratory settings or are based on questionnaires, which may have limitations with respect to scalability, ecological validity, or recall biases.

With the popularity of social media and mobile phones, in conjunction with an increased use of online crowdsourcing platforms to obtain judgments from diverse populations, scholars have started to explore crowdsourcing as a medium to obtain estimates of urban perception for both indoor [15, 32] and outdoor environments [30, 28, 25]. For outdoor environments, gathering perceptions typically involve the use of Google Street View (GSV) [30, 25, 9]; while GSV is widely available in the developed world, it is not so for the developing world [28]. In [30], the authors conducted a study to measure the perception of outdoor urban scenes on safety, class and uniqueness, based on geo-tagged images obtained via GSV in four developed cities (in the US and Austria). In a similar study on urban perception, judgments were collected to examine visual cues that could correlate outdoor places in London with three dimensions (beauty, quietness, and happiness) [25]. Our current study builds upon our previous work [28], where we carried out a crowdsourcing study to collect perceptions of six dimensions of urban awareness (dangerous, dirty, preserved, etc.) by local inhabitants of one Mexican city. Compared to [28], we collect and study data that is ten times larger and comes from three cities, define and study a larger number of urban constructs, conduct cross-city analyses, and analzye temporal effects as discussed next.

2.3 Temporal effects on urban perception

The work in the previous subsection uses temporally fixed image stimuli to obtain perceptions. However, cities are dynamic and the time of day might play an important role with respect to urban perception.In the field of urban planning, there has been significant interest to quantify perceived safety and fear of crime during nighttime [23, 20, 16]. Using on-street pedestrian surveys, the authors found that 90% of the respondents felt that the improvements in street lighting lead to a reduction in the perceived fear of crime, an increased sense of personal safety, and increased pedestrian use after dark [23]. No image stimuli were used in this study. Another study compared 16 images of outdoor scenes taken during day-time and night-time to test the effect of visibility on making a place feel safe [20]. Respondents were undergraduate psychology students who were asked to rate these scenes. The authors found statistically significant differences on ratings on perceived safety during different times of the day. A similar study was conducted using 20 photographs of night-time locations from a university campus [16]. We study not only the role of night-time or dark scenes on perceived safety, but also other psychological dimensions e.g., quietness, happy, pleasant, etc.

3. DATA COLLECTION FRAMEWORK

In this section we describe our data collection framework, including the criteria to select the studied cities in Mexico, the definition and selection of urban awareness dimensions, and the mobile crowdsourcing design to collect two image corpora.

3.1 Project Design

The image corpus used in our study was collected with an approach aimed at exploring urban environments of cities in Latin America, with an initial emphasis in Mexico. The approach was developed in the context of a larger research initiative, which aims at addressing specific urban issues by young volunteers through the use of collective action, participatory sensing and mobile crowdsourcing. The project emphasizes that empowering citizens through technological means that increase awareness and deepen the understanding of socio-urban concerns is of crucial importance. This is so because the state and evolution of their cities strongly depend on the capacity of their populations and the existence of institutional policies to create the structural conditions for sustainable development. By development, we understand the "process by which people individually and collectively enhance their capacities to improve their lives according to their values and interests" [11].

Our research project followed a transdisciplinary approach to explore the urban environment involving computer scientists and other experts on one side, and social actors on the other. Our team included specialists in computer science, social media, psychology, and visual arts, who conducted the technical and social design, as well as the development and execution of experiments on mobile sensing and crowdsourcing jointly with student volunteers, who were recruited from a local technical high school. Participating students were altruistically motivated and eager to contribute their knowledge and experiences, and to co-design all project activities to understand the urban environment of their city.

3.2 Selection of Cities

To collect images from outdoor urban spaces, we grounded our work in three small to mid-size cities in central Mexico: Guanajuato (pop. 170,000), Leon (pop. 1.5 million) and Silao (pop. 147,000). Guanajuato is a touristic city in central Mexico, and the capital of a state of the same name. Guanajuato occupies a valley, forming a complex network of narrow roads, pedestrian alleys, and stairways running uphill. Most pedestrian alleys have no car access, and other major roads run underground. Guanajuato is a historical city and a UNESCO world heritage site, with a vibrant tourism industry that is centred around the city's historical downtown area (dating from the Spanish colonial times) and several large art festivals. Guanajuato city often appears as one of top destination to visit in Mexico [26, 8].

The city of Leon is a business and industrial hub in the state of Guanajuato that drives a large part of the economical activity of the state. Leon has a strong leather industry, offering products both to the national and international markets. Leon also receives a large number of tourists. In contrast, Silao is a local hub of agricultural and industrial activity in the region, with a wide variety of farm crops, dairy packaging plants and a major car assembly plant. Due to its relatively larger size, some areas in Leon are quite inaccessible either due to safety concerns or because of the presence of large walls which typically surround up-scale neighbourhoods.

The three cities reflect a common situation in Latin American urbanization, which produces complex environments with historical sites, suburban sprawl, affluent neighborhoods, and informal settlements. For the three cities, images were captured from areas that included different neighborhoods reflecting the characteristics of each city, as well as touristic and historical sites. Figure 1 shows a sample of images from each city.

3.3 Definition and Selection of Dimensions

In order to select labels to characterize urban awareness for outdoor environments, we base our methodology on prior work [28, 30, 25]. The list of selected labels in our study encompasses the labels studied in the literature, in addition to new ones. We have chosen the following 12 dimensions in alphabetical order: *accessible*, *dangerous*, *dirty*, *happy*, *interesting*, *pleasant*, *picturesque*, *polluted*, *preserved*, *pretty*, *quiet* and *wealthy*. Three labels (*dangerous*, *dirty* and *polluted*) have a negative connotation, while the rest have a neutral or a positive connotation. Throughout the paper, we will use the umbrella term "urban awareness" to refer to these labels. Images served as stimuli to rate perceptions for 12 urban awareness labels, along a seven-point Likert scale ranging from *strongly disagree* (1) to *strongly agree* (7), as typically done in psychology and urban planning research [15, 20].

We have chosen this list of labels for several reasons. First, these labels encompass physical and psychological constructs evoked while describing socio-urban characteristics of the built environment. Second, all the three cities faces various problems including crime, prevalence of alcohol and drugs in some streets and alleys, and streets with garbage and non-artistic graffiti, to mention a few. These issues not only affect the well-being and safety of its citizens, but also hurt the image of a city e.g., as a tourist destination. Thus, it is essential to study and understand the role these perceptions play in these cities.

3.4 Mobile Crowdsourcing Design

The images used in this study were collected as part of an Urban Data Challenge (UDC). The UDC was co-designed with the aid of student volunteers from a technical school in Guanajuato city. The technical school was founded to provide high-quality education on science, technology and humanities to working class youth (about 600 students in the age group of 16–18 years old) who live in Guanajuato and surrounding suburbs.

The data challenge was carried out during a 12-week period and consisted of weekend camps, workshops, data collection, and creative use of collected data with follow-up activities. Student volunteers were organized into ten teams of ten members, each consisting of seven students, two parents and a teacher. Teams sought support from their classmates to achieve their goals, with the objective of involving a larger community in the data collection. Workshop activities included discussions about ethics, privacy, urbanism, basic techniques of photography, and the use of mobile devices for participatory sensing in urban environments. To cover Leon and Silao, student teams visited these cities in person, which are 56km and 25km respectively from Guanajuato.

Figure 1: Random selection of images from the *city-image* corpus. For privacy reasons, images showing faces have been pixelated.

Teams explored each city to document their urban concerns by photographing urban places via mobile phones. Each team was given an Android-based smartphone. However, students also used their own mobile devices for data collection. We developed a mobile application that enabled students to take pictures and upload them to our image server. The collected images covered not only urban concerns, but also captured the ebb and flow of the city highlighting different facets of urban life. Mechanisms to incentivize participation included creation of study circles to raise awareness about the importance of understanding urban phenomena through the use of mobile technology, and the role of citizens in proposing creative, community-based solutions to prevalent urban problems. The UDC produced over 7,000 geo-referenced images. All the images were taken from a first-person perspective, corresponding to the natural situation in which a person navigates and perceives the urban environment. Twelve hundred images were then selected for the crowdsourcing experiments reported in this paper.

3.5 Image Corpus

City Image Corpus: As stated before, as a result of the UDC, we collected an image corpus consisting of 7,000 geo-tagged images. For our current analysis, we focus on a random selection of 1,200 images with 400 images per city, which we call the *city-image* corpus. All images were taken between 9 AM and 5 PM during workdays. The collected image set consists of outdoor images captured at touristic hotspots, key historical sites, traditional neighborhoods, main squares, thoroughfares, main/commercial streets and downtown areas. Volunteers were asked to capture images of urban scenes in their natural setting and to avoid beautified images or applying digital filters, as is usually the case with images found in social media platforms, like Flickr or Instagram. It is important to note that the *city-image* corpus contains not only those images that document an urban concern, but also images which capture the ebb and flow of the city while depicting different aspects of urban life and build environments. Figure 1 shows a sample of images from the corpus for each city.

Evening Image Corpus: In addition, people participating in the UDC also collected images of urban areas during different times of the day in order to test if perceptions of the urban environments vary across different times of the day, along the selected dimensions. This illustrates the benefits of just-in-time crowdsourced photo taking compared to static approaches, like Google Street View. We focused our analysis on 50 urban sites in Guanajuato,

(a) Morning   (b) Evening

Figure 2: Random selection of images from the *evening-image* corpus, showing an image taken in a) Morning, and b) Evening. For privacy reasons, images showing faces have been pixelated.

where volunteers captured images of the same place during two different times of the day: first during the morning (between 10-11 AM), and then in the evening (between 6-7:30 PM). As a result, for the *evening-image* corpus, we obtained 50 images per time-slot, resulting in a total of 100 images. Figure 2 shows two images of an urban place taken during morning and evening respectively.

4. CROWDSOURCING IMPRESSIONS

To gather impressions of online annotators, we designed a crowdsourcing study on Mechanical Turk (MTurk). We chose US-based workers with at least 95% approval rate for historical HITs (Human Intelligence Tasks). To increase the reliability of annotations, we only chose "Master" annotators, a worker pool with an excellent track record of completing tasks with precision. In each HIT, the workers were asked to view an image of an urban space, and then rate their personal impressions based on what they saw along 12 labels. Additionally, workers were required to view images in high-resolution (and not just the image thumbnails). Workers were not given any information of the studied city to reduce potential bias and stereotyping associated to the city identity. We collected 10 annotations for each image and label, resulting in a total of 13,000 responses (12,000 for the *city-image* corpus and 1,000 for the *evening-image* corpus) and a total of 156,000 individual judgements. Every worker was reimbursed 0.10 USD per HIT.

We also gathered crowdworkers' demographics via an email-based survey. We asked workers about their age group, gender,

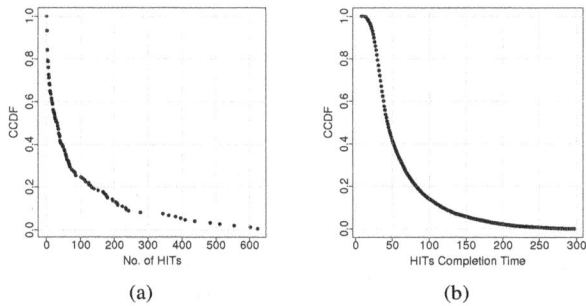

Figure 3: Worker Participation. Plot showing the complementary cumulative distribution function (CCDF) of a) Number of HITs per worker, b) HITs completion times.

Label	Guanajuato	Leon	Silao	Combined
Accessible	0.86	0.55	0.36	0.72
Dangerous	0.83	0.65	0.73	0.76
Dirty	0.85	0.72	0.70	0.78
Happy	0.82	0.76	0.61	0.78
Interesting	0.61	0.70	0.60	0.70
Pleasant	0.83	0.77	0.66	0.79
Picturesque	0.77	0.69	0.64	0.76
Polluted	0.68	0.56	0.57	0.64
Preserved	0.82	0.75	0.63	0.77
Pretty	0.80	0.69	0.66	0.76
Wealthy	0.84	0.73	0.57	0.76
Quiet	0.71	0.65	0.53	0.73

Table 1: $ICC(1, k)$ scores of 12 dimensions for each city. All values are statistically significant at $p < 0.01$.

level of education, current place of residence (categorized as rural, suburbs, small town, mid-size town, or city), and any experience of visiting any developing countries, in any region including Latin America, Asia and Africa.

4.1 Worker Participation

For a total number of 12,000 HITs available for *city-image* corpus, we observe that workers completed an average of 82 HITs, while they could potentially undertake 1,200 HITs (400 HITs per city). We had a pool of 146 workers who responded to our tasks. While 50% of the workers submitted less than 30 HITs, the worker with the highest number of HITs completed 624 assignments (Figure 3a). We observe a long-tailed distribution in HIT completion times (mean: 59 secs, median: 43 secs, max: 297 secs), as shown in Figure 3b. It is worth noting that we allocated a maximum of 5 minutes per HIT. Similar statistics were obtained for the 1,000 HITs available for *evening-image* corpus.

4.2 Worker Demographics

Of all 146 HIT respondents, 53% replied to our demographics survey. We notice a slightly skewed gender ratio (58% of workers being female), which corroborates earlier findings in the online crowdsourcing literature [27]. 80% of respondents reported their ethnicity as White/Caucasian, with 12% participants being Asian, and 3% each belonging to Hispanic/Latino and Black/African American. 45% of respondents are college graduates. Furthermore, we also notice that the worker population is relatively middle age with the most popular category (43%) being the age group of 35-50 years old (18–24: 3%, 25–34: 32%, 50+: 22%)

While only 18% of our worker pool reported to live in a big city, the majority of them (45%) are sub-urban (for the remaining categories: rural: 18%, small-sized town: 9%, mid-sized town: 9%). Only a minority (23%) of the survey respondents reported having experience visiting any country in the developing world. For those with travelling experience in developing countries, holidays and tourism were the main purposes of the visit (55%). Amongst the visited countries, 44% of these subset of respondents have travelled to Mexico, which is not surprising given that the pool of crowd-workers is based in the US.

5. RESULTS AND DISCUSSION

5.1 Annotations Quality

We begin our analysis by assessing the reliability of annotations. We measure the inter-rater consensus by computing intraclass correlation (ICC) among ratings given by the worker pool [33]. Our annotation procedure requires every place to be judged by k annotators randomly selected from a larger population of K work-

ers. $ICC(1, 1)$ and $ICC(1, k)$ values, which respectively stand for single and average ICC measures, are computed for each label and city across all images.

Table 1 reports the $ICC(1, k)$ values for all cities for $k = 10$ (due to space constraints, we omit $ICC(1, 1)$ values.) In addition to listing the individual scores for each city and label, we also report the combined $ICC(1, k)$ scores for each label and the whole dataset, where we have combined all places across cities. We observe acceptable inter-rater consensus for most labels, with all values being statistically significant (p-value < 0.01).

We notice that the inter-rater reliability for labels is above 0.7 for most of the labels and cities. This suggests that MTurk observers tend to agree on their perceptions of most dimensions. It is interesting to note that the combined label *quiet* achieves high agreement from images not showing any sound (0.73 combined score). On the other hand, the label *polluted* is the one with lowest combined ICC (0.64). We also observe that *accessibility* has low ICC for two of the three cities. Silao has overall received the lowest ICC scores compared to the other two cities.

5.2 Descriptive Statistics

Given the multi-annotator impressions, it is necessary to create a composite score for each image, given a label. To gather the individual ratings, we used an ordinal scale, which implicitly describes a ranking. It is known that the central tendency of an ordinal variable is better expressed by the median [35]. Thus, we compute the median score for each label given the 10 responses per image. Given the median scores, we then compute the mean scores and standard deviations for each label using all 400 images for each city.

Table 2 lists the descriptive statistics for each city and label, in addition to showing the aggregated scores for each label across all cities. At the level of individual annotations, the minimum and maximum values are 1 and 7 respectively for each label and city, indicating that the full scale was used by the crowd-workers. The mean scores for the majority of labels is below 4 for each city, which indicates a trend towards disagreement with the corresponding label. On the other hand, each city has urban sites that score high and low for each dimension.

In all cities, the mean scores for *accessible* are the highest amongst all labels. On all labels phrased positively (except *accessible* and *wealthy*), Guanajuato scores the highest amongst all cities, which is not surprising given that Guanajuato is a UNESCO world heritage site with a vibrant tourism industry. In contrast, *wealthy* has the lowest mean score for all cities (combined mean 2.64), which is not surprising either given that the type of cities we are study-

Label	Guanajuato	Leon	Silao	Combined
Accessible	4.62 (1.1)	5.02 (0.8)	4.41 (0.7)	4.69 (0.9)
Dangerous	2.92 (1.2)	2.86 (0.8)	3.17 (0.9)	2.98 (1.0)
Dirty	3.00 (1.2)	3.05 (0.9)	3.44 (1.0)	3.16 (1.1)
Happy	3.97 (1.1)	3.69 (0.8)	3.36 (0.8)	3.67 (1.0)
Interesting	4.38 (1.0)	3.63 (0.8)	3.50 (0.8)	3.84 (0.9)
Pleasant	4.13 (1.1)	3.83 (0.8)	3.48 (0.8)	3.82 (1.0)
Picturesque	3.55 (1.2)	3.00 (0.9)	2.73 (0.8)	3.09 (1.1)
Polluted	2.55 (0.9)	2.93 (0.8)	3.19 (0.9)	2.89 (0.9)
Preserved	4.04 (1.2)	4.00 (0.9)	3.48 (0.9)	3.84 (1.0)
Pretty	3.41 (1.2)	3.10 (0.9)	2.80 (0.9)	3.11 (1.0)
Quiet	4.08 (0.9)	3.24 (0.8)	3.10 (1.0)	3.47 (1.0)
Wealthy	2.58 (1.0)	2.90 (0.8)	2.43 (0.7)	2.64 (0.9)

Table 2: Means and standard deviations (in brackets) of annotation scores for each city and label.

ing and the intended goals of the crowdsourced collection, leaning towards documenting urban concerns.

From Table 2, we observe variation in the mean values across cities for some of the labels, but a few differences stand out. For instance, the mean differences of the *picturesque* and *interesting* attributes between Guanajuato and Silao, and the *quiet* attribute between Guanajuato and Leon and Silao all exceed 0.8, potentially suggesting differences in city perceptions. A systematic analysis to statistical testing of these differences are presented in Section 5.4.

5.3 Correlation and PCA Analysis

To understand basic statistical connections between urban awareness labels, we perform correlation analysis using the mean annotation scores for all labels. Figure 4 visualizes the correlation matrix across all dimensions using the aggregated data for all cities. We have used hierarchical clustering to re-order the correlation matrix in order to reveal its underlying structure. We color code the matrix instead of providing numerical scores to facilitate the discussion. We observe three distinct clusters. Starting from the bottom right in the first cluster, all the positive labels *happy, preserved, pretty, picturesque, pleasant, interesting* and *wealthy* are highly collinear with pairwise correlations exceeding 0.7. The second cluster consists of urban sites which are *quiet*. The third cluster (top-left) lies on the opposite spectrum with respect to cluster one, and consists of *dangerous, dirty* and *polluted*. Each of these clusters correspond to different aggregate impression, the first and third somewhat resemble "sentiment" i.e., positive/negative. As such, we can also observe significant negative correlations between dimensions in cluster one and cluster three.

To further explore the relationships between labels, we perform principal component analysis (PCA) on the aggregated annotation scores for all 1,200 images. PCA is a statistical method to linearly transform high dimensional data to a set of lower orthogonal dimensions that best explains the variance in the data [24]. In Figure 5, we show the first two principal components which explain 77% of the variance in the annotation scores along the 12 dimensions. Note that before applying PCA, the labels were scaled to unit variance. We observe that the first component, which accounts for 67% of the variance, contains labels that resemble either the positive or negative "sentiment", respectively, on the right and left side of X-axis. Furthermore, component two primarily contains label *quiet*. These results corroborate the findings from correlation analysis and have clear support from early work in environmental psychology [29].

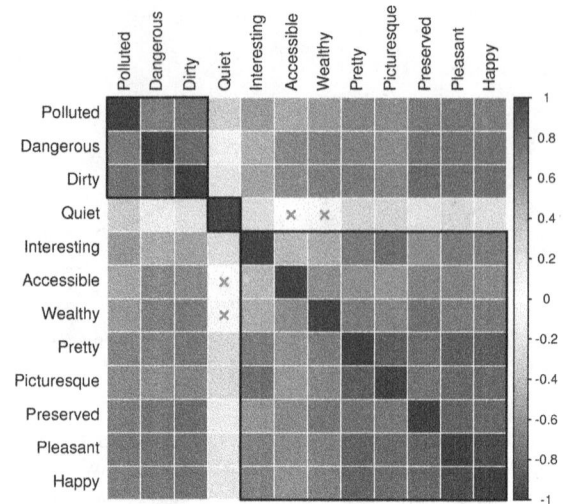

Figure 4: Plot showing the correlation matrix between dimensions. Matrix is color coded as per the palette shown in the right, with blue (resp. red) indicating positive (resp. negative) correlation coefficients. Black rectangular borders indicate the three distinct clusters found in the correlation matrix. Cells marked X are *not* statistically significant at $p < 0.01$.

5.4 Statistical Comparison across Cities

To better understand whether mean differences across cities for some of these urban awareness labels are statistically significant, we perform the Tukey's honest significant difference (HSD) test. Tukey's HSD test is a statistical procedure for groups which compares all possible pairs of mean values for each group, with the null hypothesis stating that the mean values being compared are drawn from the same population [37]. We perform the HSD test to compute pairwise comparisons of mean values between cities for each label, which results in a total of 36 comparisons (3 city-wise pairs across 12 dimensions). Out of a total of 36 comparisons, we find 30 comparisons to be statistically significant at p-value < 0.01. In Table 3, we report the top-10 significant results of the Tukey's HSD test, where the differences in the observed means are 0.6 or higher i.e., greater than half a point on the rating scale. We refrain from making claims for all smaller effect cases, following recent discussions in the statistical literature [14]. Additionally in Figure 6, we show the barplots comparing the mean annotation scores across all cities for two labels to elucidate some of the significant results from Tukey's HSD statistics. Based on these statistics we observe that:

1. Outdoor urban places in Guanajuato are perceived as more *quiet*, *picturesque* and *interesting* compared to places in Leon and Silao (rows 1,2,3,4,5 in Table 3). Overall, Guanajuato has the highest mean scores amongst all three cities on most positive labels, except *accessible* and *wealthy*, and the lowest mean scores on most negative labels except *dangerous*, as highlighted in Table 2. To highlight the differences in perception between Guanajuato and the other two cities, we present the barplot comparing the mean annotation scores of *quiet* dimension across all cities in Figure 6a. We observe that the relative percentage of places in Guanajuato which are rated higher than 4 is significantly larger than those corresponding to other cities. Similar patterns are observed for *interesting* and *picturesque*, but plots are omitted due to space constraints.

2. Silao is perceived to be more *polluted*, when compared to Guanajuato with differences in mean scores exceeding 0.6 (row 7 in Table 3). We believe these results are an effect of agricultural and industrial activity in Silao region, when compared to the historic and touristic nature of Guanajuato. When looking at the

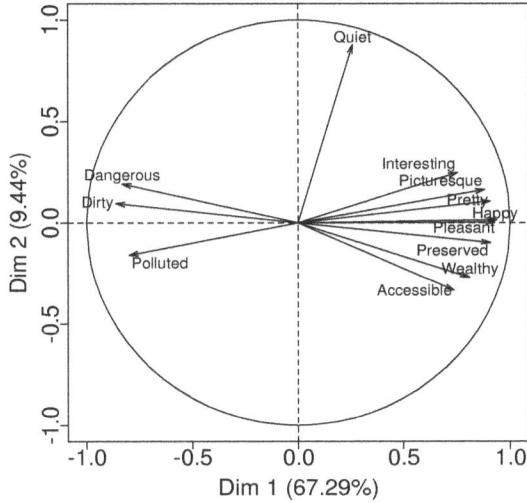

Figure 5: Plot showing the first two principal components on aggregated annotation scores on 1,200 images across all cities.

Label	City Pair	Mean Difference ± CI
Quiet	SC-GC	-0.98 ± 0.19
Interesting	SC-GC	-0.88 ± 0.18
Quiet	LC-GC	-0.84 ± 0.19
Picturesque	SC-GC	-0.82 ± 0.21
Interesting	LC-GC	-0.75 ± 0.18
Pleasant	SC-GC	-0.65 ± 0.19
Polluted	SC-GC	$+0.63 \pm 0.18$
Happy	SC-GC	-0.62 ± 0.19
Accessible	SC-LC	-0.61 ± 0.19
Pretty	SC-GC	-0.61 ± 0.20

Table 3: Tukey's HSD test statistics showing the top–10 significant results, where the differences in the observed means across cities for labels exceed 0.6. GC, LC, SC respectively refers to Guanajuato City, Leon City and Silao City. All mean differences are statistically significant at $p < 0.01$.

barplot in Figure 6b, we observe a similar pattern as highlighted above, where the relative proportion of places which are rated on a higher scale for being polluted in Silao are significantly larger than those in Guanajuato.

3. Silao is perceived to have lower accessibility than Leon (row 9 in Table 3). We believe this result is due to the fact that Leon, as a larger and more modern city, has many broad avenues and multi-lane streets. In contrast, Silao has small town streets. See examples in Figure 1.

To further validate the statistical significance of the Tukey's HSD test, we perform a series of pairwise Kolmogorov-Smirnov test (KS test) across all cities and labels. The KS test is a non-parametric test to compare the empirical distributions of two samples, with the null hypothesis being that the two samples are drawn from the same distribution [21]. We perform the KS test to compare the cumulative distribution functions of each city-pair across each label (36 comparisons) and found 32 comparisons to be statistically significant for a statistical level $\alpha = 0.01$. Results from the KS test corroborates the findings from the Tukey's HSD test.

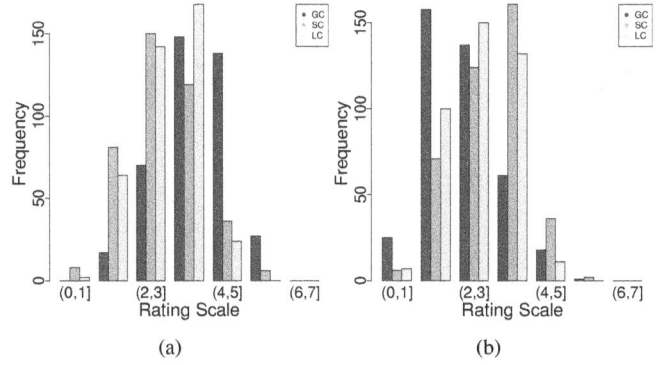

Figure 6: Barplots comparing the mean annotation scores across all cities for a) Quiet, and b) Polluted.

Label	Mean Scores		Mean Diff. ± CI	p-value
	Morning	Evening		
Accessible	4.40 (0.93)	4.38 (1.26)	-0.02 ± 0.58	0.928
Dangerous	2.86 (0.99)	3.38 (1.29)	$+0.52 \pm 0.60$	0.026
Dirty	2.89 (1.09)	3.33 (1.29)	$+0.44 \pm 0.63$	0.069
Happy	3.92 (0.98)	3.11 (1.18)	-0.81 ± 0.57	**0.0003**
Interesting	4.35 (0.74)	3.78 (1.18)	-0.57 ± 0.52	**0.005**
Picturesque	3.63 (0.97)	3.00 (1.21)	-0.63 ± 0.58	**0.005**
Pleasant	4.01 (1.03)	3.24 (1.20)	-0.77 ± 0.59	**0.0008**
Polluted	2.48 (0.86)	2.79 (1.12)	$+0.31 \pm 0.52$	0.123
Preserved	4.03 (1.02)	3.32 (1.26)	-0.71 ± 0.60	**0.003**
Pretty	3.58 (1.05)	3.03 (1.23)	-0.55 ± 0.60	0.018
Quiet	4.12 (1.01)	3.79 (1.16)	-0.33 ± 0.57	0.132
Wealthy	2.71 (1.03)	2.15 (0.92)	-0.56 ± 0.51	**0.005**

Table 4: Descriptive statistics and Tukey's HSD test statistics showing the results for morning and evening times of the day. Value marked in **bold** are statistically significant at $p < 0.01$.

5.5 Evening Corpus Analysis

In this subsection, we analyze the *evening-image* corpus to statistically test if the perceptions of the urban environments in one of the studied cities vary across different times of the day, along the selected dimensions. As described in Section 3.5, we collected 50 images of places during the morning (between 10-11 AM), and the evening (between 6-7:30 PM) in Guanajuato. In Table 4, we list the mean scores for each label across times of the day. To aggregate the impressions, we followed the same procedure as explained in Section 5.2 for each image and time-slot. Using Table 4, we notice that the mean scores for the majority of labels is below 4 for each time slot, which indicates a trend towards disagreement with the corresponding label, analogous to the results obtained with the *city-image* corpus (Section 5.2). Furthermore, we observe that the mean values of the perceptual ratings in mornings are similar to the ones observed for Guanajuato in Table 2. This is consistent with the fact that all the images from the *city-image* corpus were taken between between 9 AM and 5 PM (Section 3.5).

For the *evening-image* corpus, the mean annotation scores for all positive (resp. negative) labels are higher (resp. lower) for images taken in the morning, compared to the ones taken during the evening. In Table 4, we also report the results of of the Tukey's HSD statistics to test whether the mean scores differ across different times of the day for all labels. Based on these statistics we observe that:

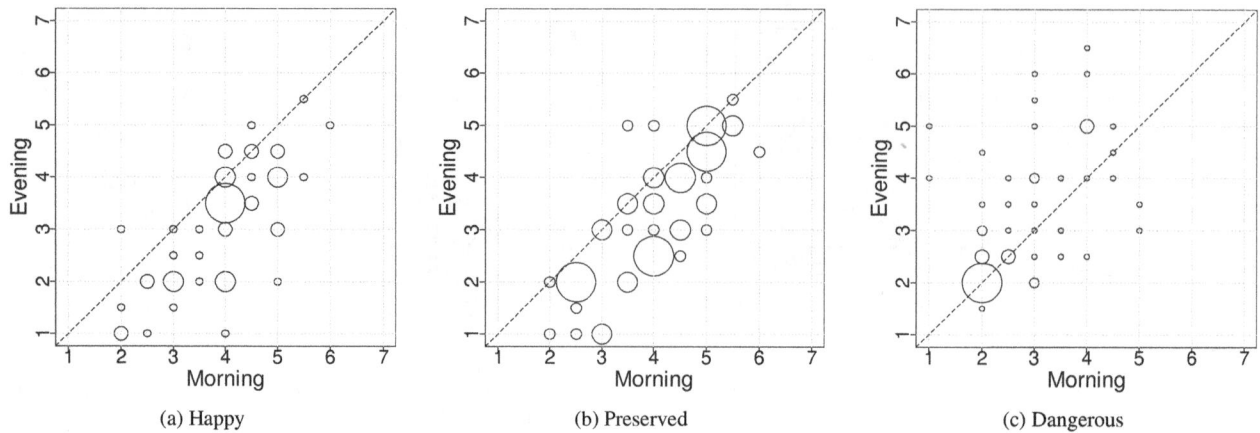

Figure 7: Scatter plots showing the pair-wise annotator scores across two different times of the day for a) Happy, b) Preserved, and c) Dangerous. Each dot corresponds to an image, with the size of the dots proportional to the number of observations. The 45° line is also shown in all the plots.

1. Evenings are perceived as less *happy*, *pleasant* and *preserved*, in comparison with morning time (differences: -0.81, -0.77, -0.71 respectively). See also Figure 7a and 7b. In addition, in Figure 8, we show a pair of images of a place where the rating between morning and evening for *Happy* differ by three ordinal scales (rated 5 and 2 respectively).

2. We do not observe statistically significant differences in the perception of *dangerous* between mornings and evenings (p-value $= 0.026$). This result is in contrast with findings from the literature [20, 16]. To put our finding in perspective, it is important to note that places are overall not perceived as *dangerous* in the *evening-image* corpus (combined mean: 3.12). See also Figure 7c.

Pair-wise Analysis: After observing that some of the perceptual ratings differ across times of the day, and in order to understand the variability of ratings for individual places, we examined the pair-wise ratings of each image between morning and evening time. We focus our pair-wise analysis on two statistically significant labels (*happy* and *preserved*), in addition to examining the non-significant *dangerous* label. Figure 7 shows the respective plots. If the perception ratings were similar between morning and evening, most of the points would have fallen on the 45° line. On the contrary, we observe that a significant majority of points lie below the line for *happy* and *preserved* (Figure 7a and 7b), indicating that places in the morning are perceived on a higher scale compared to evenings. Furthermore, it is interesting to observe a more-mixed trend for the *dangerous* label (Figure 7c). These plots further validate our findings reported in the previous section.

6. LIMITATIONS AND FUTURE WORK

In this paper, we have presented a study to examine urban perceptions in three cities in central Mexico. Our study involves data collected by locals via mobile crowdsourcing, while assessments on collected data are undertaken by an external non-local population via online crowdsourcing. In other words, we have examined the perception of places as seen by "others" rather than "locals". In our study, external observers are all US-based crowd-workers.

To elicit impressions of urban perceptions, the observer population plays an important role, whether the population is external (as is the case in our study) or local (local community who is familiar with the environment). It can be argued that the collected assessments by external observers induce bias in the ratings and thus limit the generalizability of our findings. In our survey, most

(a) Morning   (b) Evening

Figure 8: Images where the perceptual ratings differ across times of the day for *Happy*. For privacy reasons, images showing faces have been pixelated.

of the external observers reported not to have travelled to any developing country in the past (77% of our worker pool as reported in Section 4.2). We acknowledge this is one of the limitations of our work. However, we believe that the possibility of obtaining external perceptions of a city is valuable in and of itself to quantitatively characterize the urban landscape, specially when the cities have large influx of visitors (i.e. travellers, tourists, students, business people, etc.) As part of future work, we plan to engage local communities to gather responses from them and compare their impressions with the ones obtained via online crowd annotators.

As a second limitation, we believe that the lack of ground-truth on perceptual ratings makes it difficult to further contextualize some of our findings. For most of the psychological dimensions (e.g., *happy*, *pleasant*, etc.) there exist no unique ground-truth, while for the physical dimensions (e.g. *dangerous*, *polluted*, etc.), there might be proxy measures. Previous studies have examined the relationship between the perceptions of *safety* and *class* and homicides rate in New York City [30]. However, due to the lack of publicly available data in the studied cities, such analysis was not feasible. Future work could include partnerships with the city or police to investigate whether this information could be available for research.

Due to the nature of our data collection, the spatial coverage of our approach can be seen as a potential third limitation. Spatial coverage includes two aspects. The first one is the spatial sampling of regions to select urban areas. We did not perform any uniform sampling to select places for our study, which we plan to do as future work for comparison purposes. The second aspect is the spatial scalability, which involves reaching to diverse geographical regions. Our data collection methodology was limited to areas that could be reached by our local community. However, in the context of development, it is more relevant for people to explore the urban area where they live and work in order to achieve solutions to the problems they face on a daily basis. We plan to engage other communities in the future to collect diverse datasets in other cities.

We conclude by discussing the potential impact of our work. Today, the purpose of improving the urban life in developing cities depends on the collective action of citizens, communities, and governments. It is through synergistic interactions between government and self-organized citizens that complex urban issues can be tackled in the midst of chaotic urban growth and prevailing conditions of economic inequality. In this regard, educating citizens to develop a more discerning understanding of urban problems is crucial. Our work addresses this matter (beyond scientific inquiry) by contributing tools that communities could use to generate benefits for themselves. The mobile crowdsourcing approach used to collect the data enabled participating volunteers to become more aware of their urban environment. The data collected by and for the people provides an alternative and more comprehensive picture of the issues that matter to citizens, beyond a mapping exercise conducted by professional surveyors, which is often expensive and less detailed. With the objectives of informing urban planners and designing interventions in the local communities, we are teaming up with several NGOs and the local government to address some of the highlighted issues. Future development of both the academic results and community effort of the SenseCityVity project can be found here [6, 7].

7. ACKNOWLEDGEMENTS

This work has been supported by the EPFL-CODEV SenseCityVity and SNSF Youth@Night projects. We thank all the members of the SenseCityVity collective. We also thank all the student volunteers for their participation and the school authorities of CECYTE for the support to our project.

8. REFERENCES

[1] http://mapkibera.org.
[2] https://www.caminosdelavilla.org/.
[3] https://www.fixmystreet.com.
[4] http://seeclickfix.com.
[5] http://www.ushahidi.com.
[6] www.idiap.ch/project/sensecityvity/.
[7] www.facebook.com/
    SenseCityVity-1420771584831936.
[8] Top 5 cities in mexico: Readers' choice awards 2013.
    http://cntrvlr.com/1f77Jbg.
[9] M. D. Bader et al. Development and deployment of the Computer Assisted Neighborhood Visual Assessment System (CANVAS) to measure health-related neighborhood conditions. *Health & place*, 2015.
[10] B. Baykurt. Redefining citizenship and civic engagement: political values embodied in fixmystreet. com. *Selected Papers of Internet Research*, 2012.
[11] M. Castells et al. *Reconceptualizing Development in the Global Information Age*. Oxford University Press, 2014.
[12] W. Connors. Google, microsoft expose brazil's favelas.
    http://on.wsj.com/1V3X2qI.
[13] G. Esteva et al. *Grassroots post-modernism: Remaking the soil of cultures*. Palgrave Macmillan, 1998.
[14] A. Gelman et al. The Statistical Crisis in Science. *American Scientist*, 2014.
[15] L. Graham et al. Can the ambiance of a place be determined by the user profiles of the people who visit it. In *Proc. ICWSM*, 2011.
[16] K. Hanyu. Visual properties and affective appraisals in residential areas after dark. *Journal of Environmental Psychology*, 1997.
[17] K. Hara et al. Combining crowdsourcing and google street view to identify street-level accessibility problems. In *Proc. CHI*, 2013.
[18] S. F. King et al. Fix my street or else: using the internet to voice local public service concerns. In *Proc. of the 1st international conference on theory and practice of electronic governance*, 2007.
[19] P. J. Lindal et al. Architectural variation, building height, and the restorative quality of urban residential streetscapes. *Journal of Environmental Psychology*, 2013.
[20] L. J. Loewen et al. Perceived safety from crime in the urban environment. *Journal of environmental psychology*, 1993.
[21] F. J. Massey Jr. The kolmogorov-smirnov test for goodness of fit. *Journal of the American statistical Association*, 1951.
[22] A. Monroy-Hernández et al. The new war correspondents: The rise of civic media curation in urban warfare. In *Proc. CSCW*, 2013.
[23] K. Painter. The influence of street lighting improvements on crime, fear and pedestrian street use, after dark. *Landscape and urban planning*, 1996.
[24] K. Pearson. LIII. On lines and planes of closest fit to systems of points in space. *The London, Edinburgh, and Dublin Philosophical Magazine and Journal of Science*, 1901.
[25] D. Quercia et al. Aesthetic capital: what makes london look beautiful, quiet, and happy? In *Proc. CSCW*, 2014.
[26] R. Reid. Top 8 places to (safely) visit in mexico now.
    http://bit.ly/1hIjkce.
[27] J. Ross et al. Who are the crowdworkers?: Shifting demographics in mechanical turk. In *CHI*, 2010.
[28] S. Ruiz-Correa et al. The young and the city: Crowdsourcing urban awareness in a developing country. In *Proc. of URB-IOT*, 2014.
[29] J. A. Russell et al. A description of the affective quality attributed to environments. *Journal of personality and social psychology*, 1980.
[30] P. Salesses et al. The collaborative image of the city: Mapping the inequality of urban perception. *PLoS ONE*, 2013.
[31] R. J. Sampson et al. Seeing disorder: Neighborhood stigma and the social construction of "broken windows". *Social psychology quarterly*, 2004.
[32] D. Santani et al. Loud and Trendy: Crowdsourcing Impressions of Social Ambiance in Popular Indoor Urban Places. In *Proc. ACM Multimedia*, 2015.
[33] P. E. Shrout et al. Intraclass correlations: uses in assessing rater reliability. *Psychological bulletin*, 1979.
[34] F. M. Sjoberg et al. The effect of government responsiveness on future political participation. *Available at SSRN 2570898*, 2015.
[35] S. S. Stevens. On the theory of scales of measurement. *Science*, 1946.
[36] S. Sturgis. Kids in india are sparking urban planning changes by mapping slums. http://bit.ly/1LtS9S4.
[37] J. W. Tukey. The philosophy of multiple comparisons. *Statistical science*, 1991.

Janayuja*: A People-centric Platform to Generate Reliable and Actionable Insights for Civic Agencies

Tridib Mukherjee, Deepthi Chander, Sharanya Eswaran, Mridula Singh,
Preethy Varma, Amandeep Chugh, and Koustuv Dasgupta
Xerox Research Center India (XRCI), Bangalore, India
Tridib.Mukherjee@xerox.com

ABSTRACT

With the proliferation of smartphone apps, social media, and online forums, modern citizens are actively discussing and expressing opinions about city related issues in open public forums on the web. This paper presents a people-centric platform, *Janayuja*, that can act as an effective conduit between residents and civic agencies, by collecting timely information from different online sources and providing actionable insights to the agencies on pressing city issues. In particular, we elaborate on four major components of the platform: (i) *curation* of reports from heterogeneous data sources; (ii) *categorization* of individual reports into relevant issues (e.g. bus breakdown) using suitable classification techniques; (iii) *aggregation* of related reports (in the spatio-temporal sense) to identify specific issues pivoted to distinct city locations; and (iv) *verification* of issues to ensure reliability of information being provided to the agencies. Janayuja is deployed for the largest public transport agency in Bangalore, India. Based on insights generated by Janayuja, the agency can better manage their current operations, understand and anticipate new requirements from commuters (e.g. for new bus routes) and, in turn, encourage greater usage of a public transportation system.

Keywords

urban informatics; data science; trust; crowdsourcing

1. INTRODUCTION

The United Nations reports four billion people living in cities today and the number expected to double over next two decades. Bangalore, dubbed as the Silicon Valley of India; the Chinese city of Dalian, a major outsourcing center for Japanese companies; Sao Paulo, in Brazil, are glaring examples of rapid urbanization that have left civic agencies grappling with issues of scale –

---

*In Sanskrit, *Janayuja* denotes *a means of connecting to people*.

ACM DEV 2015, December 1–2, 2015, London, United Kingdom.
ⓒ 2015 ACM. ISBN 978-1-4503-3490-7/15/12 ...$15.00.
DOI: http://dx.doi.org/10.1145/2830629.2830642.

they face key infrastructural and social challenges ranging from road conditions and public transport, to women's safety, waste management and pollution. Technologies rolled out in developed countries, e.g., camera and/or sensor deployments, while being largely accurate and reliable, often become inapplicable in many developing regions due to socio-economic issues, e.g. price & maintenance overhead, devices being prone to theft and damage etc. Consequently, emerging cities are experimenting strategies to engage with residents (citizens) to be the "catalysts" of change. A broad array of platforms, like dedicated Facebook pages, Twitter handles, and hashtags are being used to discuss local issues. Solutions like the Social Networking and Planning Project (SNAPPatx [6]) in Austin, and apps like SeeClickFix [5], allow citizens to express opinions about city planning, report problems like potholes or broken roads, or simply provide feedback to the agencies.

With the ready availability of Internet connections and smart phones, citizens in developing regions are increasingly discussing their challenges in open public forums. Fig. 1 shows a snapshot of posts in various online sources regarding public transport requirements in Bangalore, India. Yet, while many of these initiatives give people a voice, and generate a lot of valuable data — there seems to be an inherent challenge in converting this data into actions. To worsen the situation, existing practices by many agencies are limited to manual surveys or call centres – that not only make the process slow and cumbersome, but are hardly scalable to growing scenarios. What is required for civic agencies (e.g., municipal, transportation, and law enforcement departments) is to not only be aware of the problems, but also to possess the necessary capabilities to analyse the severity of the problems, often judge the reliability of the informants (reporters), and act upon the identified problems in a timely, accountable manner. In this context, the premise of this work is to harness heterogeneous, large scale data from online sources and extract reliable, actionable insights from the data, for civic agencies in emerging cities.

We envision Janayuja to be such a *people-centric solution that can act as a conduit between residents and agencies by presenting actionable insights on pressing issues faced by the urban population*. Agencies, particularly in developing regions, can then manage city services towards improving their operational qualities. For example, a public transport agency may want to get insights on whether the services are commensurate with demands in various parts of the city, if there are regular incidents of crew misbehavior or route

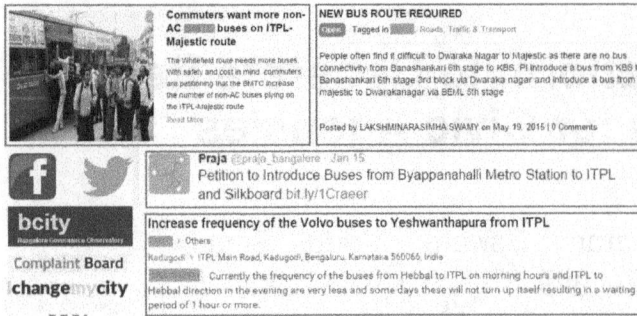

Figure 1: Sample reports from online sources

deviations, the hygiene of buses etc. However, generating meaningful insights from public opinion, as described above, is non-trivial and needs to address the following challenges.

- **Data Veracity**: Reports from unknown population may not always be truthful and often are subjective. Generating incorrect information driven by some untrusted reports is undesirable. It is therefore important to decide: *whom* and *what* to believe. Individual events such as 'Low bus frequency in Route A' may not have likelihoods that are known apriori. Social media channels may not have apriori known reliabilities; and there can be intrinsic coupling between channel reliabilities and event likelihoods.

- **Heterogeneity of Sources**: The sources are not standardized and can have open information format. Reports may vary across sources in terms of length, time-frame, intent, etc. In a complaint forum, through which people expect resolution of problems, the reports may be elaborate; whereas, in Twitter, the reports are short. Further, the reliabilities of the sources (i.e., channels) can vary for different categories, and over time depending on dynamic reporting patterns.

- **Categorization & Event Identification**: The issue/event identification needs to factor in the spatial, temporal, and category contexts of the reports. This involves classification of the *text* reports into different categories. Further, the issues need to be referenced to location landmarks in the city (e.g., bus breakdown near the Total Mall, Marathalli, Bangalore as opposed to the latitude and longitude, or broader area, Marathalli). Moreover, events can be ephemeral in nature, e.g., a bus overcrowded in peak and non-peak hours needs to be considered separately.

- **Scalability**: Manually monitoring and correlating millions of posts across hundreds of online sources in real time to analyze the severity of issues and prioritizing them is practically infeasible. Further, the fact that–reporters may not report on all channels, and may have different identities across channels– deters the maintenance of individual reporter level reliabilities at a large scale.

Our Contributions. In this paper, we propose a platform, *Janayuja*, that has four major components: (a) *curation*, (b) *categorization*, (c) *aggregation*, and (d) *verification*. The platform can curate information from a heterogeneous set of complementary data sources and generate actionable insights on city related issues for the agencies. The *curation* module standardizes the reports, across different sources, based on a space, time, category representation. The report categories are inferred by a *categorization* module by employing NLP/classification techniques. *Aggregation* of reports is then performed to identify distinct issues in an online manner where issues are pivoted to locations (landmarks) in the city. Finally, a *first-of-a-kind verification* framework is proposed that ascertains channel reliabilities and event likelihoods simultaneously. In this regard, a Maximum-Likelihood based Binomial Veracity model is used. The verification framework is scalable since it is based on determination of channel level reliabilities (as opposed to individual reporter level reliabilities, prevalent in the literature [19, 20]) and subsequent proposition of event occurrence likelihoods. Based on the event likelihood, as well as intensity and recency of reports, the *severity* of city-wide issues is modelled.

The platform is evaluated on large-scale data, 61,669 reports across 8 months, collected from around twenty–five different online sources for the city of Bangalore, India. The reports cut across ten different categories, which includes commute-related categories, such as Roads, Traffic, Illegal Parking, and Public Transport; environmental issues, such as Water, Garbage, Pollution, and Sewage; social issues, such as Crime and Electricity. We evaluate different classification techniques and obtain an accuracy of 87%. Moreover, around 92% of events (identified via report aggregation) are correctly pivoted to landmarks (bus stops) in the city. The likelihoods of the events depend on the report distribution across sources, e.g., multiple reports across multiple sources (especially ones with high reliabilities), can greatly improve the event likelihood. Janayuja has been deployed for the largest public transport agency in Bangalore. A subset of the aforementioned data (pertaining to public-transport category) is further classified to categories, in which the agency is interested in. These reports augment the existing call center channels and generate richer insights on the pressing problems faced by the regular commuters. In specific, the proposed 24X7 system curates, analyses and further visualizes the insights (in real—time) on a dashboard that has been designed for the transport department. Based on these insights, the agency can manage their operations accordingly (e.g., adding new routes, scheduling more frequent inspections on drivers & crews, etc.) and better serve the commuters.

2. RELATED WORK

Mobile Crowdsensing. Mobile crowdsourcing, crowdsensing, and human participatory sensing systems have explored the possibility of collecting implicit and explicit feedback from the residents on urban issues [2, 4, 7–9, 21]. However, in any such system, it is imperative to properly motivate the residents to report on issues, often based on some incentives. This typically translates to (a) overhead for the agencies in giving away the incentives, and (b) lower and slower penetration of such systems within the residents, so that meaningful insights can be extracted. It is thus important to complement these sources with the social media feeds and other online sources to generate rich insights on city-related issues.

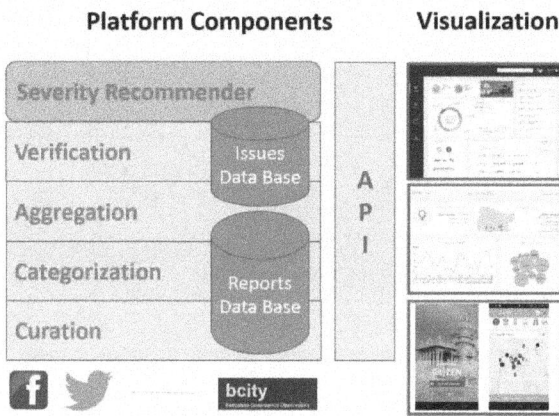

Figure 2: System components of the Janayuja platform.

Social media analysis. Analysis of social media to infer topics of interest, sentiments, etc. is well studied [10, 12, 13, 17]. However, these studies do not correlate information from other heterogeneous channels such as mobile app, public blogs, web pages, emails etc. Typically, city agencies have dedicated departments to handle complaints where complaints are received via phone calls, emails, mobile apps, and online portals. The complaints are then handled manually in the current state of the art. However, aggregation of multiple complaints across multiple channels of information for each issue, and then getting actionable insights, can lead to effective decision making and city management at a very large scale. This paper bridges the gap through the Janayuja platform that performs such aggregation to produce actionable insights for the city agencies.

Data Veracity. Ascertaining data veracity in participatory sensing systems is well studied [18–20]. However, most of the existing works assume a binary report, i.e., a source reports either a 1 (event occurred) or 0 (did not occur), our model takes any real-valued input for a report. We contend that when normalized to a scale of 0 to 1, this can be interpreted in several ways, such as the probability of occurrence of event from the source's point of view, the confidence score of the source, a severity index for the event, frequency of sighting of event, etc. This additional degree of freedom, as incorporated in this paper, helps capture and model data veracity in a better fashion.

Spatio-temporal Clustering. This paper enables an eco-system of information sources by correlating and aggregating information from heterogeneous channels such as mobile phones, social media, and other online sources. The correlation is achieved through aggregation of individual posts from different sources based on spatial, temporal, and topical relevance. Spatio-temporal clustering is a well-studied area [11] in the sensing domain in general and participatory sensing to be specific. However, generating clusters (of reports to identify distinctive issues) online while being aware of specific landmarks as well as existing issues in the city is unexplored. Such association to landmarks is essential to generate actionable insights for city agencies, where problems make more sense with reference to a landmark, rather than lat-long coordinates.

3. JANAYUJA PLATFORM

This section describes the Janayuja platform. As shown in Fig. 2, there are are four major components in Janayuja: (i) the *Curation module* (Section 3.1) gathers reports from heterogeneous online sources into a reports data base; (ii) the *Categorization module* classifies the collected reports into pre-defined categories (Section 3.2); (iii) the *Aggregation module* combines related reports to identify distinct issues/events into an issues data base (Section 3.3); and (iv) the *Verification module* ascertains the validity of these issues (Section 3.4). Finally, the severity recommender (Section 3.5) computes the severity of issues as a weighted function of event likelihood, report volume, and recency. A dashboard (or mobile app) can visualize the severity as well as other statistical summaries from the reports and issues data bases through APIs exposed by Janayuja. Sets of reports are processed concurrently by the *curation-categorization-aggregation-verification* pipeline in Janayuja. Any services (on top of the insights generated by Janayuja) can be easily instantiated based on the requirements (as demonstrated by the case study in Section 5). We now describe all the modules of Janayuja.

3.1 Curation

Janayuja collects reports from sources reporting on city-related issues using HTML parsing, accessing JSONs or public APIs. For example, for an online complaints forum, called IChangeMyCity [3], in Bangalore, India, JSON, containing complaints details, can be accessed directly. Similarly, Twitter has specific APIs for collecting public tweets. Most other online sources can be crawled using HTML parsing. Meta-data such as <location, time> and report-data such as text description extracted from the gathered reports. We observed that, in many cases, reports do not contain location information. To ascertain the location of such reports, we adopt a unique, text-based approach, which identifies proper nouns that prefix/suffix strong text-based location indicators (such as "at", "near", etc.), and queries the Google location database to infer the location. Reports gathered from heterogeneous sources are thus uniformly stored as <location,time,category> tuples in a report database.

3.2 Categorization

Reports are then subjected to a categorization process for categories such as – traffic, public transport, garbage, crime – which would be of interest to governing agencies. Each report undergoes pre-processing involving – tokenizing, spell-correction, stop-word removal and n-gram generation. Extracted reports and comments are typically integrated. For instance, let us consider the report, "Borewell dried up in M.G road. Please look into the matter. *Your issue has been assigned to the water authorities. The status has been set to resolved*", where the (italicized) comment comes together with the report in the data base. Therefore, it becomes important to filter domain-specific keywords properly. In this example, *Borewell* may be a keyword in the Water category, while the word *assigned* may appear across multiple categories. Hence, it is important to filter out these common words while generating domain-specific keywords.

We first explored a dictionary based rule engine where a dictionary of unigrams, bigrams and trigrams was

(a) Illegal Parking   (b) Garbage   (c) Public transport

Figure 3: Weighted keywords extracted for three different categories

constructed using a training set. We found the document term matrix for the relevant terms of each report; and using TF-IDF [16], we computed a relevance score for each word in each category. For instance, Fig. 3 illustrates keywords extracted for three sample categories. Words in the reports are then compared with this dictionary and categorized into one of the pre-defined categories based on the presence of some representative words. We however observed that a Support Vector Machine (SVM) based classifier, which uses category-specific keywords as feature vectors for each category, provides best accuracy results in our deployment. The keyword extraction is an off-line process and the keywords are taken as inputs to the classifier.

The accuracies of classification can be further improved in various ways. Reports may inherently belong to multiple categories. For example, a report, "Garbage dumped on footpath is making it difficult for people to walk", can be tagged as belonging to both garbage and road categories. Therefore, multi-label classification may have to be incorporated in the categorizer. We are further exploring improvements in categorization accuracies using hybrid approaches such as topic modelling, to identify events that do not directly map onto pre-defined categories (eg. a report such as, "election rally near City Market at 4PM"), and yet relate to the pre-defined categories (such as traffic).

3.3 Aggregation

Once the reports are categorized, the *aggregation* module combines multiple *related* reports together to identify distinct events or issues. We interchangeably use the terms events and issues in the paper. The reports can be considered related if they belong to the same category at a particular location (and in a given time of day, in case of ephemeral categories, such as traffic). The identified issues are stored in the issues data base (Fig. 2) by the aggregation module.

Specifically, the aggregation of reports into issues is to identify a $m:n$ mapping relationship, where m is the total number of reports in the Reports Database, n is the total number of issues in the Issues Database, and $n \leq m$ (i.e. one or more reports are attributed to each issue). To capture the ephemeral nature of issues, we allow division of time into different slots. The granularity of the slots and the total time to be divided can vary across different categories. All

reports of a category within a time slot (for the category) and within a threshold radius of a landmark (or within a threshold of each other, in case nearest landmark is beyond the threshold) can thus be aggregated into a single issue. Algorithm 1 shows the process of aggregating the reports into issues. The process takes as input the sets of—(new) reports $\mathcal{R}$, existing issues $\mathcal{I}$, landmarks $\mathcal{L}$, categories $\mathcal{C}$, and a threshold distance ρ. Based on these inputs, a new set of issues $\mathcal{I}'$ is returned. All the reports $r \in \mathcal{R}$ are aggregated into existing issues from $\mathcal{I}$ or into one or more new issues. All the new issues and the existing issues (updated with new reports) are part of the output issues set $\mathcal{I}'$.

For each report, $r \in \mathcal{R}$, it is checked if the category of the report, $\mathcal{C}(r)$ is ephemeral, i.e. if a time based aggregation is required. In such a case, the existing issues of category $\mathcal{C}(r)$, which are within the corresponding time slots, are extracted. Otherwise, all the existing issues of category $\mathcal{C}(r)$ are extracted. If the new report is just another one of the existing issues, then the issues database is updated accordingly. Otherwise, a new issue is created in the issues database. If the Euclidean distance of the issue from the nearest landmark is less than ρ, then the new issue is pivoted to the nearest landmark. On the other hand, if the nearest landmark is farther than ρ, the latitude and longitude of the report are used as the location of the issue. For a new report of an existing issue, if the issue is not pivoted to a landmark, the location is updated to the mean latitude and longitude of all the reports (including the new report).

3.4 Verification

Now we present the *verification* module, which ascertains veracity of the reports by estimating the likelihoods of the issues identified by the aggregation module. This is a key feature of the Janayuja platform to ensure *reliable* and actionable insights from the reports. In this regard, we use a maximum likelihood estimation approach to jointly determine (a) the likelihood of occurrence of the issue $z(i)$, and (b) the reliability of the channels with respect to each issue. Furthermore, the verification also incorporates the reputation of channels, if that is known a priori (so that data from the city police portal is given more weightage than a less reputed source such as a tabloid).

Let S be the set of M sources (channels) $\{S_1, S_2, ..., S_M\}$; let I be the set of N issues (events) $\{I_1, I_2, ..., I_N\}$. SI is the

Algorithm 1 Report Aggregation

```
1: Input: R, I, L, C, ρ.
2: Output: I'.
3: I' = I
4: for all r ∈ R do
5:     I'' = existing issues of category C(r) and at corresponding time
       bucket
6:     if distance(i, r) ≤ ρ ∧ I'' ≠ ∅ then
7:         add report to existing issue
8:         if ∄ l ∈ L such that location(i) = location(l) then
9:             update issue location to mean of all reports
10:        end if
11:    else
12:        create new issue i of the category C(r)
13:        l = FindNearestLandmark(r, L)
14:        if distance(l, r) ≤ ρ then
15:            pivot i (i.e., set location) to l
16:        else
17:            set location of i to r
18:        end if
19:        I' = I' ∪ {i}
20:    end if
21: end for
```

observation matrix, where each entry $S_i I_j$ is a value between 0 and 1. This can be taken as the probability or confidence with which source S_i thinks issue I_j has occurred, or as the normalized number of reports that channel S_i has received for issue I_j. Let Z be the vector of latent binary variables $[z_1, z_2, ..., z_N]$, where $z_j = 1$ when the issue is true, and 0 otherwise. Let d_j be the prior probability of occurrence of issue j. Let a_i be the probability that source S_i reports a real issue, i.e., $P(S_i I_j = 1 | I_j = true)$; let b_i be the probability of a false positive by source S_i, i.e., $P(S_i I_j = 1 | I_j = false)$. Let $\theta = [a_1, a_2, ...a_m; b_1, b_2, ..., b_m]$. The observation data SI is then treated as a binomial distribution, where for example, an entry of 0.8 is taken as 4 successes out of 5 trials in a binary event. The likelihood function is then given as:

$$L(\theta; SI, Z) = p(SI, Z | \theta)$$
$$= \prod_{j=1}^{N} \left\{ \prod_{i=1}^{M} \binom{n_{ij}}{k_{ij}} a_i^{k_{ij}} (1-a_i)^{(n_{ij}-k_{ij})} \times d_j \times z_j \right.$$
$$+ \left. \prod_{i=1}^{M} \binom{n_{ij}}{k_{ij}} b_i^{k_{ij}} (1-b_i)^{(n_{ij}-k_{ij})} \times (1-d_j) \times (1-z_j) \right\}$$
$$(1)$$

where, n_{ij} and k_{ij} are the indices of the binomial coefficient associated with $p(S_i I_j, z_j | a_i, b_i)$, which are obtained by the rational fraction approximation of $S_i I_j$.

As in [19] we use Expectation Maximization algorithm for estimating the parameters of Eq. 1, from which, we can derive $Z(j)$, a_i and b_i to be as follows:

$$Z(j) = p(z_j = 1 | SI, \theta) = \frac{A(j) \times d_j}{A(j) \times d_j + B(j) \times (1-d_j)} \quad (2)$$

, where

$$A(j) = p(SI_j, \theta | z_j = 1) = \prod_{i=1}^{M} \binom{n_{ij}}{k_{ij}} a_i^{k_{ij}} (1-a_i)^{n_{ij}-k_{ij}}$$

$$B(j) = p(SI_j, \theta | z_j = 0) = \prod_{i=1}^{M} \binom{n_{ij}}{k_{ij}} b_i^{k_{ij}} (1-b_i)^{n_{ij}-k_{ij}}$$

$$a_i^* = \frac{\sum_{j \in SC_i} k_{ij} Z(j)}{\sum_{j=1}^{N} n_{ij} Z(j)}; b_i^* = \frac{\sum_{j \in SC_i} k_{ij}(1-Z(j))}{\sum_{j=1}^{N} n_{ij}(1-Z(j))} \quad (3)$$

Our algorithm, as shown in Algorithm 2, iteratively estimates the source reliabilities θ and computes the event likelihoods Z based on the source reliabilities, until the values converge. The matrix R computed in step 15 gives the reliability of each source, i.e., the probability of the source reporting the correct state (true or false) of the event, with respect to each category of issue. If the issues have different levels of priorities or importance, the overall reliability of a source can be computed as the weighted mean of reliabilities, i.e., reliability of source i, $R_i = \sum_{j=1}^{N} w_j * R(i, j)$, where w_j is the priority of issue j.

Algorithm 2 Binomial EM Algorithm

```
1: Input: SI.
2: Output: Z, R.
3: while θ does not converge do
4:     for j = 1 : N do
5:         Compute Z(j) from Eq. 2
6:         d_j = Z(j) {To be used in the next iteration}
7:     end for
8:     for i = 1 : M do
9:         Compute a_i and b_i from Eq. 3, using Z(j) from step 5
10:        Update θ with a_i and b_i from step 9
11:    end for
12: end while
13: for i = 1 : M do
14:    for j = 1 : N do
15:        R(i, j) = Z(j) * a_i + (1 - Z(j)) * (1 - b_i)
16:    end for
17: end for
```

Often, not all sources are treated equally; some sources, such as city officials and government authorities are intrinsically more reputed than, say, a tabloid forum. In order to factor this in, we associate each source with a *reputation score*. This reputation score Ψ of a source with respect to a category, consists of a static component Ψ_{stat} and a dynamic component Ψ_{dyn}, given as $\Psi = \delta \Psi_{stat} + (1-\delta)\Psi_{dyn}$ where $0 \leq \delta \leq 1$. Ψ_{stat} comes from prior knowledge, for example, the city officials will have a higher static score than a city resident. Ψ_{dyn} evolves over time from the reliability computed by our veracity framework from past reports, based on a beta reputation score function [15] computed using the positive feedback (a_i) and the negative feedback (b_i), i.e.,

$$\Psi_{dyn}(i) = \frac{\sum_{t=1}^{T} (a_i^t + 1) \lambda^{(T-t)}}{a_i^t + b_i^t + 2}, \quad (4)$$

where $0 \leq \lambda \leq 1$ serves as a forgetting factor, and T is the time window of history. In order to capture this score in the veracity model, we modify Eq. 3 as,

$$a_i^* = \frac{\sum_{j \in SI_i} \Psi(i, j) * k_{ij} * Z(j)}{\sum_{j=1}^{N} \Psi(i, j) n_{ij} * Z(j)}$$
$$b_i^* = \frac{\sum_{j \in SI_i} \Psi(i, j) k_{ij} * (1-Z(j))}{\sum_{j=1}^{N} \Psi(i, j) * n_{ij} * (1-Z(j))}, \quad (5)$$

It may be noted that, instead of beta function, other reputation functions such as [14] may also be incorporated in a similar fashion.

3.5 Modeling Severity of Issues

Once the likelihoods of the issues are estimated by the *verification* module, the severity of the issues are computed. The severity depicts the attention an issue demands in terms of taking an action from the respective authority.

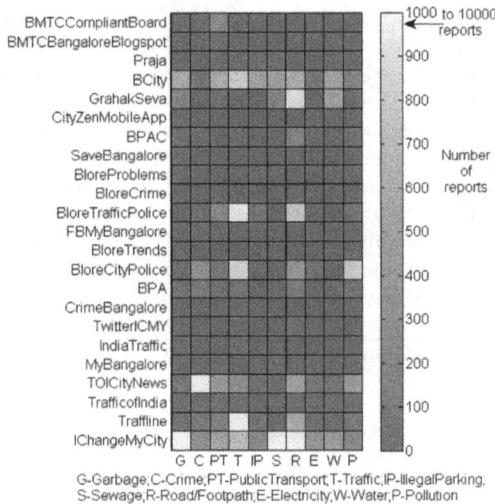

Figure 4: Source (channel) wise distribution of reports for different categories for Bangalore, India.

Severity, $\sigma(i)$, of an issue, i, is modelled as a function of three factors, namely the volume, recency and veracity of the issue. Volume of the issue is the number of reports contributing to the issue; recency of the issue points to the the time stamp of the latest report contributing to the issue, and veracity is taken as the likelihood of occurrence of the issue (Section 3.4). The factors are intuitive, as more the number of reports on a particular issue, more likely will it be to warrant action. Similarly, if the issue is unlikely to be true, then it clearly does not warrant any action. Moreover, an issue, which has been heavily reported recently, may indicate the sudden and on-going inconvenience it is creating.

As shown in the equation (4.1), for each issue, i, we calculate the volume of reports ($\nu(i)$) normalized by the maximum volume and recency normalized by the most recent issue. If $\tau(i)$ is the time elapsed after the last report came in for the issue i, then $1 - \frac{\tau(i)}{\max_{j \in \mathcal{I}} \tau(j)}$ provides a measure of recency, which becomes higher when time elapsed from last report received is lower. The volume, recency and veracity are further weighted by system design parameters, α_1, α_2, α_3 ($0 \leq \alpha_1, \alpha_2, \alpha_3 \leq 1$, and $\alpha_1 + \alpha_2 + \alpha_3 = 1$).

$$\sigma(i) = \alpha_1 \frac{\nu(i)}{\max_{j \in \mathcal{I}} \nu(j)} + \alpha_2 \left(1 - \frac{\tau(i)}{\max_{j \in \mathcal{I}} \tau(j)}\right) + \alpha_3 z(i)$$
(6)

4. EVALUATION

Janayuja has been evaluated for the city of Bangalore, India. In this regard, data from around 25 sources across social media and public web-pages are being collected every 30 minutes. In our database, we have collected more than 61,669 reports across all the sources for around 8 months. Janayuja categorizes these reports into 10 categories, such as traffic, crime, roads, public transport, garbage, pollution, water, electricity, sewage, and illegal parking etc. Fig. 4 shows the distribution of the reports across the sources for different categories. We observe that certain sources, such as IChangeMyCity [3], and BCity [1], are more popular

Table 1: Accuracy of Different Classifiers

Classification Technique	Overall Accuracy
Dictionary Rule Based	72%
Multinomial Naive Bayes	79%
Max Entropy Classifier	84%
Support Vector Machines (SVM)	87%

Table 2: Precision and Recall of SVM based classifier for different categories

Categories	Recall	Precision
Traffic	70.35%	70.00%
Water	77.05%	76.48%
Illegal Parking	58.53%	69.56%
Pollution	82.44%	81.20%
Public Transport	63.23%	66.15%
Roads	79.65%	81.78%
Sewage	79.50%	69.18%
Garbage	85.19%	92.00%
Crime	93.95%	90.00%
Electricity	88.24%	81.08%

compared to others, across all categories. However, certain sources post large number of reports on specific categories (e.g., Traffline for the traffic category).

Effectiveness of Supervised Classifiers for Categorization. Table 1 shows the accuracies of different classifiers on categorizing the reports from the aforementioned sources. Experiments are conducted on a labelled set of data, i.e. the set of data manually tagged to categories by multiple volunteers to generate ground truth (and the outcomes of the classifiers are compared with the ground truth). Accuracy of a classifier is measured in terms of percentage of true positives w.r.t. the entire labelled dataset. From Table 1, it is clear that SVM has the best accuracy. Table 2 further shows the recall and precision of the SVM for each category. *Recall* denotes the number of correctly identified items out of the total number of items belonging to a category. *Precision* denotes the number of correctly identified items of the category, in the set of items predicted as belonging to this category.

From Table 2., we observe that the recall and precision get affected to some extent by the disambiguation problem, intrinsic to text analysis. For instance, *"Poor lighting in the park"* can be misclassified as an illegal parking problem because of the presence of the keyword *park*. More importantly the categories such as <illegal parking, roads, traffic, public transport> and <sewage,water> tend to have overlapping keywords. As the discriminatory nature of the categories increase, the precision and recall tend to increase. For example, categories like, crime, pollution, garbage, electricity have discriminatory keywords, which do not overlap with other categories.

Impact of Report Aggregation. Around 5400 distinct issues have been identified by the aggregation module. The issues are mostly pivoted to landmarks (for which we have taken the prominent bus-stops in the city of Bangalore). However, not all reports could be pinned to the landmarks based on their spatial proximity (as covered in Algorithm 1). Around 450 issues (close to 8%) were not pivoted to any

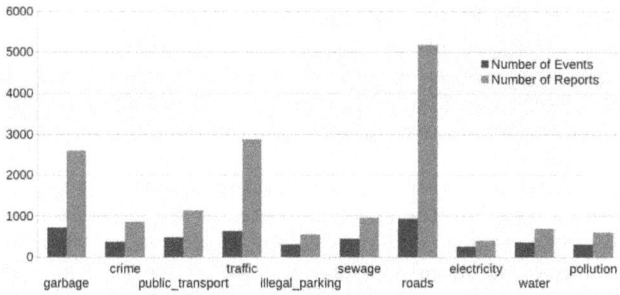

Figure 5: Overall distribution of number of reports and number of events (after aggregation) for different categories.

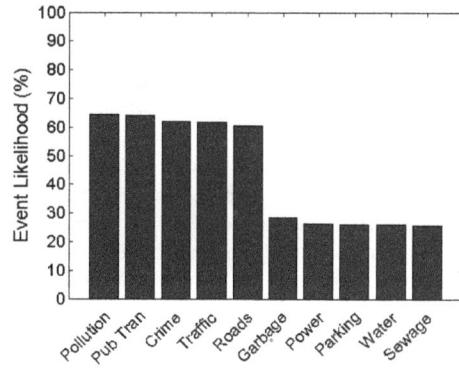

Figure 7: Event likelihood for an 80% confidence across categories

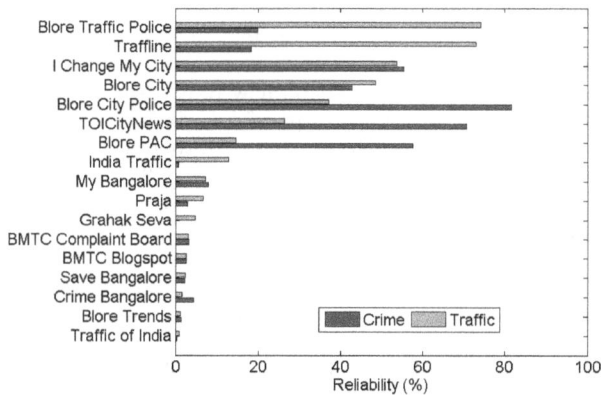

Figure 6: Source reliability for traffic & crime issues

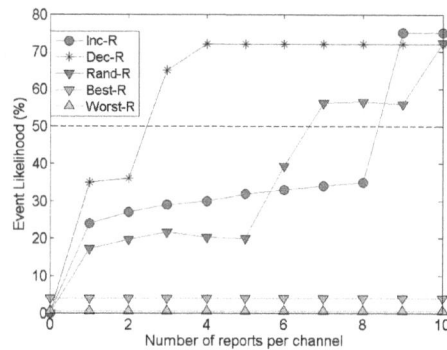

Figure 8: Event likelihood of new event for different report distributions across channels for a given category

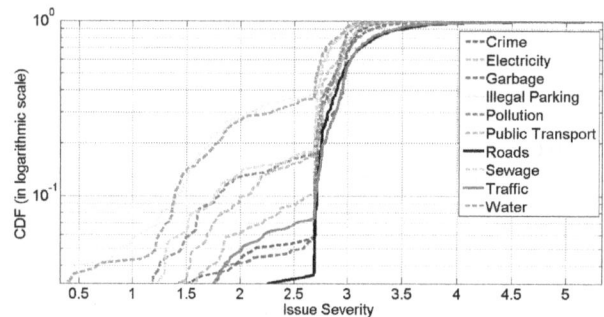

Figure 9: Cumulative Distribution Function (CDF) of issue severity across categories

landmark. Fig. 5 further shows the impact of aggregation for different categories. For example, the figure shows that the *roads* category has the highest number of reports in the city of Bangalore, and after aggregation, around 1000 distinct issues of *roads* has been found.

Estimation of Source Reliabilities. Fig. 6 shows the reliabilities of different channels for traffic and crime issues (only, due to lack of space). We see that the result from the veracity framework tallies with the known prior knowledge that the city official reporting channels such as Bangalore Traffic Police is more trustworthy for traffic information, and Bangalore City Police and Times of India news channel are more trustworthy for crime information. Interestingly, Bangalore City Police has lesser reports on crime compared to traffic (Fig. 4). However, the veracity framework can correctly estimate that the reliability of the Bangalore City Police for crime is higher than for traffic.

Estimation of Event Likelihood. Fig. 7 shows the inferred likelihood (with at least 80% confidence) of various event categories, for a given geographic location and time frame. The model computes the event likelihood based on the number of reports pertaining to that event across various channels of different reliabilities. The confidence is a measure of the estimation error associated with the event likelihoods deduced by the veracity model. It should be noted that the maximum event likelihood is around 65% because of the nature of the data available, and due to the fact that the

likelihood heavily depends on the number of reports across different channels.

We observe that as the number of reports corresponding to an event increases across different channels, the likelihood (as well as the corresponding confidence) also increase. To evaluate this, a new "event" was generated synthetically. The reports corresponding to this event were added sequentially, in the following different ways: (i) Dec-R: reports added sequentially per channel in decreasing order of channel reliabilities; (ii) Inc-R: reports added sequentially per channel in increasing order of channel reliabilities; (iii) Rand-R: reports added randomly to different channels; (iv) Best-R: reports added only to the channel with highest reliability; and (v) Worst-R: reports added only to the channel with least reliability. Fig. 8 shows the event likelihood estimated by the model for each of these policies. We see that when reports are added to the channels with higher reliabilities (as in Dec-R), the event likelihood increases to higher values (even with fewer number of reports). However, if the reports are only added to a single channel, even if it is the most reliable channel (as in Best-R), event likelihood does not increase.

Fig. 9 shows the distribution of issues across different severities (normalized in a scale of 1 to 10). To apply the severity model (Eq. 6), we have given equal weights to event likelihood, intensity, and recency (i.e., $\alpha_1 = \alpha_2 = \alpha_3$). Clearly, majority of the issues fall in the middle range (3 - 5), whereas very few issues have a very high severity. In a realistic situation, the city agencies would want very few exclusive issues to have very high severity, and the proposed severity model yields such an insight. Furthermore, it can be seen that more number of issues in roads and traffic categories have higher severity over other categories. *This corroborates the general observation that traffic and roads are the most pressing problems in Bangalore.*

5. CASE STUDY

Janayuja has been deployed for the largest public transport agency in the city of Bangalore, India. Before the use of Janayuja, the agency solely relied on their dedicated call center to get complaints and suggestions from the commuters. The call center includes data sources such as phone calls, the transportation agency's mobile app & online portal based complaint logging, emails, letters, and some print media sources. The human agents in the call center manually logs the complaints from all these different sources. There are around 15 categories the transportation agency looks into: Bus Breakdown, Bus Not Stopping, Crew Misbehaviour, Ticket Related Issue, Bus Pass Related Issue, Irregular Operation, Women Safety, Rash Driving, Irregular Operation, Traffic Violation, Accidents, Vehicle Related Issue, Bus Stand Related Issue, Route Deviation, and Lost Property. However, the amount of complaints they receive through their call center channels is on an average less than 100 complaints per month (specifically, around 850 complaints in 10 months).

Most of the people sending the complaints are non-working in general (usually, elderly population). Interestingly, the young working population, who are the majority users of transportation services in Bangalore, do not provide any specific complaints through the call center channels. On the other hand, the amount of discussions in the social media, and blog posts on-line shows a huge surge in the number of complaints and grievances people have on the services provided by the transportation agency. These are around 2400 complaints in 3 months, i.e. 800 per month on an average, which is around 10 times more than what is received through the call center channels. More importantly, the issues discussed in the online sources are often different from the ones received through the call center sources. Furthermore, there are certain new types (categories) of issues, e.g., no bus service, or new bus service

required, which are discussed in the online sources, but are not received at all through the call center channels. The transportation agency is actually unaware of such issue categories (plaguing the most frequent commuters), and hence do not even have it as part of their call-center complaints categories.

All these observations led the transportation agency to seriously look into the problem of how to tap into the "non-call-center" sources online to systematically understand the commuter feedbacks and generate actionable insights. In this regard, we instantiated Janayuja by considering a (sub)set of reports (collected from 25 different sources, as mentioned in Section 4). Specifically, the reports are filtered (during *curation* phase) using the keywords of the public transport category (Fig. 3(c)). Hence the *curation* module (Fig. 2) needed little to no adaptation. We further used the categorization module (Section 3.2) on these reports to classify them into aforementioned 15 categories for the agency, in addition to one more category of "no bus service" (which the agency was very eager to monitor from the online sources to understand demands on new routes/services). In this regard, generation of the set of keywords for the 16 categories is performed off-line. These are then fed into the classifier and the accuracy is similar to that of Table 1. The aggregation, verification, and severity recommendation (Fig. 2) needed to be adapted suitably.

Fig. 10 shows the screen-shots of the dashboard being used by the agency, as part of an ongoing pilot. Specifically, Janayuja provides the following unique offerings to the agency: (i) a single place to view a summary of complaints across various sources; (ii) ability to slice and dice complaints across locations, over time, and across sources; (iii) get suggestions on new categories (e.g., demand for new routes/services), which the agency does not get through their call center; (iv) ability to prioritize operations according to top regions of complaints and time of year to improve their services as well as leverage new business opportunities (e.g., plying on new routes, increasing number of AC buses during summer, mandating inspections to reduce ticket related issues, and so on). Additionally, the severity of the issues, color-coded in the dashboard (Fig. 11), allows the agency to get insights on which are the most discussed issues to address. Based on the visualization, the transportation agency can meet the commuter needs more effectively; and in turn can influence increased adoption of public transport in urban environment (thereby reducing congestion and improving overall social sustainability).

6. CONCLUSIONS & FUTURE WORK

This paper introduced Janayuja platform, which curates city-related issues being discussed in public forums, e.g., social media, online blogs, complaint boards etc., and generates actionable insights for the agencies to prioritize their operations accordingly. In this regard, Janayuja relies on—NLP techniques to identify categories of issues being discussed, report aggregation to identify distinct issues near city landmarks, and estimating likelihood of issues & source reliabilities—to generate actionable insights in near real-time. Key insights in designing people-centric platforms for civic agencies include: (a) requirements of multi-label classification to assign multiple categories to reports and correlation of overlapping categories; (b) unsupervised text clustering and topic modelling to identify

(a) Home Page   (b) Statistics Page

Figure 10: Dashboard Snapshots (best viewed in color)

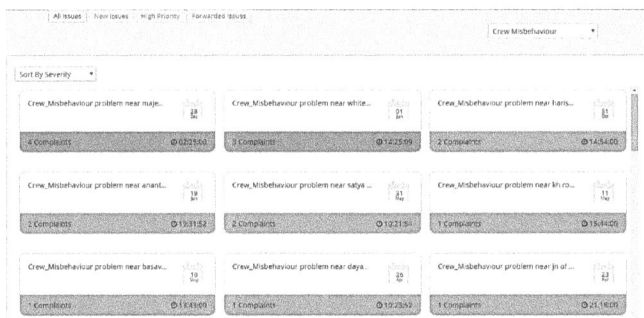

Figure 11: Dashboard Complaints Page

un-expected problem categories in an urban environment; (c) exploiting the heterogeneity of channels to determine event likelihoods with high confidence; (d) necessity to pivot issues around known landmarks of the city; and (e) ability to clearly identify and recommend the most discussed problems in the city. Future work also includes predictive analysis of reports allowing the agencies to be more proactive. Although motivated from the perspective of city agencies, the insights from Janayuja can also be consumed by a mobile app alerting residents about issues of interest (not presented due to lack of space). Based on our experience in deploying Janayuja, we contend that it can be deployed across different agencies and cities seamlessly. Janayuja platform can greatly impact citizen participation in urban planning and enable civic agencies to provide better services.

7. REFERENCES

[1] bcity. http://www.bcity.in/.
[2] FixMyStreet Platform. http://www.fixmystreet.com/.
[3] ichangemycity. http://www.ichangemycity.com/.
[4] Moovit. http://moovitapp.com/.
[5] SeeClickFix. http://en.seeclickfix.com/.
[6] SNAPPatx. http://www.snappatx.org/.
[7] Ushahidi. http://blog.ushahidi.com/2012/06/05/ushahidi-beijing/.
[8] Waze. https://www.waze.com/.
[9] Opportunities of Crowdsourcing in Russia and Ukraine, 2012. http://innovation.internews.org/blogs/opportunities-crowdsourcing-russia-and-ukraine.
[10] M. Avvenuti, S. Cresci, A. Marchetti, C. Meletti, and M. Tesconi. Ears (earthquake alert and report system): A real time decision support system for earthquake crisis management. ACM KDD, 2014.
[11] M. Budde, J. De Melo Borges, S. Tomov, T. Riedel, and M. Beigl. Leveraging spatio-temporal clustering for participatory urban infrastructure monitoring. ICST URB-IOT, 2014.
[12] F. Chierichetti, J. M. Kleinberg, R. Kumar, M. Mahdian, and S. Pandey. Event detection via communication pattern analysis. AAAI ICWSM, 2014.
[13] J. He, W. Shen, P. Divakaruni, L. Wynter, and R. Lawrence. Improving traffic prediction with tweet semantics. AAAI IJCAI, 2013.
[14] K. L. Huang, S. S. Kanhere, and W. Hu. Are you contributing trustworthy data?: The case for a reputation system in participatory sensing. ACM MSWIM, 2010.
[15] A. Jãÿsang and R. Ismail. The beta reputation system. In In Proceedings of the 15th Bled Conference on Electronic Commerce, 2002.
[16] J. Ramos. Using tf-idf to determine word relevance in document queries. In Proceedings of the first instructional conference on machine learning, 2003.
[17] N. Spasojevic, J. Yan, A. Rao, and P. Bhattacharyya. Lasta: Large scale topic assignment on multiple social networks. ACM KDD, 2014.
[18] D. Wang, M. T. A. Amin, S. Li, T. F. Abdelzaher, L. M. Kaplan, S. Gu, C. Pan, H. Liu, C. C. Aggarwal, R. K. Ganti, X. Wang, P. Mohapatra, B. K. Szymanski, and H. K. Le. Using humans as sensors: an estimation-theoretic perspective. ACM IPSN, 2014.
[19] D. Wang, L. Kaplan, H. Le, and T. Abdelzaher. On truth discovery in social sensing: A maximum likelihood estimation approach. ACM IPSN, 2012.
[20] D. Wang, L. M. Kaplan, and T. F. Abdelzaher. Maximum likelihood analysis of conflicting observations in social sensing. ACM Transaction on Sensor Networks (TOSN), 10(2):30, 2014.
[21] F.-J. Wu and T. Luo. A generic participatory sensing framework for multi-modal datasets. IEEE ISSNIP, 2014.

Understanding *Fiado:*
Informal Credit in Brazil

Heloisa Candello, *IBM Research*
David Millen, *IBM Research*
Silvia Bianchi, *IBM Research*
Rogério de Paula, *IBM Research*
Cláudio Pinhanez, *IBM Research*
Contact: hcandello@br.ibm.com

This presentation will explore insights gathered from fieldwork activities in the Northeast Brazil to design a financial application to facilitate access to credit. We interviewed 12 merchants in two cities in the northeast of Brazil and observed their everyday financial practices, their social physical networks and mechanisms to promote trust in those communities. We observed a particular kind of transaction that was common amongst our participants - called *Fiado*. *Fiado* transactions are a store credit practice in which merchants sell products to a customer based on trust that the customer will pay for it in the future. Whereas the business owners provided credit to their customers, much like a bank or store credit card, they do not appear to think of this financial activity in a particularly sophisticated manner, nor did they use this lending activity to its full advantage. For example, while the informal bookkeeping enabled monitoring of the Fiado debt, it did not easily allow for aggregation across all customers or revealing trends in lending activity due to season or some other variable of interest. The informal lending practices also did not encourage the merchants to conceptually think of these loans as future cash flows that could be used to better manage their business finance.

Our observations of the prevalence of informal lending among the small business owners have encouraged us to envision the possibility of new financial management tools. We designed a new service that may help business owners to manage, plan and predict their financial life. The system will learn from historical payment trends and be able to estimate future transactions. A digital trace of purchase and Fiado transactions will be preserved and made available in a secure way for the merchant to use e.g., as evidence of cash flows for future formal loan applications. We have created a smartphone app based on this design and are planning to field test with small business owners in Brazil.

ACM Categories & Descriptors: H.5.m Information Interfaces and Presentation (e.g., HCI): Miscellaneous.

Keywords: microcredit; economics; microfinance; Brazil; banking

DOI: http://dx.doi.org/10.1145/2830629.2830631

Revisiting the State of Cellular Data Connectivity in India

Asheesh Sharma
asheesh.csstaff@cse.iitd.ernet.in

Manveen Kaur
manveen.csstaff@cse.iitd.ernet.in

Zahir Koradia
zahir.koradia@gmail.com

Rahul Nishant
mcs122818@cse.iitd.ac.in

Sameer Pandit
mcs122821@cse.iitd.ac.in

Aravindh Raman
aravindh.csstaff@cse.iitd.ernet.in

Aaditeshwar Seth
aseth@cse.iitd.ernet.in
IIT Delhi
New Delhi, India

ABSTRACT

The count of mobile Internet users in India has been growing at a rate of 27% annually and is expected to reach 300M by 2017. There is however limited understanding of whether this rapid growth is happening while also ensuring that good quality of service is provided to users. To find out, building upon our earlier work [17] we deployed a measurement framework in 20 rural, semi-urban, and urban sites in North India and probed four leading 2G and 3G telecom providers to measure performance metrics such as availability, throughput and latency. We also observed some design and configuration aspects of cellular networks that affect the quality of service perceived by users. Our results point to many instances where misconfigurations or inadequate provisioning or poor monitoring of cellular networks led to significantly low performance provided to users. We are now using these results to argue for more robust QoS regulation in the country, and show how the current regulations for 2G and 3G services are not sufficient to hold providers accountable for the quality of service provided by them.

Categories and Subject Descriptors

C.4 [**Performance of Systems**]: Reliability, availability, and serviceability

General Terms

Measurement, Performance, Reliability

Keywords

Cellular data networks

ACM DEV 2015, Dec 1 – 2, 2015, London, United Kingdom
ⓒ 2015 ACM. ISBN 978-1-4503-3490-7/15/12 ...$15.00.
DOI: http://dx.doi.org/10.1145/2830629.2830649.

1. INTRODUCTION

The rapid proliferation of mobile phones seen around the world, and optimistic projections for the growth of mobile Internet in developing regions in the next few years, have indeed become legendary tales in the information technology revolution of the 21st century. In fact, persuading voice users to convert to using data services has spawned an industry in itself with initiatives such as Internet.org and startups such as Apps Daily and Jana, using a variety of techniques to influence users to come online. A recent study by McKinsey [13] projects India as one of the largest markets for mobile Internet, but also highlights challenges of infrastructure, user capability, affordability, and availability of relevant content and services, which if not enabled well can become impediments to the adoption of data services. In this paper, we focus on the first challenge, that of infrastructure quality, and investigate the quality of service currently provided on 2G and 3G networks in India.

While acquiring new users, telecom providers need to expand their infrastructure in tandem to cater to the increased demand. However, consumer complaints are noted commonly in India that providers are not able to meet the quality of service committed by them [7]. The regulatory environment in India is quite proactive, and TRAI (Telecom Regulatory Authority of India) has taken several measures to hold providers accountable for meeting minimum QoS requirements. In the voice calling space, the providers submit quarterly QoS reports on call drops, base station failures, etc which are also audited by third party agencies appointed by TRAI. In fact, very recently the issue of call drops has received significant attention and has become a tussle between the government and telecom providers both pushing back on each other [20]. The telecom providers claim that too little spectrum is available to them and the government also does not help subsidize or acquire sites for the providers to put up new cellphone towers, while the government claims that they have been quite responsive to telco requests and the telecom providers need to utilize their infrastructure more efficiently. Similar regulations on mobile data services are not as mature as yet – a test methodology to measure key QoS parameters has been prescribed by TRAI [26], but the quarterly data is not audited as in the case of voice calling, and penalties or other mechanisms are not in place if the providers do not meet some minimum QoS standards.

A consultation was organized by TRAI recently to discuss whether minimum QoS guarantees for mobile data should be mandated or not [27], and the providers reverted with an argument that any guarantees for 2G or 3G would be hard to ensure because of user mobility, and also linked it with the net neutrality argument in some manner [1].

In this paper, we make an effort to strengthen the argument for having more robust QoS regulations for 2G and 3G services in India. We do this by collecting performance data on throughput, latency, and availability from 20 sites in rural, semi-urban, and urban areas in North India, and give concrete evidence that the QoS provided differs considerably from advertised values, and is widely different in different locations. We then compare these measured values with data reported by the providers to TRAI, and show that the values differ substantially and that more realistic test environments should be mandated by TRAI to mimic the actual user experience with cellular data services. We also show through two examples that better infrastructure monitoring and more careful network configurations can help improve the QoS even with the current infrastructure – providers who have configured smaller buffer sizes in their network elements are able to provide better latency, and similarly providers who have configured less reactive switching between 2G and 3G are able to avoid certain detrimental interactions with the higher layer TCP protocol that impacts the final throughput achieved. Overall, we highlight the need for telecom providers to manage their networks more efficiently and provide better QoS to consumers, who currently do not seem to be getting the service to which they are entitled. As part of a larger effort in this project, we have partnered with a consumer rights organization to now take these findings to TRAI and other regulatory bodies, and push for urgent revisions on QoS regulation in the country.

2. RELATED WORK

In terms of methodology, our work comes closest to that of tools like Netalyzer [18] and research on largescale measurement of broadband networks [23, 19, 2, 8, 10], all of which have highlighted the need to understand network conditions from the end user's point of view. Users are impacted by policies and capacity provisioning of edge ISPs with aspects like buffer sizes and traffic shaping having a significant impact on the QoS experienced by the users. Our measurement architecture is similar to Netalyzer, and we have also borrowed several techniques from these papers to probe firewalls, caching, etc reported in our earlier research [17]. Similar work of largescale probing of the network edge is however not common in the cellular data connectivity space. Cellular network measurement research has actively covered TCP behavior on cellular networks [14, 12, 4, 5], and has also seen interest in understanding hardware characteristics such as the radio wake up latency and scheduling policies [3, 9, 21, 25] with the broad objective to tweak protocols so as to obtain better performance on cellular data networks. Our own focus in this paper is not on network protocol modifications to get better performance, but to conduct measurements on 2G and 3G networks in the developing region context of India to understand the current state of QoS experienced by the users. Our goal is to specifically use the measurements to reason about appropriate regulatory mechanisms that can help ensure that telecom providers will work towards better quality of service provisioning for the users.

A similar focus on using measurements to push for stronger regulatory mechanisms is also seen in [24] where it is proposed that providers should publish a "nutrition label" with details about the QoS provided by them, just like how it is mandatory for packaged food items to carry information about their ingredients and nutrition levels. Although telecom providers in India do disclose this information to TRAI which is published on the TRAI website, it is arguable that many consumers may not know about it or consult the website, and therefore a nutrition label like disclosure will help improve consumer awareness. We have included this proposal in our recommendations to TRAI. Another example in more mature regulatory environments as in the United States, is the federal appointed agency Sam Knows [16] which maintains thousands of broadband gateways installed in consumer homes around the country, and collects measurements from these devices to get controlled yet unbiased measurements directly from the end-users. This is another recommendation we have made to TRAI. Our work is therefore taking network performance research and situating it in the context of consumer rights, to lobby for stronger quality of service regulatory mechanisms.

Much of the works cited above conducted measurements in the developed parts of the world. Developing regions are likely to exhibit interesting characteristics though, and several researchers have worked in this context. [15] profiled Internet usage in a small community in Zambia which got its backhaul connectivity through a low bandwidth satellite link, but with fast wireless meshes within the community. It revealed the need for efficient caching and peer to peer solutions to keep the traffic local. [29] conducted measurements in Ghana and found that due to a lack of server infrastructure locally, complex web pages which involved multiple redirections and DNS resolutions led to very high latencies for web browsing. [6] measured broadband and mobile Internet performance in South Africa, and arrived at a similar conclusion that the lack of inter-connectivity between ISPs and distance of the content from the users, led to poor performance and reliability. Our work is along similar directions, of conducting measurements in a developing region. We too draw attention to the degree of connectivity between ISPs and peering with CDNs, along with keeping a focus also on the quality of network configuration and monitoring by different telecom providers in India.

3. METHODOLOGY

As reported in an earlier paper [17], during 2013 we collected 2G and 3G measurements from 7 rural and urban locations, having probed each location for a period of at least 3 months. We have since then repeated the measurement exercise in more locations, bringing the count of the total number of rural and semi-urban sites probed to 15, and urban sites to 5. The methodology followed was the same as in our earlier work. We wrote a measurement suite on Linux based Netbooks which were placed at these sites, and were configured to run tests to measure the throughput, latency, availability, etc of 2G and 3G connections provided by different telecom providers. On each Netbook, we attached three Huawei USB modems to be able to probe three different telecom providers simultaneously.

We leveraged our existing relationship with several social enterprises and NGOs, to identify sites where we could safely place our equipment for a long stretch of time over several months, and also refer to local staff members working out of these locations to check or restart the Netbooks if required. With help from the organizations PRADAN and Vikas Samvad, we identified 11 sites in the state of Madhya Pradesh, which were either local offices of these organizations or the homes of their staff members and volunteers. Similarly, with help from the social enterprises Air Jaldi and Gram Vaani, we identified 5 sites in the state of Jharkhand. 3 sites were used in the state of Rajasthan which were homes of family members of some of the authors of this paper. Finally, 1 site was in Delhi out of our lab itself. For all sites, the SIM cards for the 2G and 3G connections were procured locally, and only those providers were probed which steadily gave a high signal strength of at least 20 ASU at the sites. Wherever 3G services were available, we probed both 3G and 2G performance. Note that 3G services are however available only in urban and semi-urban areas, therefore 2G measurements prevail in our dataset. This is reflective of the adoption of 3G services in the country, which was approximately half of 2G adoption during the time we conducted the tests.

The choice of using Netbooks was primarily motivated because of the long battery life of commodity Netbooks, so that the deployments would not require any complex setup with UPSes or solar powered units to manage power failures. We however had to handle several other challenges, which often required strong support from the local staff or friends and family at these locations. One such challenge was that the 2G and 3G connections we bought locally were prepaid connections and hence had to be recharged periodically. We did build watchdogs on the Netbooks which would use AT commands to query the remaining usage quota on the connections, and according send us alert emails so that we could add money through APIs provided by prepaid recharge vendors. There however were several instances when the SIMs lost their validity and had to be replaced. Another challenge was that the USB modems would sometimes hang. Despite watchdogs which would attempt to first re-mount that particular USB modem, failing which the Netbook would be rebooted automatically once tests on other connections had completed, the only failsafe was to unplug and plug the modem for which we had to seek help of the local staff. Finally, due to disk failures or misconfigurations, and massive floods in one site in Madhya Pradesh, the Netbooks themselves had to be replaced at a few locations and required us to travel to the sites with replacements. For these reasons we could not use all the measurement data produced, and had to select for our analysis only those sites and providers for which we got long stretches of good quality data.

Table 1 summarizes the providers and access technologies we were able to probe successfully at the different locations. EDGE and UMTS are 2.5G and 3G technologies respectively belonging to the GSM family, and 1xRTT and EvDO are 2.5G and 3G technologies belonging to the CDMA family. For ease of exposition, we refer to EDGE and 1xRTT as 2G, and UMTS and EvDO as 3G technologies. Among the GSM based providers, we chose BSNL, Airtel and Idea which are among the largest providers in the country, and refer to them as G_1, G_2 and G_3 respectively with the G meant to denote GSM. Reliance is the only operator providing CDMA based services, and we refer to it as C_1 with the C meant to denote CDMA. Labels R_1 to R_{11} refer to rural locations, S_1 to S_4 are semi-urban locations, and U_1 to U_5 are urban locations.

Table 1: Measurement locations/service providers

	G_1 (BSNL)	G_2 (Airtel)	G_3 (Idea)	C_1 (Reliance)
R_1 (Lamta, MP)	EDGE	EDGE	-	1xRTT
R_2 (Paraswada, MP)	EDGE	EDGE	EDGE	-
R_3 (Ukwa, MP)	EDGE	EDGE	EDGE	-
R_4 (Amarpur, MP)	EDGE	EDGE	EDGE	-
R_5 (Samnapur, MP)	EDGE	-	-	1xRTT
R_6 (Janakpur, MP)	EDGE	-	-	-
R_7 (Manjha, MP)	-	EDGE	-	1xRTT
R_8 (Hanumanpura, RJ)	EDGE	EDGE	EDGE	-
R_9 (Kulhi, JH)	EDGE	UMTS	-	-
R_{10} (Gondlipokhar, JH)	EDGE	UMTS	-	-
R_{11} (Getalsud, JH)	UMTS	EDGE	-	1xRTT
S_1 (Dindori, MP)	EDGE	-	-	-
S_2 (Panna, MP)	EDGE	UMTS	UMTS	-
S_3 (Jatadungari, MP)	-	-	EDGE	-
S_4 (Ormanjhi, JH)	-	EDGE	UMTS	-
U_1 (Pondi, MP)	EDGE	-	-	1xRTT
U_2 (Jaipur, RJ)	UMTS	UMTS	EDGE	-
U_3 (Sikar, RJ)	UMTS	UMTS	EDGE	-
U_4 (Ranchi, JH)	EDGE	UMTS	-	-
U_5 (Delhi)	UMTS EDGE	UMTS EDGE	UMTS EDGE	EVDO

Figure 1 shows the key components of the measurement architecture we deployed. The Netbooks consult a control server to get a list of tests and test parameters to execute, and then run these tests such as upload and download iperfs to a different measurement server. Yet another data server is used to collect data from the Netbooks when they are not running the measurement tests. We used virtual machines hosted on Linode for the measurement and control servers, and a server at IIT Delhi as the data server. Interested readers are referred to our earlier paper [17] for more details and reasons behind our choice of this architecture.

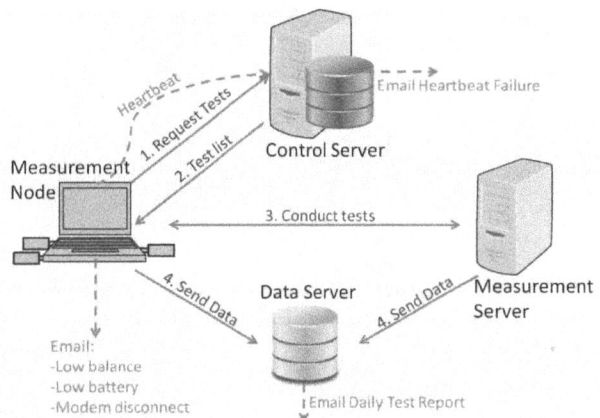

Figure 1: Measurement architecture. Solid lines test execution steps. Dashed lines show suite health monitoring components

4. QOS MEASUREMENT RESULTS

With the objective to understand the QoS provided by telecom providers, we probed three key metrics: availability, upload and download throughput, and latency, at all the measurement sites. We then compared this data with the values reported by telecom providers to TRAI.

4.1 Availability

For each service provider at each location, we evaluated the fraction of time for which connectivity was available. To do so we timestamped network connection and disconnection events reported by the USB modems during the time when the upload/download/latency experiments ran on the modems, and also noted any modem down times during this period when the modem was not responding and re-mounting attempts were being made by watchdog scripts. Using this we calculated the availability as:

$$availability = \frac{connected\_time}{(measurement\_duration - down\_time)}$$

where $connected\_time$ is the duration in seconds for which connectivity was available, $measurement\_duration$ is the time for which experiments ran on the modems, and $down\_time$ is the duration for which the USB modem may have been in a hung state. Figure 2 shows the availability of service providers across different locations. It is alarming that in some cases the availability is as low as 35%, which means that the modem was able to successfully remain connected to a base station for only 35% of the time for which it tried. Further, we notice that with the exception of C_1, availability is typically lower in rural and semi-urban locations than in urban locations. This is probably an artifact of misconfigurations or insufficient monitoring of rural cellular sites, some of which we bring to notice again in subsequent sections.

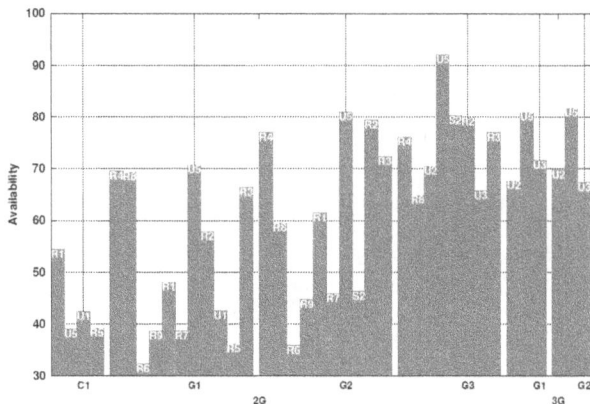

Figure 2: Availability of service providers across rural and urban locations for 2G and 3G access

4.2 Throughput

We used long duration single threaded TCP tests with iperf on the uplink and curl on the downlink to measure the throughput. Figure 3 shows the 2G and 3G uplink/downlink throughput values. The observations are similar as for the availability data, that some providers like G_3 provide consistent performance, but there is a high degree of variability with other providers. We will also bring to notice apparent evidence of misconfiguration in subsequent sections where we show that TCP connections can actually get stalled for tens of seconds at times, thus affecting the throughput, and pointing towards the need for better monitoring and configuration of cellular sites.

What is also alarming is the extent to which the obtained throughput is often much lower than the values advertised by the service providers. Table 2 shows these advertised values. In fact, misleading advertising which promise speeds of "up to 14.4 Mbps" are common sites on wall paintings and billboards all across India, and the Supreme Court even challenged such advertisements [22]. TRAI needs to take note of misleading advertisements which are not only uncompetitive but also hinder the awareness of the consumers in terms of knowing what QoS are they actually entitled.

4.3 Latency

We used ping and traceroute measurements to find the latency values to the first IP hop in the network, arguably the GGSN or the PDSN gateway in the cellular network. We also compared this to the end to end latency to the Linode measurement server, to understand what proportion of the latency is spent in the radio access network.

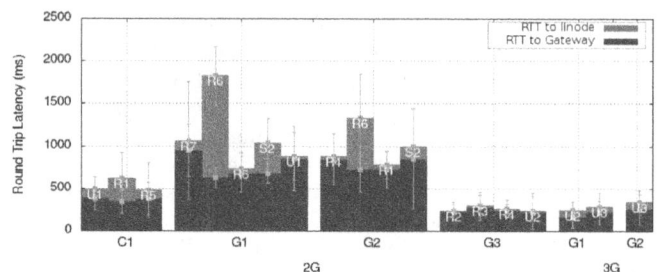

Figure 4: RTT to the measurement server and cellular gateways

Figure 4 shows the round trip latencies to the measurement server, and its sub-component to the gateway node in the network. It is interesting to note that providers like G_3 are able to provide almost 3G like latencies on 2G connections, but other providers have much higher latencies and also show wide variations across different locations, again pointing towards different network configurations which probably cause these variations. We confirm this by measuring the buffer sizes on the downlink and uplink by sending a train of UDP packets and spotting the first packet which was lost. Figure 5 shows the buffer sizes, and we can observe that providers G_3 and C_1 with the smallest buffers are also the ones with the smallest latencies. Large buffers are known to lead to high latencies and the bufferbloat problem, where interactive flows suffer when co-existing with long flows [10]. We therefore argue that just more careful network configurations can alleviate several QoS problems, without any need to provision additional infrastructure.

Another observation from Figure 4 is that the latency beyond the gateway is also lower for G_3 and C_1, indicating that these ISPs are likely to have better connectivity with

Table 2: Throughput values advertised by service providers

	2G Uplink	2G Downlink	3G Uplink	3G Downlink
C1	-	20 Kbps	-	256 Kbps
G1	144 Kbps	144 Kbps	14 Mbps	14 Mbps
G2	256 Kbps	256 Kbps	21.1 Mbps	21.1 Mbps
G3	236 Kbps	236 Kbps	5.7 Mbps	21 Mbps

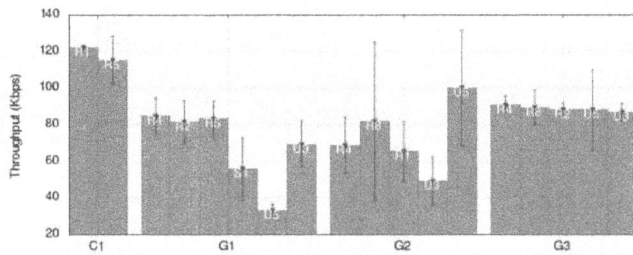

(a) 2G Uplink Throughput

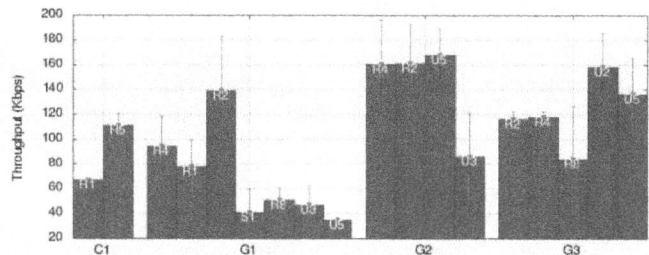

(a) 2G Downlink Throughput

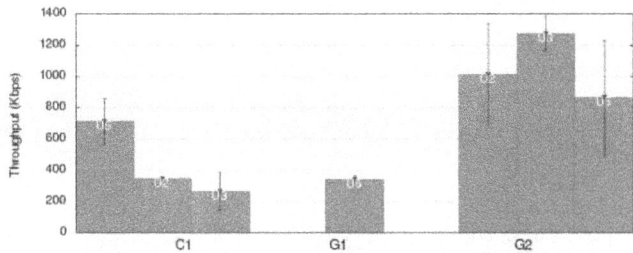

(c) 3G Uplink Throughput

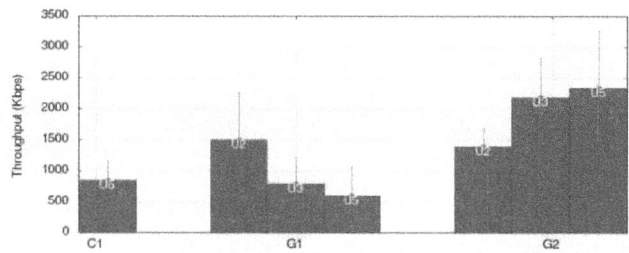

(d) 3G Downlink Throughput

Figure 3: Measured throughput values across various locations and service providers

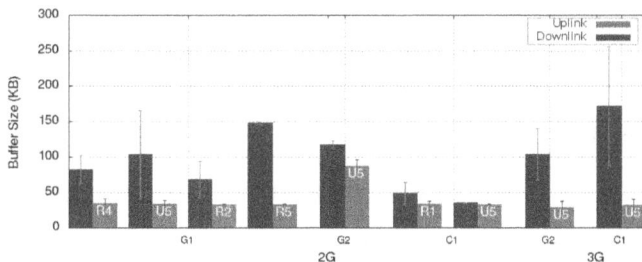

Figure 5: Uplink and downlink buffer sizes (KB)

the rest of the Internet. We explore this in greater detail in subsequent sections when we look at inter ISP connectivity.

4.4 Comparison with TRAI reported values

TRAI releases a quarterly report on the quality of service provided in different states for cellular data services [28]. These are self reported values by the telecom providers, based on a test methodology specified by TRAI [26]. On the surface the test methodology looks similar to our own, where TRAI specifies the file size and number of tries for upload and download to measure throughput, and the use of ping to find latencies. The tests however are actually conducted in a controlled environment most likely from network elements located deeper inside the radio access network which does not accurately mimic the real world environment that users actually experience. Table 3 shows the data from the TRAI report for the service provider Airtel (G_2), and compares it with the parameters as measured by us during the same period. Broadly, the throughput values are of the same order, the latency values measured by us are quite higher, but the greatest difference is in the availability values where the provider actually reports 100% availability in most cases!

The takeaways therefore from a QoS regulation standpoint is for TRAI to mandate more realistic environments for providers to conduct network tests, or to depute third party agencies such as Sam Knows in the United States to report measurements collected from actual user devices [16]. These measures would bring more data to the public domain and thus draw attention to the widely different QoS provided in different locations by different providers. Proposals such as nutrition labels [24] could also help empower consumers by making them more aware of the QoS to expect and then use the information to make better choices when buying data plans. However, unless TRAI does not mandate some minimum QoS standards to which providers can be held accountable, or the published information is not made available to consumers easily to be able to exercise their choice in selecting providers, even these stronger regulatory measures may arguably not yield much benefits. We therefore believe that TRAI should continue to mount pressure on the providers to manage their networks better since our data indicates that just careful network configurations alone can help to a significant extent.

5. NETWORK CONNECTIVITY

We next explore inter-ISP connectivity and CDN linkages of cellular providers because these aspects influence the quality of service perceived by users [29, 6].

We start with listing some common CDN providers, and then use traceroute and the RIPE database to chalk out AS hops to these CDN networks from the four cellular providers probed by us. Figure 6 shows the consolidated AS map. We can see from the map that Bharti Airtel and Tata Communications (which acquired a controlling stake in the state owned VSNL network in 2002 [11]) hold dominant positions in providing backbone connectivity for India with the rest of the world. We also interestingly find that providers like G_3

Table 3: Comparison of performance metrics observed by us with TRAI reported values by service providers

Location		Observed Values			TRAI Values		
		Availability (%)	Throughput (kbps)	Latency (ms)	Availability (%)	Throughput (kbps)	Latency (ms)
RJ	2G	59.49	131.02	308.45	100	116.5	206.3
	3G	69.73 - 71.58	1394.03- 2187.13	128.84 - 256.89	100	2476.3	191.8
JH	2G	41.97 - 57.64		453.85 - 1040.75	100	199.7	244.8
	3G				100	3485.2	64
MP	2G	36.37 - 80.17	85.89 - 160.72	405.16 - 936.45	99.83	131.8	119
	3G	73.66	907.80	476.57			
Delhi	2G	81.44	167.82	310.58	100	130.2	173.3
	3G	91.69	2332.25	540.41		2369.4	80.4

(Idea Cellular) do not own any backbone links of their own, but use service from G_2 (Bharti Airtel) and other providers, and are still able to provide better latency values.

It it also clear that the telecom providers are well networked with CDNs. Akamai has its servers located in all the provider networks except Idea. Most providers also peer directly with many CDN providers, showing that they are cognizant of the benefits of CDNs. To study this further, and to see implications of the AS connectivity on the quality of experience for web browsing, we measure the page load times for several webpages accessed from different providers.

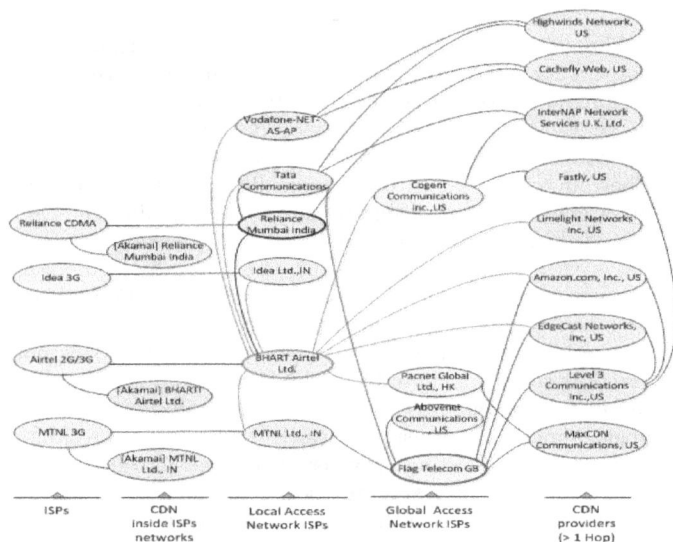

Figure 6: AS map for inter-ISP connectivity

Page load time is certainly not the best or the only metric to assess the quality of experience for web browsing, but we chose it as a first step which could be executed easily. We used the Selenium browser automation framework with the Chrome driver on the Netbooks, to probe a number of different websites and collect HAR traces which could be analyzed to find the page load times and other HTTP dynamics. We ran this test in New Delhi for different categories of websites including news websites, government websites, and e-commerce websites. The websites were chosen carefully as those which use a CDN provider to serve at least 80% of their content, and those which do not use CDNs at all. We also ensured that the websites we selected had similar cumulative page sizes of between 2-3MB.

Figures 7 (a) and (b) show page load times for webpages that do not use CDN providers to host their content, and Figures 7 (c) and (d) show page load times for webpages that do use CDNs. Tables 4 and 5 gives the list of webpages probed. A comparison for webpages with and without CDNs shows that with 2G access technology, the page load times are better by almost 50% when using CDNs, and with 3G access technology they are almost 25% better. The second observation is that irrespective of whether or not CDNs are used, G_2 (Airtel) consistently gives the best page load times followed by G_3 (Idea), and G_1 (BSNL) gives the worst. Since most of the CDN using websites we probed use Akamai, Airtel was able to do quite well thanks to its close linkage with Akamai. BSNL however despite its close linkage has a poorly configured network, and is not able to utilize its CDN linkages. This clearly shows that network configuration and connectivity both have important implications on the quality of experience that providers can ensure to their users.

We also advocate that a crowdsourcing platform which collects such QoE parameters for different websites and telecom providers, across locations, can help consumers make better choices when buying data plans. This would in turn usher more competition between the providers. TRAI itself could host such a platform, or help create a platform run by neutral agencies.

Table 4: Pageload time for websites without CDN

Website alias	Page alias
http://www.ibps.in/	W1
http://www.incredibleindia.org/en/	W2
http://india.gov.in/	W3
https://www.irctc.co.in/eticketing/loginHome.jsf/	W4
http://www.kerala.gov.in/	W5
https://www.maharashtra.gov.in/	W6
https://morth.eproc.in/ProductMORTH/publicDas/	W7
http://www.odisha.gov.in/portal/default.asp/	W8
https://www.sbi.co.in/	W9
http://www.tn.gov.in/	W10

6. CONNECTION STALLS

In our earlier work [17] we reported a curious observation that large file downloads on TCP would sometimes stall for long periods of time of up to tens of seconds. During these stall events, a lost packet would result in multiple timeouts and get retransmitted repeatedly. However, unlike regular

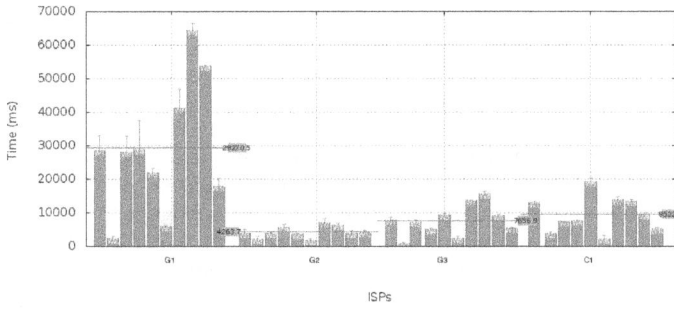

(a) 2G : without CDN

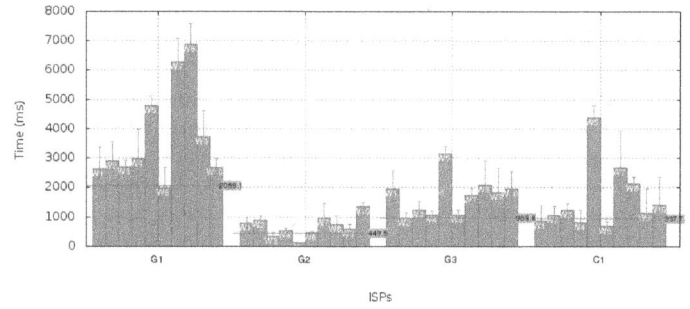

(b) 3G: without CDN

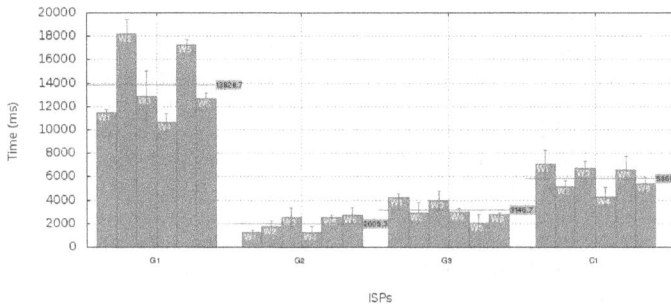

(c) 2G : with CDN

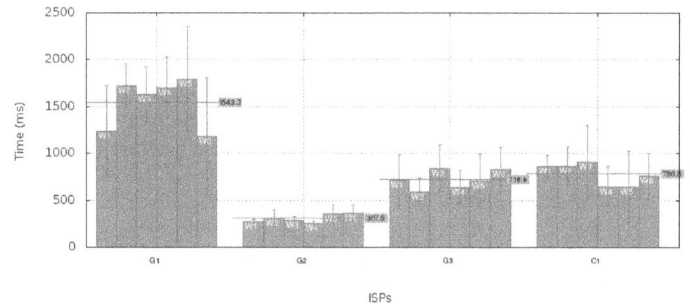

(d) 3G : with CDN

Figure 7: Comparison of Page Load times for websites using and non using CDN services

Table 5: Pageload time for websites with CDN

Website alias	Page alias	CDN provider
http://timesofindia.indiatimes.com/	W1	Akamai
http://www.espncricinfo.com/	W2	Akamai
http://www.bbc.com/bbc/	W3	Fastly
http://www.bostonmagazine.com/	W4	Internap
http://www.news.com.au/news/	W5	Akamai
http://www.yatra.com/yatra/	W6	Akamai

timeout situations where all packets following the lost packet are also lost and later retransmitted, in this case the packets were not lost but would sit in some buffers along the way and eventually reach the receiver without requiring any retransmissions. We found that the occurrence of these stalls was quite frequent in some locations and detrimental for performance because they would cause the entire TCP connection to pause and later initiate a slow start. We validated earlier that the stalls were not an artifact of the modem, or the server, or due to any middleboxes that might be buffering out of order packets, and we had not been able to satisfactorily explain the phenomenon. We now have an answer and it has to do with device and network configurations which cause the USB modems to search for other networks periodically, and thereby temporarily suspend data transfer – the signal strength drops to zero and a new connection has to be initiated after the search procedure is over. Since this happens more in some sites than others, it again points towards

configuration problems that lead to such events.

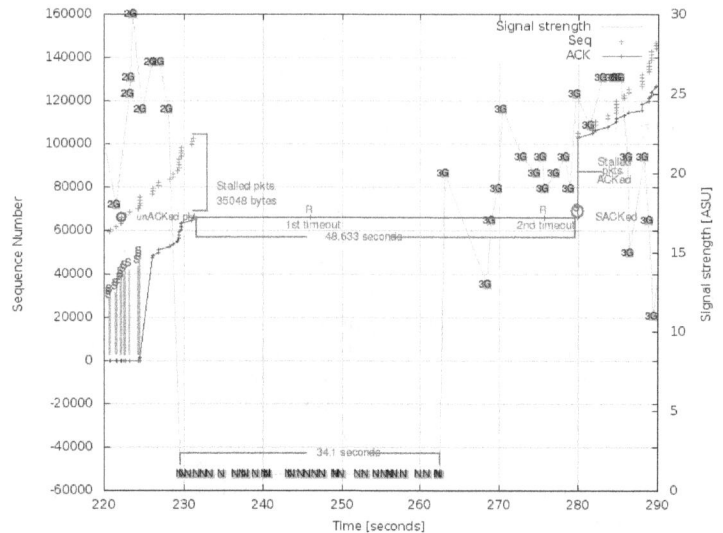

Figure 8: Example of a stall event

Figure 8 shows such a stall event on the sender side trace. The signal strength at the receiver is also plotted on the same graph. We can see that when acknowledgements are not received after time 232, the first unacked packet is retransmitted twice during timeout events, and finally when

155

the acknowledgement is received at time 240, it is soon after followed by an acknowledgement for the stalled packets without requiring any retransmissions for these packets. This shows that the stalled packets were actually transmitted just once before time 232; these packets were then waiting in some buffers along the way and reached the receiver together with the retransmitted packet. The signal strength trace shows that during this stall event, the receiver actually switched from a 2G to a 3G connection, and registered a signal strength of zero when the switching was in progress. A similar analysis of the receive side trace showed that the seemingly lost packet was actually received during its first transmission itself but the ack could not be transmitted because the device lost its signal. Therefore, due to the switching not only did the connection stall for more than 50 seconds, but TCP also went into repeated timeouts.

We investigate this in more detail. Figure 9 (a) shows the latency during different kinds of switching events that happen. Locations such as R_5 and R_6 on connection G_1 only had 2G available and see switching from 2G to 2G with latencies as high as 20 seconds. Thus, even in the case of zero mobility, the modems go into a search phase like in a handoff. Other locations which had 3G available, see switching from 3G to 2G, 2G to 3G, and 3G to 3G, pointing to even more drastic outcomes from the search process. We do not know whether the search process was initiated by the mobile or the network, since both GSM and CDMA technologies allow both kinds of handovers, but the essential point this observation highlights is to reduce unnecessary events either through better configuration settings or more intelligent algorithms.

Figure 9 (b) shows the frequency of switching, with many locations witnessing a switching event every 40 seconds on average. The negative axis on this figure shows how often these switches led to stall events where there was at least one timeout, and many locations have such stalls once every minute. There are however also combinations of providers and locations with low switching frequencies, but such cases of good configuration settings are seemingly rare.

Figure 9 (c) plots the duration of these stall events. As in the example shown earlier, these stall durations run into tens of seconds. The events are therefore detrimental in the case of any long transfers since almost every minute some tens of seconds of connectivity goes unutilized, and in the case of TCP this further sends the connection into timeouts.

A deeper analysis of some locations reveals that 3G-2G switches are the most frequent, and in almost 50% of the cases these switches lead to stall events. This is shown in Figure 9 (d) for location R_7 with G_1 (BSNL). Other kinds of switches such as 3G-3G and 2G-3G are less frequent, and also lead to fewer stalls. A possible reason behind this observation that 3G-2G switches have the worst outcome, is that when a connection is in 3G before the switch then the latencies are lower and therefore there is a higher chance of timeouts occurring because of the switch.

Overall, we found that long duration downloads in most locations had stalls more than 40% of the time, and in some cases almost 90% of the downloads had stalls. Downloads without stalls gave a throughput 25% higher than downloads with stalls in the case of 2G, and 65% higher in the case of 3G connections. This seems like it could be an avoidable penalty: In the case of sites with only 2G access, repeated searching could be disabled, or at least made less frequent.

With sites having 3G and 2G access, a deeper analysis of the provider logs should be done to check if 3G access is being deliberately downgraded to 2G by the providers because their networks are underprovisioned, or the networks are just misconfigured and cause unnecessary switches.

When considered in perspective with the latency and throughput measurements in the earlier sections, it is clear that some providers are able to provide more consistent performance than others, and some sites are better configured than others. These observations therefore point towards the need for providers to be more careful in managing their networks, which can either be ensured through stronger and more appropriate regulations or through greater consumer awareness, so that the providers can be pushed to work harder at delivering better performance.

7. CONCLUSIONS

We showed through our measurements that the quality of service obtained by users differs considerably from advertised values by the telecom providers, and from values reported by them to the telecom regulatory authority in India. We also showed that in many cases just more careful configurations of the cellular networks could lead to better performance. We are now working together with a consumer rights organization to take up this evidence to the government regulators and argue for stronger QoS regulations in the country.

8. ACKNOWLEDGEMENTS

This work was supported with funding from the Ford Foundation. We are deeply grateful to our field partners, PRADAN, Vikas Samvad, Air Jaldi, and Gram Vaani, who provided invaluable support to run the experiments. We also acknowledge the strong support that CUTS (Consumer Unity and Trust Society) has provided to help us understand the QoS regulatory framework in India, and have partnered with us to work towards stronger regulations in the country.

9. REFERENCES

[1] Personal communication with TRAI officials, June 2015.
[2] A. Akella, S. Seshan, and A. Shaikh. An Empirical Evaluation of Wide-area Internet Bottlenecks. In *Proc. IMC*, 2003.
[3] J. J. Alcaraz, F. Cerdan, and J. Garcia-Haro. Optimizing TCP and RLC Interaction in the UMTS Radio Access Network. *Network Magazine of Global Internetworking*, 2006.
[4] P. Benko, G. Malicsko, and A. Veres. A Large-scale, Passive Analysis of End-to-End TCP Performance Over GPRS. In *Proc. INFOCOM 2004*, 2004.
[5] R. Chakravorty, A. Clark, and I. Pratt. GPRSWeb: Optimizing the Web for GPRS Links. In *Proc. International conference on Mobile Systems, Applications and Services*, 2003.
[6] M. Chetty, S. Sundaresan, S. Muckaden, N. Feamster, and E. Callandro. Measuring Broadband Performance in South Africa. In *Proc. ACM DEV*, 2014.
[7] 3G consumer. Pathetic Internet Speeds on 3G, http://bit.ly/1KH1JT5, http://bit.ly/1KH1JT5, Sept 2015.
[8] M. Dischinger, A. Haeberlen, K. Gummadi, and S. Saroiu. Characterizing Residential Broadband Networks. In *IMC*, 2007.
[9] A. Elmokashfi, A. Kvalbein, J. Xiang, and K. Evensen. Characterizing Delays in Norwegian 3G Networks. In *Proc. PAM*, 2012.
[10] J. Gettys. Bufferbloat: Dark Buffers in the Internet. *Internet Computing, IEEE*, 15(3):96–96, 2011.
[11] Tata Group. Tatas Vault Ahead in Telecom, Acquire 25% Stake in VSNL, http://bit.ly/1V5WxyN, February 2002.
[12] H. Inamura, G. Montenegro, R. Ludwig, A. Gurtov, and F. Khafizov. TCP over Second (2.5G) and Third (3G)

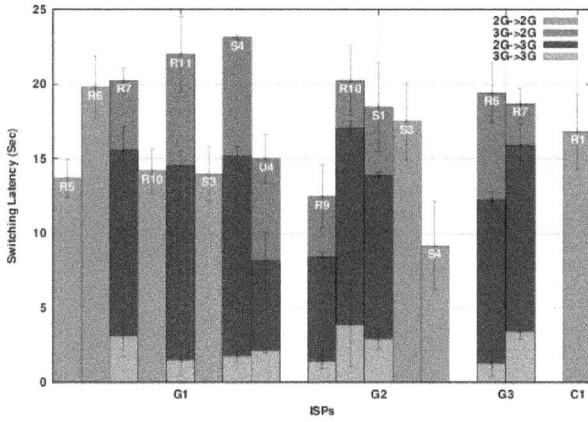

(a) Switching latencies

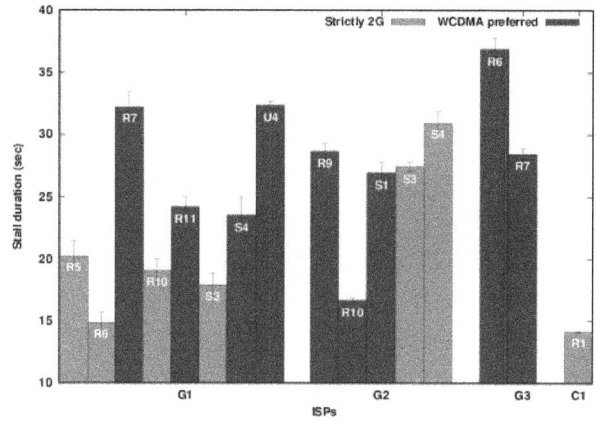

(b) Stall durations

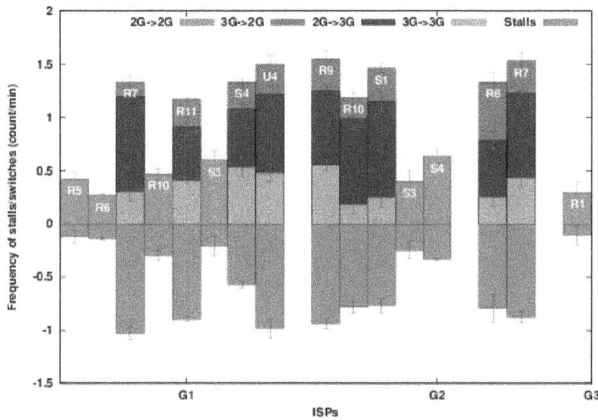

(c) Frequency of stalls and switches

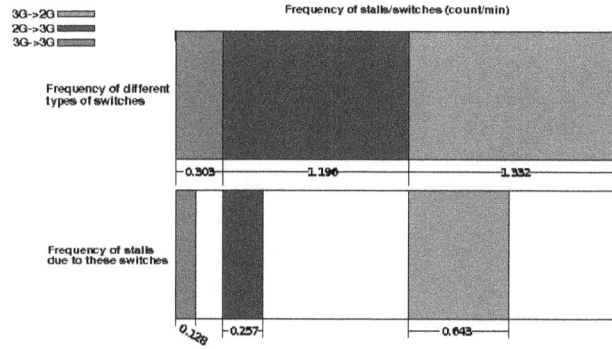

(d) Proportion of switches leading to stalls

Figure 9: Switches and stalls at different locations

Generation Wireless Networks. RFC 3481 (Best Current Practice), February 2003.

[13] McKinsey Inc. Offline and Falling Behind: Barriers to Internet Adoption, http://bit.ly/Ztobeu, September 2014.

[14] H. Jiang, Y. Wang, K. Lee, and I. Rhee. Tackling Bufferbloat in 3G/4G Networks. In *Proc. IMC*, 2012.

[15] D. Johnson, E. Belding, K. Almeroth, and G. Stam. Internet Usage and Performance Analysis of a Rural Wireless Network in Macha, Zambia. In *Proc. NSDR*, 2010.

[16] Sam Knows. https://www.samknows.com/, September 2015.

[17] Z. Koradia, G. Mannava, A. Raman, G. Aggarwal, V. Ribiero, A. Seth, S. Ardon, A. Mahanti, and S. Triukose. First Impressions on the State of Cellular Data Connectivity in India. In *ACM DEV*, December 2013.

[18] C. Kreibich, N. Weaver, B. Nechaev, and V. Paxson. Netalyzr: Illuminating the Edge Network. In *Proc. IMC*, 2010.

[19] K. Lakshminarayanan, V. Padmanabhan, and J. Padhye. Bandwidth Estimation in Broadband Access Networks. Proc. IMC, 2004.

[20] N. Narajayan and Scroll.in. Tower Shortage, Spectrum Crunch and an X Factor - Why Call Drops are Common in India, http://bit.ly/1N5ltAx, August 2015.

[21] J. Prokkola, P.H.J. Perala, M. Hanski, and E. Piri. 3G/HSPA Performance in Live Networks from the End User Perspective.

In *IEEE International Communications Conference*, 2009.

[22] PTI and Times of India. Delhi Highcourt to Test MTS's 9.8 Mbps Internet Speed Claims, http://bit.ly/1QTUGY1, 2014.

[23] S. Sundaresan, W. de Donato, N. Feamster, R. Teixeira, S. Crawford, and A. Pescapè. Broadband Internet Performance: A View from the Gateway. In *Proc. ACM SIGCOMM*, 2011.

[24] S. Sundaresan, N. Feamster, R. Teixeira, A. Tang, K. Edwards, R. Grinter, M. Chetty, and W. Donato. Helping Users Shop for ISPs with Internet Nutrition Labels. In *Proc. ACM SIGCOMM Workshop on Home Networks*, 2011.

[25] W. Tan, F. Lam, and W. Lau. An Empirical Study of 3G Network Capacity and Performance. In *Proc. IEEE INFOCOM*, 2007.

[26] TRAI. The Standards of Quality of Service for Wireless Data Services Regulations, 2012, http://bit.ly/1V5UlY9, 2012.

[27] TRAI. Consultation Paper on Amendments to the Standards of Quality of Service for Wireless Data Services Regulation, 2012, http://bit.ly/1QTUGY1, April 2014.

[28] TRAI. Quality Performance Monitoring Report (PMR) on Quality of Service of Wireless Data Services, http://bit.ly/1FY1MV6, March 2015.

[29] Y. Zaki, J. Chen, T. Potsch, T. Ahmad, and L. Subramanian. Dissecting Web Latency in Ghana. In *Proc. IMC*, 2014.

Analysis of End-User QoE in Community Networks

Bart Braem, Johan Bergs,
Chris Blondia
University of Antwerp - iMinds
Middelheimlaan 1
Antwerpen, Belgium
first.last@uantwerpen.be

Leandro Navarro
Universitat Politècnica
de Catalunya
Jordi Girona, 1-3
Barcelona, Spain
leandro@ac.upc.edu

Sabine Wittevrongel
Ghent University
Sint-Pietersnieuwstraat 41
Gent, Belgium
sw@telin.ugent.be

ABSTRACT

Community networks are a potential model for the Future Internet, where the users form and operate the network instead of a central, commercial entity. Socio-economic studies show that community networks are an excellent model to develop networking infrastructure commons (as common-pool resources or public goods) that promote sustainable development, with greater effects in less developed areas. The performance of parts of community networks has been studied extensively, often focusing on routing protocols or applications on top of community networks. This work focuses on the end-to-end quality of Internet access in community networks, as a validation of the technical applicability of this concept in under-served regions. A comparative analysis with other ISPs per country shows the effectiveness of these community networks in providing satisfactory networking services to end-users, particularly effective for underserved areas or people.

1. INTRODUCTION

Community networks are often referred to as *bottom-up broadband*, where the people form the network instead of the network being pushed on the people, with a price tag[5]. While network sharing is not a novel idea, the availability of cheap off-the-shelf wireless hardware in the nineties has led to a strong adoption of wireless mesh networks as the backbone for community networks, which now span entire regions. For thousands of users in both developed and under-served countries, community networks form the only means to access the public Internet or even just local community services.

From a sociological point of view, the concept of community networks closely aligns with the availability and sharing of information and services within a community[9]. Especially for developing countries, but even in higher income countries, to most users the local information regarding e.g. crop prices or bus times is an important piece of information. As an illustration, even in the European Union many

ACM DEV 2015, December 1–2, 2015, London, United Kingdom.
ⓒ 2015 ACM. ISBN 978-1-4503-3490-7/15/12 ...$15.00.
DOI: http://dx.doi.org/10.1145/2830629.2830639.

regions are underserved by traditional ISPs, because of technical reasons but often also because of economic reasons. If the distance between the nearest high bandwidth fiber loop and a particular location is too large, ISPs tend to charge the end-users for their costs. In many cases this cost becomes prohibitive, e.g. in the case of mountainous areas.

Today a large number of community networks are operational around the world, from Argentina to Tibet[2]. Some networks consist of just a few nodes, others are composed of hundreds and even thousands of nodes in the case of AWMN in Greece and guifi.net in Spain[23]. Notice that in the latter case parts of the network do not have access to the public Internet and other parts can only reach the Internet through proxy servers with varying performance[18]. The equipment used to build and operate the network is often low-cost or even DIY, the software running on top of it is usually open source[12, 8].

In this paper we present the results of a large-scale measurement campaign, where we specifically analyse the network performance as experienced by the end-user in community networks in comparison to other ISPs. To the best of our knowledge, this is the first end-to-end measurement study of the quality of Internet access in community networks, as a validation of their deployment for development projects.

The rest of this paper is structured as follows: in section 2, we describe the tools we used to perform measurements on nodes in a network and how these tools are then deployed in existing community networks, described in section 3. In section 4, we describe and compare the results obtained from our measurements. In section 5, we discuss the implications of these results in developing regions and some of the requirements for that to happen. Finally, in section 6, some conclusions are formulated.

2. MEASUREMENT TOOLS

In order to evaluate the performance of a network accessing the Internet, measurements need to be performed. For this, we selected several tools to be deployed in three community networks.

RIPE ATLAS provides a widely deployed tool for measurement of end-user experience[4]. The project has deployed small hardware, called RIPE ATLAS probes, all over the world in thousands of locations. These provide an excellent vantage point within the network. However, the RIPE ATLAS project requires custom hardware by design, to provide very strict guarantees on measurements. For reasons of cost deploying the required amount of RIPE ATLAS probes within the community networks under study was not possible.

Project BISMark wants to measure home network performance, and it realises this by means of custom gateway firmware[20]. It is however not feasible to deploy this specific firmware on all nodes in a community network.

NLNOG-RING is a non-profit software project designed to share shell access in participating ISP (core) networks to study and debug network behaviour[16]. The approach is elegant, however it requires connecting existing servers to this ring network in order to increase the sharing scope. Therefore, it was not an option for this study.

Finally, perfsonar-ps is a suite of measurement tools which can be deployed freely, containing a number of systems and techniques to study the performance of networks[6]. Data gathering and open data set publication and analysis is more out of scope for this project, therefore and for support reasons we chose Measurement Lab for the measurement of Internet access, combined with the Community-Lab testbed for launching the measurements from inside of several community networks.

2.1 Measurement-Lab

We selected the Measurement Lab[11] (M-Lab) platform to perform our measurements on. M-Lab is an open, distributed server platform on which researchers can deploy open source Internet measurement tools. The data collected by those tools is released in the public domain. M-Lab was founded by the New America Foundation's Open Technology Institute (OTI), the PlanetLab Consortium, Google Inc. and academic researchers. M-Lab servers are distributed globally, but most of the servers are located in North America and Europe. The M-Lab platform offers a number of measurement tools, enabling its users to do different kinds of measurements, such as Paris traceroute and reverse traceroute[1, 14], testing for application-specific blocking or throttling, testing for traffic shaping, checking up- and download speeds and more. The tool we selected to use in our measurements of Internet access is called "Network Diagnostic Test" and is described in more detail below.

2.2 Network Diagnostic Test

The Network Diagnostic Test (NDT) reports upload and download speeds. It tries to determine the cause of limited speeds and checks for proxies, NAT devices or middleboxes between the machine running the test and one of the M-Lab servers[7]. Therefore it can provide several objective indications of the user's experience of an Internet connection. Below, we included the output of a typical run of the NDT tool:

```
Testing against host ndt.iupui.mlab1.ath02.measurement-lab.org
Testing network path for configuration and performance problems  -- Using IPv4 address
Checking for Middleboxes . . . . . . . . . . . . . . . . . . . Done
checking for firewalls . . . . . . . . . . . . . . . . . . Done
running 10s outbound test (client to server) . . . . . 4.45 Mb/s
running 10s inbound test (server to client) . . . . . . 45.92 Mb/s
sending meta information to server . . . . . . Done
The slowest link in the end-to-end path is a 10 Mbps Ethernet or WiFi 11b subnet
Information: Other network traffic is congesting the link
Server 'ndt.iupui.mlab1.ath02.measurement-lab.org' is not behind a firewall.
[Connection to the ephemeral port was successful]
Client is probably behind a firewall. [Connection to the ephemeral port failed]
Information: Network Middlebox is modifying MSS variable (changed to 1410)
Server IP addresses are preserved End-to-End
Information: Network Address Translation (NAT) box is modifying the Client's IP address
Server says [79.131.35.128] but Client says [ 10.255.18.237]
```

The most important values in this output for the analysis in this paper are the bitrates for the upload and download tests. What is not included in this output is the RTT value.

In addition to producing this output, the NDT tool logs all test data to M-Lab. This data can later be queried using Google BigQuery.

2.3 Google BigQuery

Google BigQuery is a tool to analyse big data in the cloud[21]. It offers an SQL-like interface to query data stored in the cloud. The NDT tool described above logs all results to M-Lab, which can then be queried using BigQuery. The data logged by the NDT tool contains much more information than the output shown above. It contains RTT values, node identifiers, IP addresses, geolocation information and more. The node identifier can be manually specified by the user running the NDT test and can as such be used to group measurement results for each node.

2.4 Community-Lab

To gather the data required for the analysis performed in this work, we have used the CONFINE Community-Lab testbed[1]. Community-Lab supports experimentally-driven research on community networks developed and operated by the European FP7 CONFINE Project. To allow researchers to perform experiments it has more than 200 nodes integrated in five existing community networks: guifi.net (Spain), FunkFeuer (Austria), AWMN (Athens Wireless Metropolitan Network), Sarantaporo.gr (Greece), Wireless Belgium (Belgium) and Ninux.org (Italy). Three of these networks have been studied in this paper: guifi.net, Ninux.org and AWMN.

Using the Community-Lab testbed, it is possible to deploy virtual machines on so-called "research devices". Research devices are connected to the community network through a "community device", a node in the community network, but research devices do not have to adapt to the requirements of the community network. This approach allows researchers to flexibly deploy virtual machines throughout a community network without having to configure the VMs specifically for each individual network. Additionally, by separating the research devices from the community devices, the community networks themselves need not explicitly support the research tools deployed on the network. Figure 1 shows the Community-Lab nodes used in the experiment.

We have deployed the NDT tool on virtual machines running on all the available nodes (211) in the Community-Lab testbed. The tool was scheduled to run once every hour. The data of the test runs are logged to Measurement-Lab to allow access via Google's BigQuery service.

3. COMMUNITY NETWORKS

All over the world citizens and organisations pool their resources and coordinate their efforts to build network infrastructures. The coverage of underserved areas and the fight against the digital divide are the most frequent driving factors, but motivations such as contributing to development of a new telecommunications model or just for pleasure are also often mentioned by community network contributors. Technologies employed vary significantly, ranging from very-low-cost, off-the-shelf wireless (WiFi) routers to expensive optical fibre equipment[2].

Models of participation, organisation, and funding are very diverse. For example, some networks are freely acces-

---

[1] https://community-lab.net

sible, others are cooperative based, some are run by federations of microISPs, etc.

Community networks (CNs) correspond to the subset of these networks that is characterised for being open, free, and neutral. They are open because everyone has the right to know how they are built. They are free because the network access is driven by the non-discriminatory principle; thus they are universal. And they are neutral because any technical solution available may be used to extend the network, and because the network can be used to transmit data of any kind by any participant, including commercial purposes.

We have selected three main community networks involved in the Community-Lab testbed considering the number of network nodes and the number of research devices available for experimentation. These are the Athens Wireless Metropolitan Network (AWMN) in Greece, guifi.net in Spain, and Ninux in Italy[2]. All of them consist of thousands of links, mostly wireless, but gradually they also integrate optical fibre and optical wireless links. The fundamental principles of these networks, defined at the start to be fully inclusive, revolve around:

- Non-discriminatory and open access to the network infrastructure. The access is non-discriminatory because contributions, either economic or in-kind, are cost-oriented instead of market-oriented. It is open because everybody has the right to join the infrastructure.

- Open participation. Everybody has the right to join and participate (construction, operation, governance) in the community.

These fundamental principles applied to an infrastructure result in a network that is a *collective good*, *socially produced*, and governed as a *common-pool resource (CPR)*, as defined by E. Ostrom [17].

Started in 2002 in Athens, Greece, the Athens Wireless Metropolitan Network (AWMN) is a grassroots wireless community, taking advantage of state of the art wireless technologies, to connect people and provide services. The network comprises (as of July 2015) 2385 active nodes out of 12233 registered nodes, 1238 backbone nodes, 2655 links, 835 access points, 744 active services.

guifi.net started in 2004 in Gurb, a rural and underserved area in Catalonia, Spain. It combines several technologies, mainly wireless and optical fibre. Due to its affordability, accessibility, and ease of deployment, WiFi was the first technology to be used and is still the most popular. The initial nodes of guifi.net were deployed by 2004. Optical fibre was first introduced in 2009[3] and currently there are around 100 optical links. As of October 2015, guifi.net has a total of 29,664 nodes declared as operational, accounting for about 34,000 WiFi links (31,000 AP-Client and 3,000 Point-to-Point) resulting in a total length of 55,000 Km. Most of the nodes (29,600) are located in Spain.

Ninux.org was born in Rome around 2002 and now spans all over Italy. Its name currently stands for "Neighborhood Internet, Network Under eXperiment". Ninux.org is a network of computers connected without wires, created by a community of geeks, radio amateurs and fans in Italy. The network comprises (as of October 2015) 349 active nodes out of 2120 potential nodes, 176 links, and 25 access points.

---

[2]AWMN: `http://www.awmn.net/`, guifi.net: `http://guifi.net/`, Ninux: `http://ninux.org/`
[3]`http://guifi.net/node/23273`

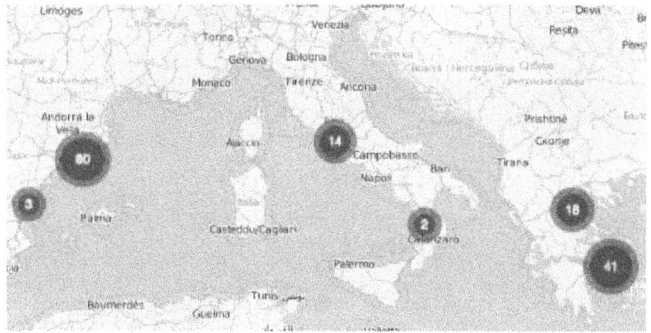

Figure 1: Nodes in the experiment

4. RESULTS AND ANALYSIS

To analyse the behaviour of nodes in a community network accessing the Internet, we have used the measurement data on Ninux.org, guifi.net and AWMN from June 9, 2015 to August 31, 2015 (158 nodes in these three networks). We only have valid data starting from June 9, as the version of the NDT tool used prior to that date could not tag individual nodes with a unique identifier. We need to be able to do this, since we are running our tests across different community networks, which use the same (private) IP address ranges internally. This means that we cannot distinguish nodes based solely on their IP address, as different nodes (on different networks) might be using the same IP. As the Community-Lab testbed already uses internal unique identifiers for each node, we re-used those identifiers as the node identifier in the NDT tests, enabling us to uniquely match each measurement result to the node running the test. During the measurement period, 21,483 download tests have been run on AWMN, 18,907 on guifi.net and 20,171 on Ninux. For the upload tests, we have 21,854, 19,380 and 20,881 measurements, respectively.

4.1 Round-Trip-Time Measurements

The Round-Trip-Time (RTT) is one of the measures to assess the "quality" of a community network. Not only high RTTs are an indication of degraded QoE, but also the degree of variation in RTT is important to take into account.

Figure 2 shows the cumulative distribution of RTT values in the three community networks considered. The RTT measurements are taken from the download tests. The maximum RTT in the graph is capped to 1,000 ms. Figure 2 shows that the distribution of RTTs is very different depending on the community network considered. In the Ninux network, low RTTs are the norm, with 90% of the measurements being less than 200 ms. In AWMN, very low RTTs are uncommon. Most RTT measurements on this network are situated between 100 and 300 ms. The situation in guifi.net, however, is very different. Although a significant amount of measurements show low RTTs (less than 200 ms), the distribution has a very long tail, with 10% of the measurements taking more than 1 second.

This cumulative distribution is taken over all nodes during the entire period considered. As this only gives an indication of the RTTs one can expect in these networks, time information is not included in this graph. Therefore, figures 3, 4 and 5 each show the measured RTT values for two nodes in AWMN, guifi.net and Ninux, respectively. The

161

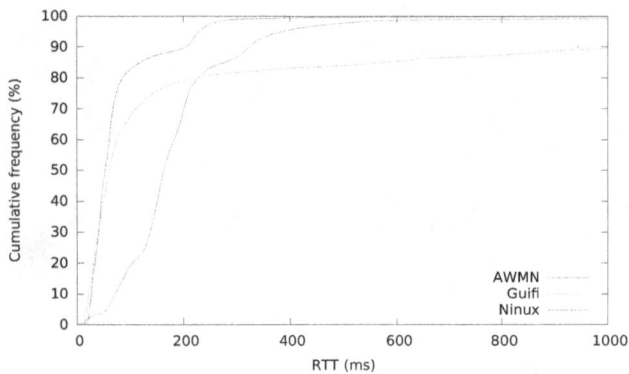

Figure 2: Cumulative distribution of RTT measurements, capped to 1s

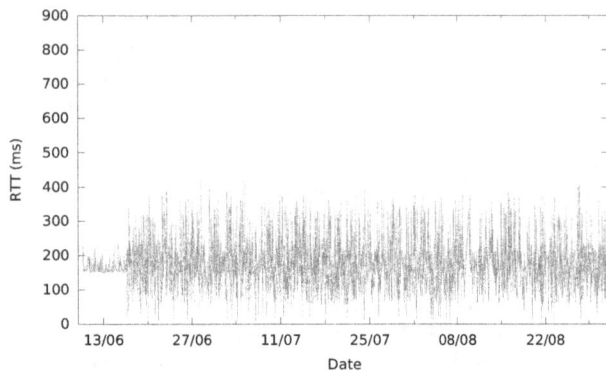

Figure 3: RTT measurements, AWMN

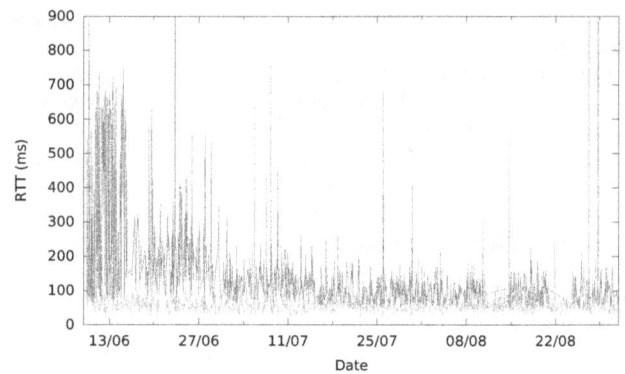

Figure 4: RTT measurements, guifi.net

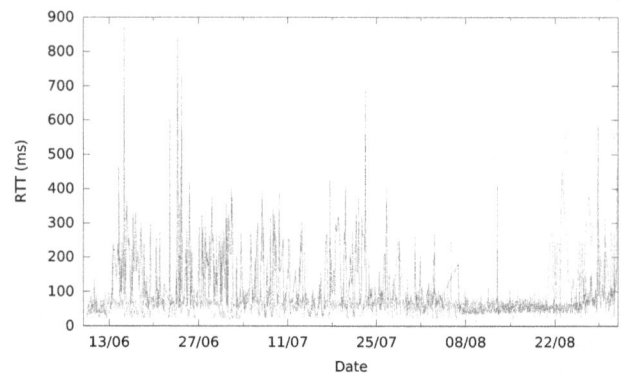

Figure 5: RTT measurements, Ninux

nodes were chosen randomly amongst those that contained sufficient and realistic measurements. With this we mean that some of the nodes that ran the tests are located in data centers belonging to e.g. universities that participate in the community networks. These nodes skew the results, as they tend to have very fast and reliable Internet access, while a typical end-user node does not have this luxury. The graphs clearly show the unstable nature of the networks. In the AWMN network, both nodes behave similarly. From June 9 to June 16, they both experience a relatively high but constant RTT around 160 ms. However, on June 16, something changed in the AWMN network, causing the RTT values to become very unstable. These unstable RTT values are observed continuously for the rest of the measurement period. Also visible on figure 3 is that one of the nodes (represented by the green line) has gone offline for a period of about two weeks, in August. When looking at the guifi.net network, it is clear that one node consistently has a very low RTT, apart from some rare anomalies, whereas another node exhibits a very unpredictable behaviour. The same is true for the nodes in Ninux, in figure 5. Not only does this graph show that RTT values can be very different for different nodes in the network, but also that the behaviour can change over time: the first few days of the measurement period, both nodes experience constant, low RTT times, until something changes in the Ninux network, affecting only one of the two nodes. At the end of the measurement period, another event leads to a sudden change in RTT values for the second node.

These measurements indicate that the network quality in all three networks considered is variable, both in time (the same node may experience good or bad RTT values over time) and in place (different nodes might exhibit a different behaviour).

4.2 Throughput Measurements

In addition to RTT measurements, the other measure to assess "quality" is throughput, both upload and download. This is also measured by the NDT tool. Figures 6 and 7 show the cumulative distribution of download and upload measurements on the three community networks considered. Both graphs are capped to a maximum throughput of 400 Mbps, as they contain long tails.

Figure 6 shows that a user on the the AWMN network on average experiences lower download speeds than on Ninux and guifi.net. The Ninux network especially logs many very high-speed download tests, as 30% of the measurements exceed 400 Mbps. Although of course very promising results, we consider these to be measurement errors where the nodes were located in data centers or other less realistic locations, as explained above. Because of the setup and the configuration of Community-Lab combined with M-Lab NDT, these results are hard to filter out. Figure 7, on the other hand, shows that the upload speed measurements show less difference between the three networks.

Figure 8 shows the download speed measurements on the same two nodes in the Ninux network as in figure 5. What is immediately visible, is that the download speeds are very

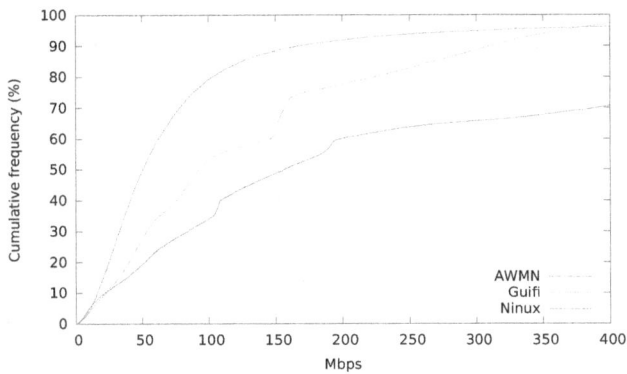

Figure 6: Cumulative distribution of download measurements, capped to 400 Mbps

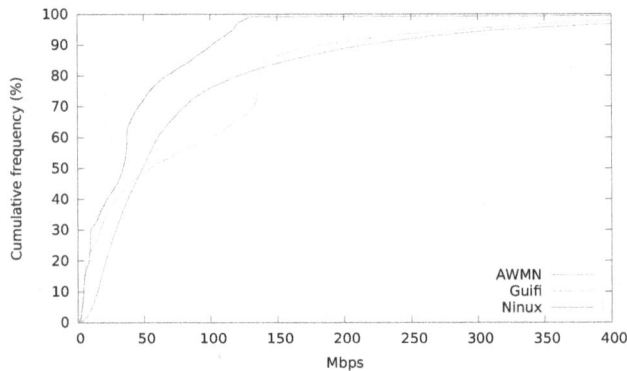

Figure 7: Cumulative distribution of upload measurements, capped to 400 Mbps

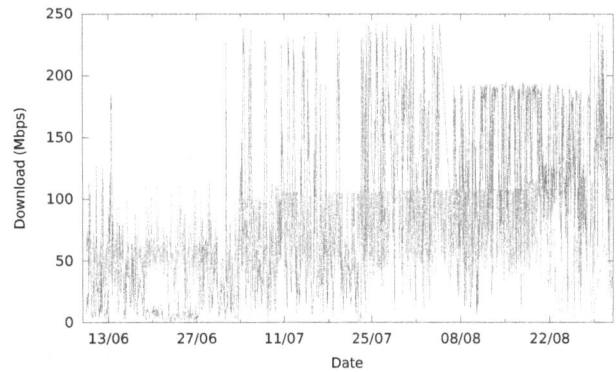

Figure 8: Download speeds, Ninux

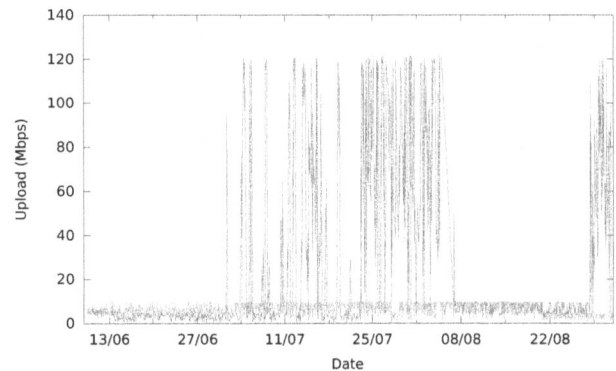

Figure 9: Upload speeds, Ninux

variable. However, for the green node (the one with relatively stable RTT times), most measurements lie around the same average throughout the duration of the tests. The red node, on the other hand, shows more erratic behaviour. For a relatively long duration in June, the download speeds measured are very low. These are encountered during a time when the RTT values are very high and unstable. However, in July the RTT values are still high and unstable, while the download speeds are considerably higher. This shows that RTT measurement based monitoring of the quality of a community network is insufficient to assess the overall performance experienced by the end-user.

Figure 9 shows the upload speed measurements for the same nodes in the Ninux network. Again, the results for the red node change suddenly at several points in time, while the values for the green node remain stable throughout the entire measurement period.

4.3 Comparison with Other ISPs in the Region

The experiment reported in this paper using Community-Lab nodes embedded in the three community networks has helped to raise the number of measurements contributed to M-Lab to allow comparisons with other ISPs. On the Ninux (through the FusoLab AS), guifi.net (through the guifi.net Foundation, labelled as "Fundacio Privada per a la Xarxa Lliure") and AWMN (as part of the LANCOM AS) net-

works, the number of measurements has reached the threshold of 200 samples within the same month, which enables the comparison with other ISPs in the respective countries.

A comparison of results of our measurements in M-Lab with equivalent measurements from top ISPs in the same countries should show how well community networks can serve its users. The resulting performance, measured by M-Lab tools such as NDT, for the three community networks under evaluation is among the top eight ISPs in each country. Figure 10 shows the results for the most typical measurement of median upload and download speed and median latency. The three networks are among the top eight ISPs in download speed. guifi.net is ranked first in Spain both in median upload speed and best median latency; Ninux (FusoLab) is ranked second in upload, and fourth in best latency; AWMN (part of LANCOM) is first in upload speed, 8th in best latency. In the area of Barcelona, where guifi.net has its connections to Internet carriers, the results are excellent: first in upload speed (guifi.net 7.82 Mbps, the Academic network 4.23 and Cableuropa ONO 3.31), third in download speed (Cableuropa-ONO 18.1 Mbps, the Academic network 9.8, guifi.net 9.79) and first in best latency (guifi.net 14 ms, Vodafone 25, Cableuropa-ONO 35).

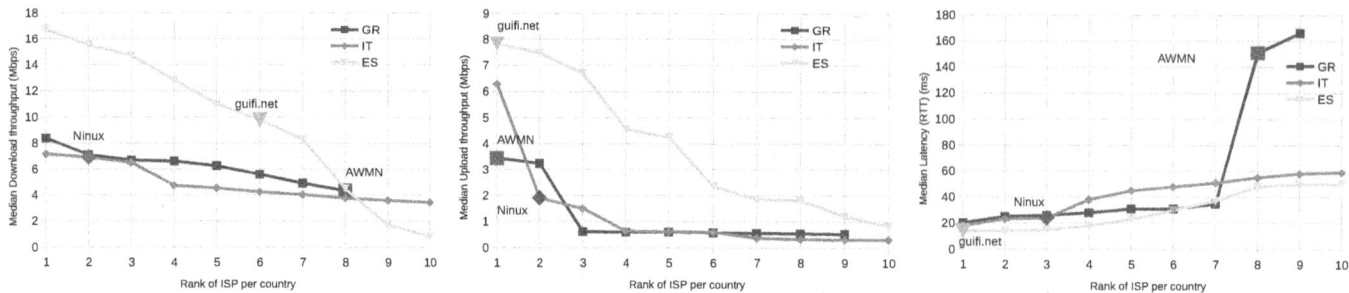

Figure 10: Median Download and Upload throughput (Mbps) and Latency (RTT in ms) per Country and ISP, sorted by Download speed (M-Lab July 2015)

Table 1: Values in Figure 10

ISP in Greece	Down	Up	RTT	ISP in Italy	Down	Up	RTT	ISP in Spain	Down	Up	RTT
Lancom (AWMN)	4.33	3.44	151	GARR	6.51	6.28	38	guifi.net	9.78	7.82	14
OF-Larissa	8.37	3.24	166	Fusolab (Ninux)	6.91	1.91	24	Telecable Ast.	14.7	6.69	18
TELLAS	6.69	0.61	26	Telecom IT	3.77	1.50	58	Euskaltel	15.51	4.55	15
FORTHNET	6.62	N/A	31	Convergenze	4.72	0.63	55	CESCA	9.79	4.23	48
Greek Research	8.85	N/A	20	UNIDATA	7.15	0.61	18	Cableuropa-ONO	12.83	2.36	37
OTE	4.90	0.58	31	FastWeb	3.44	0.60	45	CableTel Galicia	10.97	1.82	50
CYPRUS TA	6.26	0.56	25	Vodafone O.	4.02	0.37	59	PROCONO	16.73	1.2	23
ON	7.08	0.55	35	NGI	3.58	0.33	23	Jazz Telecom	3.19	0.67	76
Hellas OnLine	5.59	0.53	28	Tiscali IT	4.54	0.31	48	Iberbanda	0.8	0.61	99
				Wind Tel	4.23	0.31	51	Telefonica	1.72	0.54	74

5. IMPLICATIONS ON COMMUNITY NETWORKS FOR DEVELOPMENT

The study shows several areas to explore by researchers in networking, social and economics, practitioners and regulators.

The measurement results, despite being more favourable than we initially expected, all come from a well-know third party (M-Lab). Without going too far, we can easily say that the user experience perceived from users located where the probes are must be good to excellent. It is also relevant to see that, at country level, the three community networks are first or second in upload speed, with very symmetric transfer rates, a clear signal of good quality (QoE) and lack of the typical distinction between asymmetric client-oriented broadband connections versus much more expensive server-oriented connections. We encourage additional community networks to setup measurement points or encourage its users to contribute measurements that allow expanding this analysis.

Although it cannot be directly extrapolated to other countries, particularly in developing areas, the experience from many community networks around the world in all continents shows that community-driven cooperative initiatives can create network infrastructures run as a formal or informal network commons and bring connectivity to disconnected or under-served areas, as shown around the world[2] with contributions from nine community networks in North America, three from South America, six in Europe, and one in South Africa. Collaboration over the last two years with UWC in South Africa in the development of a local community network has shown in detail how remote rural communities can bootstrap network infrastructure offering voice and more recently data services to local communities where no commercial models would initially work. The resulting model is described in [19] and in a booklet[25]. These re-

sults show how community networks can satisfy the local needs of citizens, administration and businesses. Instead of extracting money from the community towards big Telecom operators, the study shows ways where the money flow can go to local entrepreneurs and start-ups who do maintenance, troubleshooting, and computer help for local users, including local schools and community groups. This can create a sustainable ecosystem, even a competitive market, of local businesses that contribute to local development. In fact, guifi.net has enabled local business models, with about 270 professional installers involved, including about 15 local micro-ISPs. However this socio-economic impact has only been studied with sufficient detail in guifi.net.

Regarding measurable impact in population from underserved areas guifi.net has collected evidences. guifi.net is mainly deployed in the region of Catalonia, starting from a rural area with very bad or nearly no connectivity [3]. Statistical data is available from a large scale survey about penetration of the bandwidth and Internet access in the households of Catalonia in 2013, released by the public Catalan Statistics Institute (IDESCAT)[4] detailed for each of the 42 counties in Catalonia. Despite the fact that Catalonia is about three points above the Spanish average, it is still seven points below the European average. The Catalan county with the best results and the only one above the EU average, is Osona, where guifi.net was born. It is surprising to see higher penetration than in Barcelona, the largest urban area in the region of study. Moreover, it is the only county where broadband access is above Internet access (showing that guifi.net is a local broadband infrastructure where most but not everyone use it to reach the Internet, and many also use it for internal communication). The indicators of other counties where guifi.net presence is significant, such

---

[4]http://www.idescat.cat Data source: http://www.idescat.cat/novetats/?id=1724&lang=en

as Bages and Baix Ebre, are also larger when compared to similar counties but where guifi.net presence is irrelevant.

While Ninux and AWMN are yet limited to their own countries, local initiatives following the guifi.net network commons model [3] and using its tools are starting or have developed in other regions of the world. In Africa a few nodes are operational in Ethiopia (about 20 are planned). More are planned in Morocco, Nigeria and Occidental Sahara. In Asia there is one operational node in Pakistan and 8 planned nodes in India. In America there are 5 operational nodes and 22 planned or under construction in Argentina, 5 operational in Colombia, for a total of 169 nodes in different states of development, including in Bolivia, Brazil, Chile, Cuba, Ecuador, El Salvador, Haiti, Mexico, Nicaragua, Paraguay, Peru, the Dominican Republic, the United States of America, Uruguay, and Venezuela.

The principles, governance mechanisms, and results, in terms of service (QoE) and coverage, shown by these community networks among many other around the world demonstrates the effectiveness of the model to serve the needs for connectivity and participation in the digital society for all, particularly for the underserved by other commercial or public offerings. These community networks become a *collective good* or a peer property in which participants contribute their efforts and contribute goods (routers, links, and servers) that are shared to build a computer network. Its development is a *social production* or a peer production because the participants work cooperatively, at local scale, to deploy an infrastructure and build network islands. The resulting infrastructure is governed as a *common-pool resource (CPR)* to avoid the tragedy of congestion or destruction by abuse and to become a key resource for widespread participation and socio-economic development.

In fact, the International Telecommunication Union in its report[22] in 2008 proposed regulatory reforms to promote widespread, affordable broadband access, rooted in enabling and promoting diverse practises of sharing. Similarly as with competition, sharing is seen as very beneficial in multiple aspects such as passive infrastructure like ducts, civil works, towers, poles, rights of pass, radio spectrum, international gateways, undersea cables, mobile roaming, content distribution. A recent study[15] also confirms the opportunities, economic benefits, and its growth, with best practises identified in Africa (Kenya, Nigeria, South Africa, Uganda, Côte d'Ivoire, Mozambique), and Asia (India, Indonesia, Thailand and the Philippines). Therefore infrastructure sharing appears to be a good principle for national regulators to promote cost effective and therefore sustainable network infrastructures, that can enable competitive service offers.

African countries are known for network inefficiencies: excessive latency due to circuitous routing paths, going many times across Internet exchanges in Europe to connect two nearby countries[13], and lack of local caches and servers[24]. Our measurements show that the observed communities rank among the best infrastructures in median upload speed and median latency, with allows and promotes the production and provision of local content. The network commons model enables and promotes traffic exchange among nearby networks. This is demonstrated by guifi.net acting as a de-facto regional 10 Gbps backbone Internet exchange that interconnects with small local ISPs reducing latency and widening the offer of local services and content. In fact, these non-profit neutral initiatives can help build cooperative efforts that can result in the bootstrapping of local markets for connectivity and services.

Recent studies by the European Commission[10] show that many studies conclude that broadband has a significant and positive impact on economic growth (measured by GDP) through improvements in productivity, a positive relationship between broadband speed and GDP, with greater effects for countries and regions with lower income. The study arguments that high-speed networking service shares characteristics of a public good (such as street lighting) that can be supplied by different levels of public and private sector collaborations. Although this is part of the EU Broadband Vision, it applies globally, and community networks appear to be a successful model to cooperative build and improve infrastructures to achieve that vision under a network commons model.

In fact, the feasibility of a community network and its network commons model of a local network infrastructure requires the support of local governments, as they regulate access to public spaces, a neutral telecom regulation that allows and promotes low barriers for new infrastructures, a local community that has the need, motivation and experience to manage a commons resource, and a team of local champions that have the vision, will, leadership and credibility of the locals.

6. CONCLUSION

In this paper we presented the results from the first end-to-end measurement campaign in community networks using the M-Lab measurement infrastructure and the Community-Lab experimental testbed embedded in several community networks. The results from a user perspective with NDT show promising network performance in general, however with high variability over time and over different nodes. This is clearly illustrated by measurement results which exceed multiple seconds.

The contribution of many more NDT measurements to M-Lab originating in community networks from our experiments has enabled a comparison with other ISPs of the performance of the Internet access service and the quality of experience (QoE) from a user perspective. The country results show that each community network is among the top eight ISPs in its country in end-user network metrics, and achieves top results for upload speeds, which shows the symmetry of connectivity compared to the typical asymmetric service from commercial ISPs.

Despite several community networks have proven their feasibility with sustainable local infrastructures and society impact, our experimental results can not be considered conclusive so far. Therefore, we believe more prolonged and extensive measurements are necessary.

Moreover, we plan future work to consider additional quantitative analysis of Quality of Experience in community networks, as end-users from the communities are fairly happy with the results shown in this work. Additionally, it would make sense to correlate the end-to-end data with more information on the underlying network, including topology and e.g. routing algorithm knowledge. Given the requirements of real-time, correlated data, this might be particularly hard to realise.

Results from community networks and recommendations from global organisations such as ITU, Deloitte, APC and the European Commission show the great direct and indirect impact of cooperative (sharing) efforts to develop networking infrastructure and services under a commons model of governance. Supportive regulation and financial support of these initiatives can have a major impact in local socio-economic development and quality of life improvements, even with greater effects in developing areas.

7. ACKNOWLEDGEMENTS

This work is supported by the European Community Framework Programme 7, FIRE Initiative projects "Community Networks Testbed for the Future Internet" (CONFINE), FP7-288535, and by the Spanish government under contract TIN2013-47245-C2-1-R.

8. REFERENCES

[1] B. Augustin, X. Cuvellier, B. Orgogozo, F. Viger, T. Friedman, M. Latapy, C. Magnien, and R. Texeira. Avoiding traceroute anomalies with paris traceroute. In *Proc. ACM SIGCOMM Internet Measurement Conference*, 2006.

[2] J. Avonts, B. Braem, and C. Blondia. A questionnaire based examination of community networks. In *Wireless and Mobile Computing, Networking and Communications (WiMob), 2013 IEEE 9th International Conference on*, pages 8–15. IEEE, 2013.

[3] R. Baig, R. Roca, F. Freitag, and L. Navarro. guifi.net, a crowdsourced network infrastructure held in common. *Computer Networks*, 2015.

[4] V. Bajpai, S. J. Eravuchira, and J. Schönwälder. Lessons learned from using the ripe atlas platform for measurement research. *ACM SIGCOMM Computer Communication Review*, 45(3):35–42, 2015.

[5] B. Braem, C. Blondia, C. Barz, H. Rogge, F. Freitag, L. Navarro, J. Bonicioli, S. Papathanasiou, P. Escrich, R. Baig Viñas, et al. A case for research with and on community networks. *ACM SIGCOMM Computer Communication Review*, 43(3):68–73, 2013.

[6] P. Calyam and M. Swany. Research challenges in future multi-domain network performance measurement and monitoring. *ACM SIGCOMM Computer Communication Review*, 45(3):29–34, 2015.

[7] Carlson. http://e2epi.internet2.edu/ndt/, 2015.

[8] T. Clausen and P. Jacquet. Optimized link state routing protocol (olsr). Technical report, 2003.

[9] J. Crowcroft, A. Wolisz, A. Sathiaseelan, J. Crowcroft, A. Wolisz, and A. Sathiaseelan. Towards an affordable internet access for everyone: The quest for enabling universal service commitment (dagstuhl seminar 14471). *Dagstuhl Reports*, 4:78–1377, 2014.

[10] E. C. DG-CONNECT. Note on the socio-economic benefits of high-speed broadband. 2015.

[11] C. Dovrolis, K. Gummadi, A. Kuzmanovic, and S. D. Meinrath. Measurement lab: Overview and an invitation to the research community. *ACM*

[12] P. Escrich. https://libre-mesh.org/, 2014.

[13] A. Gupta, M. Calder, N. Feamster, M. Chetty, E. Calandro, and E. Katz-Bassett. Peering at the internet's frontier: A first look at isp interconnectivity in africa. In *Proceedings of the 15th International Conference on Passive and Active Measurement - Volume 8362*, PAM 2014, pages 204–213, New York, NY, USA, 2014. Springer-Verlag New York, Inc.

[14] E. Katz-Bassett, H. Madhyastha, V. Adhikari, C. Scott, J. Sherry, P. van Wesep, T. Anderson, and A. Krishnamurthy. Reverse traceroute. In *USENIX Symposium on Networked Systems Design & Implementation (NSDI)*, 2010.

[15] D. LLP. Unlocking broadband for all: Broadband infrastructure sharing policies and strategies in emerging markets. 2015.

[16] NLNOG. http://ring.nlnog.net//, 2015.

[17] E. Ostrom. *Governing the commons: the evolution of institutions for collective action*. Cambridge University Press, Nov. 1990.

[18] P. Pitarch Miguel. Proxy performance analysis in a community wireless network. 2013.

[19] C. Rey-Moreno, Z. Roro, W. D. Tucker, M. J. Siya, N. J. Bidwell, and J. Simo-Reigadas. Experiences, challenges and lessons from rolling out a rural wifi mesh network. In *Proceedings of the 3rd ACM Symposium on Computing for Development*, ACM DEV '13, pages 11:1–11:10, New York, NY, USA, 2013. ACM.

[20] S. Sundaresan, W. De Donato, N. Feamster, R. Teixeira, S. Crawford, and A. Pescapè. Broadband internet performance: a view from the gateway. In *ACM SIGCOMM computer communication review*, volume 41, pages 134–145. ACM, 2011.

[21] J. Tigani and S. Naidu. *Google BigQuery Analytics*. John Wiley & Sons, 2014.

[22] I. T. Union. Trends in telecommunication reform 2008: Six degrees of sharing. 2008.

[23] D. Vega, L. Cerda-Alabern, L. Navarro, and R. Meseguer. Topology patterns of a community network: Guifi. net. In *Wireless and Mobile Computing, Networking and Communications (WiMob), 2012 IEEE 8th International Conference on*, pages 612–619. IEEE, 2012.

[24] Y. Zaki, J. Chen, T. Pötsch, T. Ahmad, and L. Subramanian. Dissecting web latency in ghana. In *Proceedings of the 2014 Conference on Internet Measurement Conference*, IMC '14, pages 241–248, New York, NY, USA, 2014. ACM.

[25] Zenzeleni. *Zenzeleni. Do It For Yourselves: An Introduction to Community Telecomunications Networks*. University of Western Cape, September 2015.

Optimizing Mobile Application Communication for Challenged Network Environments

Waylon Brunette[1], Morgan Vigil[2], Fahad Pervaiz[1], Shahar Levari[1], Gaetano Borriello[1], and Richard Anderson[1]

[1] Department of Computer Science and Engineering, University of Washington, Seattle, WA,
{wrb,fahadp,levaris,gaetano,anderson}@cse.uw.edu

[2] Department of Computer Science, University of California Santa Barbara, Santa Barbara, CA,
mvigil@cs.ucsb.edu

ABSTRACT

Designing mobile applications for challenged network environments necessitates new abstractions that target deployment architects, non-developers who are charged with adapting an ensemble of off-the-shelf software to a deployment context. Data transfer is integral to mobile application design and deployments have inherent and contextual requirements that determine what data should be transferred and when. In this paper, we investigate building mobile applications in challenged network environments by focusing on abstractions to support disconnected environments and areas of sparse heterogeneous connectivity. We explore and characterize various methods of transmitting data using: existing synchronization tools, peer-to-peer communication, and sparse networks. We also introduce a new software tool called ODK Submit to help streamline application customization to challenged network environments.

Keywords

mobile devices; Open Data Kit; application framework; multiple-channel communication; peer-to-peer networking; multi-network

1. INTRODUCTION

Network connectivity is a persistent concern for organizations working in resource-constrained contexts because 1) connectivity is not always present, 2) the type of connectivity often varies by location, 3) data transmission costs may be too high for limited budgets, and 4) administrative protocols restrict how data can be transmitted and stored. These constraints can inhibit a mobile application's capabilities, implying that deploying organizations need to adapt their application to factor in connectivity and other contextual limitations. Various ICTD research projects have focused on improving connectivity by extending communication infrastructures (e.g., long distance WiFi, village base station, mesh networks). However, customizable software frameworks could help improve mobile applications' capabilities in challenged network environments until universal connectivity is available and affordable everywhere.

Mobile devices often have several built-in transmission capabilities (e.g., GSM, WiFi, peer-to-peer) but lack a flexible framework to systematically adjust to changing network conditions based on an application's deployment requirements instead of simple connectivity available recognition. Data transfer is integral to an application's usage and context making it difficult to create a universal solution to address diverse requirements. This paper argues for creating a software tool that selects appropriate data for transmission over available network channels and can be customized by deployment architects. Deployment architects are generally non-programmers who adapt an ensemble of off-the-shelf software to a deployment context. Providing flexible transmission management to deployment architects could improve the feasibility of deploying mobile information systems in challenged network environments by enabling application-level communication optimizations.

Challenges for deploying applications in developing regions have been documented [10] and include: low literacy, limited technical personnel, use of inexpensive multipurpose devices, and context-specific customization. Research initiatives that address some of these challenges have focused on interface design [16, 28] and rapid customizability [19] to produce frameworks such as Open Data Kit (ODK) [11, 19] and CommCare [17]. These frameworks focus on lowering technical barriers to assist organizations in deploying information services in resource-challenged contexts and are designed for disconnected operation. However, ODK leaves decisions about when and how to transmit data to the end-user which leads to possible inefficiencies with respect to transmission costs or deadlines.

In this paper, we examine options to enable non-developers to adapt their mobile application to various network conditions. To motivate the need for a configurable data transmission tool that operates in sparse connectivity, we discuss challenges with existing paradigms, characterize the performance of popular data transfer apps from different locations, and formalize sources of transmission meta-data into three perspectives. We then propose an (ODK) extension called ODK Submit that uses an organization's deployment parameters to guide communication decisions. Submit enables application-level communication optimization of sparse heterogeneous networks by sending appropriate data over available network infrastructure or peer-to-peer communications. We also investigate and characterize Android peer-to-peer transfer methods to better understand deployment trade-offs for different use cases.

ACM DEV 2015, December 1–2, 2015, London, United Kingdom.
© 2015 ACM. ISBN 978-1-4503-3490-7/15/12 ...$15.00.
DOI: http://dx.doi.org/10.1145/2830629.2830644

2. CHALLENGES BUILDING MOBILE APPS

Building and deploying mobile data collection and decision support applications can be challenging, particularly because the task of bridging the design-reality gap [20] is left to the non-programmer deployment architect. In this section, we outline some of these challenges and discuss assumptions that inhibit deployment customization across diversely challenged networking environments.

2.1 Existing Paradigms

Challenges with deployments are often magnified in resource-constrained environments because of insufficient design paradigms.

Uniform Data: Existing routing paradigms often assume that inherent data properties are sufficient to determine the appropriate network technology for data transmission [15, 24]. This assumption overlooks the fact that data is not uniform but instead has two distinctive qualities: inherent qualities *and* contextual qualities. Inherent qualities of data, such as data types and sizes, are independent of the application in use. In contrast, contextual data qualities are necessarily dependent on use scenarios. Examples include data priority, data importance, deadlines, and precedence. Contextual qualities such as an organization's data policy and local laws can also affect how data is stored and transmitted (e.g., private medical records vs public data).

Single-Task Mobile Apps: Resource-constrained environments often lack enough technical personnel to build and customize information systems. This leads organizations to use productivity software (e.g., MS Excel, MS Word) to create solutions that can be customized by staff having little programming expertise. These tools have been designed for conventional PCs that are poorly suited to these limited infrastructure environments. Although mobile devices are well-suited to scarce connectivity and sporadic grid power, mobile software tools do not yet offer the same range of features as customizable PC productivity tools. Instead, several small apps focused on single tasks are created leading to specialized apps with minimal customizability. Mobile frameworks, such as ODK 2.0 [11], are needed to help organizations customize and refine their apps to their context while maintaining the single-task paradigm. Additionally, with single-task apps there is often limited coordination of system resources making it challenging to conserve resources. For example multiple apps could simultaneously attempt to communicate when connectivity becomes available.

Similar Transmission Cost: Developers often choose a single transport protocol such as TCP/IP or SMS because of systems abstractions and availability of networks for the original deployment location. However, the cost associated with connectivity can vary across different regions creating feasibility issues for deploying applications in varying contexts. For example, a 500MB post-paid mobile broadband subscription in Europe costs 1% of per capita GNI. By contrast, the same subscription costs 38% of the average per capita GNI across Africa [6]. Even as the cost of broadband subscriptions falls globally, an entry-level broadband connection continues to cost over 100% of per capita GNI in less developed countries, as compared to only 1% of per capita GNI in more developed countries [3]. Even in developed regions, there are communities yet to be covered. In the US, broadband coverage on Native American reservations is less than 10% per capita [5], despite coverage of over 70% for the rest of the country. Although technologies with universal connectivity options like satellite uplinks exist, financially constrained organizations cannot afford them. Restricting data transmission to a single protocol can lead to missed opportunities in optimizing transmission costs based on contextual qualities of data.

2.2 Example Usage Scenarios

Based on our deployment experiences, we outline scenarios that highlight networking challenges and the benefits of leveraging contextual data properties when making data transmission decisions.

Scenario 1 - Site Visits: The Government of Punjab's Health Department (Pakistan) used ODK to document the workload, staff attendance, and available medical supplies at health clinics. To identify shortages it dispatched inspectors to verify inventory and photograph workers for attendance verification. This information was transmitted to ODK servers; however, only the medical supply data was time-sensitive. The photographic verification of attendance was a human resource concern and did not require urgent delivery, yet the non-urgent piece of data dominated the transmission cost because the size of the photos are large.

Scenario 2 - Forest Monitoring: The Surui, an indigenous Amazonian tribe, uses ODK to inventory their forests for selling carbon credits in voluntary carbon markets to create a tribal income stream and protect their environment. Workers hike or boat into remote areas with little connectivity and spend days or weeks conducting carbon inventories. Workers inventory a section of the forest to determine the amount of carbon stored in the trees and upload this data on their return. Data loss and/or corruption can be expensive since expeditions are time-consuming. A simple solution to combat data loss is to replicate data in the field across multiple devices. When workers are in the field they also record signs of illegal logging activity. In contrast to inventory data, reports of illegal activity should be quickly transmitted to authorities via any available connectivity (possibly expensive) to increase the likelihood of catching the perpetrators.

Scenario 3 - Community Health: Community Healthcare Workers (CHW) frequently travel to villages to provide basic care. Their visits at households or low-end clinics provide an opportunity to document patients, perform a quick analysis of whether a patient requires referral for further attention, and educate people about best-practices[16, 26]. For example, AMPATH's home-based HIV/AIDS counseling and testing program in Kenya used ODK to reach over a million patients at home. However, CHWs' duties can vary per organization and country thus producing variation in data priority. For example, supervisors may need to receive updates frequently about which tasks have been completed (via SMS or cellular data) but the transfer of patients' medical data may be postponed until a WiFi connection is available. Ministries of Health would likely want an immediate notification on the detection of Ebola or Polio to rapidly quarantine Ebola areas to contain an outbreak or quickly deploy polio vaccination teams to surrounding communities.

2.3 Existing Synchronization Tools

Cloud-based data storage and synchronization systems often serve as building blocks for application development. To better understand the performance of existing tools, we evaluated the operation of three popular cloud-based systems: Dropbox [1], OneDrive [2], and Google Drive [3]. We measured performance on Android devices using libraries provided by the cloud services since we are evaluating developer options for creating mobile data applications. Since not all contexts suffer from challenged networks, we chose three cities (Lima, Peru; Kisumu, Kenya; & Lahore, Pakistan)in somewhat resource-constrained countries. Large cities have better infrastructure than their rural counterparts demonstrating best-case scenarios for countries with resource constraints. To provide context for the

---

[1] https://www.dropbox.com/home
[2] https://onedrive.live.com/
[3] https://www.google.com/drive/

Table 1: Network measurements from various locations

LOCATION	RTT (ms)	BANDWIDTH (Mbps)	LOSS (%)
Lima	1173.0	1.05	0
Lahore	207.0	1.05	0
Chowchilla	154.6	1.69	0
Pala	63.0	6.93	0
Seattle	39.2	11.00	0

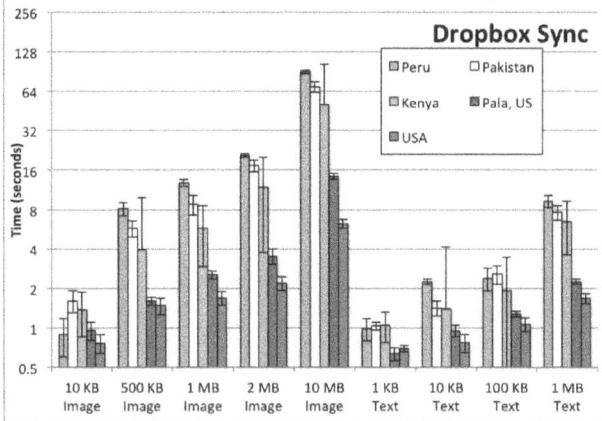

Figure 1: Dropbox file synchronization performance with varying file sizes using mobile data connection. (Log Scale)

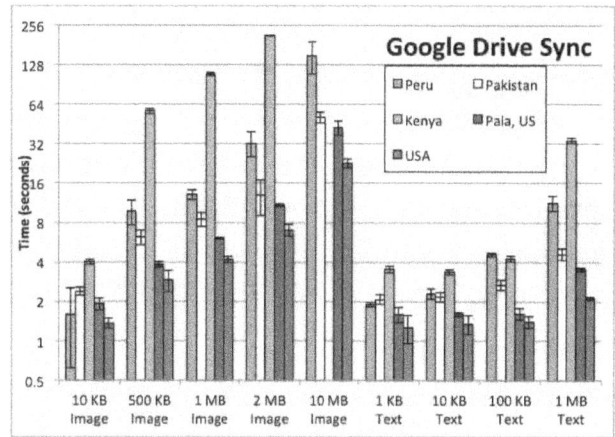

Figure 2: Google Drive file synchronization performance with varying file sizes using mobile data connection. (Log Scale)

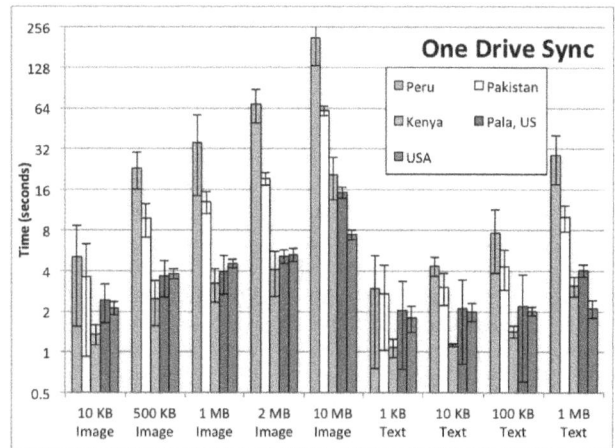

Figure 3: OneDrive file synchronization performance with varying file sizes using mobile data connection. (Log Scale)

performance divide between urban and rural areas, we also evaluate the performance differences of an urban city in the U.S. (Seattle, WA) and rural towns in the U.S. (Chowchilla and Pala, CA), which have populations of ~600K, ~18K and ~1.5K respectively. Service carriers used in the experiments include Claro (Lima), Telenor (Lahore), T-Mobile (Seattle), Verizon (Chowchilla) and AT&T (Pala). File synchronization was measured 15 times per service using 10KB, 500KB, 1MB, 2MB, and 10MB of image files and 1KB, 10KB, 100KB, and 1MB of text files.

Table 1 shows network statistics recorded using ping and iperf tools. Cellular networks in Lima and Lahore tend to be highly latent with low bandwidth capacity with Lima experiencing the longest round trip times at 1,173 ms. Seattle was 5 and 30 times faster than Lahore and Lima respectively. Mobile network connectivity in rural US test sites was significantly lower as Chowchilla had 1.69 Mbps (154.6ms RTT) and Pala had 6.93 Mbps (63.02ms RTT) compared to Seattle's 11 Mbps (39.2ms RTT) high speed bandwidth. We emphasize that network availability and performance in Chowchilla and Pala represent a best case for rural connectivity in the US, as measurements were taken from the more densely populated town centers. We also note that poor network infrastructure is not just a problem for developing countries, but for rural parts of developed countries as well.

Results from the performance tests shown in Figure 1, 2 and 3, reveal that Dropbox performs better with all tested file sizes. This is unsurprising as the Dropbox API compresses all files prior to transmission, while Google Drive and OneDrive do not. OneDrive only performed differential synchronization of Microsoft Office files, which excludes many large media files. Google Drive did not use differential synchronization for any file, causing it to use the most bandwidth per file update of the three evaluated options. When accessed via the developer API, Dropbox does not provide differential synchronization, though it does perform data compression prior to transmission. We also note that OneDrive experienced higher variability in file transfer times than Google Drive and Dropbox, with a standard deviation of 5.2 seconds compared to 2.3 seconds for Dropbox and 4.6 seconds for Google Drive. Even though Lahore, Kisumu, and Lima have access to mobile Internet, the performance of the connections were inconsistent and more prone to high latency and limited bandwidth than connectivity in Seattle.

Our measurements demonstrate that common data synchronization platforms experience issues in varying network environments as they all experienced longer file transfer times and greater variability in transfer time in resource-constrained environments. Based on our experiments, Dropbox would be the preferable 'off-the-shelf' solution, followed by Google Drive, then OneDrive. However, there are still issues that these cloud synchronization platforms do not address such as: 1) they lack support to enable organizations to treat data differently based on contextual data qualities; and 2) they are TCP/IP based and do not allow for alternative connectivity options in challenged network environments.

3. PERSPECTIVES

Data is often transmitted using whatever protocol a software developer selected when developing the software. Dynamic selection of available protocols based on a deployment's context and user location could improve connectivity in challenged network environments. To better facilitate dynamic selection the traditional concept of the TCP/IP Application Layer [27] should be extended to include: 1) metadata from the platform about connectivity; 2) data properties from the software/application developer; and 3) contextual constraints from an deployment architect. The deployment architect is the domain expert who deploys the software in the field and customizes it to meet the needs of their business or organization. The deployment architect and the software developer both

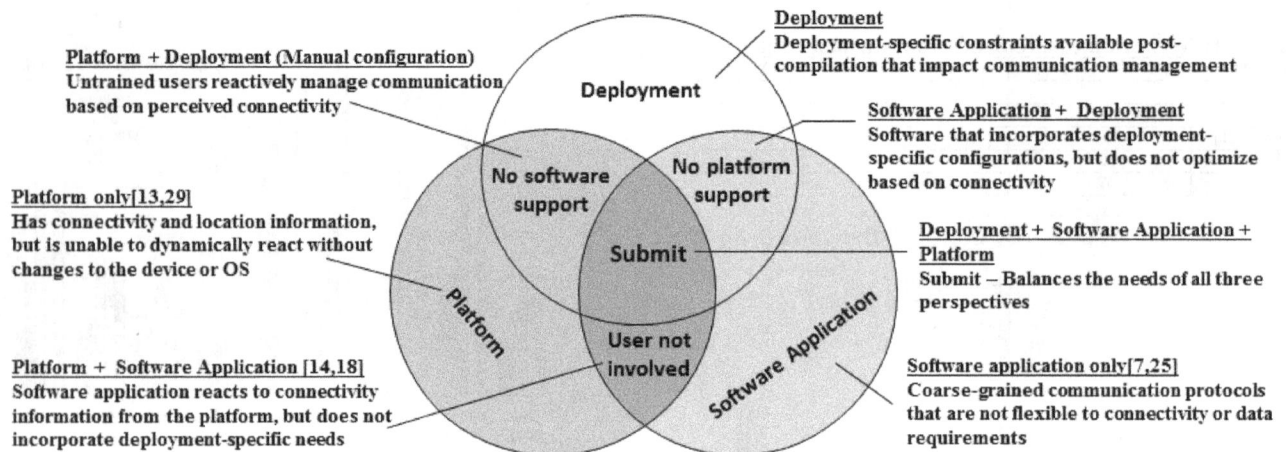

Figure 4: Design space of communication solutions for utilization of heterogeneous networks

provide vital information that is necessary to understand an application's communication context and constraints. Our approach of breaking the application layer into parts is similar to Martins et al.'s approach to coordinating different perspectives on system power[22]. We find their multi-perspective approach to optimizing battery life suitable to optimizing communication resources. As Martins et al. point out: *"the user needs to drive"*; claiming: *"1) The OS cannot always know the resource priorities of all applications; 2) applications cannot always know the functionality priorities of the end-user; and 3) users should choose the right level, trading off functionality versus lifetime."* Overall we agree with these insights with the exception of focusing on the end-user. Instead, there is often a deployment architect that handles organization-wide restrictions and imposes constraints derived from deployment considerations. The focus on a deployment architect in addition to the end-user is an important distinction, as grouping developer, deployment architects, and end-users into a single concept can make system optimizations difficult. Figure 4 shows how Submit aims to combine information from the network perspectives of the platform, software developer, and deployment architect to efficiently manage communication resources to relieve the end-user of communication management.

Platform Perspective - The platform perspective encompasses the device and operating system perspectives on connectivity and mobility. For instance an Android device can: detect the type of available network connectivity, detect device mobility, estimate available data capacity, and estimate the device's geographical location. Location and mobility information enable Submit to possibly infer the duration of a connection and apply regional data policies. However, the platform is unaware of what policies, financial restrictions, and other data priorities a user or organization may want applied. There are numerous works related to a platform-only communication management scheme as multiple communication channels can be dynamically allocated based on availability or bonded to create compound channels with greater throughput capacity[14, 30]. While Submit dynamically schedules traffic based on channel availability, it does so without modifying the underlying platform to combine or bond channels.

Application Developer Perspective - The application developer perspective encompasses issues relating to the functionality of a mobile application. A developer understands the inherent properties such as the type and typical size of data that can help Submit develop an appropriate cost model. Unfortunately, a developer may be biased towards a particular communication medium and may not bother including functionality to support alternatives such as: local off-line storage to support disconnected operation or transmission

of summary data over SMS. Thus, developers constrain communication resources via software design and protocol selection. Some examples of developer limitations include apps that communicate over 2G and 2.5G networks exclusively rather than 3G data networks[7, 29]. Likewise, a single protocol limits what an app can effectively communicate, for example, transmitting binary over SMS is non-optimal. Furthermore, a developer likely does not fully understand how a future user may want to deploy the application in varying context with limiting data policies and budgets.

Application Deployment Perspective - The deployment perspective encompasses issues relating to contextual deployment requirements that should be incorporated by a deployment architect, as the dynamic contextual information is not available when the developer compiles the software. A deployment's requirements can provide important metadata including information prioritization, and financial restrictions that may change during the lifetime of the project. ODK tools are designed to be general-purpose and have been deployed in a variety of settings including public health, environmental conservation, and census applications. These domains have different needs and real-time information may change how data is transmitted. For example, in a health application, a CHW may find a patient needing immediate referral to a care facility. This message is urgent and should be sent with a different priority than updating a healthy patient's medical record. Usage context is not predictable by the developer nor can the platform impose that one particular channel be used as that channel may not be available. Depending on the urgency of the data it may be necessary to send the same data over multiple channels to ensure delivery or possibly reach multiple destinations. Submit seeks to remove the user burden of actively monitoring the status communication events.

Overlapping Perspectives - There are points where each of these perspectives overlap and interact. The most commonly combined perspectives are those of the platform and software application. Opportunistic off-loading approaches combine the connectivity awareness of the platform with software application protocol decisions [9, 18, 21]. While this approach provides more guidance than either platform or software developer perspectives alone, it results in coarse-grained communication automation. In contrast, web applications exemplify the absence of the platform perspective [4, 1]. While there is value to platform-independent systems, platform information about connectivity and location is necessary for maintaining historical connectivity models. Submit's design incorporates information from the different perspectives and attempts to hone how and when information is transmitted in challenged networking environments.

4. ODK SUBMIT

To address challenges faced by deployment architects trying to customize their deployments in challenged network contexts, we introduce ODK Submit. Submit combines information from the three perspectives to optimize data transmission in challenged network environments by utilizing multiple heterogeneous networks (e.g., cellular, Wi-Fi, peer-to-peer) based on contextual data properties and available connectivity. Urgent data can be transmitted over more pervasive, higher cost networks, while less urgent data can be transmitted opportunistically over less pervasive, lower-cost networks. ODK deployments are common in rural environments with sometimes sparse connectivity. In a May/June 2015 online survey of the ODK community by Cobb and Sudar et al. [13], 48 out of 56 respondents who deploy mobile devices for data collection reported deployments in rural environments. Respondents from all environments reported that the total size of data collected varied considerably with 19.6% collected gigabytes, 53.6% collected megabytes, 10.7% collected kilobytes of data, and 16.1% did not know. Transmitting gigabytes over expensive connections could potentially be cost prohibitive so understanding how important a piece of data is crucial when deciding to transmit over expensive connections.

The data transmission method selected should be based on an organization's usage model and priorities, as a one size fits all solution will not work for the variety of ICTD use cases. Examples outlined in Section 2.2 have varying requirements from the deployment perspective. For example, forest workers do not have reliable access to electricity, potentially for weeks, making battery life the highest priority. Occasionally replicating data between devices in the field can reduce the chance of data loss. Data importance and other data properties set by a deployment architect should determine when and how much data to replicate to conserve battery life. In contrast, CHWs have better access to power and experience variation in the frequency in which they come into range of inexpensive connectivity (e.g., Wi-Fi at a clinic) and how often they meet other CHWs in the field. As CHWs meet in remote areas, peer-to-peer technologies could be used to transfer data so that a CHW with more clinic visits could act as a Data MULE [25] and transport information with low priority, reducing the amount of data that needs to be sent over costly cellular networks.

To facilitate diverse application requirements, Submit leverages ODK 2.0's XLSX format to specify parameters. ODK users already utilize the XLSX format to specify names of input data fields, define the field's data type, provide question text, flow logic, and other information. We are exploring the use of a basic set of parameters that deployment architects can input into the XLSX system in relative terms (1-10 scale), including data priority (how quickly the data should be transmitted) and data importance (how important it is that the data not get lost). Additionally, we are investigating the provision of deadlines in terms of delta after the data was collected. To minimize the burden on the deployment architect, all parameters are kept optional and - if unspecified - automatically set to lowest values, causing the system to optimize for low-cost routing. Since network costs vary across geographies, Submit requires an organization to create a cost model by specifying a configuration file with cost per byte or cost per message for each transmission medium.

Submit helps to simplify mobile app development by managing connections, providing a user interface (UI), and abstracting various transmission protocol libraries. For long periods in disconnected environments Submit supports peer-to-peer data transfer using Wi-Fi Direct, Bluetooth, both versions of NFC available on Android, and QR Codes. Submit simplifies the process of leveraging Android's peer-to-peer networking capabilities by notifying users when to exchange data and includes abstractions that simplify

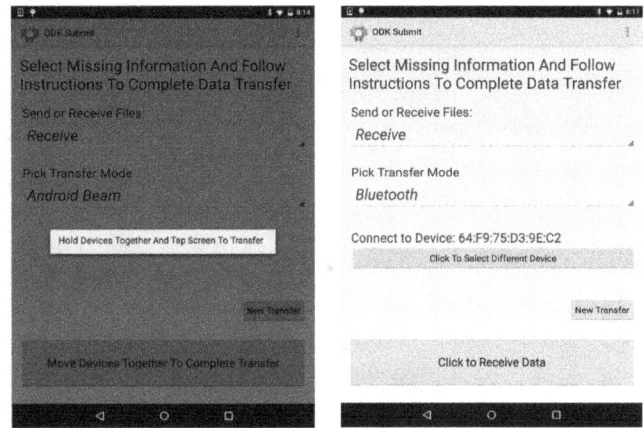

Figure 5: Submit's peer-to-peer transmission screen showing an example of NFC (left) and Bluetooth (right) transmission.

peer-to-peer connection setup. Deployment architects can predetermine parameters for peer-to-peer communication, such as which transfer mode to use. If necessary, Submit presents an unified peer-to-peer interface (shown in Figure 5) to the user prompting them for missing information (e.g., select Bluetooth device to transmit). Additionally, since many synchronization protocols are complex and possibly proprietary, it would be difficult to create a generic tool that conformed to all possible synchronization protocols. Instead, Submit functions as a module that enables developers to flexibly integrate their app-specific protocols with Submit's networking logic. For example, Submit only requires an app to provide contextual properties and metadata (e.g., type, size, priority) and allows a mobile app to maintain ownership of transmission protocols. This means the choice to use Submit does not preclude the use of another sync protocol or encryption schemes as an app can leverage Submit's communication management for only a subset of its data.

4.1 System Design

Submit is an Android service that coordinates data communication by providing channel monitoring and transmission scheduling mechanisms to Android apps. For the purposes of this section, the term client app refers to any Android app that binds to Submit's Android service. Submit provides software developers with an interface that abstracts communication channels and flexibly handles data ownership and application-specific synchronization issues. Submit is designed to separate application logic from the network routing logic with a communication system that provides extensibility in terms of: 1) adding transmission channels; 2) modifying transmission channel selection; and 3) handling complex data ownership and application-specific synchronization issues. Submit's service API exposes communication scheduling mechanisms that client apps use to either 1) delegate responsibility of transmitting data to Submit; or 2) register to receive notifications when appropriate network channels are available. When using Submit for notification purposes, a client app takes responsibility to transmit its data with its own possibly proprietary or complex protocol.

Client apps specify two types of objects to interface with Submit: 1) the DataPropertiesObject and 2) the SendObject. The DataPropertiesObject contains metadata that describe the data to be transmitted. The properties supplied include: data size, data urgency, data fragmentability, and reliability requirements. The inherent properties are derived from the perspective of the developer representing "normal" sized data for the client app as an app that primarily transmits responses to survey questions has larger "normal" data than an app that primarily transmits simple reminders the size of SMS

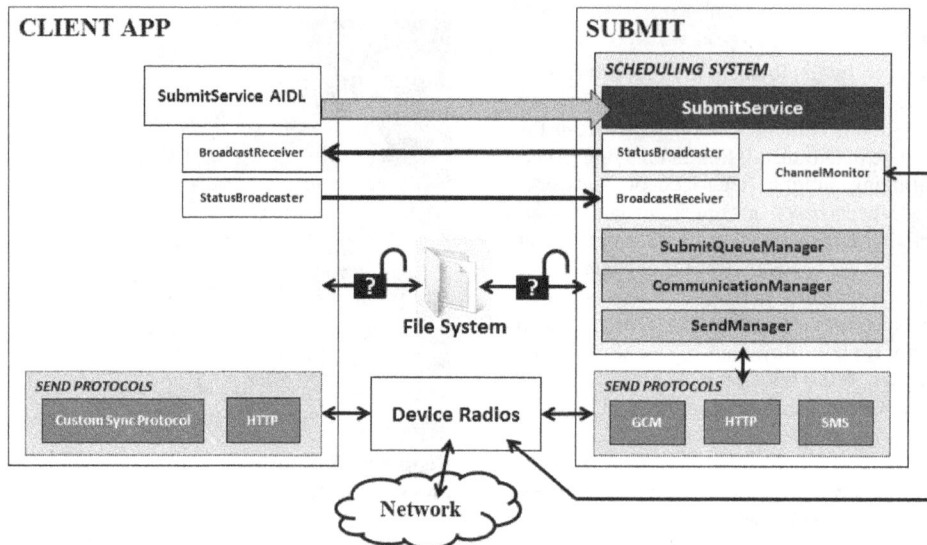

Figure 6: Architecture diagram showing how Submit interacts with a client app and Android system resources

messages. By obtaining the software apps perspective on data size, Submit is able to calibrate its routing mechanisms to best handle the common communication case on a per app basis and select appropriate channels. The SendObject contains a list of DestinationAddresses that define the type of transport as well as the necessary parameters to use for the transport. For example, to utilize HTTP POST, the DestinationAddress would contain a URL; to utilize an SMS channel the DestinationAddress would include a phone number. By implementing DestinationAddress as an abstract type, Submit is extensible to various communication protocols. SendObjects also contain the file path to, or string representation of, the data to be sent on behalf of the client app.

Shared data between Submit and client apps could create race conditions as apps are often dependent on their internal data stores being correct and consistent. Submit addresses ownership issues by removing ambiguity through the assumption that the client app owns the data until it explicitly grants Submit temporary ownership rights when it delegates transmission responsibility to Submit. If an app only provides a DataPropertiesObject which has no pointers to the data, Submit assumes the app is maintaining ownership of the data as the client app is only asking for a notification of when to send the data. In contrast, if the client app provides a SendObject containing the actual data or a pointer to an accessible external file, Submit retains ownership of delegated external data until it notifies the client app with the final status of the transmission. Since both the client app and Submit can be responsible for sending data, they must communicate the success or failure of data transmission. Broadcast intents are used to synchronize the sending status. When Submit is responsible for transmitting the data, it broadcasts the status of the communication exchange to the client app. Likewise, if a client app has been notified it is the appropriate time to send the scheduled data, the client app broadcasts the transmission result status to update Submit's internal state.

If the client app delegates responsibility for sending to Submit, the SendManager selects an appropriate network to transmit the data based on the DestinationAddresses and the protocols suited to the available network. By providing multiple client libraries that implement various protocols, Submit increases a client app's ability to communicate using various protocols without requiring expansion of the client app's code base. Currently implemented communication protocols include HTTP/SSL and SMS.

Submit's CommunicationManager is responsible for determining whether an available channel is appropriate for submitted data.

The CommunicationManager gauges an available channel's bandwidth capacity and costs. The ChannelMonitor listens to system broadcasts for changes in connectivity, including WiFi events, ad hoc communication opportunities, and cellular events. It reports back the current state of connectivity to the SubmitService when a change is detected. The SubmitQueueManager iterates continually over the pending data that needs to be transmitted (described by DataPropertyObjects). With each pass through the queue, it updates the state of each pending data item based on the results from Submit's protocol modules.

4.2 Related Work to Submit

Previous research has explored leveraging a variety of networks for data transmission [8] and splitting data over multiple networks based on cost and availability [9, 18, 21]. While work exploring simultaneous data transmission over multiple interfaces has been shown to improve mobility, power efficiency, and network capacity [8], our work focuses on selecting a single network from a heterogeneous combination of different transmission opportunities in a manner specialized to the deployment context. Submit is most similar to work that focuses on identifying the best type of network for data transmission given various contexts and policies. Multi-Nets [23] proposes real-time switching between different network interfaces on mobile phones using policies based on power, data offloading, throughput, and latency. However, policies are configured by the user and are applied to every app that uses the device. In contrast, Submit provides a library that allows deployment architect to configure policies that will only be applied to apps relevant to the application. In this way, Submit is most similar to Delphi [15], a transport layer module that selects the most appropriate network for data transmission given policies set by applications. However, Delphi assumes operation in an environment with ubiquitous connectivity and focuses on the transport layer not the application layer. While it attempts to provide a systematic evaluation of various networks for data transmission, it does not address many of the issues of developing contexts including intermittent connectivity and regional pricing policies. Also in contrast to Delphi, Submit also uses information about data (e.g., time-sensitivity, importance) to identify the best method for transfer. Haggle [24] is another solution that separates application logic from inflexible pre-programmed transport bindings so that applications can communicative in dynamic networking environments. Haggle and Submit both provide API's to developers but Submit goes further and

Table 2: Average latency for a client app sending data using Submit and without using Submit

	Wi-Fi w/ Submit	Wi-Fi w/o Submit	3G w/ Submit	3G w/o Submit
10 KB	0.12s	0.10s	0.59s	0.47s
100 KB	0.40s	0.28s	1.66s	1.28s
1 MB	2.53s	2.03s	10.93s	7.86s
10 MB	22.55s	20.58s	83.95s	80.35s

provides constructs for deployment architects who are not programmers to adjust their composable mobile information system. Another issue with Haggle is that it proposes a general form of a naming notation to allow for late-binding that is independent of the lower-level address. While a good idea, the infrastructure is not currently available to support some of these assumptions. In contrast, Submit is designed to work with existing infrastructure to enable applications to "just work" in different environments with limited infrastructure. Our work distinguishes itself from previous research in that it seeks to provide a network management module at the application layer that enables flexible control to an organization deploying a customizable app in areas of limited connectivity.

5. EXPERIMENTS

5.1 Splitting Data Transmission

To measure the baseline impact Submit has on a client app's communication performance, we integrated a simple file upload app with Submit to evaluate network usage and latency. The test involved the client app using HTTP POST to upload data from a client to a server with and without Submit. Performance was measured in two scenarios: Wi-Fi only and 3G only. The tests were performed on a Samsung Galaxy running Android 4.3 using either 3G or Wi-Fi networks. The results in Table 2 show the average latency for each file size for the ten uploads. As expected, there is slight latency overhead associated with Submit due its use of remote procedure calls and broadcast intents to communicate with a client app for each uploaded file.

Submit's latency additions are counterbalanced with its ability to minimize network usage according to user preferences. To verify the reduction of cost for network usage a small experiment was performed for ten minutes where Wi-Fi was disabled, leaving only 3G accessible. In this experiment, the client app uploaded a randomly selected file between 5 KB and 100 KB from a directory of files. For the client using Submit, a threshold value was set that prevented any file over 7 KB from being sent over a mobile broadband network. After ten minutes, the Wi-Fi was re-enabled for 10 minutes. After the entire 20 minutes the number of packets sent over Wi-Fi was compared to the more costly 3G network. The client without Submit sent over 380.6 KB over 3G whereas the client using Submit only sent 12.8 KB over 3G. Thus, Submit selectively uses one network while waiting for cheaper channel to become available.

To understand Submit's effects on deployment scenarios a small sampling of 85 actual site visit records were used to calculate data transmission reductions for the Site Visit scenario described in section 2.2. Table 3 shows the calculated average reduction if Submit managed ODK Collect's data submission process. By simply separating transmission of the text portion of the data and delaying the transmission of the photo's binary data until the device is in free Wi-Fi range would mean 0.37% of the total data would be transmitted via cellular and 99.53% of the data would be transmitted over Wi-Fi. Using Submit's concept of data priority could further reduce cellar transmission to 0.1% of total bytes by only transmitting the information about medication inventory.

Table 3: Reduction of transmission if record is split by data type or data priority for site visits scenario

	Bytes	Percent
Avg Total Record Transmission Size	330,773	100.00
Avg Data Size	1,213	0.37
Avg Photo Size	329,217	99.53
Avg Priority Data Size	343	0.10

5.2 Peer-To-Peer Transmission

We evaluate the performance of peer-to-peer transmission methods by comparing 5 methods of transferring data between Nexus 7 devices positioned 0.5 meters apart running Android 4.4.4. WiFi Direct and Bluetooth were tested using transfer sizes of 1 KB, 10 KB, 100 KB, 1 MB, 10 MB, 100 MB, and 1 GB of data. NFC transfer sizes were limited to data transfer times that were feasible for generic peer-to peer use (large transfers took too long). NFC with Bluetooth was tested up to 10 MB, while NFC only was tested up to 100 KB. Additionally, peer-to-peer transfer using QR codes was tested by having one Nexus 7 display QR Codes on its screen while another Nexus 7 read the QR codes with its built-in camera from 0.3 meters away. The ZXing library was used to generate and scan the QR Codes. While QR Codes specifications state transmission up to 4 KB of data [2], our results show that transfers are unreliable past 1 KB of data. The time it takes to scan a QR Code is fairly consistent as the size of data increases, but the error rate increased to over 60% for file sizes larger than 1 KB.

Bluetooth and NFC were the fastest transfer options for smaller amounts of data as shown in Figure 7. As the data size increases WiFi Direct emerges as the fastest mode of transfer. Until data sizes exceed 100 MB, the total time for WiFi Direct remains essentially constant because establishing the connection dominates the transfer time [12] as shown in Figure 8. WiFi Direct is a realistic choice for data on the order of 1 MB or larger, for anything lower than 1 MB Bluetooth may be a better option. Figure 7 also shows that NFC only is significantly slower than Bluetooth enabled NFC[4]. QR scanning had the largest variance in the duration of file transfer. While increasing the error correction level of the code can help remedy this issue, for data sizes close to 1 KB the QR Code was too dense to accurately and consistently be scanned.

Since battery life is important in disconnected environments, we evaluated the power performance of WiFi Direct, Bluetooth, and QR codes. For each test a connection was established between two fully charged Nexus 7's and data was continuously transmitted from one device to the other until the sending device's battery was depleted. For consistency the device screens remained on at all times since the QR method requires the screen to be on and active usage of devices would cause the screen to be active some percentage of the time. The experiments revealed that despite being able to leave the device in airplane mode, the QR Code scanner consumed more battery than traditional data transfer methods. The QR scanner took 6.8 hours to drain the battery to a 10% level while WiFi direct transfer only lasted 0.33 hours longer. In comparison it took about 9.3 hours of Bluetooth transmission to drain the battery to a 10% level. The results suggest that the power required to continually use the camera and process bar codes resulted in greater battery consumption over time than WiFi or Bluetooth transmission.

The main factors for selecting a peer-to-peer method include transfer time and battery efficiency. Per byte, WiFi is more battery efficient, but within the range of 100 KB to 1 MB, Bluetooth is faster. In the case of forest inventory workers, opportunity to charge the devices is the limiting factor and WiFi should probably be selected, since it is more efficient per byte. For the CHWs, avoiding the slightly more cumbersome connection process of WiFi might

---

[4]http://developer.android.com/training/beam-files/

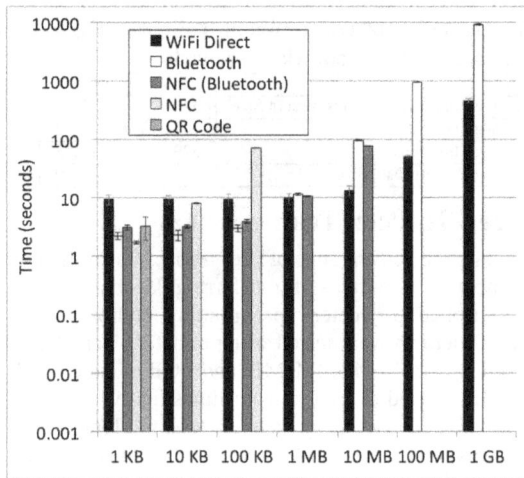

Figure 7: Data transfer times associated with peer-to-peer technologies with different file sizes. (Log Scale)

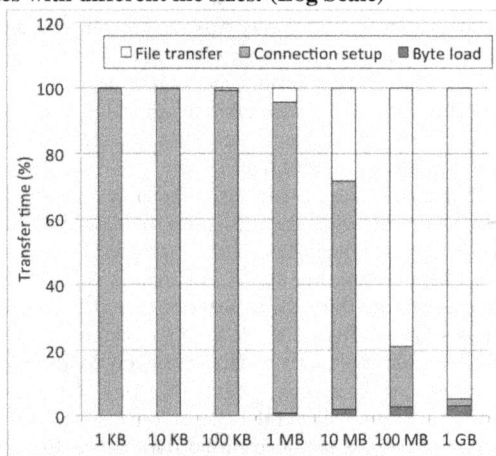

Figure 8: Percent of time spent in different phases of WiFi Direct transfer. Connection setup time dominates small file size transfer.

be more important. The main disadvantage of both Bluetooth and WiFi Direct is the difficulty for the user to confirm which device they connected to. While this may be less of an issue in a forest inventory setting, it is one of the primary concerns in a clinical setting. With both Bluetooth and WiFi Direct, someone attempting to steal data can spoof their device name and MAC address, potentially deceiving a user. NFC and QR Code communication allows users to visually clarify that the correct device is receiving the data. This can be an important advantage when the information is confidential such as medical data. The results show that the QR Code scanner is slower and less power efficient than NFC with Bluetooth. However, there is the possibility of hand-to-hand contact from using NFC when the two devices are brought close together to establish the connection. Hand contact could be a disadvantage in a remote clinical setting where hygiene practices might restrict such contact. A key advantage of Bluetooth over WiFi Direct is the ability to pair devices ahead of time, allowing users to more confidently send their data to the correct person. However, if NFC is not an acceptable option due to hand-to-hand contact or data size, white-listing Bluetooth devices could increase security in a clinical setting.

5.3 Usability of Peer-To-Peer Transfer

To understand the overhead of using different peer-to-peer modalities we conducted basic usability tests with 22 participants. The

participants' ages ranged from 18 to 56, with a mean age of 25. After initial demographic information was collected, participants were given a short training session on how to use Submit's manual peer-to-peer transfer screen. Participants were then given a list of ten 1KB transfers tasks to complete, one sending and one receiving for each of the five transfer methods. The order of the task list was randomized across participants so that each transfer method appeared with similar frequency at each position. The first two tasks for each user used a specific transfer mode (e.g., send using NFC, then receive using NFC). After the first two tasks, participants were asked to complete the NASA TLX[5] form to rate the difficulty of the specific transfer mode. Once completed, participants proceeded with the eight remaining tasks. After the ten tasks were completed, a semi-structured interview was used to solicit feedback about the most confusing part of the transfer process and to help identify possible improvements to Submit's peer-to-peer transfer. Participants were also asked to rank the five transfer methods based on ease of use (on a rank scale from 1 to 5, where 1 was the easiest transfer method to use and 5 was the most difficult), and rank them based on efficiency (on a rank scale from 1 to 5, where 1 was quickest transfer method and 5 was the slowest method).

Usability results confirmed the results from transmission performance. Users found that using a QR Code to transfer data was both the least efficient ($p < 0.001$) and the most difficult method ($p < 0.001$) to use[6] with a mean efficiency rank of 4.7 and a mean difficulty rank of 4.6. In three cases, users were unable to successfully scan the QR Code due to the lighting conditions of the room. Users also found that Bluetooth and WiFi Direct were the fastest ($p < 0.001$) and easiest ($p < 0.001$) to use.[6] WiFi Direct had a mean efficiency rank of 2.3 and a mean difficulty rank of 2.3. Bluetooth had a mean efficiency rank of 1.9 and a mean difficulty rank of 1.8.This slightly differs from the data gathered during channel testing. Due to the longer connection setup time, WiFi Direct should have been outperformed by all four of the other transfer methods. This discrepancy can be explained by the fact that users had to select more information during the user testing. The time it takes to select all this information causes the actual speed of transfer to matter less when compared to the overall time spent using the application. Additionally, the time it takes to move the devices together for NFC, and the time it takes to line up the devices for QR Code scanning was not accounted for in the evaluation of performance. These usability issues dramatically increase the overall time it takes to transfer using NFC and QR Codes. Testing results showed QR Codes take an unreliable amount of time due to user and environment conditions such as reflections due to lighting. However, based on the data collected from the NASA TLX form, there was no significant difference between the average level or type of stress users experienced while using the different transfer modes ($p = 0.57$)[7]. This implies that while users do prefer some transfer methods above others, the difference between them is relatively small compared to the overall ease.

While users found Bluetooth and WiFi Direct to be the fastest and easiest methods and QR Codes to be the slowest and most cumbersome, results were more varied for the NFC options. Some users liked the strong visual and physical cues associated with holding the devices together and touching the screen to beam the data between devices. Users also appreciated that the receiving NFC user does not have to select any options since the parameters, such as from whom you are receiving, are all automatically inferred

---

[5] http://humansystems.arc.nasa.gov/groups/tlx/
[6] Significance calculated using the Kolmogorov-Smirnov Test.
[7] Significance calculated using the Kruskal-Wallis Test.

when you hold the devices together. Other users felt uncomfortable with the inevitability of hand to hand contact that comes from holding the devices together with NFC. Other users expressed concern surrounding potentially dropping the device. Most users held the tablets together with one hand, and tapped the screen with their other hand. They thought NFC was slightly more inconvenient than other mediums, but would not mind using it.

6. CONCLUSION

Configurable mobile data transmission frameworks can enable deployment architects with limited programming skills to adapt mobile devices to meet diverse application requirements in challenged network environments. High-level data and networking abstractions can improve mobile app design paradigms by making single-purpose apps more malleable to resource-constrained contexts where issues such as affordability, infrastructural constraints, institutional capacity, and technical support are nontrivial. Submit improves deployments by supporting variations in deployment contexts in a systematic manner. Submit's abstractions decouple data and connectivity to enable application-level optimization of sparse heterogeneous networks. Submit identifies available connectivity in challenged networking environments and sends appropriate data over available channels in limited resources settings.

Experiences from the field highlight the fact that the selection of appropriate technologies for data transmission involves accounting for inherent data properties, contextual data properties, and network properties. Submit enables deployment architects to shape the communication priorities of the components comprising a larger application. Several deployment scenarios of interest benefit from peer-to-peer connectivity when centralized infrastructure is unavailable for data transmission. Which peer-to-peer transfer method to use should also be based on inherent properties (e.g. data size), contextual properties (e.g. data importance, security), and battery constraints. Our experiments showed the most significant barrier to peer-to-peer transmission is the time it takes for users to set up a peer-to-peer connection. In order to address these challenges, Submit handles peer-to-peer connections internally and automatically populates most settings before providing a unified UI to the user.

Creating software tools that enable application-level communication optimizations through the selection of appropriate data for transmission over available network channels represents a necessary complement to infrastructural improvement. Data communication needs to be adaptable to deployment conditions and solutions that focus on optimizations to the network transport layer do not have the flexibility to leverage the sparse challenged network conditions that exist. Therefore, adaptable frameworks that create abstractions that target application-level users (as opposed to developers adapting to network transport layers) are needed to empower deployment architects to easily customize application deployments to match an organizations requirements. For mobile tools to be successful in resource-constrained environments they should be composable by non programmers, deployable by resource-constrained organizations, usable by minimally trained users, and robust to intermittent power and networking outages.

7. ACKNOWLEDGMENTS

We thank Samuel Sudar for his help on this project. We also thank Neha Kumar and Elizabeth Belding for their insightful feedback on the paper. The material in this paper is based upon work supported by NSF research grant IIS-1111433, NSF Graduate Research Fellowship grants DGE-0718124 and DGE-1144085, and USAID contract AID-OAA-A-13-00002.

8. REFERENCES

[1] Obami. http://www.obami.com/portals/obami/about_obami.
[2] Qr Code. http://www.qrcode.com/en/about/version.html.
[3] The World in 2011: ICT Facts and Figures. https://www.itu.int/en/ITU-D/Statistics/Documents/facts/ICTFactsFigures2011-e.pdf, 2011.
[4] My MedLab. http://www.mymedlab.com/, 2013.
[5] Tribal Initiatives. http://transition.fcc.gov/indians, Mar 2013.
[6] The World in 2013: ICT Facts and Figures. https://www.itu.int/en/ITU-D/Statistics/Documents/facts/ICTFactsFigures2013-e.pdf, 2013.
[7] M-pesa. http://www.safaricom.co.ke/m-pesa/, 2014.
[8] P. Bahl, A. Adya, J. Padhye, and A. Walman. Reconsidering Wireless Systems with Multiple Radios. *SIGCOMM Computing Communication Review*, 34(5):39–46, October 2004.
[9] A. Balasubramanian, R. Mahajan, and A. Venkataramani. Augmenting Mobile 3G Using WiFi. In *Proc of the 8th International Conference on Mobile Systems, Applications, and Services*, MobiSys '10, pages 209–222, 2010.
[10] E. Brewer et al. The Challenges of Technology Research for Developing Regions. *IEEE Pervasive Computing*, 5(2):15–23, 2006.
[11] W. Brunette et al. Open Data Kit 2.0: Expanding and Refining Information Services for Developing Regions. In *Proc of the 14th Workshop on Mobile Computing Systems & Applications*, HotMobile '13, 2013.
[12] D. Camps-Mur, A. Garcia-Saavedra, and P. Serrano. Device-to-Device Communications with Wi-Fi Direct: Overview and Experimentation. *Wireless Communications, IEEE*, 20(3):96–104, June 2013.
[13] C. Cobb, S. Sudar, R. Anderson, F. Roesner, and T. Kohno. Work in progress, 2015.
[14] L. B. Deek, K. C. Almeroth, M. P. Wittie, and K. A. Harras. Exploiting Parallel Networks Using Dynamic Channel Scheduling. In *Proc of the 4th Annual International Conference on Wireless Internet*, WICON '08, pages 1–9, ICST, Brussels, Belgium, Belgium, 2008.
[15] S. Deng, A. Sivaraman, and H. Balakrishnan. All Your Network Are Belong to Us: A Transport Framework for Mobile Network Selection. In *Proc of the 15th Workshop on Mobile Computing Systems & Applications*, HotMobile '14, 2014.
[16] B. DeRenzi et al. E-IMCI: Improving Pediatric Health Care in Low-income Countries. In *Proc of the Conference on Human Factors in Computing Systems*, CHI '08, pages 753–762, 2008.
[17] B. DeRenzi et al. A framework for case-based community health information systems. In *Global Humanitarian Technology Conference (GHTC), 2011 IEEE*, pages 377–382. IEEE, 2011.
[18] B. Han et al. Mobile Data Offloading Through Opportunistic Communications and Social Participation. *IEEE Transactions on Mobile Computing*, 11(5):821–834, May 2012.
[19] C. Hartung et al. Open Data Kit: Tools to Build Information Services for Developing Regions. In *Proc of the 4th ACM/IEEE Int Conf on Information and Communication Technologies and Development*, ICTD '10, 2010.
[20] R. Heeks. Avoiding eGov Failure: Design-Reality Gap Techniques. www.egov4dev.org/success/techniques/drg.shtml, 2008.
[21] Y. Li, G. Su, P. Hui, D. Jin, L. Su, and L. Zeng. Multiple Mobile Data Offloading Through Delay Tolerant Networks. In *Proc of the 6th ACM Workshop on Challenged Networks*, CHANTS '11, pages 43–48, 2011.
[22] M. Martins and R. Fonseca. Application Modes: A Narrow Interface for End-user Power Management in Mobile Devices. In *Proc of the 14th Workshop on Mobile Computing Systems and Applications*, HotMobile '13, 2013.
[23] S. Nirjon et al. MultiNets: Policy Oriented Real-Time Switching of Wireless Interfaces on Mobile Devices. In *Real-Time and Embedded Technology and Applications Symposium (RTAS), 2012 IEEE 18th*, pages 251–260, April 2012.
[24] J. Scott et al. Haggle: A Networking Architecture Designed Around Mobile Users. In *WONS 2006: Third Annual Conference on Wireless On-demand Network Systems and Services*, pages 78–86, 2006.
[25] R. C. Shah, S. Roy, S. Jain, and W. Brunette. Data MULEs: Modeling and Analysis of a Three-tier Architecture for Sparse Sensor Networks. *Ad Hoc Networks*, 1(2âĂŞ3):215 – 233, 2003.
[26] K. Shirima et al. The Use of Personal Digital Assistants for Data Entry at the Point of Collection in a Large Household Survey in Southern Tanzania. *Emerging themes in epidemiology*, 4(1):5, 2007.
[27] R. W. Stevens and G. R. Wright. TCP/IP Illustrated: Vol. 2: The Implementation, 1995.
[28] M. Vitos, J. Lewis, M. Stevens, and M. Haklay. Making Local Knowledge Matter: Supporting Non-literate People to Monitor Poaching in Congo. In *Proc of the 3rd ACM Symp on Computing for Development*, ACM DEV '13, 2013.
[29] L. Wei-Chih et al. UjU: SMS-based Applications Made Easy. In *Proc of the First ACM Symposium on Computing for Development*, ACM DEV '10, 2010.
[30] K.-K. Yap et al. Making Use of All the Networks Around Us: A Case Study in Android. In *Proc of the 2012 ACM SIGCOMM Workshop on Cellular Networks: Operations, Challenges, and Future Design*, CellNet '12, pages 19–24, 2012.

Author Index

www.ingramcontent.com/pod-product-compliance
Lightning Source LLC
Chambersburg PA
CBHW081529220326

41598CB00036B/6373